Changing Moods

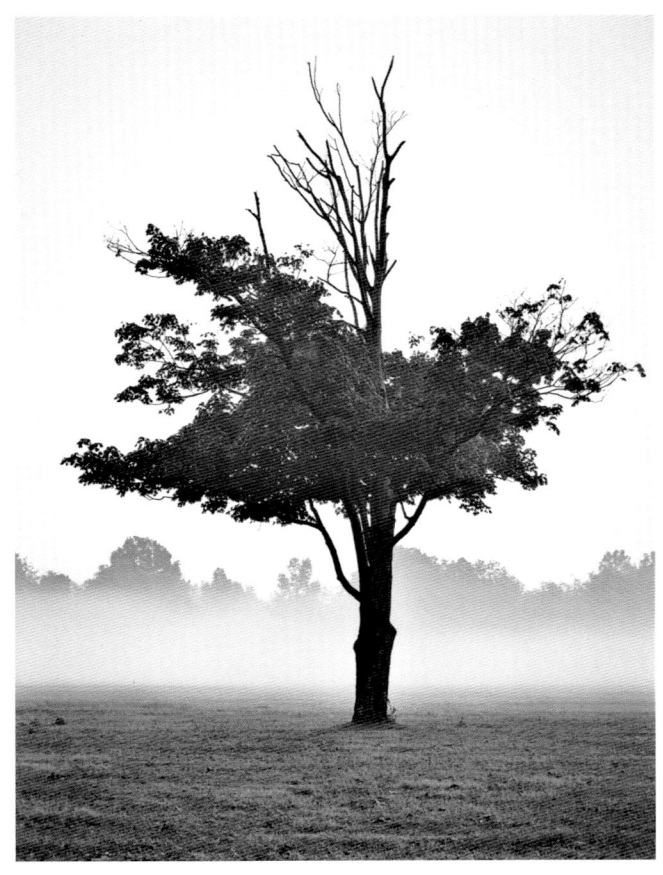

ALSO BY JOHN ALEXANDER DERSHAM

Fort Payne (Postcard History Series)

My Alabama: John Dersham Photographs a State

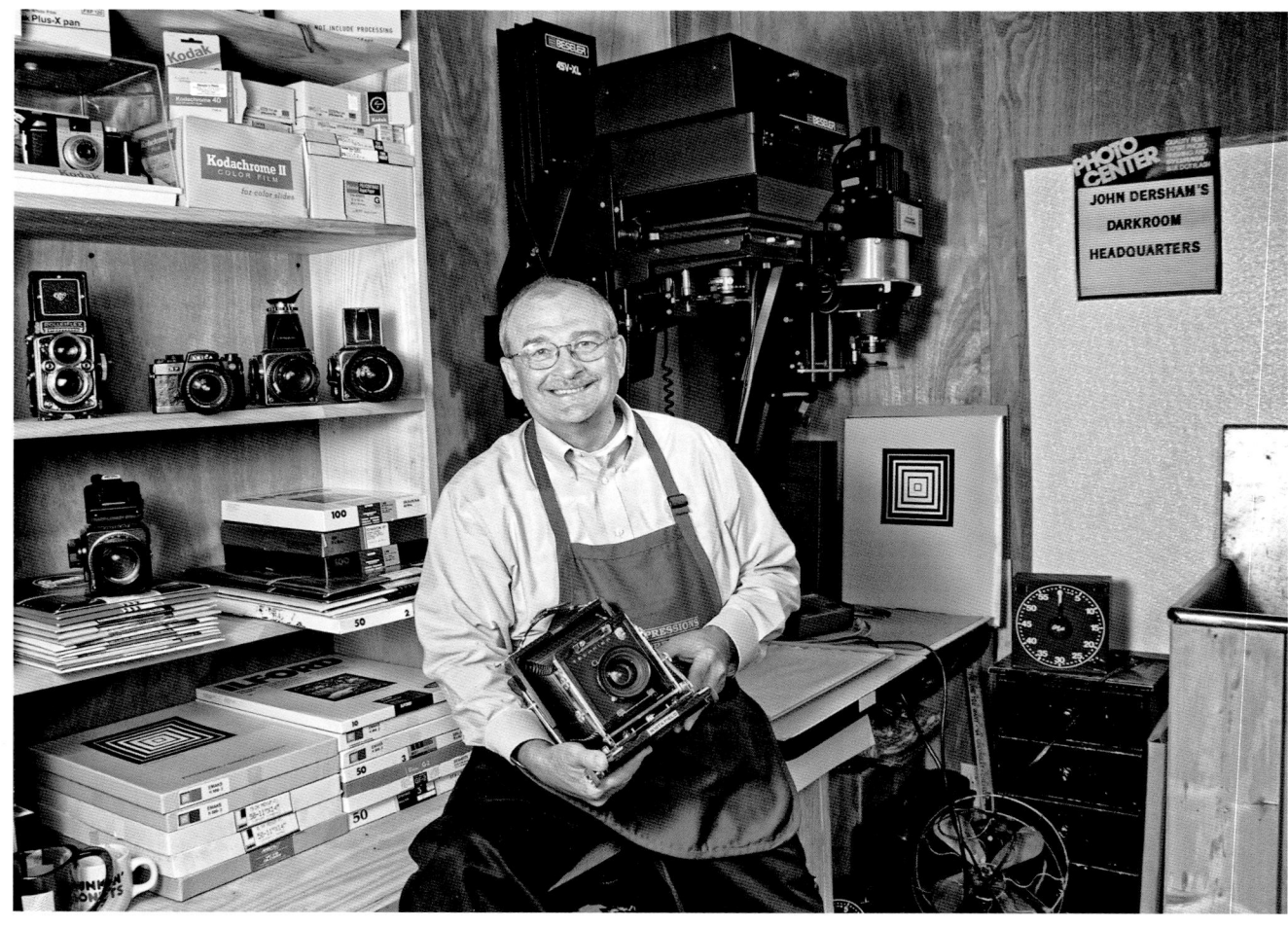

John Dersham in his darkroom, by Steven Stiefel, October 8, 2013.

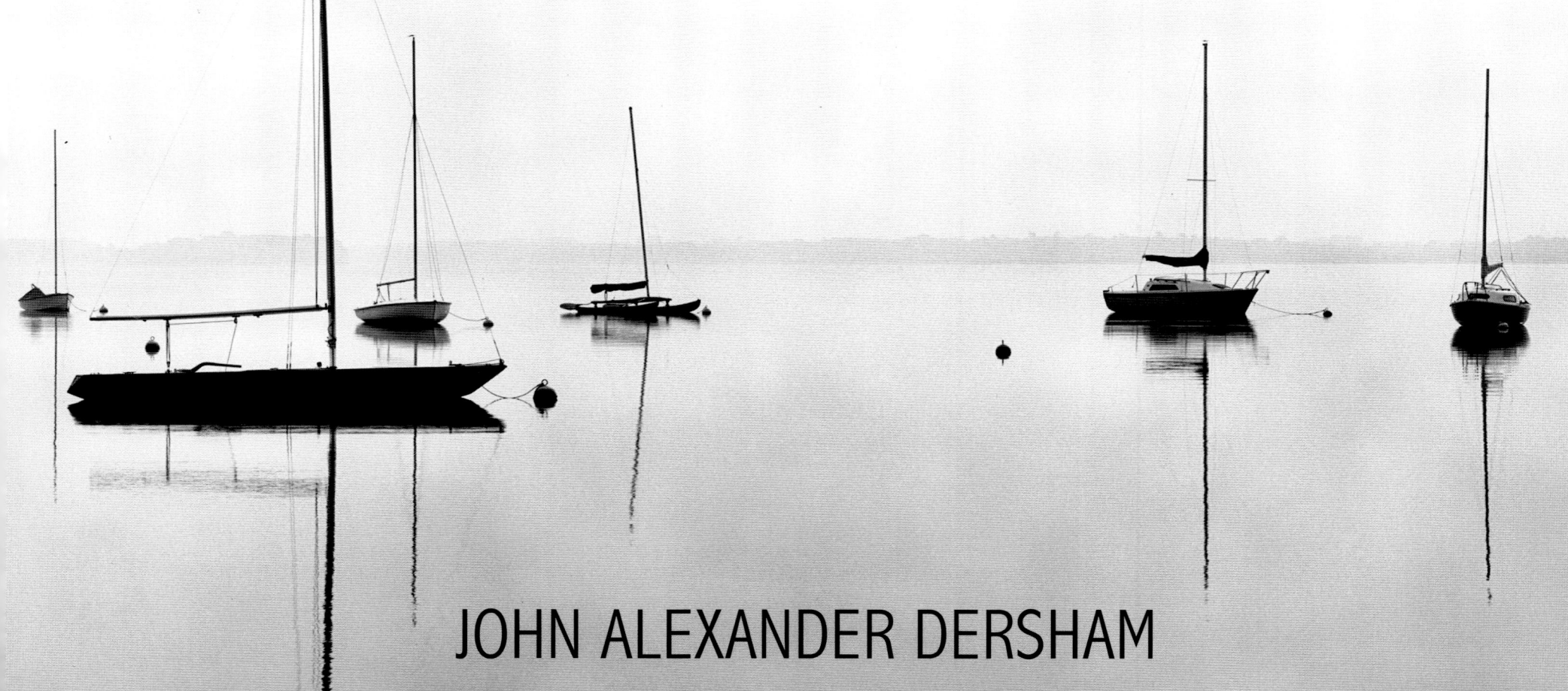

CHANGING MOODS

SIXTY YEARS IN BLACK AND WHITE

JOHN ALEXANDER DERSHAM

FOREWORD BY ALAN ROSS

NewSouth Books | Montgomery

NewSouth Books
105 S. Court Street
Montgomery, AL 36104
www.newsouthbooks.com

PUBLISHER'S CATALOGING-IN-PUBLICATION DATA
Names: Dersham, John, author, photographer.
Title: Changing moods: Sixty years in black and white / John Dersham ;
foreword by Alan Ross.
Description: Montgomery, Alabama : NewSouth Books, [2021] | Includes
annotations and index.
Identifiers: LCCN 2020951178 (print) | ISBN 9781588384324 (print)
Subjects: Art—Photography. | Art—Photography—Black and white. |
Art—Photography—Large format. | Art–Artists' books—Individual artists. |
Biography—Photographers.

Design by Randall Williams

Printed in South Korea by Pacom

On the front endsheet: Yellowstone River at daybreak, Yellowstone National Park, Wyoming, 8-18-1988; Linhof Technika V 4x5 camera; 120mm Schneider Symmar S lens; Kodak Tmax 400 4x5 film; Kodak HC110B developer.

On the half-title page: Lone maple tree in morning fog at Washington Crossing State Park, Bucks County, Pennsylvania, 10-29-1985; Toyo 8x10M camera with 5x7 back; 300mm Schneider Xenar lens; Kodak Tri X Pan Pro 4x5 film; Kodak HC110B developer.

On the title page: Silver Lake in morning fog, Bucks County, Pennsylvania, 7-7-1984; Linhof Technika V; 210mm Schneider Symmar lens; Kodak Tri X Pan Pro 4x5 film; Kodak HC110B developer. I traveled to Silver Lake, about thirty miles from where we then lived in Philadelphia. I arrived just as the sun was coming up. A nice layer of fog was hanging over the water, and it was a very pretty scene to look at and oh, so peaceful and quiet. I did not see a single person my entire time at this location. Later that same day I processed my sheet film from the day's shoot. In those days, prior to digital scans, you had to make a contact sheet just to see the image as a positive. I always viewed my negatives on a light box, thus determining what I would print. This image did not look good to me on the light box, and I never printed it. After processing and drying the film, I put the negatives in an archival poly negative sleeve which goes inside the archival paper sleeve. I then wrote the date, location, angle of the sun, and technical detail about the making of the image on the other outer paper sleeve. It was not until I scanned this negative in 2010 that I realized I loved this shot. Sometimes with film you just don't know what you have till you can view an image as a positive and enlarge it.

On the back endsheet: Devils Tower, Wyoming, 6-19-1988; Toyo 810M camera; 300mm Schneider Xenar lens; yellow K2 filter; Kodak Tri X Pan Pro 8x10 film; Kodak HC110B developer.

Acknowledgments

I want to thank my family who over many years supported my many long hours consumed while I was out taking photographs or working in the darkroom to produce them: my wife, Kyle, daughter Jennifer, and son Jad (John).

A special thanks to NewSouth Books—Suzanne La Rosa, Randall Williams, Matthew Byrne, Lisa Harrison, Lisa Emerson, Samantha Stanley, Kelly Snyder, and Beth Marino—for supporting this project 100 percent to make this a dream-come-true book for me. Thanks also to Alan Ross, a mentor from afar for decades, and to printing consultant Jared Stevens, who helped NewSouth shepherd the book through the manufacturing process.

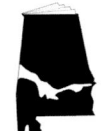

The Black Belt, defined by its dark, rich soil, stretches across central Alabama. It was the heart of the cotton belt. It was and is a place of great beauty, of extreme wealth and grinding poverty, of pain and joy. Here we take our stand, listening to the past, looking to the future.

To my mentors, Roger Berg, Andy Tau, and Milton Shanklin,
who taught me their art and craft.
And to my parents, Watson and Rosalie Dersham,
who witnessed my young passion for photography and gave me unlimited support.

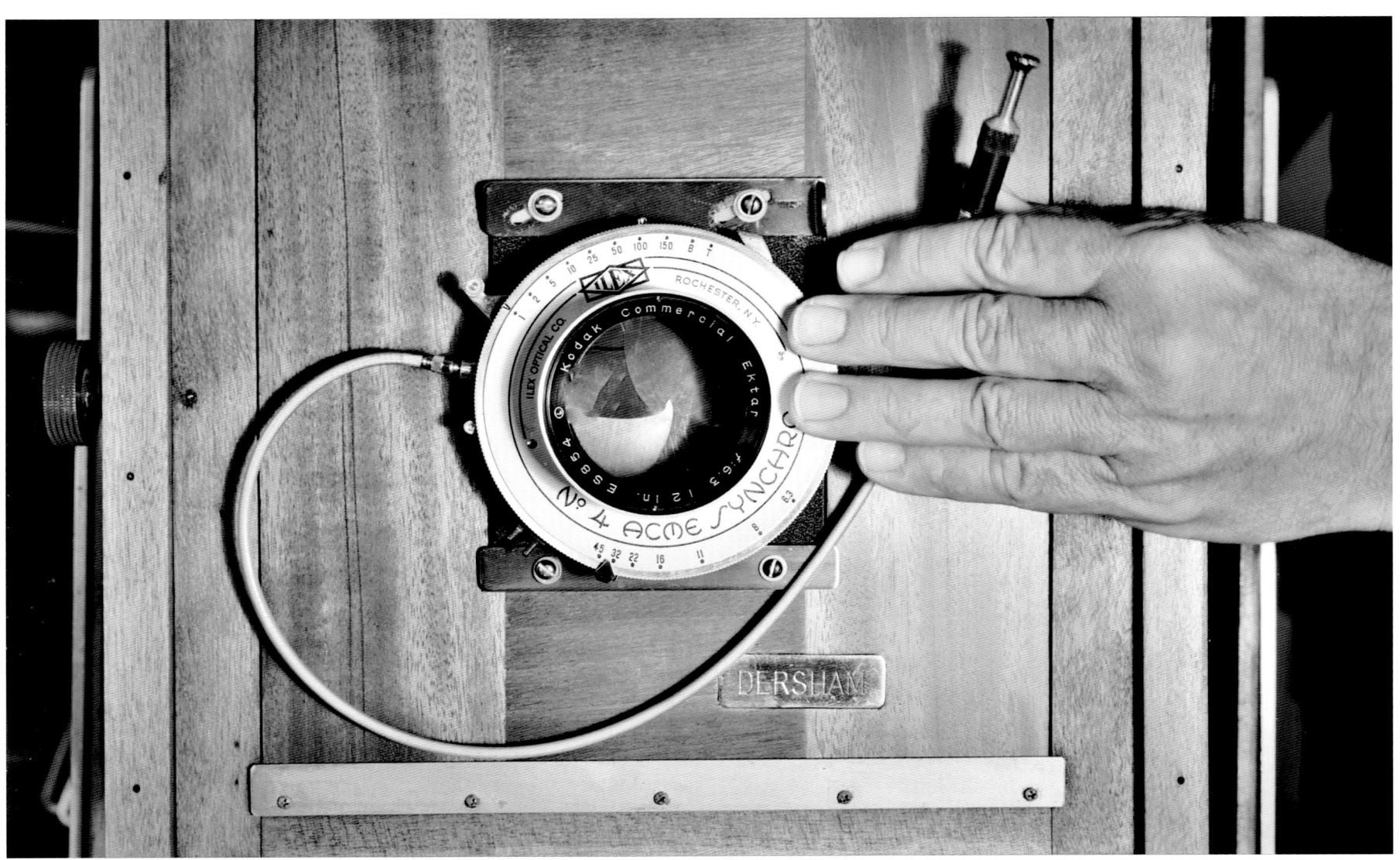

Selfie by John Dersham of 11x14 Burke and James field camera, 3-8-2008; Toyo 8x10M camera; 240mm Schneider G Claron lens; Kodak Tmax 100 8x10 film; PMK Pyro developer.

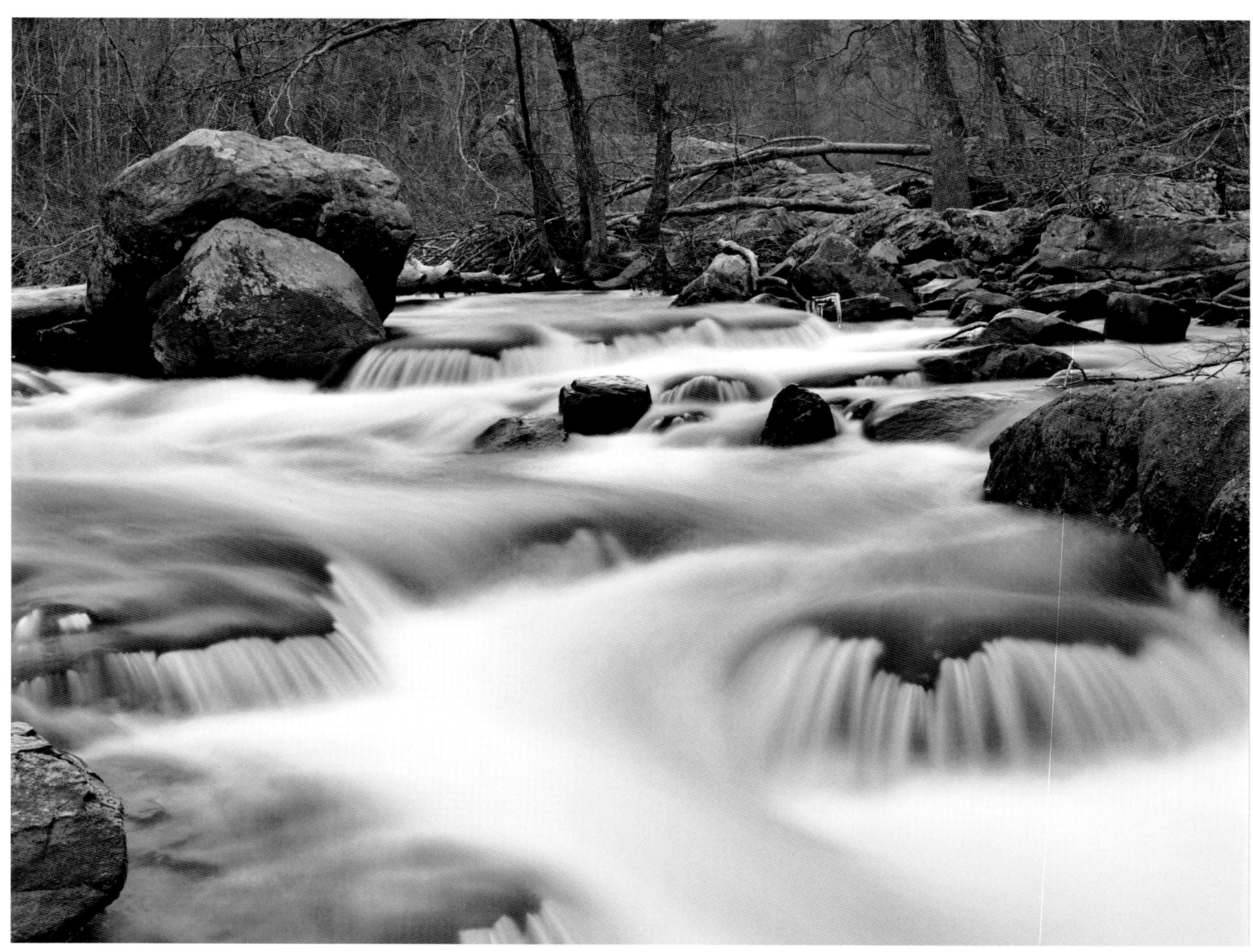

West Fork of the Little River, DeKalb County, Alabama, 1-12-2003; Linhof Technika V; 210mm Schneider Apo Symmar; Kodak Super XX 4x5 film; Kodak Xtol developer.

Contents

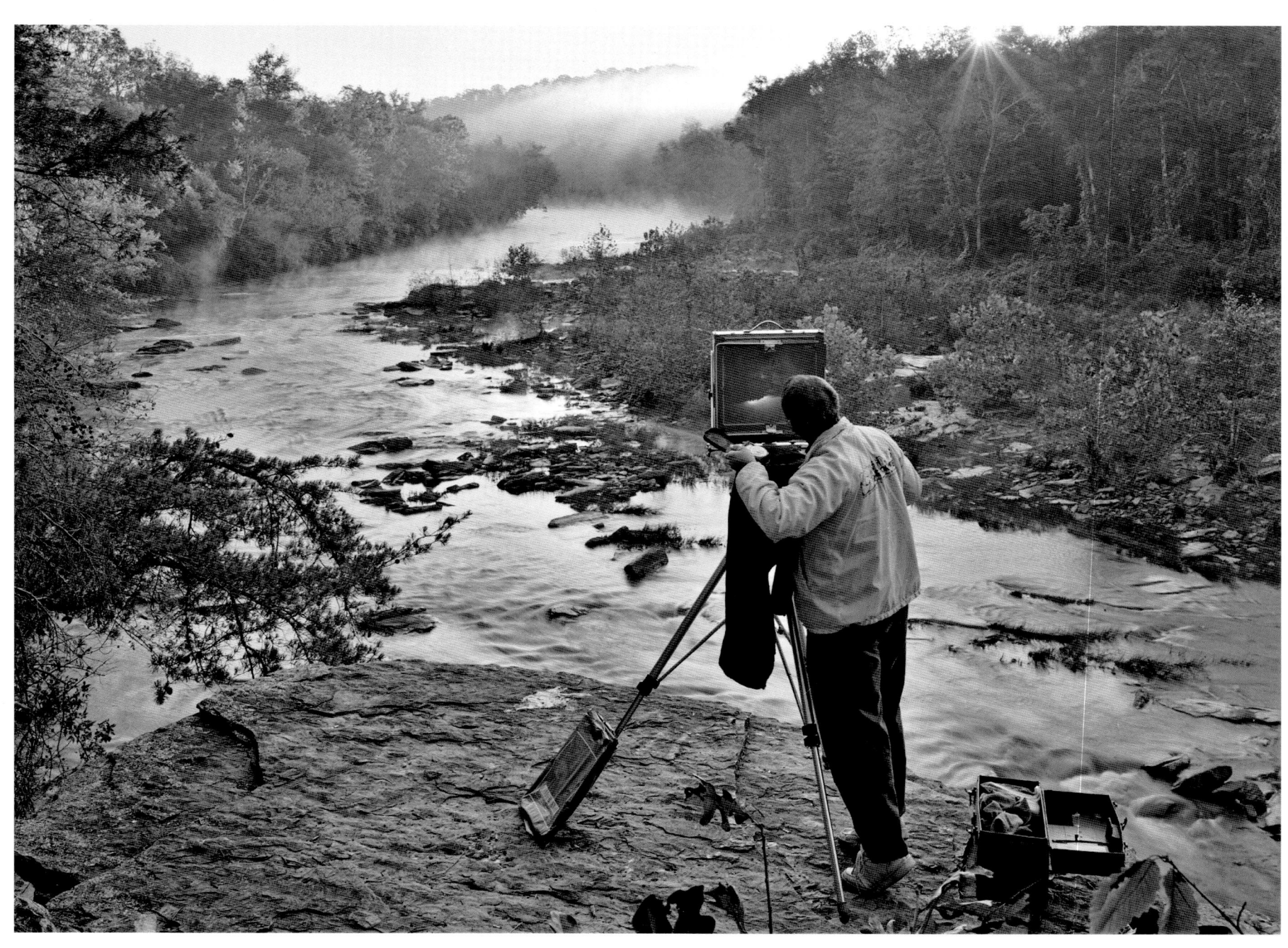

John Dersham, Mulberry Fork of the Warrior River, Alabama, October 22, 1995,
shooting 11x14 film at sunrise; photo on 4x5 film by David Haynes.

Foreword

ALAN ROSS

I have long held that photography is very much a sort of language. It can be as practical and no-frills as an entry in an encyclopedia. It can tell a story or report wartime agony. In a series, it can be a set of instructions or the great American novel. Alone, a photograph can be a graceful haiku. And for those of us to whom words do not come easily, a photograph becomes the language that allows us to express who we are, what we feel, or how we respond to the world around us.

In his latest book, John Dersham uses the language of photography to reveal his passion for black-and-white large-format imagery and the visual feast of everyday life. He tells us a love story.

This love is evident in his images that evoke the peace to be found on quiet country roads and friends gathered together, or in trees and towns, roads and rivers, an old general store next to a quiet leaf on a wet river rock.

Dersham's photographs are masterfully seen and clearly demonstrate his passion for his craft. They also transcend the everyday snapshot to showcase the photograph as an expressive art. His photographs of people are not just pictures of people—they tell a story *about* the people in the image. A photo of a winding road leading to some buildings beckons the viewer to imagine standing there in person, captivated by the scent of the grasses.

The exclusive use of black-and-white monochrome images adds layers of richness and personalization to the story. By its very nature, black-and-white is an abstraction of reality. With color, unless the photographer is doing something clearly "different," there is an inescapable expectation of reality. A green sky or purple skin just looks wrong. Black-and-white, by contrast, allows for interpretation and freedom from the reality in front of the lens without looking "wrong." And a black-and-white image offers the viewer an opportunity to insert his or her own imagination and interpretation of what the photographer is trying to share.

Dersham's choice of camera also speaks volumes about his dedication to craft and mastery. I like to say that different kinds of cameras are simply different tools. One tool may be better suited to a particular task than another. A person can drive a screw with a hammer, but it may not be the effective tool for the task.

A large-format camera can be big and a bit slow to work with, but it provides a large negative capable of recording an immense level of detail and very smooth and nuanced tones. Unlike making a quick snap with a cell phone, a photographer working with a large-format camera necessarily works with methodical intent. The set-up itself is a labor of love, and the resulting image is a matter of creative passion and craft. Another part of Mr. Dersham's love story.

Changing Moods: Sixty Years in Black and White, then, is an eloquent expression and sharing of Mr. Dersham's feelings about land, lore, and people, told through the language of photography.

Alan Ross is not only a great large-format black-and-white photographer in his own right, but his teachings and work following his career as Ansel Adams's assistant have enriched countless photographers around the world. He continues to be the exclusive printer of the Yosemite Special Edition negatives, an assignment Adams personally selected him for in 1975. Alan makes each print by hand from Adams's original negatives using traditional darkroom techniques.

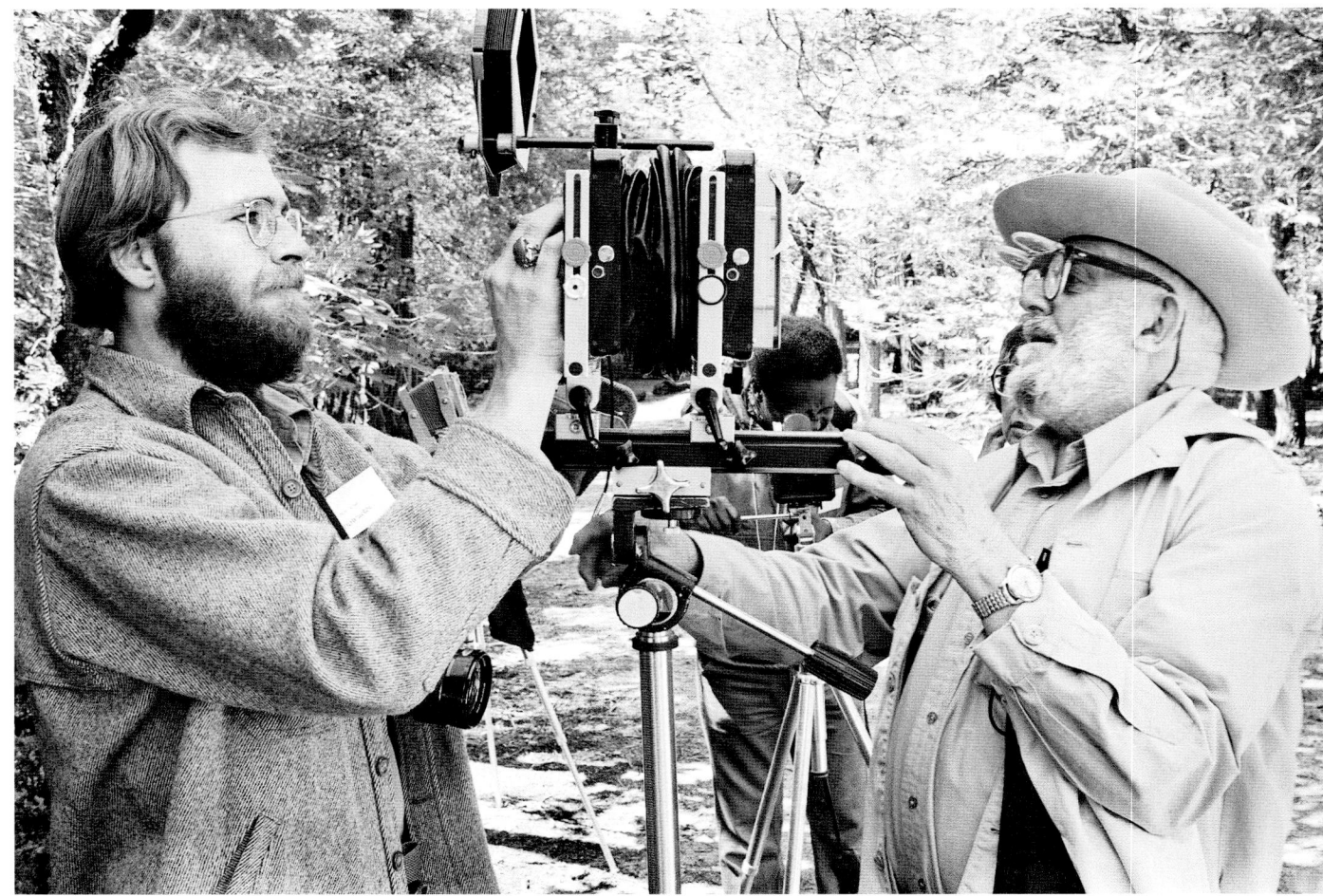

Alan Ross, left, with Ansel Adams, by Frank Neimeir, Yosemite, June 1977.

Preface

Within these pages lies one man's journey through sixty years of photography. Over the decades, I have undertaken paid photography jobs and assignments: photography for travel guides, photo books, postcards, weddings and portraits, magazine pictures for articles, and for my magazine and newspaper columns. Many of my paid assignments were for the tourism industry, where good photography lures visitors to scenic locations. Quite a few were specific assignments for tourism trail guides: highlighting waterfalls in North Alabama, historic sites, and niche interests hike historic churches and scenic motorcycle routes. In most cases, these were for printed guides handed out at welcome centers, hotels, attractions, restaurants, and mini markets. They also are mailed to visitors who request them from tourism websites.

I chose not to become a full-time paid professional photographer for a couple of reasons. One, I liked having a regular income. Two, I liked to shoot pictures that I wanted to take, not ones I was required to take. My photography has been a lifetime pursuit of satisfying my personal artistic palate. It has been a lifelong ambition that the viewers of my work will enjoy viewing my images as much as I have enjoyed producing them.

I have partaken in two lengthy careers, first thirty-five years in the photographic industry, mostly at Eastman Kodak and subsidiaries, and second in the tourism industry. In the first, my background in photography was a direct benefit, and in the second, photography has been an associated skill set that has benefited me as a photographer but also has benefited tourism organizations nationwide—and in fact worldwide—that have used my photography for marketing and promotion of scenic, cultural, and historic visitor attractions.

MY FIRST MENTORS WERE my parents, Watson and Rosalie Dersham. I owe them a lifetime of gratitude for their 100 percent support in my photographic endeavors from day one. They witnessed my young passion for photography and provided tutoring and educational support that allowed me the equipment, film, and darkroom supplies necessary to learn photography as an art and a craft.

Mom was always interested in my brother Tom and me getting into sports and other hobbies. Dad and I were tropical fish enthusiasts. We had a tropical fish hobby/business in our basement when I was in my middle teens. Dad purchased a score of aquariums, fish food, heaters, filters, gravel, lights, etc. We raised a lot of baby fish, and when they were about half grown, we sold them to Mattingly's five and dime store in Columbia, Missouri. Roger Berg, the manager, had turned a section of Mattingly's into the best tropical fish store in Columbia, filling an entire wall with aquariums. He was a hobbyist himself and had built quite a following at his store. I kept the money from selling the fish while Dad spent his money to buy all the supplies. I still have a handwritten journal entering our fish sales and the money I received. Helping Dad with the aquariums was my first job. That is how my parents were. They helped fund interests that they thought were good for my brother and me and that kept us out of trouble.

When I was very young, Dad was director of health education for the city of Cincinnati, Ohio, which issued him a 4x5 Speed Graphic camera to take pictures of unhealthy local conditions in the late 1940s and early 1950s. He learned photography quite well because the Speed Graphic required an excellent understanding of aperture, shutter speed, depth of field, and how to handle and load sheet film. Probably because of his interest, I got my first photographic developing kit the Christmas of 1964. I did not quite know how to use it—Dad never had a darkroom but took his 4x5 negatives to a neighbor and watched him process them.

Meanwhile, Mom and Dad were both avid newspaper readers. Mom in particular was always looking at the human-interest stories. Thus, I was made aware of my first true teacher of photography and a primary mentor when Mom gave me an article in the *Columbia Missourian* about a man named Roger Berg. Obviously, Dad and I were already friends with Roger because we sold fish to him. But until Mom gave me the article about him being an avid photographer who had just won a major photo contest, Dad and I had no idea of that side of Roger.

From that point on, Dad and I went to Mattingly's almost every evening. I began talking photography with Roger in addition to fish. Roger later purchased Capens' Camera Store (later Columbia

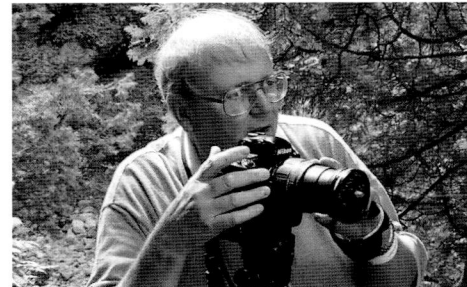

Roger Berg, Columbia, Missouri (contributed photo).

Photo) when Mr. Capens retired after having the store for fifty years.

Roger took me, a fourteen-year-old, under his wing. He taught me film developing and printing in his darkroom. I also joined the Mid Missouri Camera Club, and for the next several years of junior high and high school, Roger and fellow club leaders Milton Shanklin and Andy Tau taught me composition, lighting, and the darkroom fundamentals. In those pre-computer days, the fine darkroom print was the only way to properly view an image. Great care was taken to print each negative. My mentors were perfectionists and quite well known as masters of their craft, extremely disciplined on the compositional value of a photograph but also on the camera and darkroom technique.

The Mid Missouri club was very active and before long Roger, Milt, and Andy had me entering in contests pictures I processed and printed in a makeshift darkroom in our basement at home. The quality of the image had to be really good or it did not get far in the judging.

Over the years, I stayed in touch, gradually losing touch with Milton and Andy in their later years. Both passed away decades ago. I kept up with Roger Berg until he died in 2007. He had continued to operate Columbia Photo and Portrait Studio.

BY THE TIME OF my first high school summer job in 1968, I had already amassed eight years of experience in taking and processing pictures. Camera club member Milton Shanklin was a professor of biology at the University of Missouri and was another of my primary mentors. Because of his interest in photography, Milt was given a special project at the University of Missouri to take a time-lapse photo of the sky every minute. These were used for tracking cloud patterns. He hired me as his darkroom technician and lab engineer. I worked in his darkroom at the university for the summers of my junior and senior years in high school. My classmates, none of whom were in the camera club, could never figure out how I got a much better summer job than theirs. I was the only young person in the photography club at that time. On Friday evenings, rather than being out with my friends or on dates, I was with the camera club. We'd go to Shakey's Pizza Parlor after each meeting for conversation, music, and, for them, beer.

Milt drove a Volkswagen Beetle filled with photography equipment. He left that car unlocked no matter where he parked it. He used to drive me around for supplies, or I would go out picture taking with him. When Milt got angry at another driver, he would, in a couple of seconds rant, spout out every cuss word in alphabetical order. It was almost poetic. The first time I heard him do it I laughed to the point of serious pain.

My third mentor was the aforementioned Andy Tau. He was well-known locally as an instructor for the camera club and as a photographer for the University of Missouri, which had one of the world's best schools of photojournalism. Andy was from Missouri but had lived in San Francisco where he was a protégé of Ansel Adams and a member of his F64 Club, for serious large-format photographers only. Edward Weston was affiliated also. We are talking about some of the most famous photographers in history. F64 is an aperture setting found only on large-format lenses. It is a

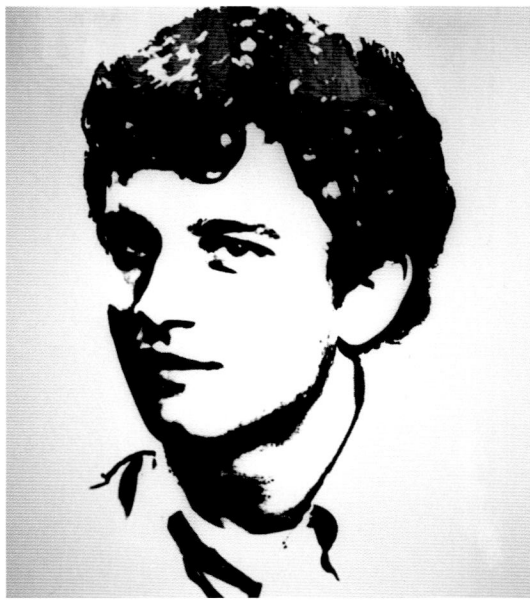

Tone-line photograph of John Dersham by Milton Shanklin, July 7, 1970.

very small aperture that allows increased depth of field—similar to 35mm or medium-format cameras at F22—for the longer lenses needed to cover large-format film.

ROGER, MILT, AND ANDY were dedicated large-format photographers and any film size less than 4x5 would not produce the print quality they considered acceptable. They taught me the art of the fine print. This meant the print in itself was a piece of art. It needed to be perfect. It had to be on archival double-weight silver halide paper, perfectly exposed for that particular paper. It had to be dodged and burned at just the right places to enhance the total image quality. You had to use archival processes for chemical preservation and washing of the print prior to drying, flatting, mounting, and ultimately framing.

Even though I was in my middle teens and my mentors were in their forties and fifties, they dedicated their valuable time and knowledge teaching me hands-on principles of photography. They helped me learn to compose and properly expose the image on film, process the film, and print the negatives to make fine-art prints worthy of camera club competitions and gallery exhibitions.

These mentors followed the wave of fine art large-format photography popularized by Ansel Adams. They were instrumental at the beginning of my sixty years in black-and-white photography, and to this day their teaching, along with the insights of Ansel Adams, is still present in the methods that I use in the darkroom.

The average person today looks at their pictures almost exclusively on a computer screen, smartphone, or notebook. This is true of amateur and professional photographers as well. Images all look good on these devices; it does not matter if they are 4-megapixel or, as my 8x10 negatives are, 600-megapixel. The technology only allows you to view images at a greatly reduced resolution, making those of the best and the worst quality look about the same.

The art of the fine print is just that. These are photographs taken with the intent of being a piece of art that can hang on a gallery wall, just like a painting, to be judged as a finished material object, not a fleeting screen image. To make fine art prints from digital or from film requires hard work, but from film the work required is more exhausting. Physical labor is needed along with an understanding of the darkroom chemicals, paper, enlarger, exposure, cropping, dodging, burning, toning, washing, drying, mounting, and framing. This may take hours and days in the darkroom. The digital image has fewer steps, and, for me, is less rewarding than the perfected finished result of a film image.

In the past couple of decades, large-format photography and the fine art of darkroom printing are no longer topics in many mainstream photography circles. These have become niche arts, with a small but loyal following. Many people like me have been doing it for decades. Worldwide, young enthusiasts new to large-format and print-making grew up in the digital age, but somewhere along the way discovered large-format film and fell in love with what they saw in a fine-art print. Such prints from the masters like Ansel

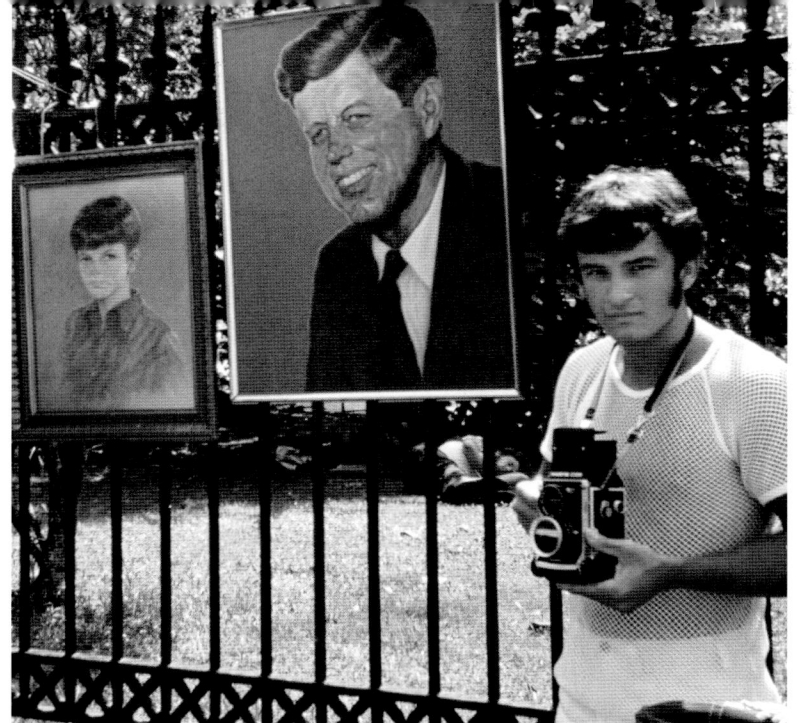

John Dersham, Washington Square, New Orleans, 1970.

Adams and Edward Weston sell for thousands and thousands of dollars because there is no way to make an exact duplicate in the darkroom. A digital image, once perfected in Photoshop, can result in multiple identical images. The gallery value of a digital print will never reach the value of individually made darkroom prints.

FILM PHOTOGRAPHY REQUIRES A lot of time. It is expensive and a million things can go wrong. It is also what makes it more challenging, more fun, and, I feel, more interesting to look at than digital. I find digital sterile and perfect to the point of being uninteresting.

Beyond family and work, photography and all its aspects define my life. From early morning picture outings, to processing the film and printing late at night into the following morning, I love to study the craft to find ways to improve. I use archival storage methods for the negatives and prints. I like playing with the equipment and always looking for new stuff I need or want to help improve my work.

I love collecting photo equipment, showing my prints in galleries, and teaching photography workshops. I enjoy engaging in the photo community in person and on social media. I like working on photo projects for books, magazines, and travel guides. These activities have consumed many wonderful hours of my life.

I am very grateful that at such a young age I became so inspired and had the parents and the mentors to keep me learning and improving. It has truly been a lifelong passion.

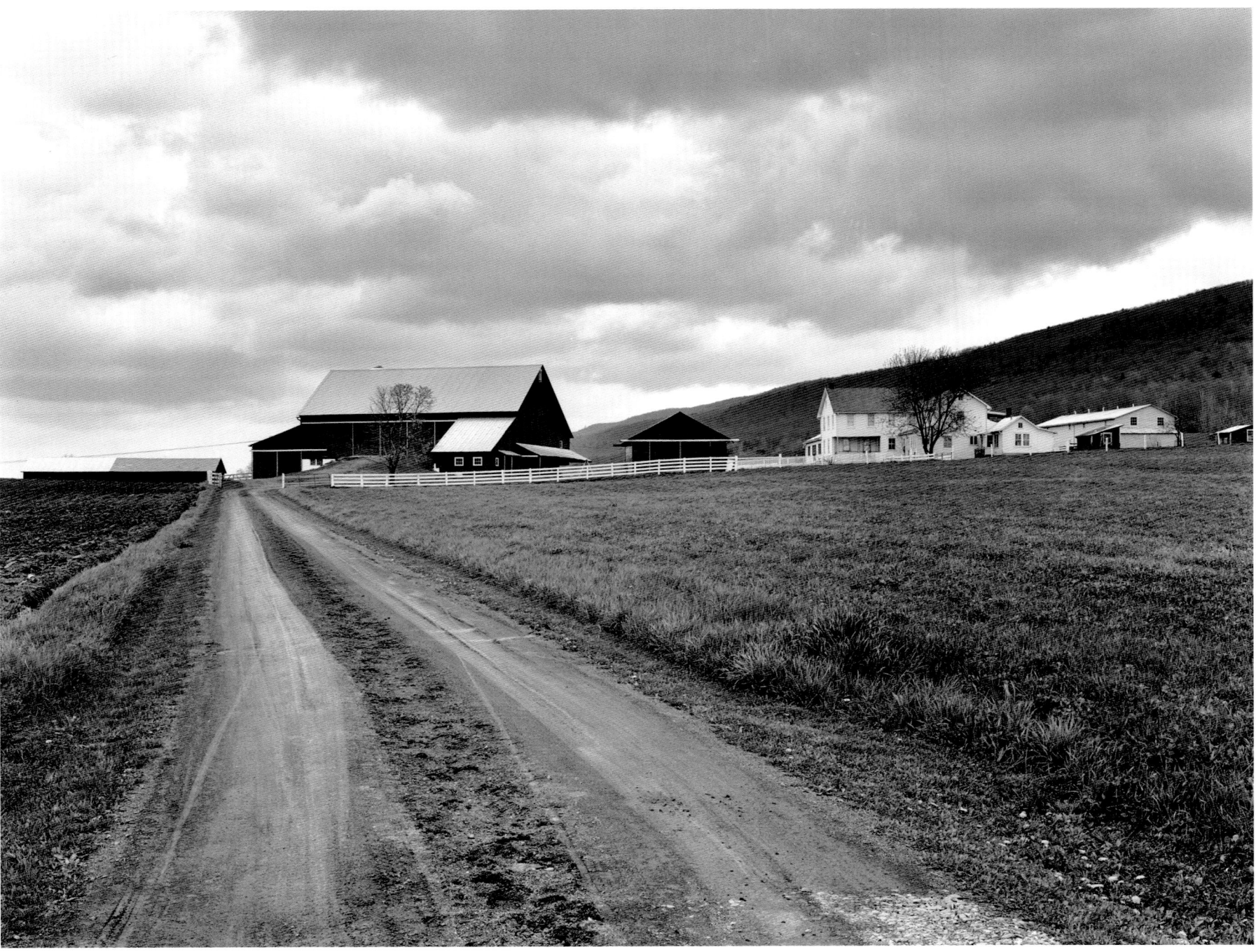

Amish farm in Big Valley near Lewistown, Pennsylvania, 5-5-1984; Cambo View 4x5 camera; 150mm Schneider Symmar S lens; Kodak Tri X Pan Pro, 4x5 film; Kodak HC110B developer.

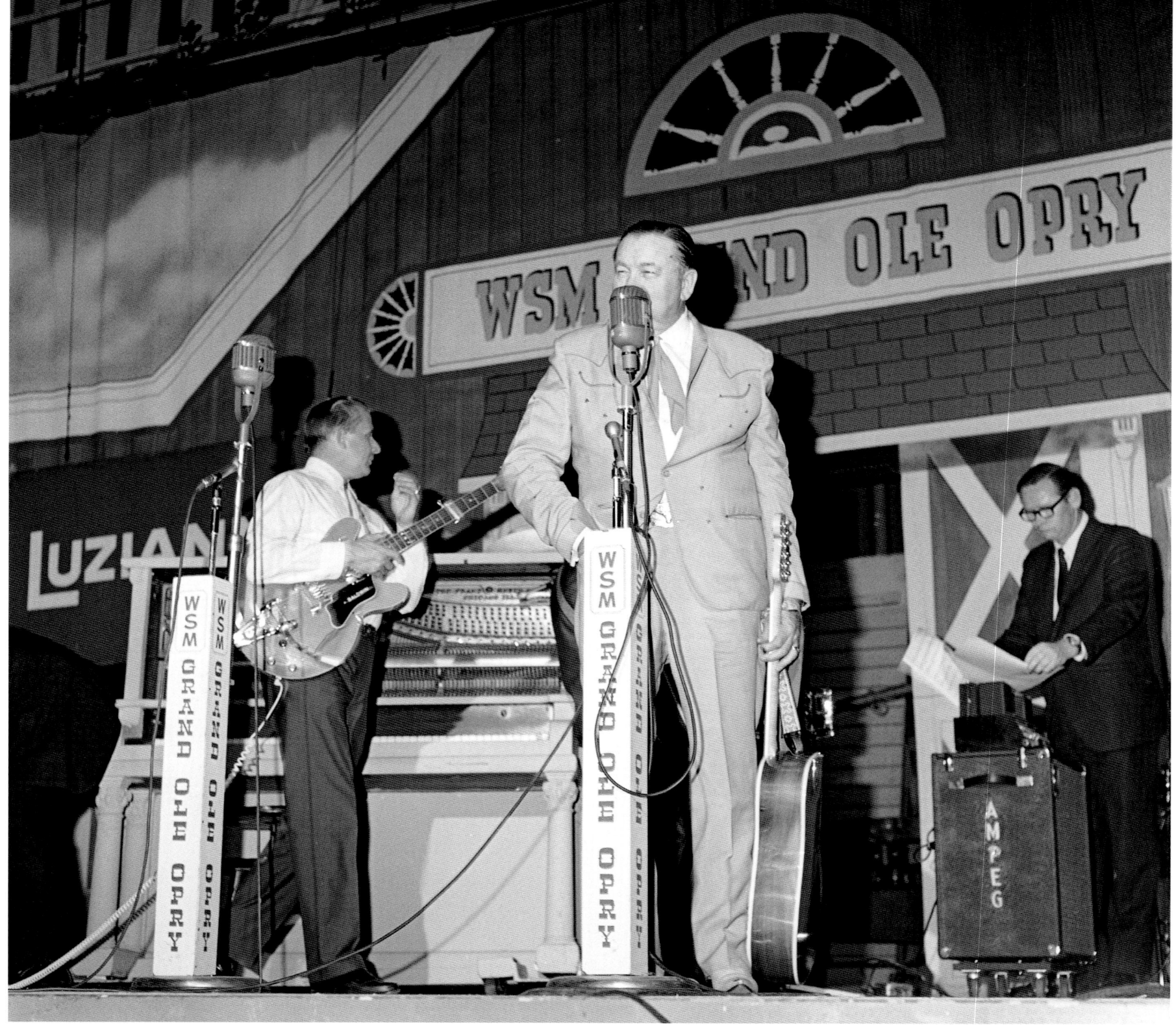

Tex Ritter at the Grand Ole Opry, Ryman Auditorium, Nashville, Tennessee, 6-1969; Mamiya C220 camera; 80mm Sekor lens;Kodak Verichrome Pan 120 film; Edwal FG7 developer.

1

The 1960s: The Passion Begins

My parents are from Pennsylvania. My dad, Watson Winaford Dersham, was from Mifflinburg, a small farming borough in the central part of the state that was settled by German immigrants. My Dersham descendants have deep roots in his area. Mifflinburg was once known as "Buggy Town" because it produced more horse-drawn vehicles per capita than any other town in Pennsylvania and was among the top producers in the United States.

Dad got his degree from Pennsylvania State University in 1940. Penn State helped him line up a teaching job in Knox, Pennsylvania, just shy of a hundred miles northeast of Pittsburgh. In the fall of 1940, Dad began teaching health and physical education at Knox High School, and he met my mom, Rosalie Wanda Gross, who was born and raised in the small community. Mom was out of high school and working in the local 5 & 10 store. Dad met her at the counter. They began dating in 1940. At the end of 1941, Dad was drafted into the U.S. Army. He went through boot camp and basic training at Camp Shelby in Hattiesburg, Mississippi.

In May 1943, Dad was ordered overseas and he and Mom decided to get married. He told Mom he wouldn't be home until the war was won. He was sent to North Africa, Germany, and Italy, where he served as an artillery sergeant during his two and a half years in the war. With the end of hostilities, Dad made good on his promise and came home to Mom to restart their lives together.

He and Mom moved to State College, where he used the G.I. Bill to return to Penn State to get his master's in public health education. Following graduate school, he went to work for the American Cancer Society out of Harrisburg.

In 1947, Dad left the American Cancer Society when he was offered and accepted a job of as director of public health education for the city of Cincinnati. It was in there in January 1949 that my brother Tom was born. I followed in 1951. Since my parents and all of our family were from Pennsylvania, I have always considered Pennsylvania my home state.

Early in 1957, Dad was solicited by the American Heart Association and became its western regional consultant. The organization's headquarters were in New York City on East 23rd Street. We moved to my grandmother's home in Mifflinburg for the last half of my kindergarten school year. Dad had begun working in New York, but we did not have a house yet, since the one in Cincinnati had to be vacated after it was sold. In June of 1957, with the help of my mother's aunt, Mabel Broadhead, and other members of her family, we found a house in a New York City bedroom community—New Rochelle, New York (considered in the early 1900s one of the first American suburbs). We moved into a neighborhood of Cape Cod and English Tudor homes. Every morning, Dad took the train to Manhattan for work.

His territory included ten western states. He was gone for weeks at a time. Because of the daily commute, often long travel out of state, and a young family at home, Dad began asking the Heart Association for a different position. After nearly four years in New York, he was offered the vice presidency of the American Heart Association at the Missouri affiliate in Columbia. So, in early September 1960, we packed up again and migrated to the Show Me State. This would be the last move for my parents. They lived there for the remainder of their lives, in the same house for nearly fifty years.

I TOOK MY FIRST picture on November 1, 1960, one day after my ninth birthday (on Halloween).

In 1930, Eastman Kodak celebrated its fiftieth anniversary. The company had an anniversary promotion to inspire young people to begin taking pictures. Via a coupon from some magazine or newspaper, all kids turning twelve years of age in 1930 could receive a free Kodak Brownie loaded with black-and-white film. Dad was one of

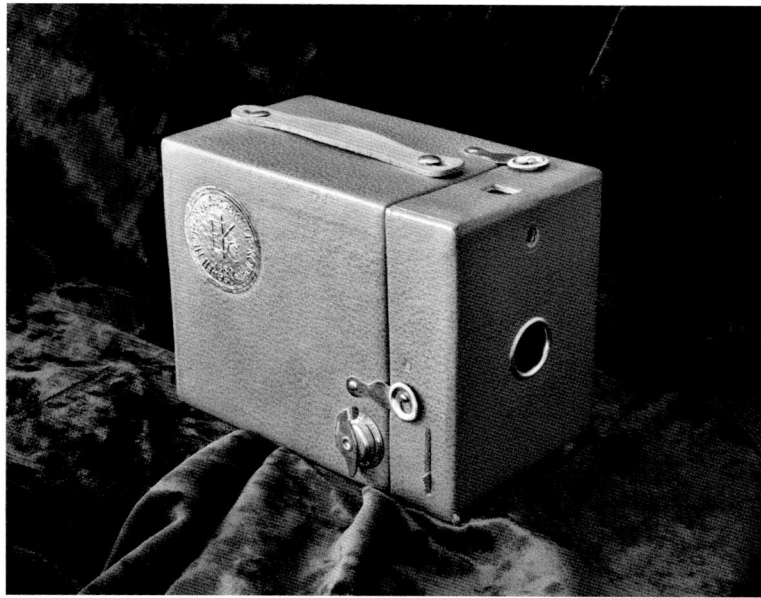

1930 Eastman Kodak 50th Anniversary Brownie.

those five thousand-plus twelve-year-olds who got the now collectors' item 1930 Brownie with a Kodak fiftieth anniversary seal on its side.

Dad had rediscovered his Brownie during our move to Columbia. On my birthday, I asked Dad if I could take some pictures with his camera on a trip the family was taking to Cape Girardeau the next day. He said yes, so we went to the drugstore and bought a roll of 620 Kodak Verichrome Pan film. I remember being thrilled by the prospect of taking pictures on the trip.

We hit the road in our 1959 Ford Country Sedan wagon, white with red interior and a 352-cubic-inch V8 engine. Mom and Dad sat up front and Tom and I sat in the backseat, being rowdy as usual. Between spurts of laughter and arguing with Tom, I kept a watchful eye out for something to photograph. On old U.S. Highway 61 between St. Louis and Cape Girardeau, I spotted an antique store with a covered wagon sitting out front. I yelled for Dad to stop so I could take a picture. He obliged and pulled to the side of the road. I recall Mom telling me to be careful since we were right on the edge of the road, but I was thoroughly occupied. It was here that I shot my first picture. One frame is all I shot and we moved on to Cape Girardeau where before the end of the day I had shot all eight frames. The camera had a 6x9 format which meant only eight pictures were available on the 620 rolls. Many cameras using 620 films were square format, which would allow twelve exposures.

As soon as we got home Dad showed me how to unload the

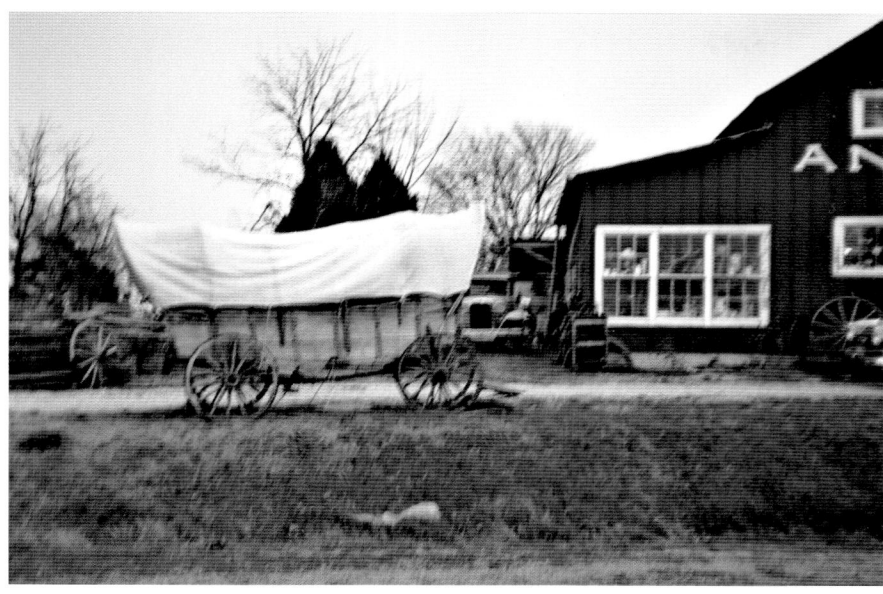

Left, my first picture, Highway 61 near Cape Girardeau, Missouri, November 1, 1960.

1930 Kodak Brownie camera; Kodak Verichrome Pan 620 film; Smith Studio, Columbia, Missouri, processed.

Below left, my parents soon bought me a Yashica D medium format twin lens reflex, a professional camera.

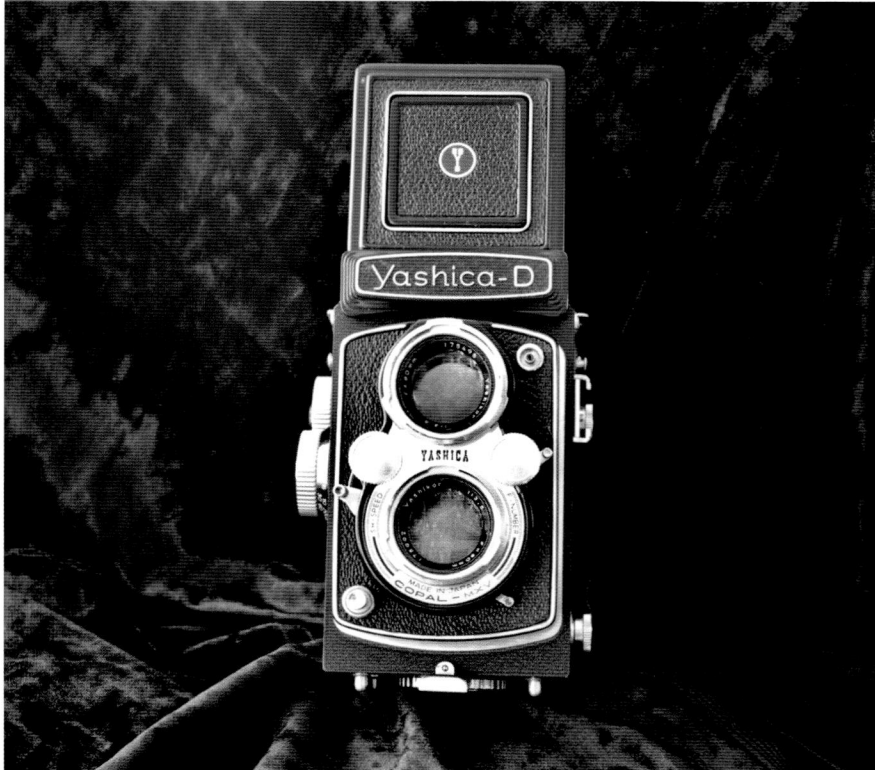

camera, and the next day we took the film to Smith Studio in Columbia for processing. Smith was a portrait studio but they also sold cameras and processed film for local drugstores, camera shops, and drop-off customers. Two days later we picked up the pictures. I had suddenly garnered a big case of the photo bug that has been a permanent part of my life ever since. I was captivated by photography from that day forward; it has been an intimate and enduring aspect of my life.

One year later, on my tenth birthday, my parents bought me a more advanced Kodak Brownie. I wore it out taking pictures of anything and everything. I would send these photos to Smith Studio in Columbia to be processed.

On my thirteenth birthday in 1964, my parents bought me a professional-quality Yashica D twin lens reflex medium-format camera. They wanted me to have a quality camera, especially since I had shown so much interest from the very first roll that I shot. Dad bought the camera at Smith Studio. The Yashica D was the camera most used during the 1960s and into the 1970s for high school and college photography classes. These rugged cameras used 120 film and produced a 2¼x2¼ square negative.

Dad asked Mr. Smith if I could come in after school and see how the film processing and printing was done. Mr. Smith agreed,

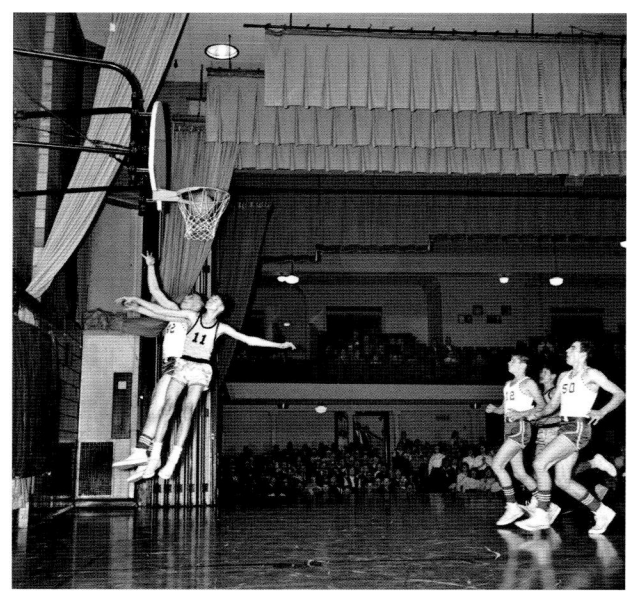

Yearbook photograph for Jefferson Junior High School, Columbia, Missouri, November 1966.

Yashica D camera;
Kodak Verichrome Pan
120 film; FoJo Studio,
Desoto Missouri
processed.

and I became an apprentice at Smith Studio. It was a busy lab, so commercial equipment was necessary. I learned to process film in high volume and how to print on Kodak 5S printers. I would later utilize this experience when I worked for Kodak in their mega processing labs.

My family settled well in Missouri. In the 1960s, I went from fourth grade to my first year in college.

My brother and I were avid baseball players. Back in New Rochelle, I had been the first eight-year-old to make the majors of Little League. Johnny Carson's sons, Christopher and Cory, played in our league and we became acquainted. This was back when Johnny was the host of the game show, *Who Can You Trust*, prior to his tenure on the *Tonight Show*. At age fifteen and playing senior Little League, I was the only player to be voted to the all-star team by every coach in the league. I played baseball through high school, and Tom played golf in high school and college. Tom

was an impressive golfer. He was featured in the "Who's Who" of college golf.

In Columbia, high school began as a sophomore. Freshman were considered junior high. I went to Hickman High School, home of the Hickman Kewpies. Rose O'Neill, creator of the famous Kewpie doll, lived most of her life in Missouri. Having a Kewpie doll as our team mascot did not incite much fear from our opponents, but we were always highly ranked statewide in all sports.

I was one of only two sophomores who made the varsity baseball squad in 1967. We went to the state finals. In the game that we lost, Jerry Reuss, who went on to have an illustrious major league career, pitched against us. I got the only hit against him in that game.

Aside from baseball, I was an aquarist, an interest I mentioned earlier that I shared with my dad. We always had aquariums, and I carry on the tradition to this day.

By 1966, photography was beginning to dominate my time. I was the yearbook photographer in junior high and high school. I was active in the Mid Missouri Camera Club and won awards in my first several photo contests. I also began to exhibit prints in our high school lobby, the local camera store, and the library. In an era when no picture could be seen electronically, getting to exhibit my prints was a great source of pride.

In the fall of 1969, I began college at Northeast Missouri State University (now Truman State). I had a great year, making lifelong friends along the way. At the end of my freshman year in 1970, I pledged a fraternity (Sigma Tau Gamma).

Many of my classmates knew I was a photographer, so I was asked to photograph people and events. In those days, photographers were much rarer. Most people used Instamatic cameras casually; it was not like it has been since the advent of digital photography and smartphone cameras.

Frosted Maple Leaf

Much of my photography has been done by driving around looking for interesting subjects at the moment I am there. If the subject is great but there is not enough time or light to shoot it, I make a note of the subject and location and estimate the time of day the scene would look better. Then go back and shoot it.

A large percentage of my images are "found" while driving on photo trips for the sole purpose of photography. I have had a lifetime of these, beginning with trips with my parents before I could drive. Only a small percentage of my photo outings are specifically to get a particular picture.

My trips usually have a general destination, such as a city, a park, a body of water, or a region of a state. I start by leaving the house very early to be able arrive at my proposed shooting area prior to daylight. I love doing this because the craft is all about where the light is and how it illuminates the subject. Pictures are created from being at the subject when the light is just right.

The simple picture at right is one of those. This image was taken in October 1967 in the countryside near Columbia, Missouri, with my mother driving because I was only fifteen. This image of a frosted sugar maple leaf won a prize at the Mid Missouri Camera Club contest that same year and was displayed in a local bank that always showed the winning images from the camera club. I printed this on 11x14 double weight Kodak Ektalure photographic paper and selenium toned it for image warmth and to help preserve the image. Half a century later, the print still looks new.

Frosted Maple Leaf, near Columbia, Missouri, 10-1967; won third place at Mid Missouri Camera Club annual gallery competition; Yashica D camera; Kodak 120 Verichrome Pan film; 80mm Yashinon lens; Edwal FG7 developer.

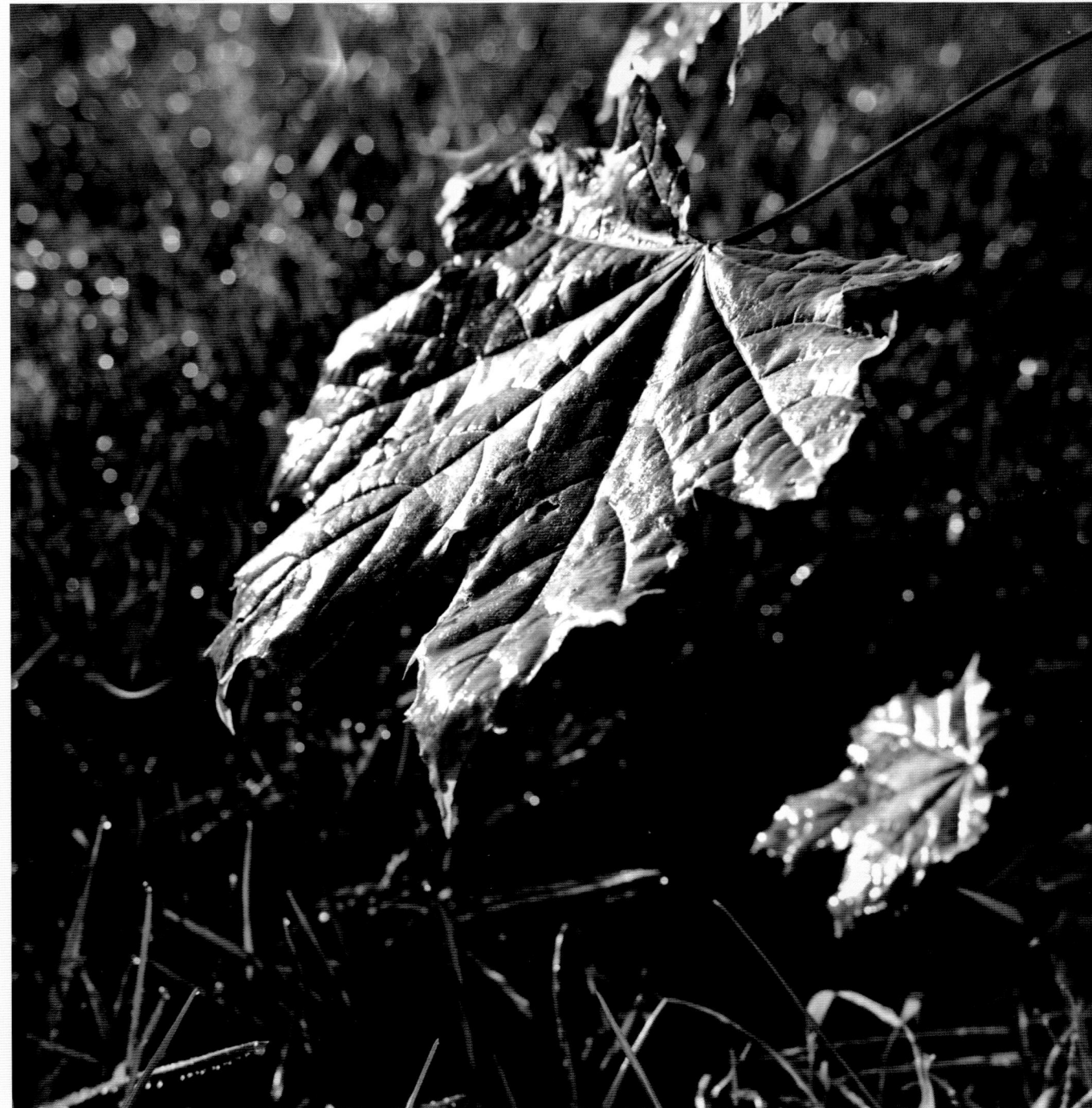

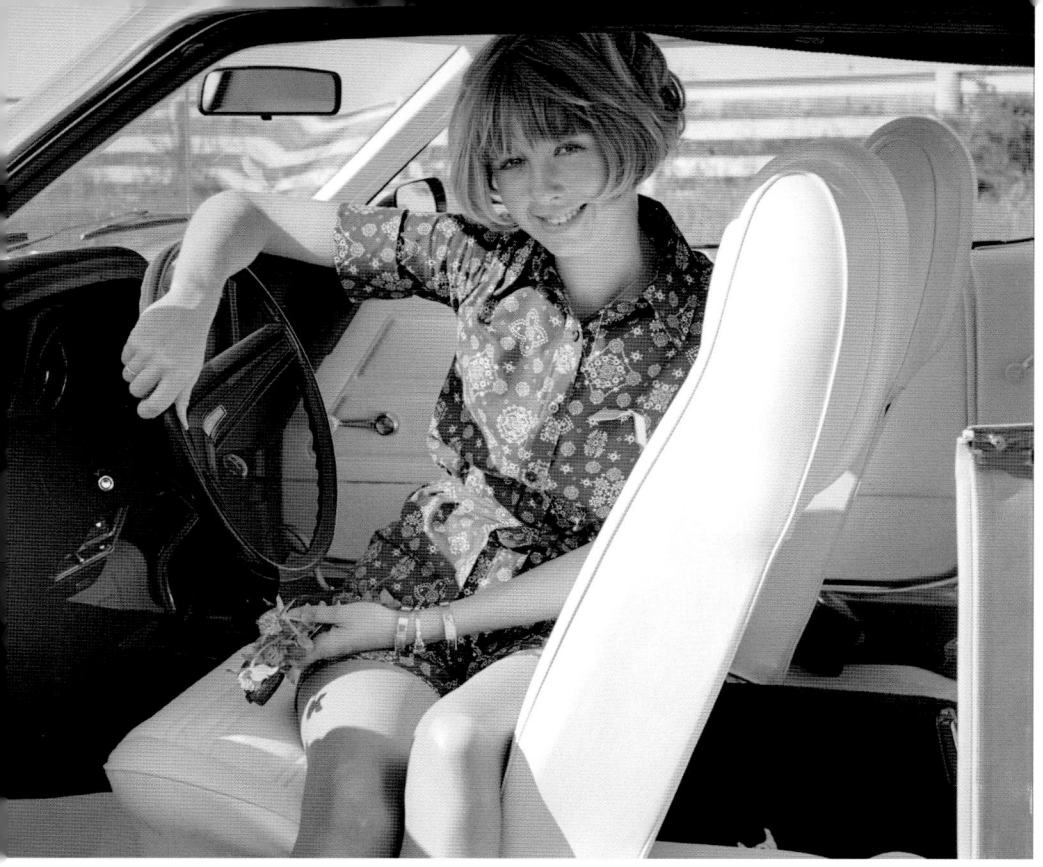

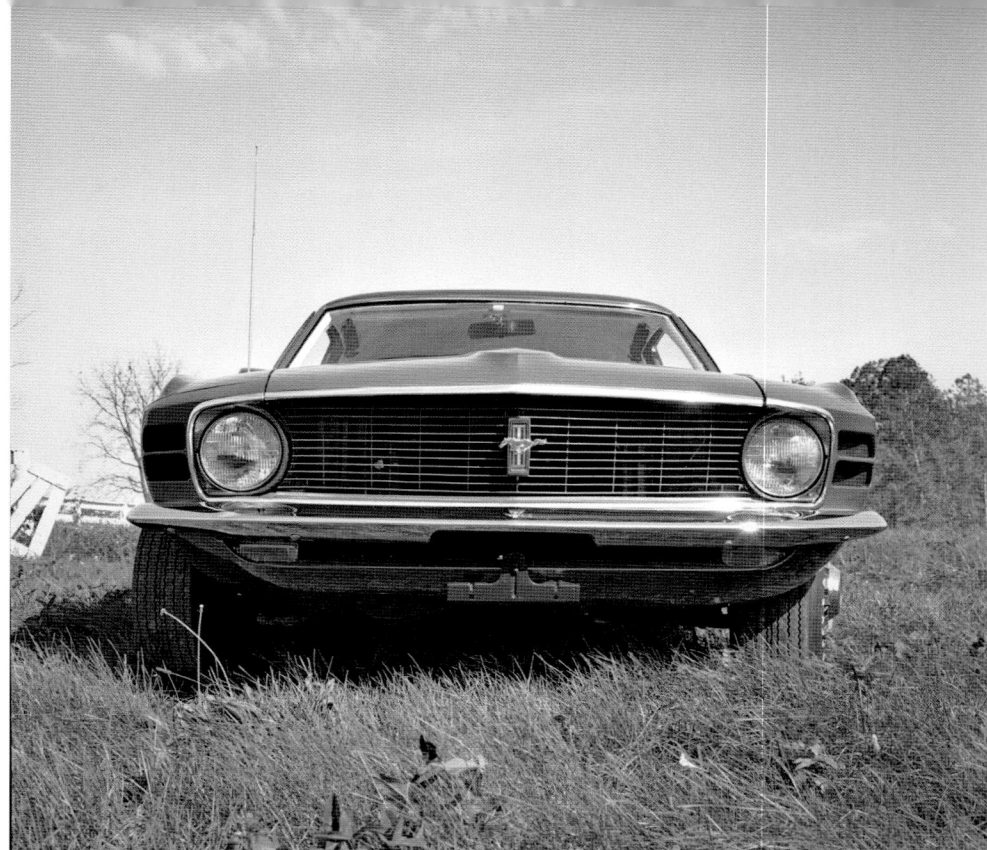

Columbia, Missouri, Ann Payne with my new 1970 351-cubic-inch Mustang coupe, October 1969.

Mamiya C220 camera; 80mm Sekor lens; Kodak Plus X Pan 120 film; Edwal FG7 developer.

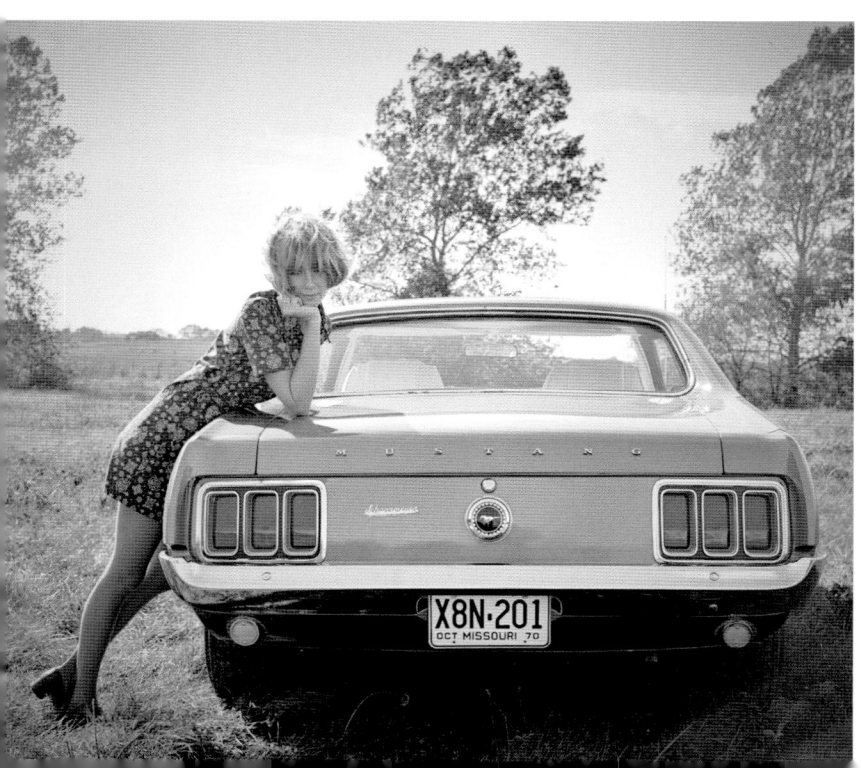

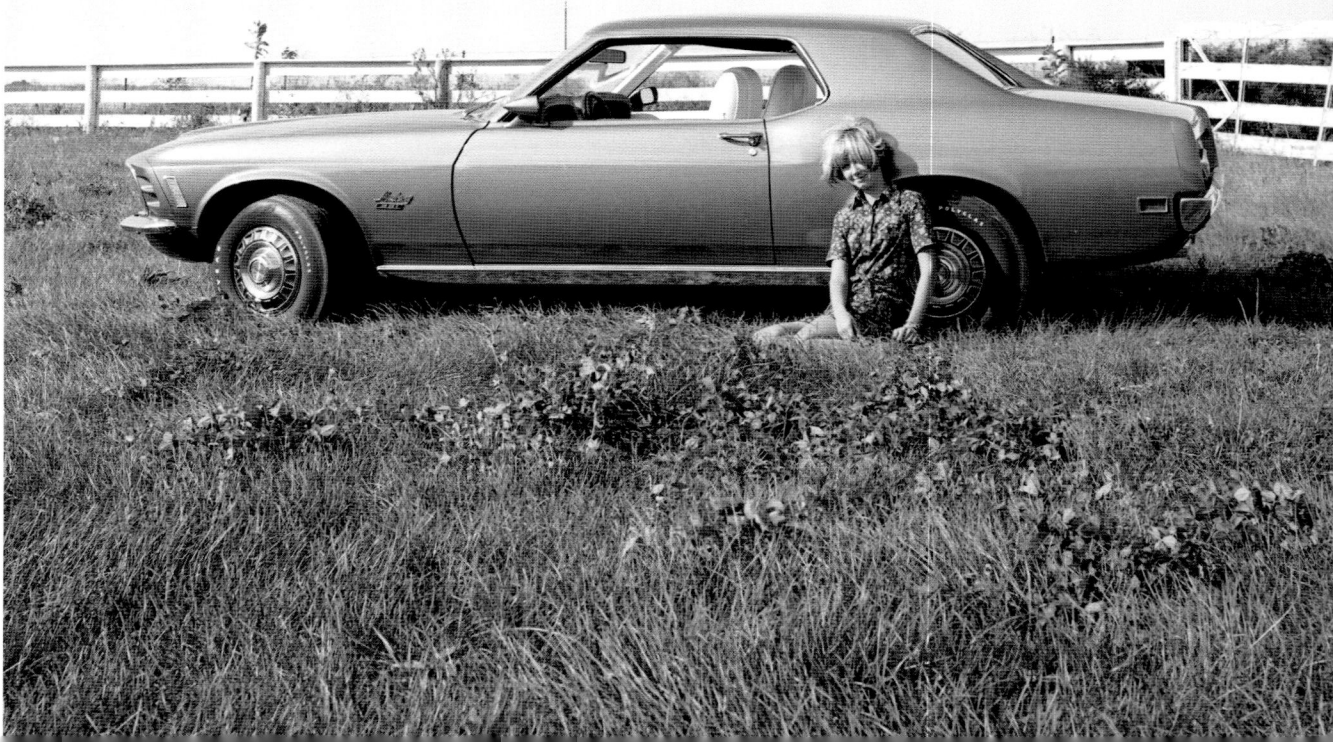

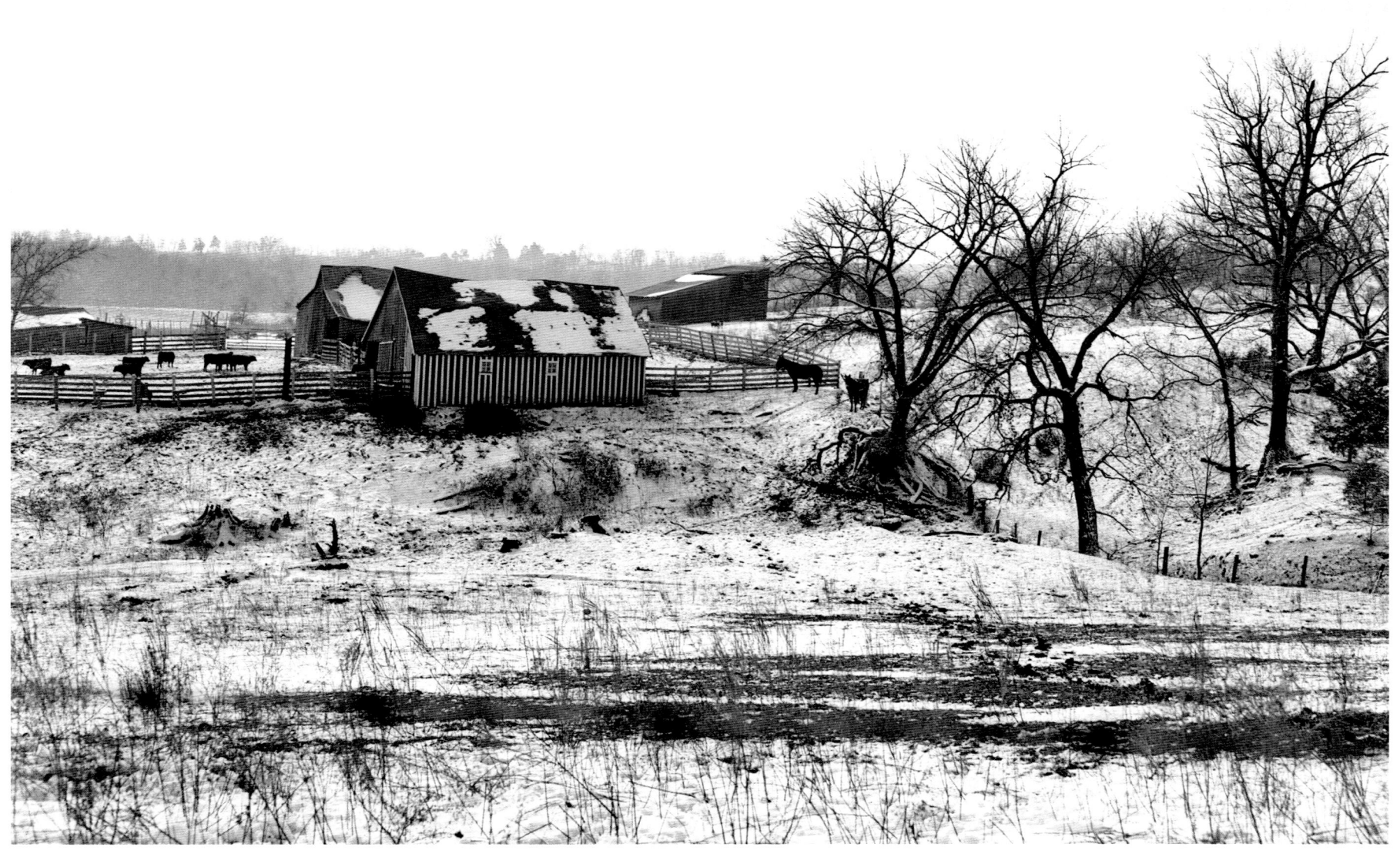

Farm near Columbia, Missouri, 12-1968; Busch Pressman 4x5 camera; 135mm Zeiss Jena Tessar lens; Kodak Royal Pan 4x5 film; Edwal FG7 developer.

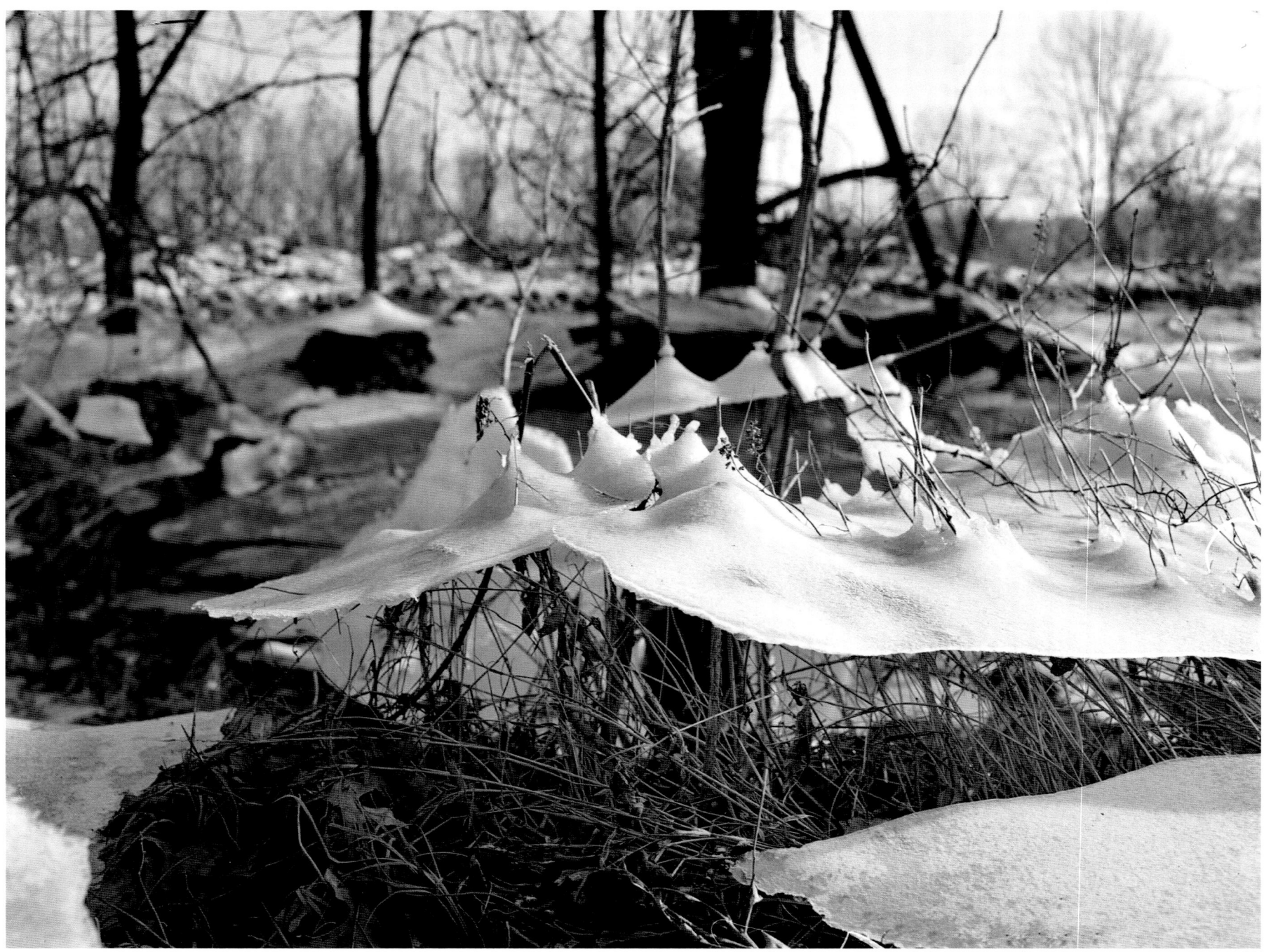

Ice sheets near Columbia, Missouri, 12-26-1968; Busch Pressman 4x5 camera; 135mm Zeiss Jena Tessar lens; Kodak Royal Pan 4x5 film; Edwal FG7 developer.

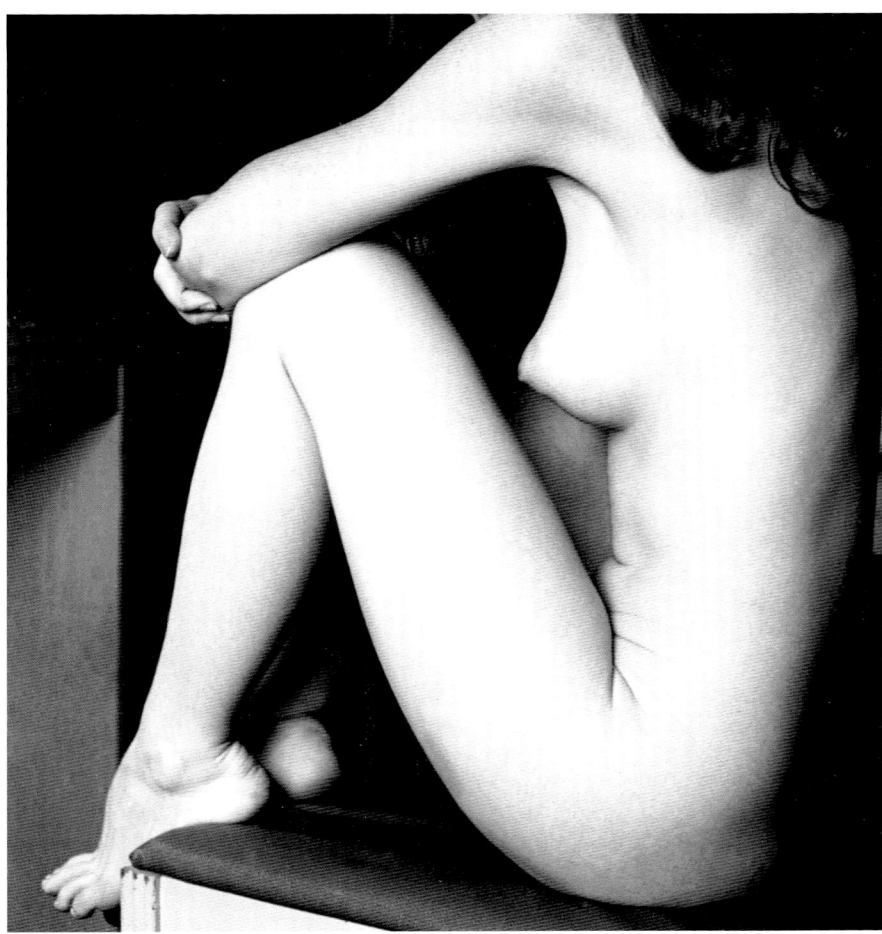

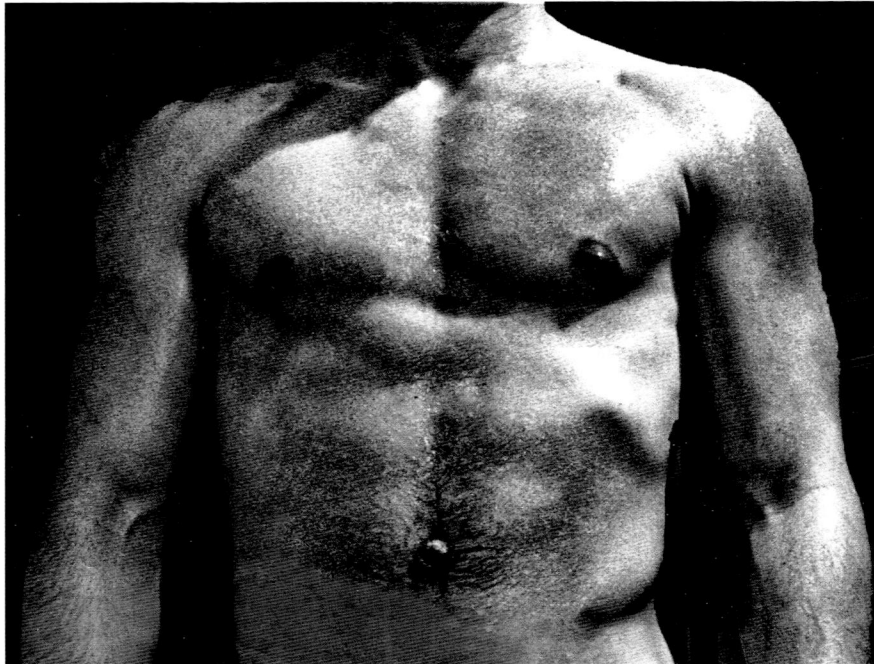

Though my primary photographic interest—and the bulk of my portfolio—has been landscapes and Americana, I have also done portrait and figure photography. Here are two early examples from a college photography class assignment: male and female nude studies from photo class models using natural light, 12-1969; Mamiya C220 medium format camera; 80mm Sekor lens; Kodak Plus X Pan 120 film; Edwal FG7 developer.

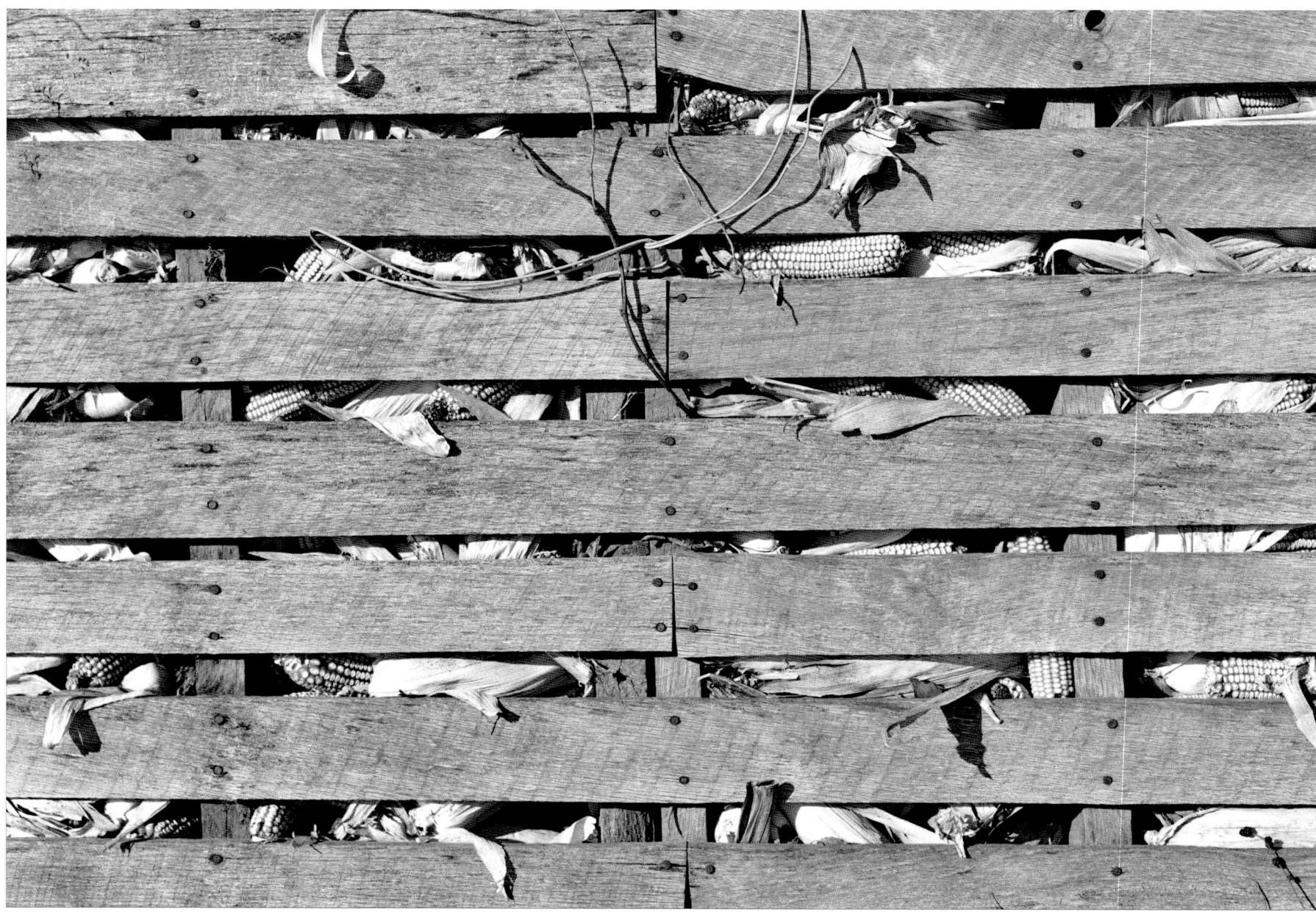

My first large-format picture, Corn Crib near Columbia, Missouri, 12-26-1968: On Christmas Day 1968 my parents gave me a used 4x5 Busch Pressman camera with a 135mm Zeiss Jena Tessar lens, uncoated from the WWII era, and some Kodak Royal Pan 4x5 film, which I used to take the picture on this page. I already had eight years of picture-taking and four years of darkroom experience. Large-format photography opened a new chapter for me, even though I continued with smaller formats too. Each film size had its advantages for particular types of shooting and subject matter. Large-format was hands down the best for landscape photography, which was my primary focus.

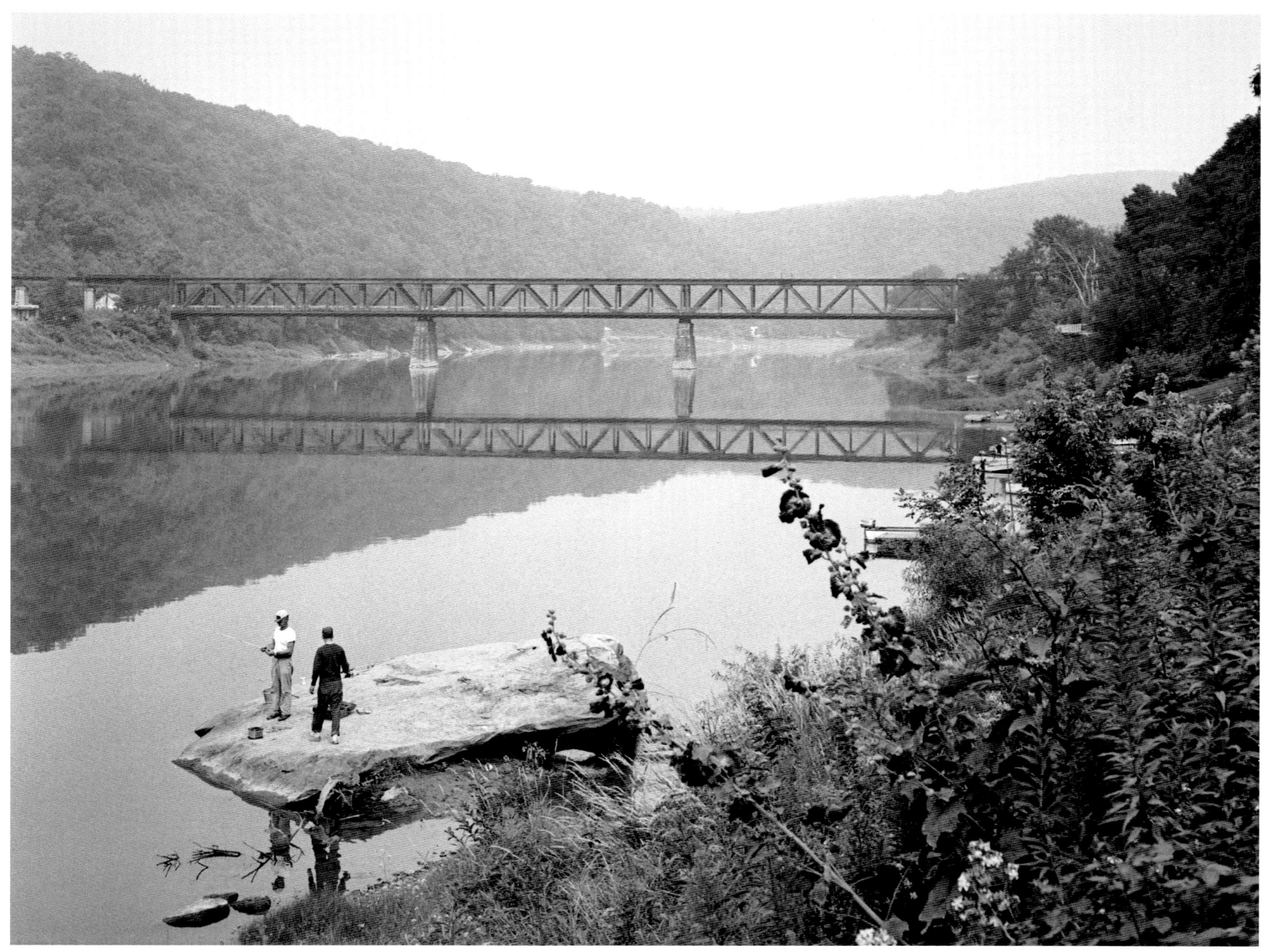

Emlenton, Pennsylvania, Allegheny River, 8-1969. Mamiya C220 camera; 80mm Sekor lens; Kodak Plus X Pan 120 film; Edwal FG7 developer.

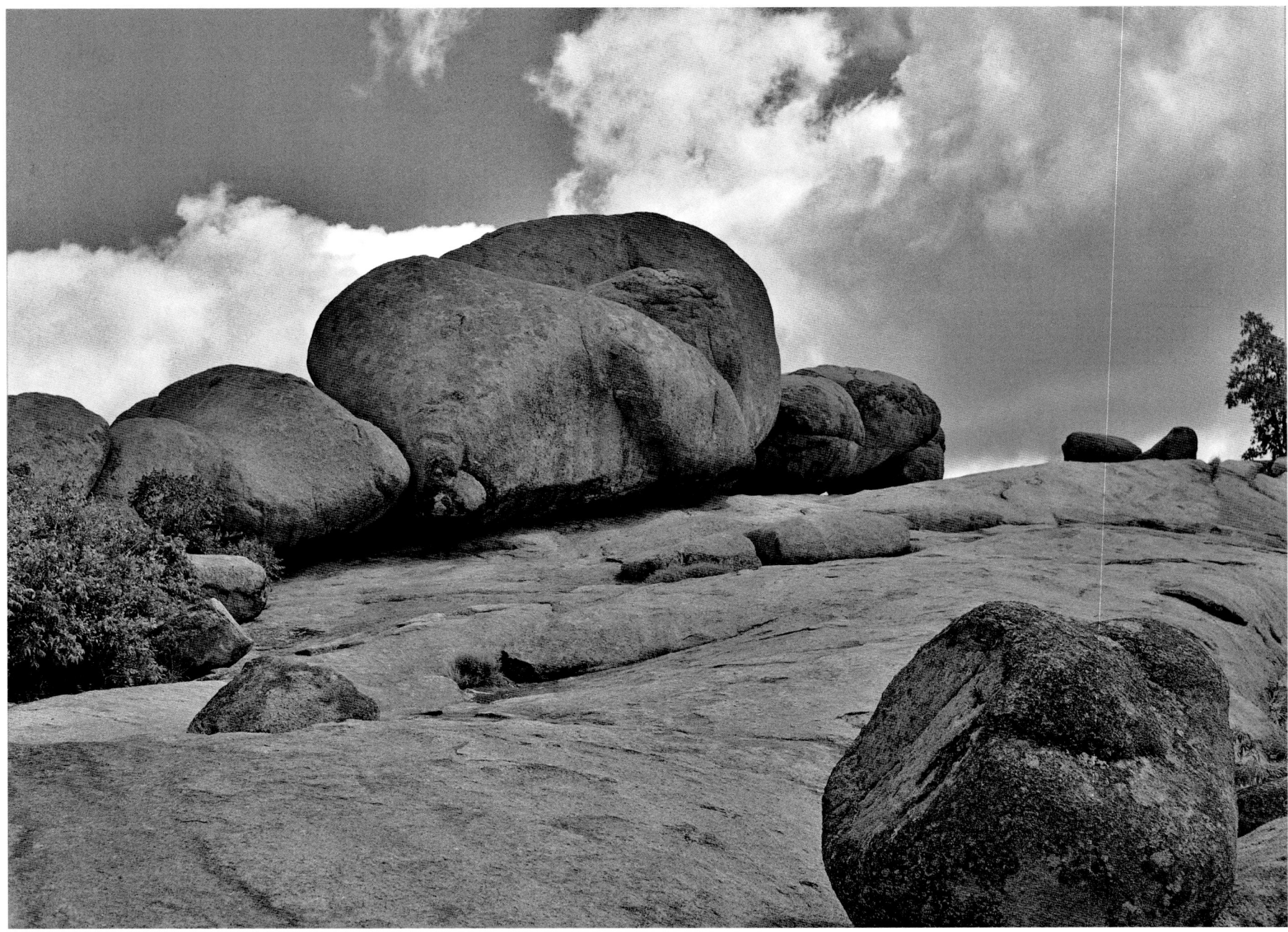

Above: Elephant Rock State Park, Missouri, 7-1969; Mamiya C220 camera; 80mm Sekor lens; yellow K2 filter; Kodak Plus X Pan 120 film; Edwal FG7 developer.

Facing page: Johnson's Shut-Ins State Park, Missouri, 7-1969; Mamiya C220 camera; 80mm Sekor lens; Kodak Plus X Pan 120 film; Edwal FG7 developer.

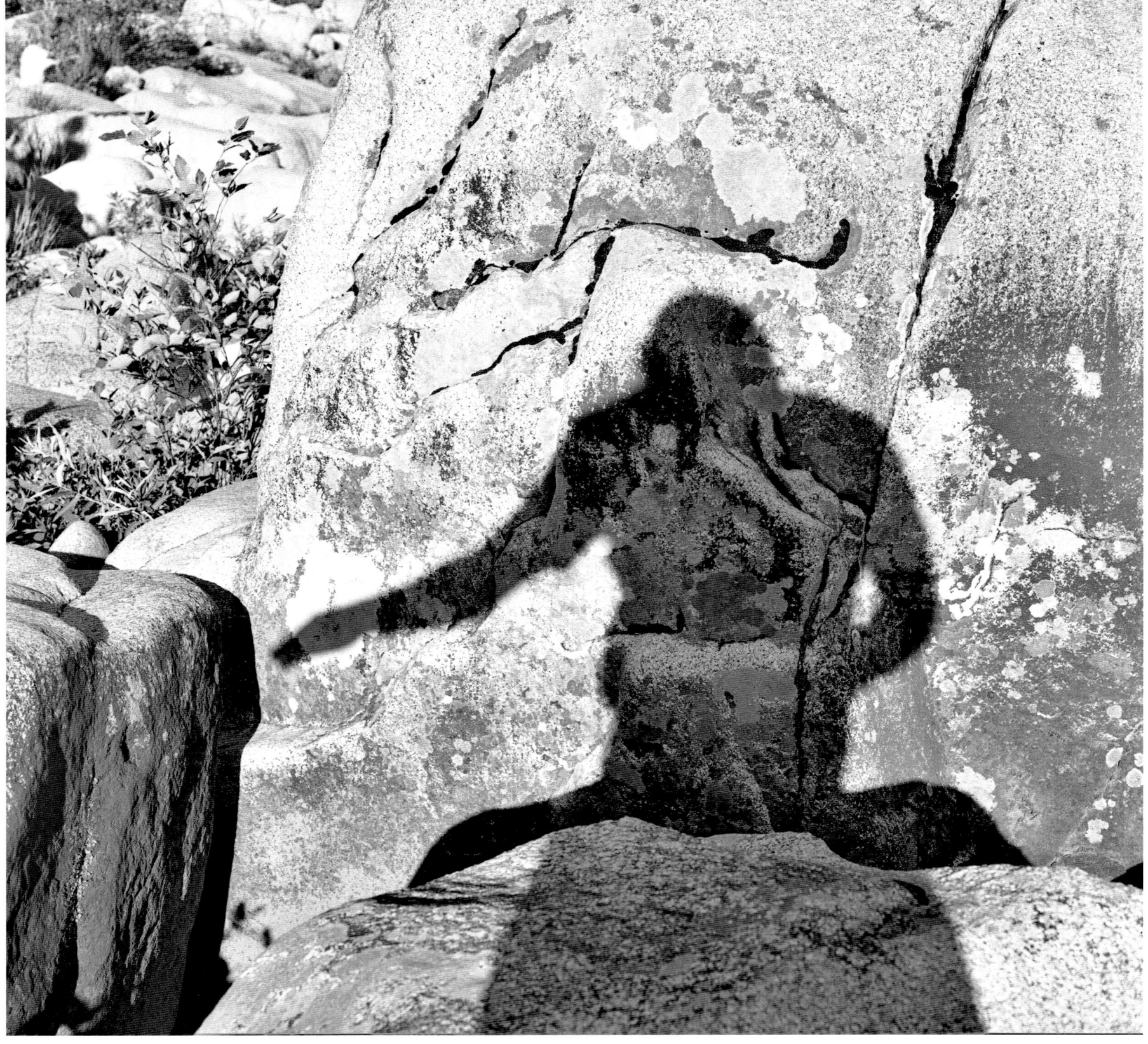

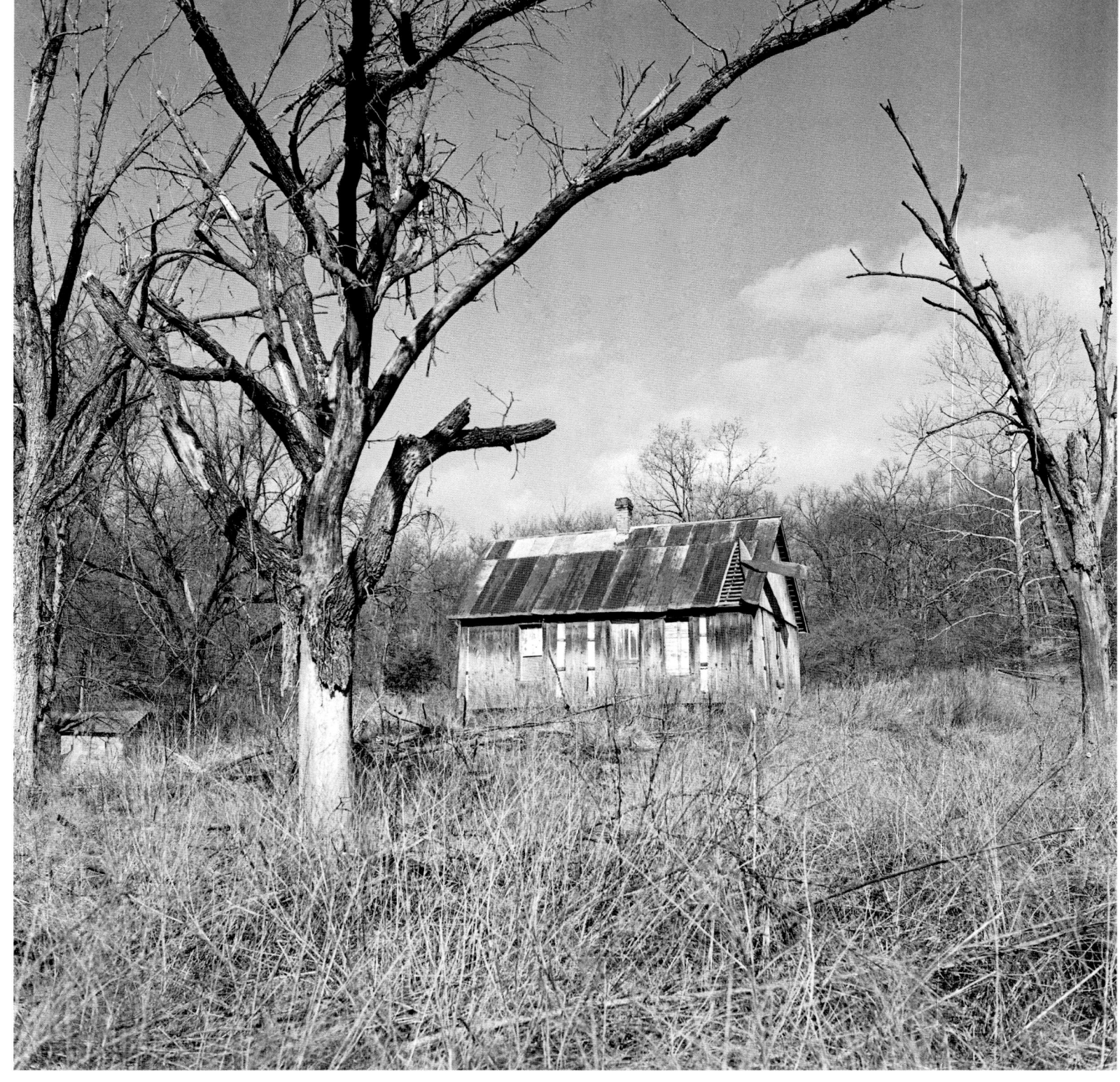

Above: Rural Southern Missouri, 3-1969; Yashica Mat TLR camera; 80mm Yashinon lens; Kodak Verichrome Pan 120 film; Kodak D76 developer.

Facing page: Rural Southern Missouri, 3-1969; Yashica Mat; 80mm Yashinon lens; Kodak Verichrome Pan 120 film; Kodak D76 developer.

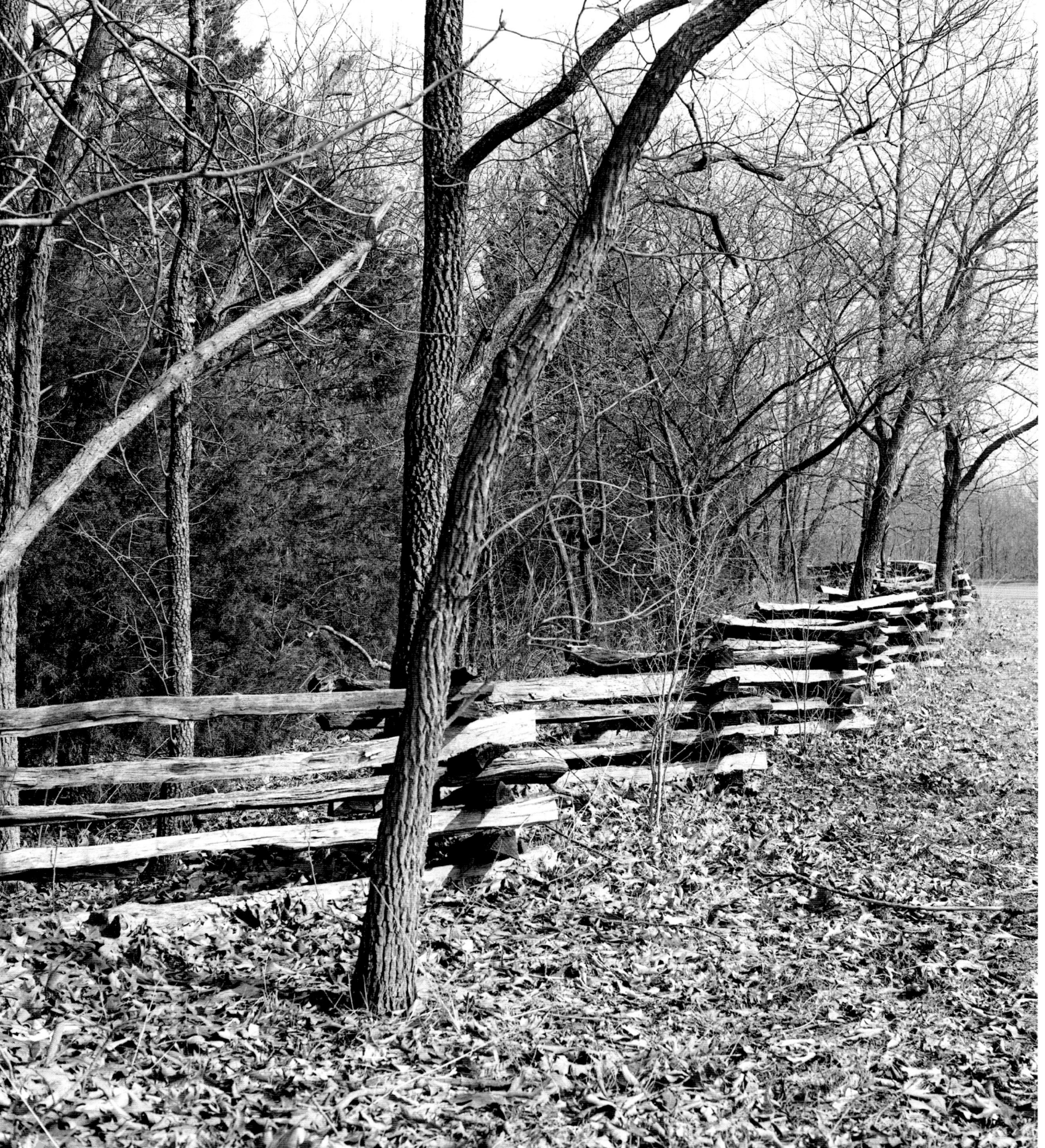

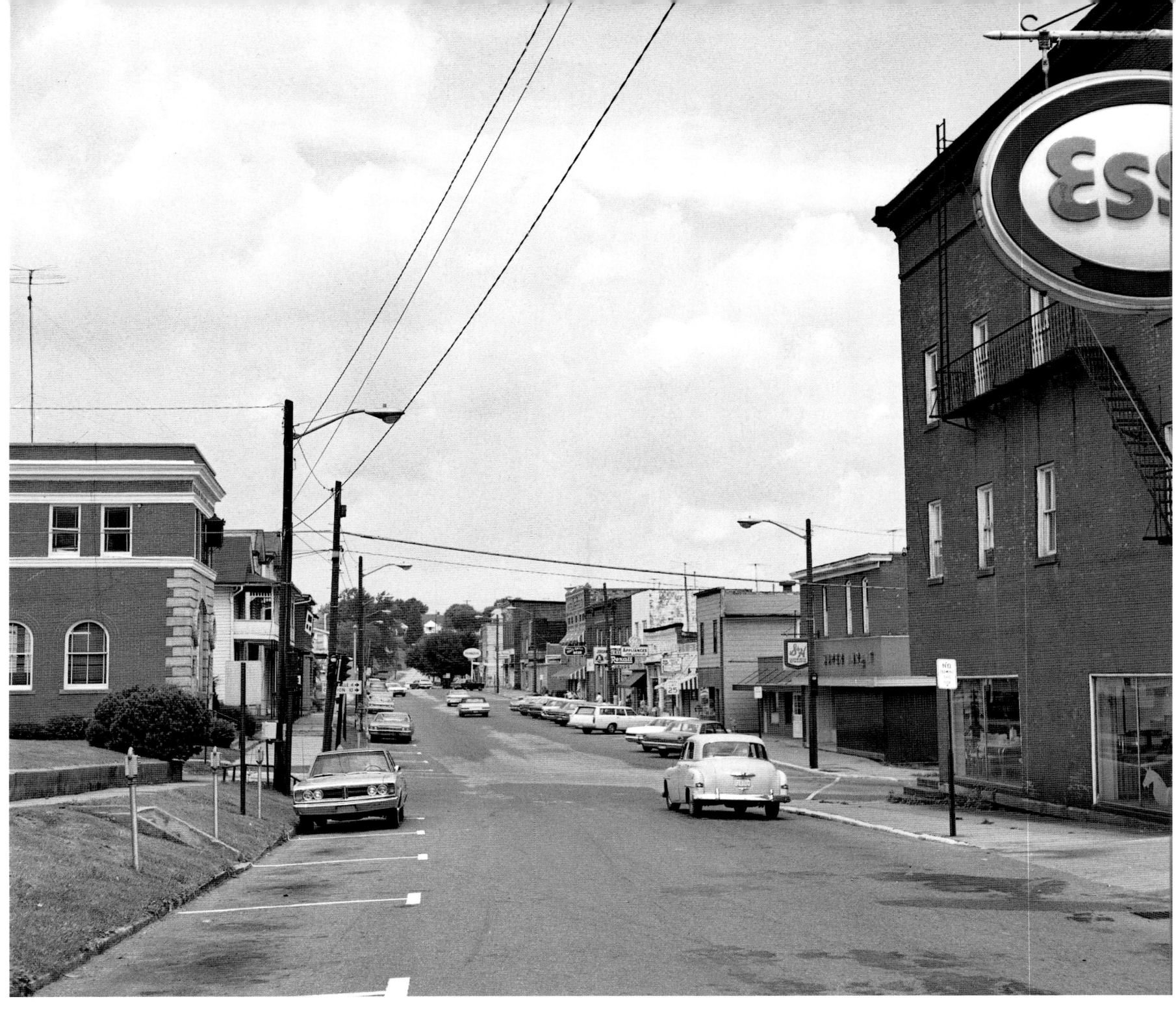

Above: Knox, Pennsylvania, 8-1969; Mamiya C220 camera;80mm Sekor lens; Kodak Plus X Pan Pro 120 film; Edwal FG7 Developer.

Facing page: Rural area near Columbia, Missouri, 10-1967; Yashica D camera; 80mm Yashior lens; Kodak Verichrome Pan 120 film; Edwal FG7 Developer.

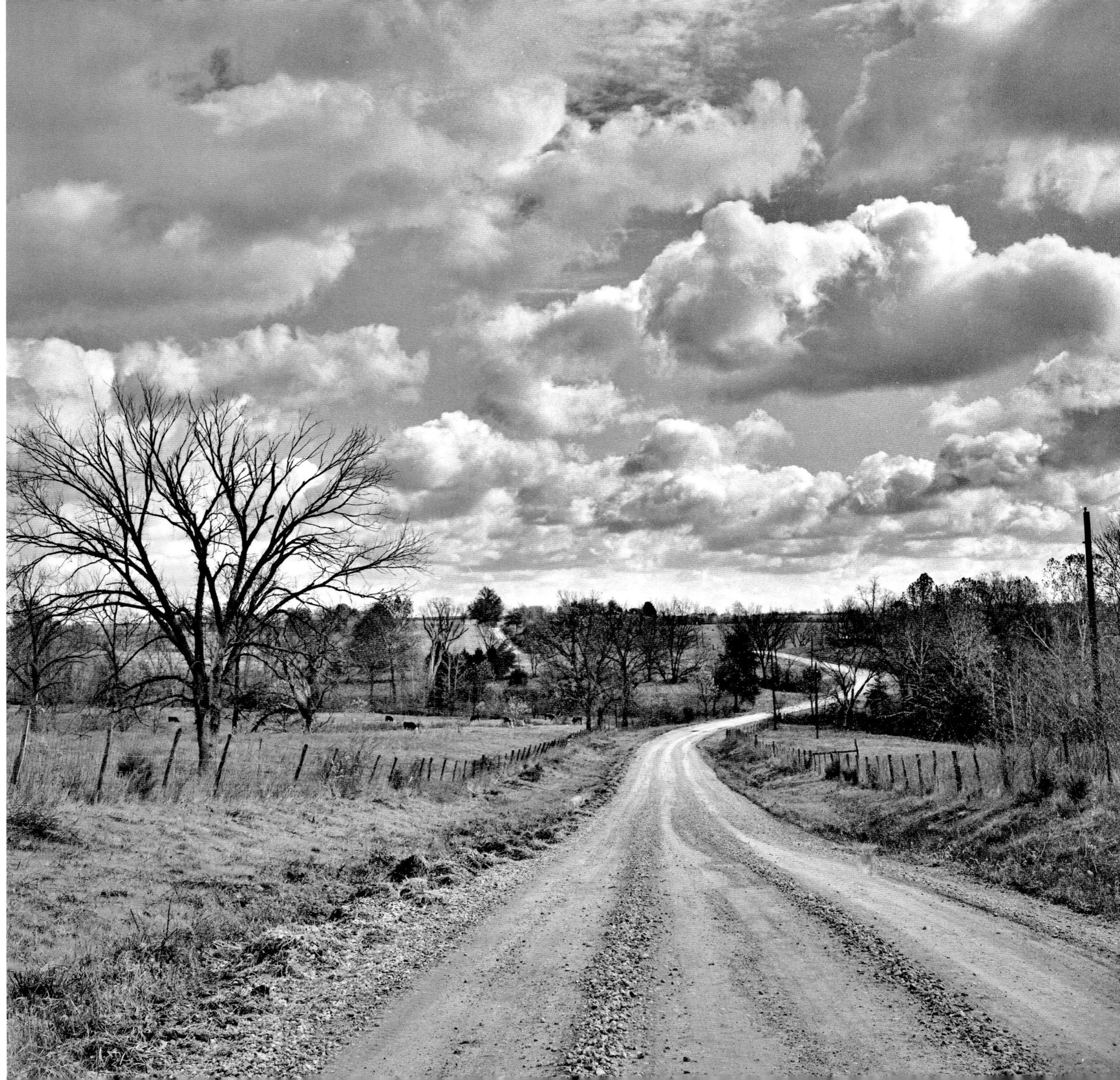

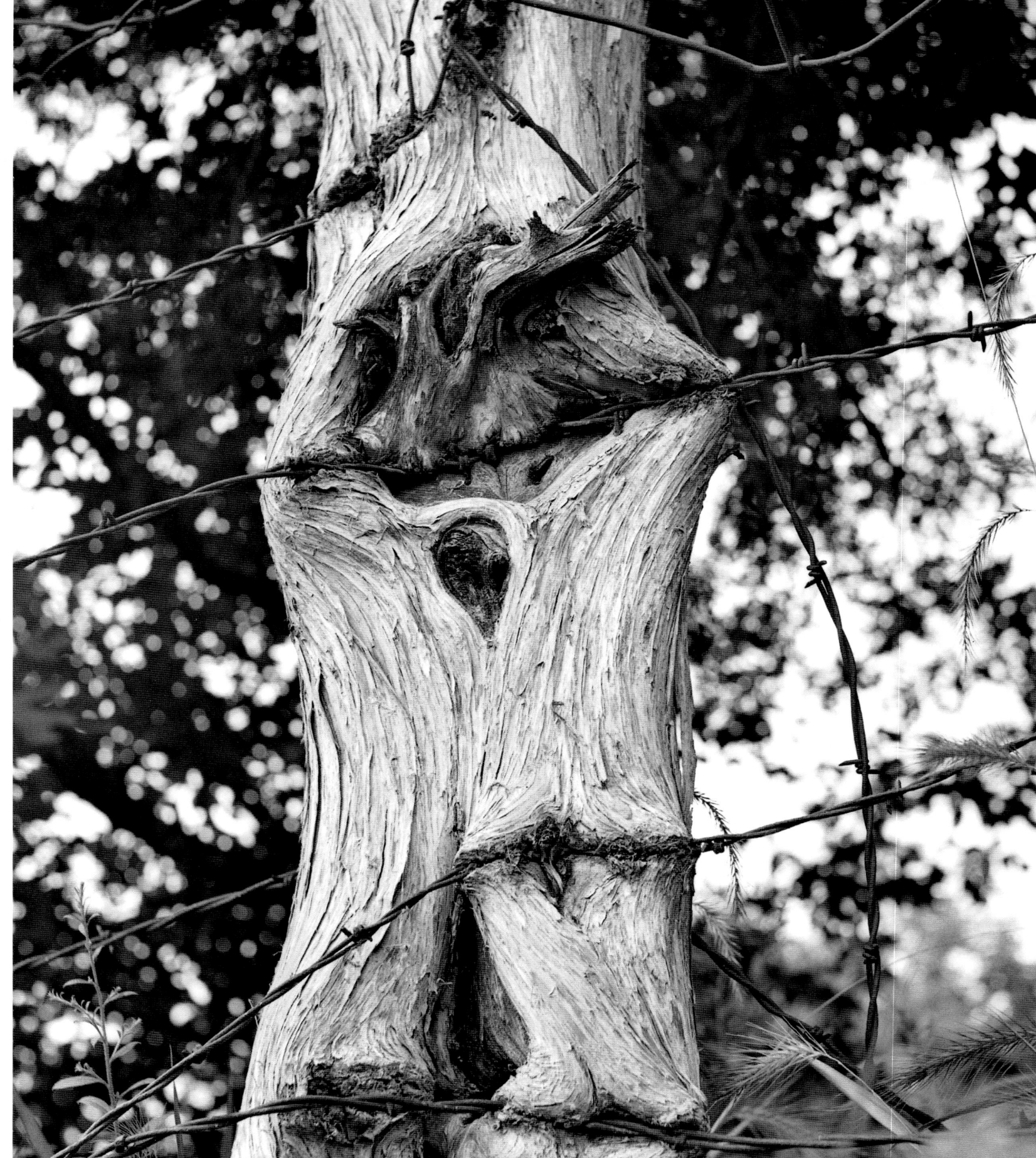

Barbed wire in red cedar tree, rural Boone County, Missouri, 7-1968; Mamiya C220 camera; 80mm Sekor lens; Kodak Verichrome Pan 120 film; Edwal FG7 developer.

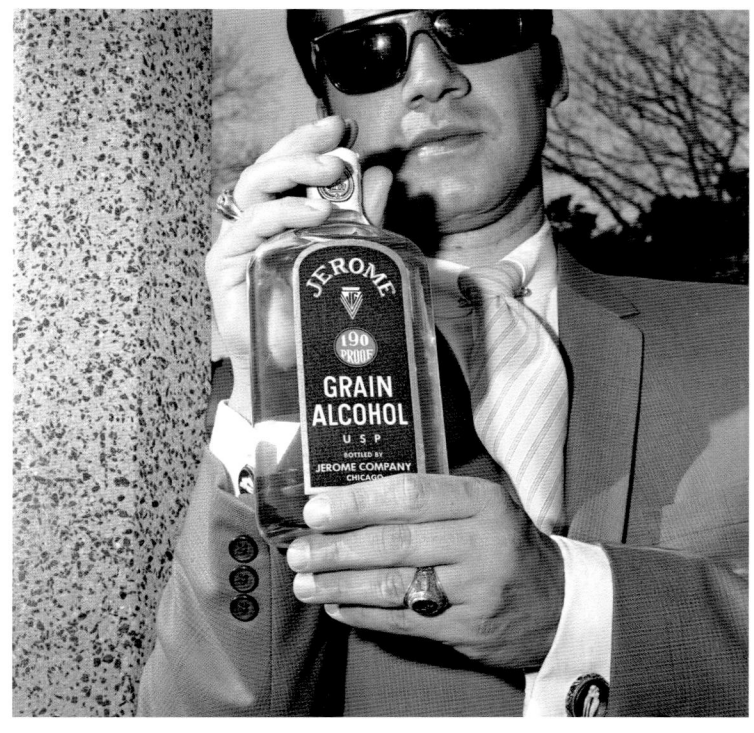

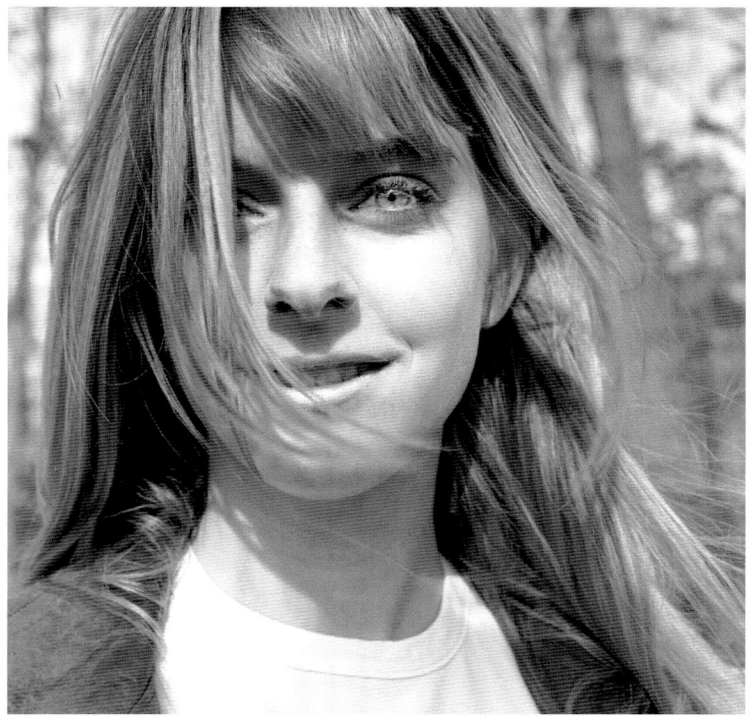

Top left: Sal Costa for advertising shot for college freshman photography class, 10-1969; Busch Pressman 4x5 camera; 135mm Zeiss Jena Tessar lens; Kodak Royal Pan 4x5 film; Edwal FG7 developer.

Top right: Emily Schroeder, countryside near Columbia, Missouri, 12-1969; Mamiya C220 TLR camera; 80 Sekor lens; Kodak Plus X Pan 120 film; Edwal FG7 developer.

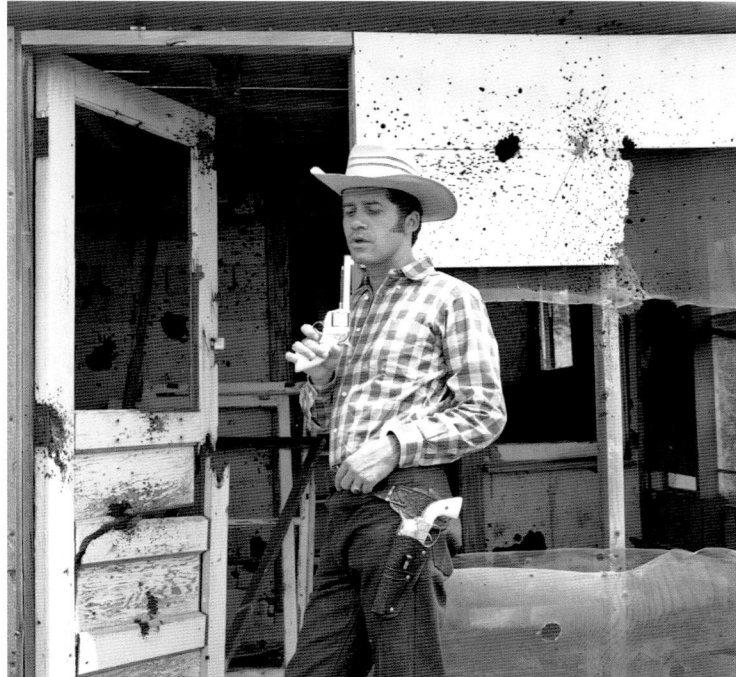

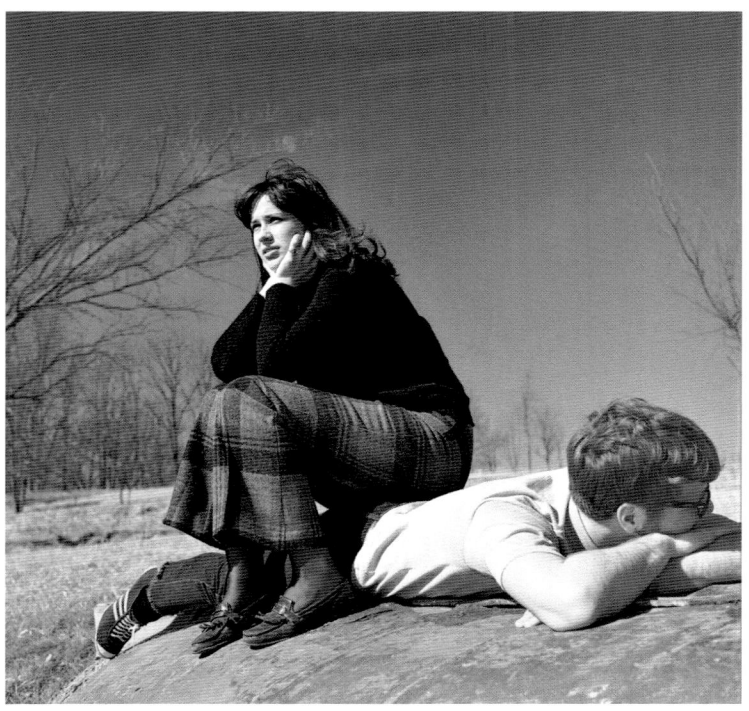

Bottom left: College photography class; photograph a person in a theater or movie setting; Sal Costa, 9-1969; Mamiya C220 TLR camera; 80mm Sekor lens; Kodak Plus X Pan, 120 film; Edwal FG7 developer.

Bottom right: College photography class; topic, a male and a female in an outdoor setting, Thousand Oaks State Park, Kirksville, Missouri,11-1969; Mamiya C220 TLR camera; 80mm Sekor lens; Kodak Plus X Pan, 120 film; Edwal FG7 developer.

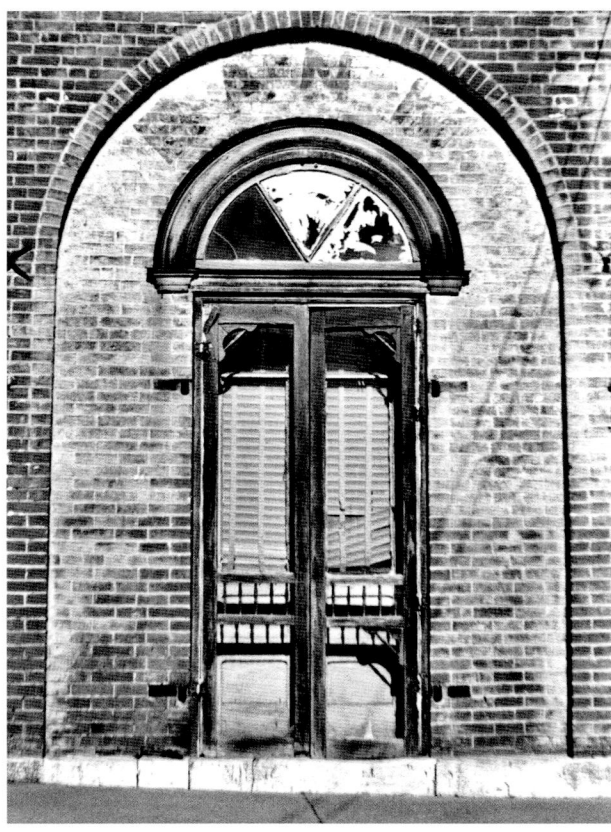

Above: Arrow Rock, Missouri, 1961; Kodak Brownie Hawkeye camera; 620 Verichrome Pan film; Smith Studio, Columbia, Missouri, processed.

Right: Church at Silver Dollar City, Branson, Missouri, won honorable mention at the annual Mid Missouri Camera Club gallery exhibit, 8-1965; Yashica D TLR camera; 80mm Yashinon lens; Kodak Verichrome Pan 120 film; Edwal FG7 developer.

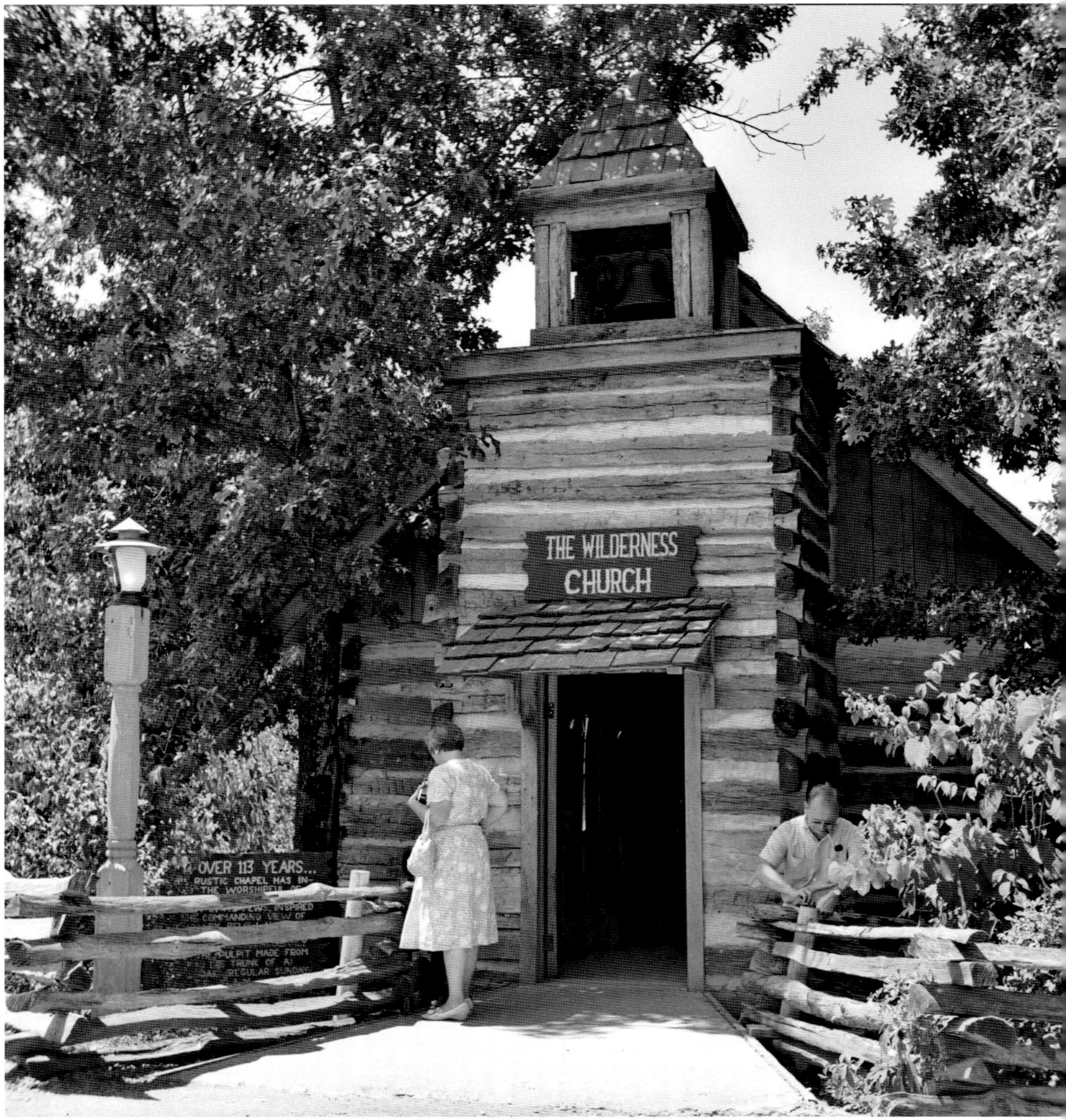

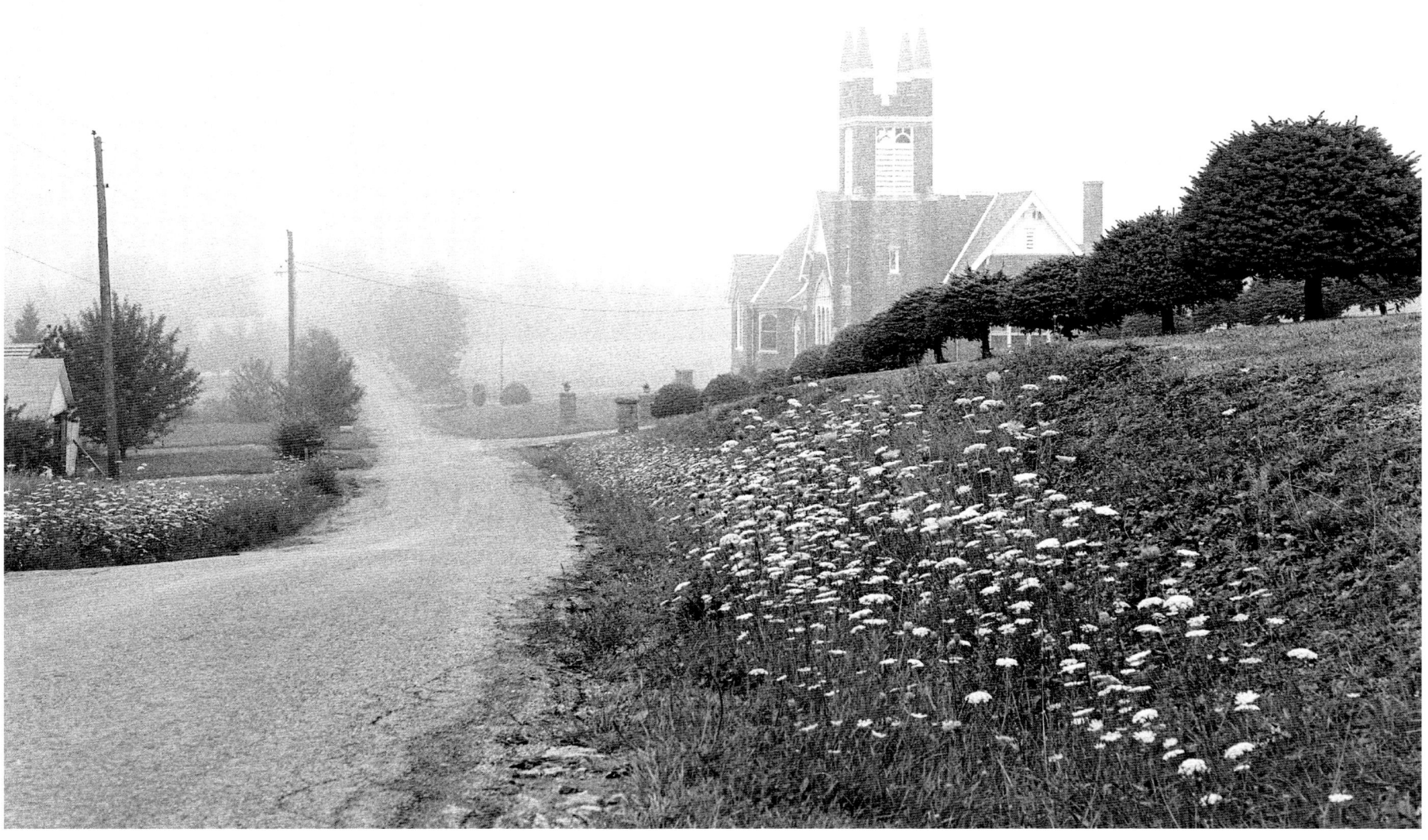

Church in fog, rural western Pennsylvania, 8-1969; Mamiya C220 TLR camera; 80 Sekor lens; Kodak Plus X Pan 120 film; Kodak D76 developer.

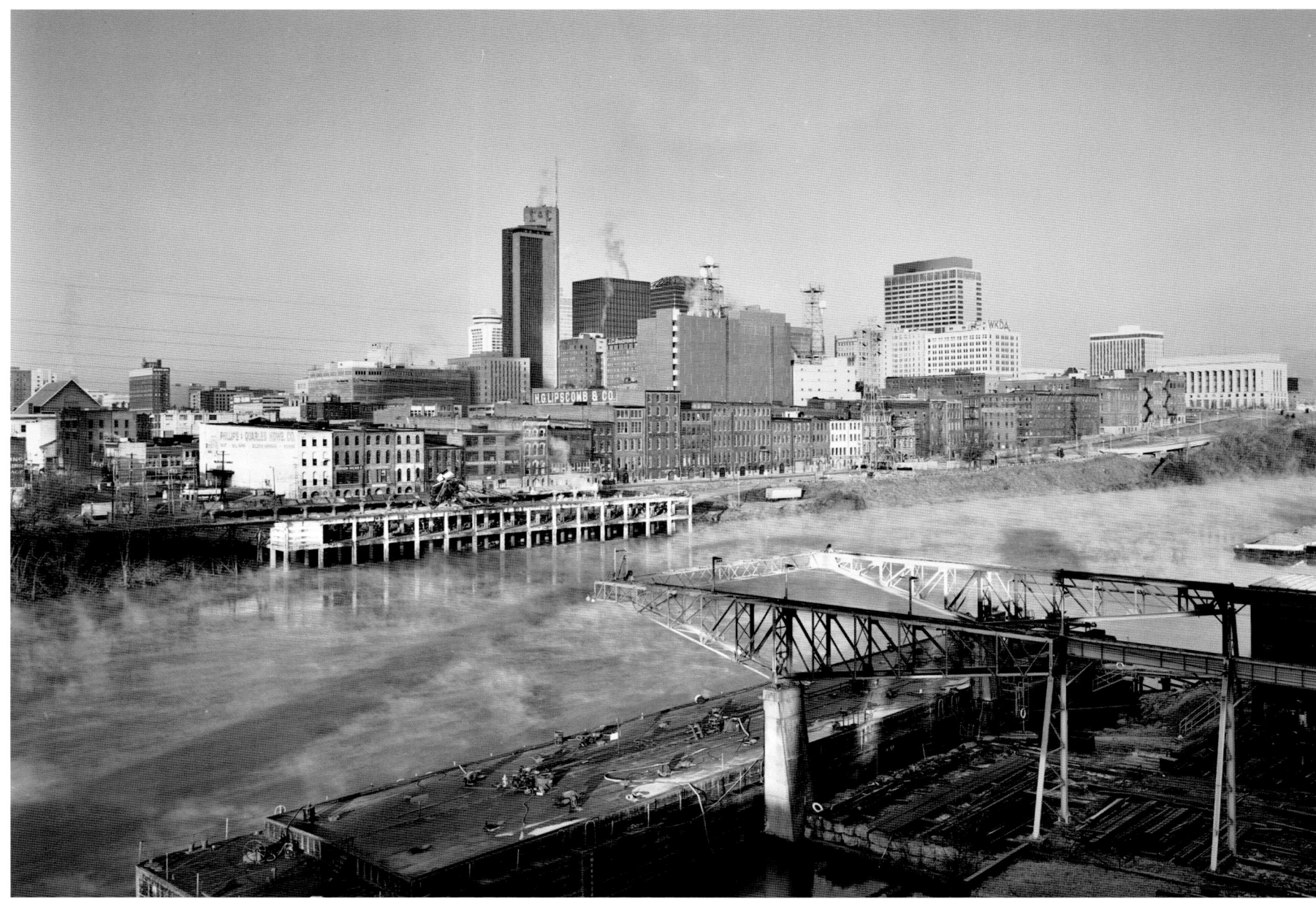

Nashville from the Shelby Street bridge overlooking the Cumberland River, 12-7-1979; Crown Graphic 4x5 camera; 135mm Schneider Xenar lens; yellow G filter; Plus X Pan Pro 4x5 film; Edwal FG7 developer.

2

The 1970s: Perfecting the Craft

I consider the 1970s my favorite decade. Not only because of my increased immersion in photography, but also because a number of wonderful things happened to me over the course of the decade.

By my sophomore year (1970–71) at Northeast Missouri State University, my photography had become popular on campus. I was asked to take the yearbook group photographs for the fraternities and sororities. It was a time of free-spirited people and social change; no one wanted traditional college portraits. I posed people standing in a lake, laying down on the grass, hanging from trees, leaning out fraternity house windows, etc. I tried anything that I thought was original and weird. I was living in a rental house with my college roommate, Sal Costa. The house had a basement that was perfect for a darkroom to process and print these pictures. Despite clever ideas for the shots, I remember being horrified by the results of my yearbook photography. I refused to get a copy of the yearbook myself. I saw it one time at the university library and vowed never to look at it again.

In 1971, I transferred from Northeast Missouri State University in Kirksville back home to Columbia to attend the University of Missouri. I was taking photography and photojournalism but was unsure if I wanted to continue the major. At that time, I was pursuing a lot of other interests. I started writing poems my junior year of high school, which blossomed into songwriting. By 1971, I had melodies to pair with some of my poems. I began playing guitar and singing around this time. I loved Nashville and was a country music fan, but I was more interested in light rock and adult contemporary. It was the singer/songwriter era, and I thought I could make a career of it.

On February 2, 1972, I moved to Nashville with $285 and a 1970 Mustang that Mom and I had been sharing. My parents agreed to let me have the car if I would pay them back at a later date, which I did when my Aunt Maude died later that year and left me some money.

I did not know a soul in Nashville and had no job prospects. None of that could dampen my spirits. I did have a slight acquaintance with Jim Ed Brown and his sister, Maxine. During the Nashville Sound era, Jim Ed, Maxine, and Bonnie Brown had country crossover hits like "The Three Bells," "The Old Lamplighter," and "Scarlet Ribbons" (in 2015, the Browns were inducted into the Country Music Hall of Fame). The sisters had retired in 1967, and Jim Ed was recording for RCA as a solo act. I had met the Browns

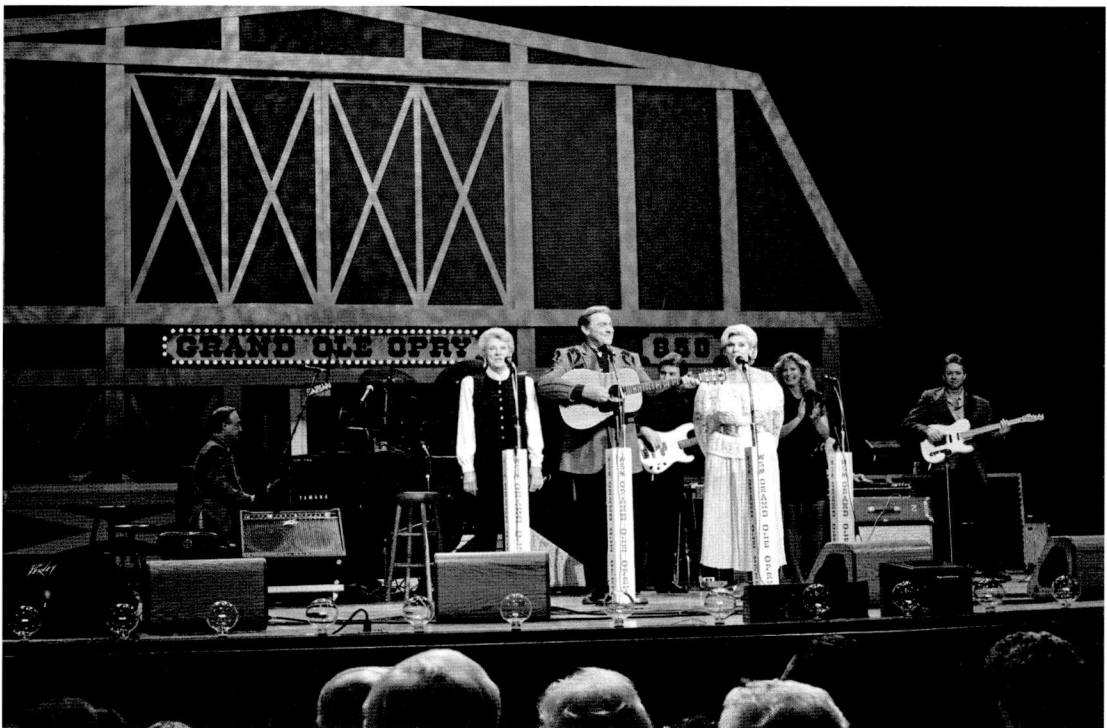

The Browns at the Grand Ole Opry, Nashville, Tennessee, August 1996. The Browns are members of the Country Music Hall of Fame, and this picture is used in the Hall.

at a concert where I took pictures of the show. I sent the pictures to them and Jim Ed lined his office walls with them. Maxine was living in Little Rock, Arkansas, and had a recording studio there. I decided on my way to Nashville that I would go to Little Rock first to show her my songs.

When I left Maxine, she handwrote a letter for me to give to Jim Ed. She asked him to help me out. On February 4, after my first night in Nashville in a cheap hotel, I drove down to Demonbreun Street near Music Row and visited Jim Ed in his office. He was located in the Faron Young Building, which housed Young, also a

Hall of Famer, and several other artists.

Jim Ed read his sister's letter. He remembered me from the pictures that were sprawled all over his office wall. He took me to lunch at Minnie Pearl's Fried Chicken (Bill Anderson and Eddy Arnold were among the other Nashville stars who got into the restaurant franchise business). After lunch Jim Ed promised to have his band, The Gems, work up a couple of arrangements of my songs. I was twenty, so I think Jim Ed wanted to look after me. He even called Mom from his office to let her and Dad know that I had arrived in Nashville and was safe.

Over the years, I stayed in touch on and off with Jim Ed, Maxine, and, occasionally, Bonnie. Four decades later, when Maxine wrote her auto-biography *Looking Back to See* (the title of an early Browns hit), I had been communicating with her about some pictures I took of the Browns in 1996 at a Grand Ole Opry reunion; she wanted to donate those pictures to the Country Music Hall of Fame for the Browns display.

In 2018 Maxine wrote a Facebook response to my photography, noting our meeting all those years prior:

Through the years, I have met & shook hands with a lot of people. I remember very few, but of those few I often wonder what happened to them.

One winter day in 1972, a nice young, good-looking man found his way to mine & my sister Bonnie's recording studio in North Little Rock, Arkansas. He had written some songs & wanted our opinion . . . He held us spellbound as we listened intently to his velvet voice, watched his big smile, & those big blue eyes. He was very good, but Bonnie & I had retired from show biz & had pretty well lost contact with anyone who was honest & who we could recommend he go talk to. . . . However, I gave him a few names to contact in Nashville. . . . Several years passed. I never heard from him. Then, all of a sudden, someone was sending me pictures of the Grand Ole Opry & making nice comments on my computer. It never dawned on me who that person may be. . . . Then, I started seeing some great pictures of the rural South, cotton fields, farmhouses, or shacks, the way life was back in the Depression years, & my life growing up during those years in Dallas County, Arkansas. These pictures inspired me & they were my life . . . They are priceless!!!!! The friend I met in 1972 made a lasting impression on me . . . His name is John Dersham.

Over the next few days, I found an apartment, and my experience with tropical fish helped me land a job at Doctor's Pet Center at 100 Oaks Mall in Nashville. At the pet store I met Robin Rice, a Peabody College student who loved pets. We hit it off immediately and for the next several years had an on-again, off-again relationship. Eventually we became good friends and we stayed in touch till she passed away in 2017.

In June 1972, I went to work as manager for the camera department at J. C. Penney, which also was at 100 Oaks Mall. I put in a job application mostly because of all the pretty girls working there. I did not know the store was looking for a camera department manager, but my prior jobs written on my application all revolved around photography. In a few days store manager Ray Moore called me to ask me to come in for an interview, then hired me at $2.50 an hour, which was double what I had been expecting as a store clerk. I worked at J. C. Penney for the next three and a

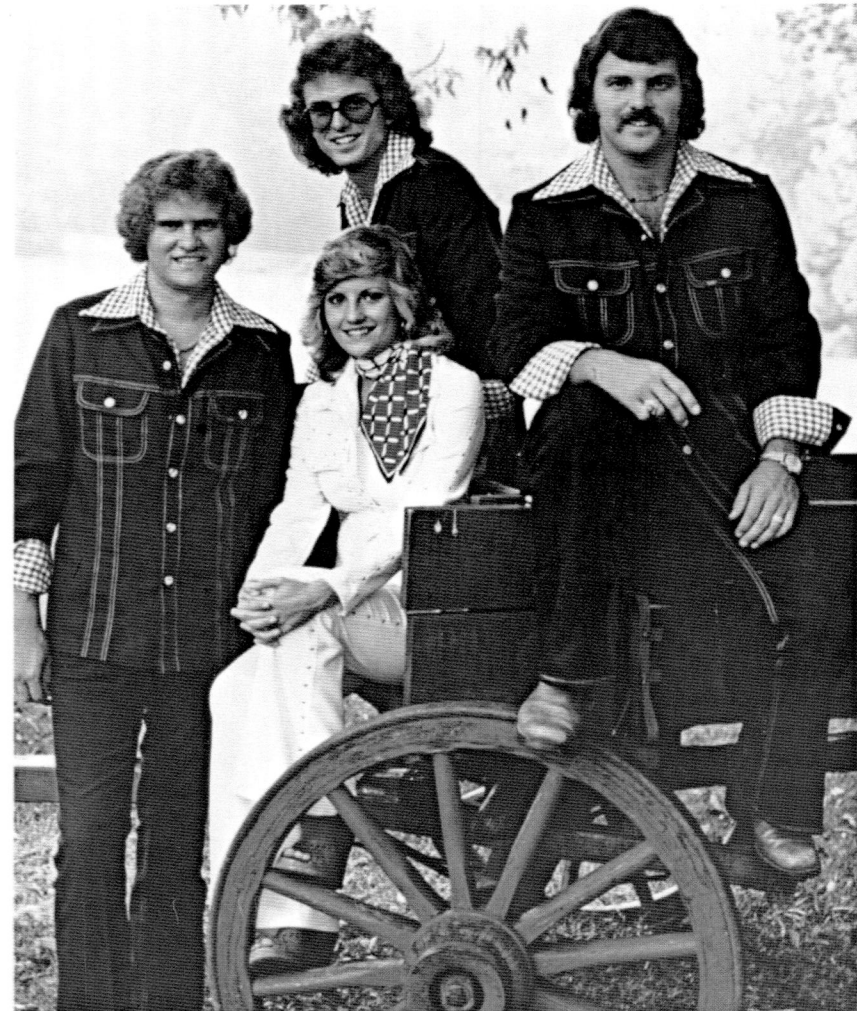

YOUNG COUNTRY

Young Country promo shot, 1975; LaDonna, Rudy, and Steve Gatlin and Tim Johnson (standing, left). Brother Larry Gatlin was a solo act at the time.

Olympus OM1 camera; 50mm Zuiko lens; Kodachrome film; Kodak processed.

half years, dating girls, writing songs, and having a wonderful time.

I met lots of people in the music industry, though I found it much easier to get their attention as a photographer than as a songwriter. I soon got jobs doing album covers and promo pictures for well-known artists like Jim Ed Brown and the Browns, the Gatlins, and the Blackwood Singers.

From 1972 to 1974, I was writing songs and pitching them to artists. I had befriended Rusty Thornhill, who played music at the Holiday Inn at the foot of the capitol building in Nashville. I started to see him fairly often. He invited me over to the new recording studio he built in the basement of his house. He owned a publishing company, Pen Shanty Music, and a private label record company, BRT Records. Thornhill liked my songs and my voice, so his company got three of my songs recorded by other artists and one by him. I became an American Society of Composers, Authors and Publishers (ASCAP) writer and ended up recording under Thornhill's label two of my songs: "Love Is My Gift to You" and "Dixie Feeling." They were not hits, but I made lots of friends and got a few small royalty checks. I heard two of my songs played on local radio stations, which was incredible. Meanwhile, I never stopped working a regular job and never performed live.

IN LATE 1975 AND 1976, I partnered with Larry Scot Little, who had moved to Nashville from Miami. He was there for the same reason I was. We both loved easy-listening music by the likes of John Denver, Bread, Lobo, America, Don McLean, Gordon Lightfoot, and the Carpenters. We worked on several projects together, none of which was financially fruitful, but we became good friends. We hung out a lot, contemplating out loud life, philosophy, and other thought-provoking subjects.

In 1973, my parents bought me a duplex in Nashville. They let me live on one side and manage the tenants and the rent on the other side, letting the rent pay the house note. What a deal! I was in a neighborhood called Crieve Hall, only a few

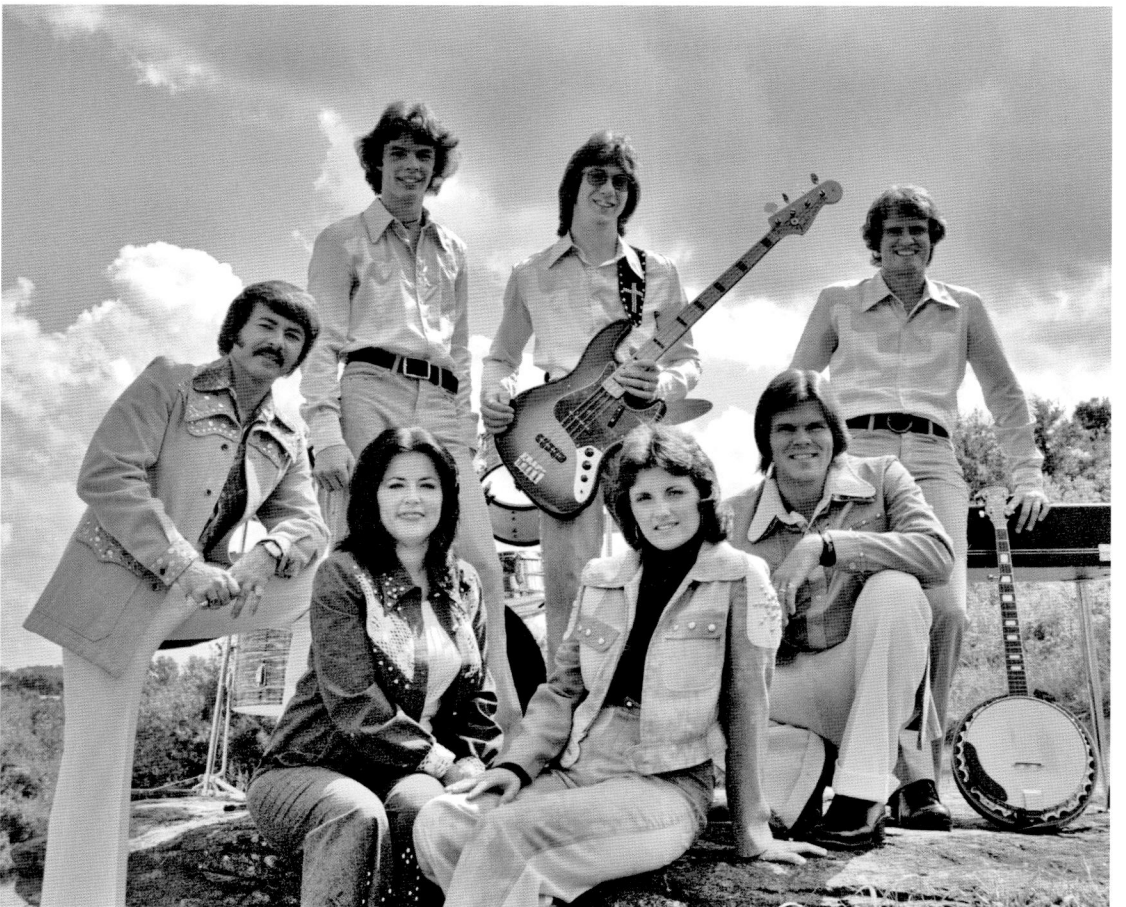

The Blackwood Singers, Nashville, Tennessee, 9-1974; promotion shot; Yashica 635 TLR camera; 80mm Yashinon lens; Kodak VPS 120 film; Meisel Photochrome processed.

minutes from work and just a short interstate drive to downtown Nashville. The house had an acre of yard, which I loved. I enjoyed yard work, having done it at home growing up. Dad taught me a lot about flowers and trees.

When we bought the house, unbeknownst to me, the Legendary Blackwood Singers lived on the other side of the duplex. Winston and Ron Blackwood were grandsons of founding member Roy Blackwood and sons of legendary R. W. Blackwood of the Blackwood Brothers Quartet. They were arguably the most beloved Southern gospel group of all time. The Blackwood Singers had a show in Branson, Missouri, for many years and still perform today. I soon became good friends with Winston and Ron and their band members. I did photography for the band, as well as for the individual members.

My duplex was especially nice. It looked more like a single-family home. My door was on the side and almost unnoticeable. The front door was for the other side of the house. Unlike most duplexes of that era, this one had a full basement, so I immediately put in a darkroom. I had been without a darkroom for a little more than a year. At that point I had ten years of darkroom experience, so not having one was a loss. It had become a part of my culture and picture-taking did not seem finished until I completed my work in the darkroom.

While working at J. C. Penney, I became good friends with Connie Rhodes. She worked in the record department, next to the camera department. She began inviting me to her house to eat dinner since I was alone. Connie lived near the mall, and our homes were not far from each other, so it was easy to spend time with each other. We kind of dated on and off for the next three years. We both dated other people, too, so we never got too serious about each other. Connie had long blond hair that hung almost to her knees and she was about five-nine. Her younger sister, Cindy,

was in early high school and was an all-state gymnast.

Connie's parents really liked to have me over to their house, so I was there a lot. The Rhodeses' house had a second floor, with the stairwell open to the living room below. Cindy would sit on the stairs and talk to Connie and me sitting on the couch.

In 1976, Cindy was working at Opryland USA as a singer and dancer. She used her athleticism in her dancing, which eventually landed her in the spotlight. She went on to record records, and star in movies (screen name, Cynthia) like *Dirty Dancing, Staying Alive, Flashdance, Xanadu,* and *Runaway.* She later married singer/writer/producer Richard Marx and retired from show business to raise a family.

IN EARLY DECEMBER OF 1975, Wayne Martin, general manager of Colorcraft Corporation, the photo processing service for J. C. Penney nationwide, visited me at the store. Wayne and I had become friends, and we often went for a cup of coffee in Penney's downstairs restaurant (hard to believe they had a full-service restaurant in mall stores at the time). Wayne asked if I knew anyone with photo experience who might work for Colorcraft. This was a sideways job offer, since it was a standing rule that vendors not recruit employees of retailers; he could have lost his job. But I let Wayne know I might be interested, and he let me know opportunities the job would open up for me and how much money I would make. Plus, I would get a company car. The pay was higher than my income at J. C Penney and there was an incredible benefit package. I gave a two-week notice and left Penney on December 23, 1975, just in time to go home for Christmas to see my parents and family.

I began my new job as the regional representative for Colorcraft on December 28, 1975. Ultimately, Colorcraft would become an Eastman Kodak Company, and I would become an Eastman Kodak manager. Counting my Colorcraft time, I worked at Eastman Kodak for thirty years. I spent most of my time in the photo processing side of the business, but later dealt with consumer products that included film, cameras, batteries, videotapes, and photo processing. While I worked at J. C. Penney, sales representatives from the photographic industry called on me—Jim Hodges from Fox Photo, Ed Zeigler from Minolta, Buzz Ashenburg and Spike Bloom from Eastman Kodak, and Wayne Martin from Colorcraft. I ended up working with and remaining friends with all these reps as Kodak mostly consolidated their former businesses.

I REMAINED FRIENDS WITH Connie Rhodes and would see her regularly. She told everyone I was her best guy friend. Connie began to date Jeff Van Wye, also a singer and dancer at Opryland. Through Connie, I got to meet Jeff. I would go with her to Opryland to see Jeff and Cindy perform. Unbeknownst to me, Jeff had a sister who would change my life forever.

In July 1976, I took pictures of Connie for her to use in seeking modeling jobs. I had photographed her several times already. Her long, strawberry-blond hair stuck out to everyone who saw her. I shot color film this time instead of my usual black and white, which I processed and printed. I was not processing color film at that time, so I had to send it off.

In the meantime, I went to Mifflinburg to meet my parents and my brother and his wife. The Dershams went to visit family in Pennsylvania every August all of the years Tom and I were growing up, so as adults we kept up that tradition as long as we could.

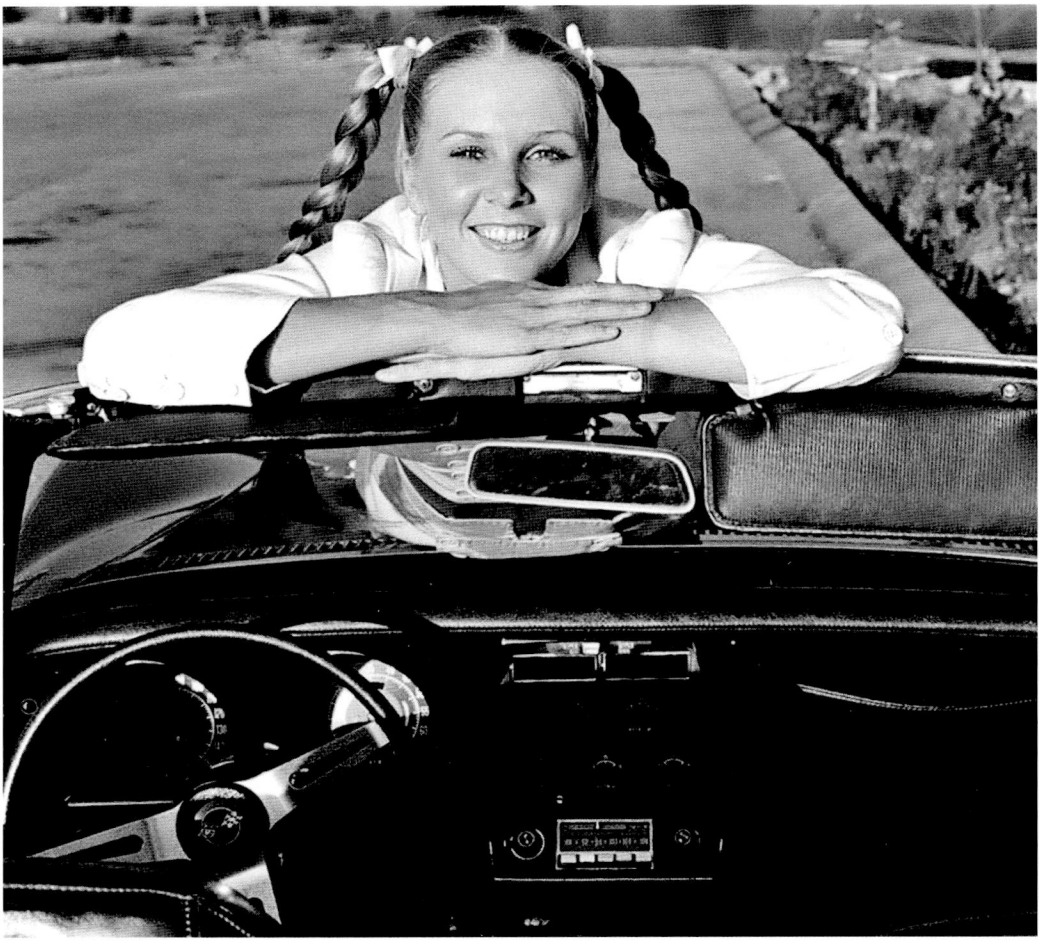

Connie Rhodes, Nashville, Tennessee, 8-1976; Olympus OM1 camera; 70-150 Zuiko lens; Kodak VPS 35mm film; Meisel Photochrome processed.

When I returned home from Pennsylvania, the pictures of Connie were waiting for me. I called Connie to come over and take a look.

Connie always came through my basement door and came up the steps from the basement to visit me. She knocked on the basement door, and when I opened it, I saw another face with her. This face was beautiful, with giant hazel (greenish-brown) eyes. She looked at me with no real expression, but I will never forget seeing her standing on the stairwell. Connie introduced her as Jeff's sister, Kyle.

They came in and we went to my music room and Kyle sat on my bean bag on the floor as I showed Connie her pictures. My high school/college friend Tim Drennan was visiting me. Connie asked me to please play Mickey Newbury for Kyle. Mickey Newbury ("American Trilogy," "Just Dropped In") was our new favorite singer/songwriter. Kyle instantly loved him too.

Connie and Kyle soon left. The next day, I took Tim over to Connie's house, and Kyle was there, so we chatted for a while. Suddenly, Jeff called to say their dad had had a heart attack, and they immediately left for their home in Shelbyville, Indiana. (Their dad recovered fine.)

I did not see Kyle again for a number of days. She had gotten an apartment near Jeff, and Connie called and asked if I wanted to hang out at the pool in Kyle's apartment complex. At that time, I had another friend from J.C. Penney with me, Gary Zulauf. We hung out with the girls at the pool for a while and by late afternoon Kyle offered to make her famous white bean soup. Gary said he had to leave, but I stayed and hung out with Kyle. She did not make the soup that night, and instead I took her to Centennial Park in Nashville. We sat on a bench swing and talked for a long time.

Over the next couple months, we were together most of the time when we were not working. I was not dating anyone, and she had just moved from Indiana to distance herself from the boyfriend she had just broken up with. We really did not show signs of real attraction to each other at first; we just loved to be together and we had a good time when we were together.

Kyle had grown up with a horse and loved to ride. She suggested we go to Percy Warner Park in Nashville and ride horses. By that time, you would say we were dating. Kyle smoked, which was a point of contention between us. I had always refused to date anyone that

smoked. When we got to the park, I just stopped and told her I was sorry, but I could not stand the smoking. I took her home. On the way, she said she would stop smoking. I did not really believe her, because I had seen how that habit hooked people.

I still had a lot of friends at Penney's, and Kyle started working there in the junior's department. I got word from friends at Penney's that Kyle really was not smoking. I finally went to see her at the store, and she insisted she had stopped. We were both eager to hang out again. It only took three months of being with Kyle almost daily before the subject of marriage arose. It happened one night at the Kwik Sak near her apartment while we were sitting in the car drinking soda pops. There was no proposal; we just agreed to be married.

KYLE DECIDED TO GO home to her parents after Christmas of 1976 and stay there to help with the wedding plans. Meanwhile, my parents had bought another duplex just down the street from the one I lived in. I managed both, maintaining them and keeping them rented, and collecting the rent that covered my parents' mortgage payments for both houses. Just before Kyle left town, we began looking at houses in Hendersonville, just outside of Nashville. We found two houses on the same street that we loved, especially one with a Cape Cod look. While she was away in Indiana with her parents, my parents and I managed to buy both houses in Hendersonville and sell both houses in Nashville. My parents' equity made it worth it for us to live in one single-family house and take care of maintenance and rental on the other. (We kept and rented both Hendersonville houses, even after we moved, until 1985, when we sold them and my parents made a nice profit.)

On March 5, 1977, we had a small wedding at her parents' house in Shelbyville, and a bigger reception at her aunt's house in

Columbus, Indiana. After we got married, her parents got us a hotel room just outside of Columbus. We were going to Disneyworld for our honeymoon. I told Kyle we needed to stop back at home in Nashville to pick up some stuff for the trip, since it was on the way. She became quite suspicious when I turned off at the exit that went to Hendersonville, but I insisted since we were in the area we stop by and see the house we liked. When we got to the house, I handed her the key. It was one of those moments we will never forget.

I had managed to get most of our stuff moved in, but it was piled up. We spent the night there and headed for Orlando the next day. We had a fun several days in Orlando and at DisneyWorld, but we were eager to get back to make a new home together. My career was taking off with Colorcraft, and Kyle got a job processing film for a national school portraits photofinishing lab in Hendersonville.

COLORCRAFT WAS QUICKLY BECOMING the largest wholesale photofinisher in the country. It serviced the major retail stores, drugstores, and camera stores that offered private label photofinishing. At places like Kmart, it was advertised as Kmart photofinishing even though Colorcraft did the processing. Over the next several years, my job grew from me being the only representative in the Nashville area to having three full-time route drivers picking up unprocessed film and delivering the finished packages.

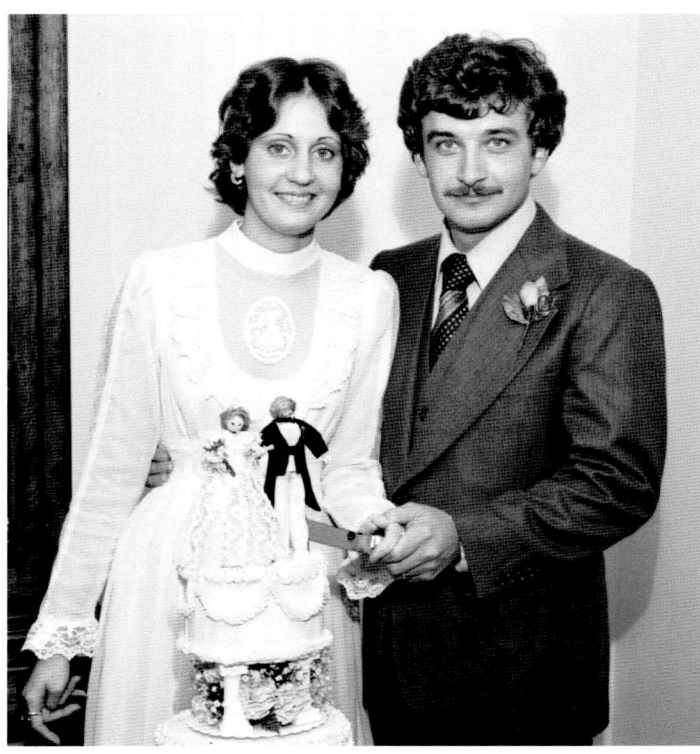

John and Kyle, March 5, 1977.

My songwriting had ended as I became more interested in my career, marriage, and my passion for photography. Once Kyle and I were moved into our house in Hendersonville, I quickly got my darkroom up and running in the basement. There were two, large, finished rooms in the basement. One was a den with a fireplace and the other was half of a two-car garage that had been redone. I was able to build the darkroom and have plenty of space for a studio.

In 1977, I got back into large-format photography which I had begun a decade earlier but had not regularly practiced in recent years. In early 1978, I got a Burke and James Saturn 75 view camera with 4x5 and 5x7 backs. At the same time, I upgraded my Yashica twin lens reflex to a German-made Rolleiflex TLR with a Zeiss lens.

I began doing portraits and weddings, and taking lots of early morning trips to the country to shoot landscapes. At the same time, I was meeting serious photographers who worked in camera stores or were customers at the stores. In my job with Colorcraft, I was the representative calling on those stores.

During the last three years of the 1970s, my passion for photography reached a new level. My advancement from the 1960s and early 1970s had become obvious in regard to the capturing of each image to the darkroom work required to present a really well-done print.

On August 26th, 1978, our daughter, Jennifer Christy Dersham, was born at Baptist Hospital in Nashville. Kyle and I took Lamaze classes together and Jennifer was born in a birthing room for natural child birth. Two years and thirteen days later on September 9, 1980, our son, John Alexander Dersham III (Jad), was born in a natural birthing room in Hendersonville.

Our home was full of people and love. Close friends and family visited often. My parents in Missouri came about four times a year. Kyle's parents in Indiana were physically closer and came more often than that. We made trips to both family homes several times a year as well.

Meanwhile, Kyle found a new career as a veterinary technician at the Hendersonville Animal Clinic, working for Drs. Jerry Flatt and William Shannon. Kyle had always been an animal person, so the fit was perfect.

BY THE END OF the 1970s, I was entrenched in everything to do with photography at work, as well as exercising my passion for photography as an art. I was shooting regularly and working in the darkroom a few times a week.

I was getting my work exhibited around the Nashville area and meeting and getting to know other photography enthusiasts. A group evolved that we called the Nashville Photo Boys, consisting of John Lucas, Steve Jackson, Claude Gibson, Joe Pass, Harold Martin, and me. We all used large-format cameras and had much fun shooting together in the wee hours of the morning, then getting back together at a later time to show our finished darkroom prints.

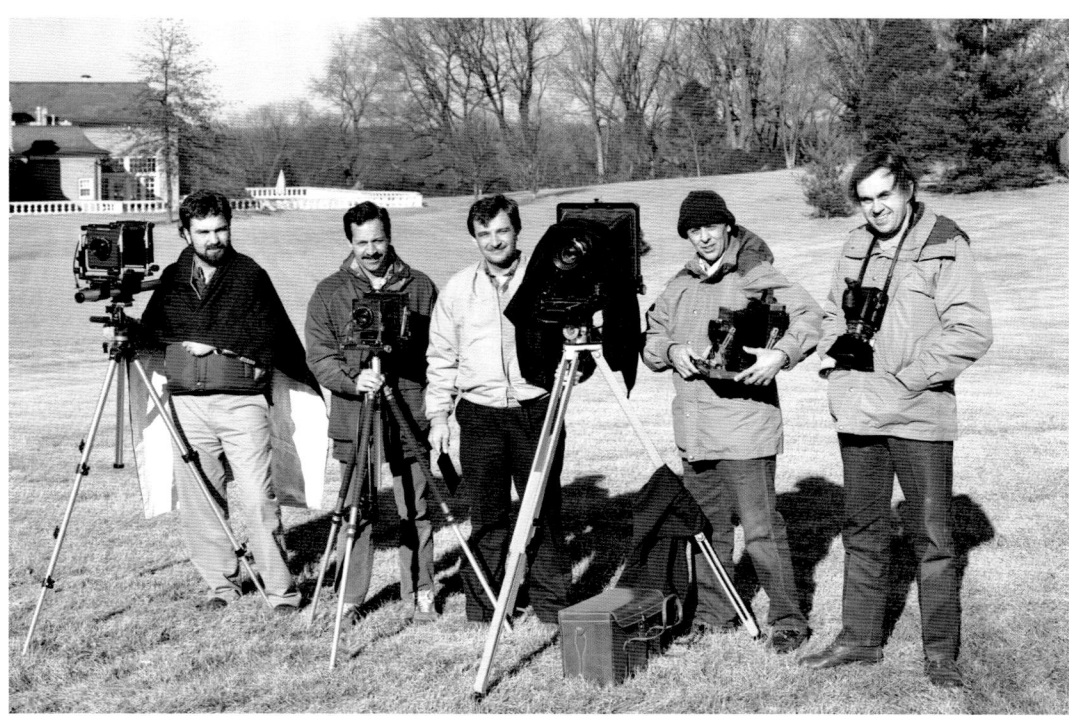

The Nashville Photo Boys, December 31, 1985; from left, Steve Jackson, John Lucas, John Dersham, Claude Gibson, and Joe Pass.

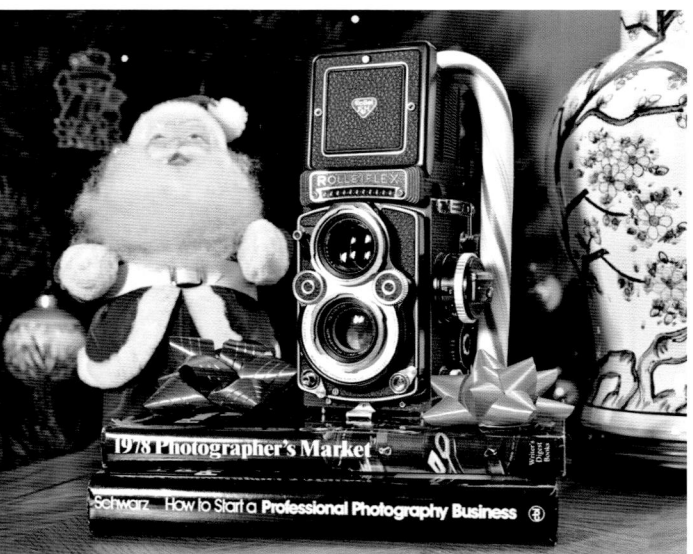

Linhof Technika V 4x5 camera; 150mm Schneider Symmar lens; Kodak Plus X Pan Pro 4x5 film; Kodak HC110B developer.

My new Rolleiflex 3.5F with Schneider Xenotar lens, December 1978.

Saturn 75 view camera with 4x5 back; 12-inch Gundlack Radar lens; Ilford FP4 4x5 film; Edwal FG7 developer.

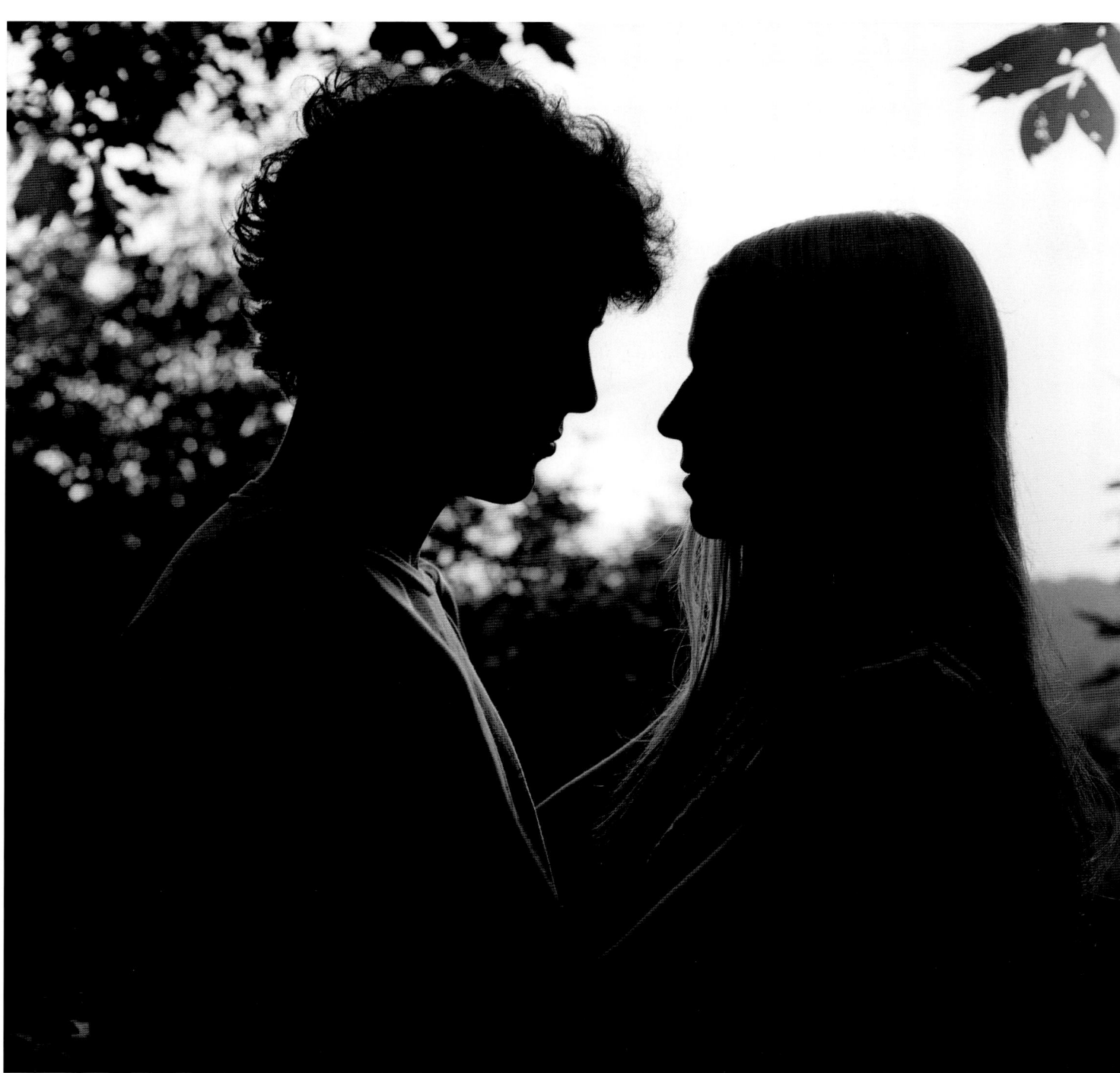

Ralph and Phyllis, sunset
silhouette, Columbia,
Missouri, 8-1970; Mamiya
C220 TLR camera; 80mm
Sekor lens; Kodak Plus X 120
film; Edwal FG7 developer.

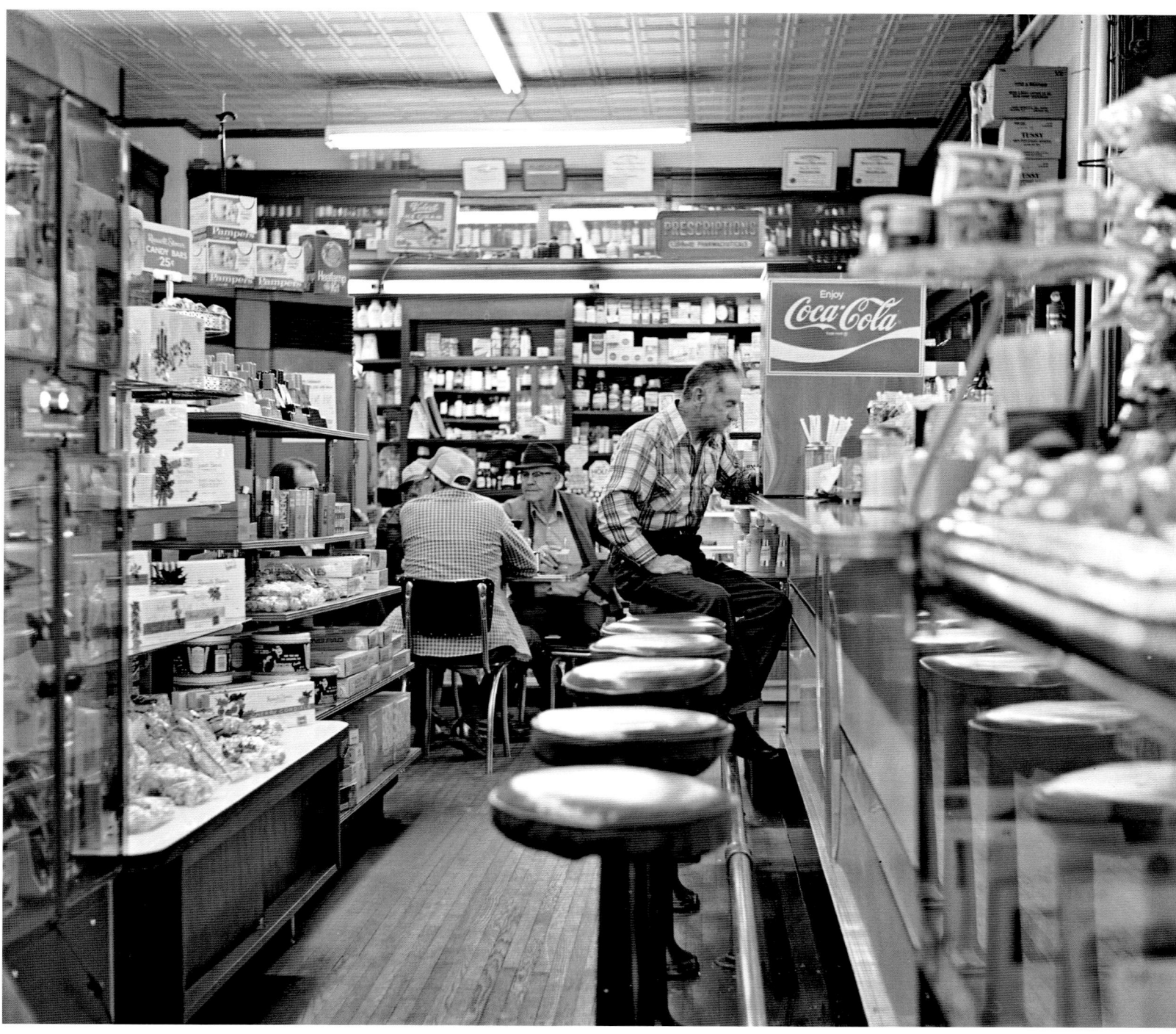

Ledbetter
Drugstore,
Lawrenceburg,
Tennessee,
12-20-1978;
Rolleiflex TLR
120 camera;
80mm Zeiss
Tessar lens;
Kodak Plus X,
120 film; Kodak
D76 developer.

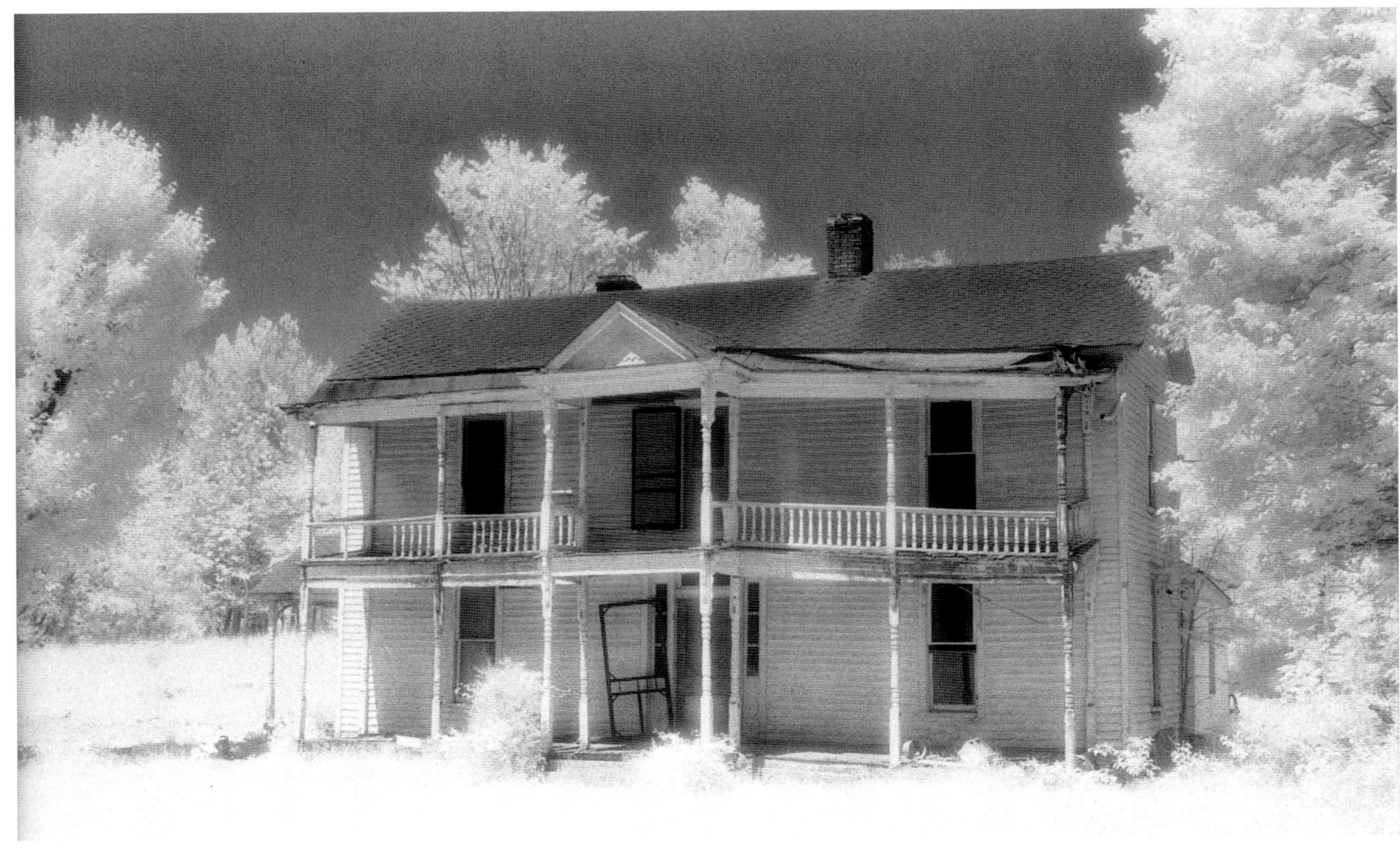

Old house near Gallatin, Tennessee, 10-1974; Miranda Sensorex 35mm camera; 50mm lens; red filter; Kodak High Speed Infrared film; Kodak D76 developer.

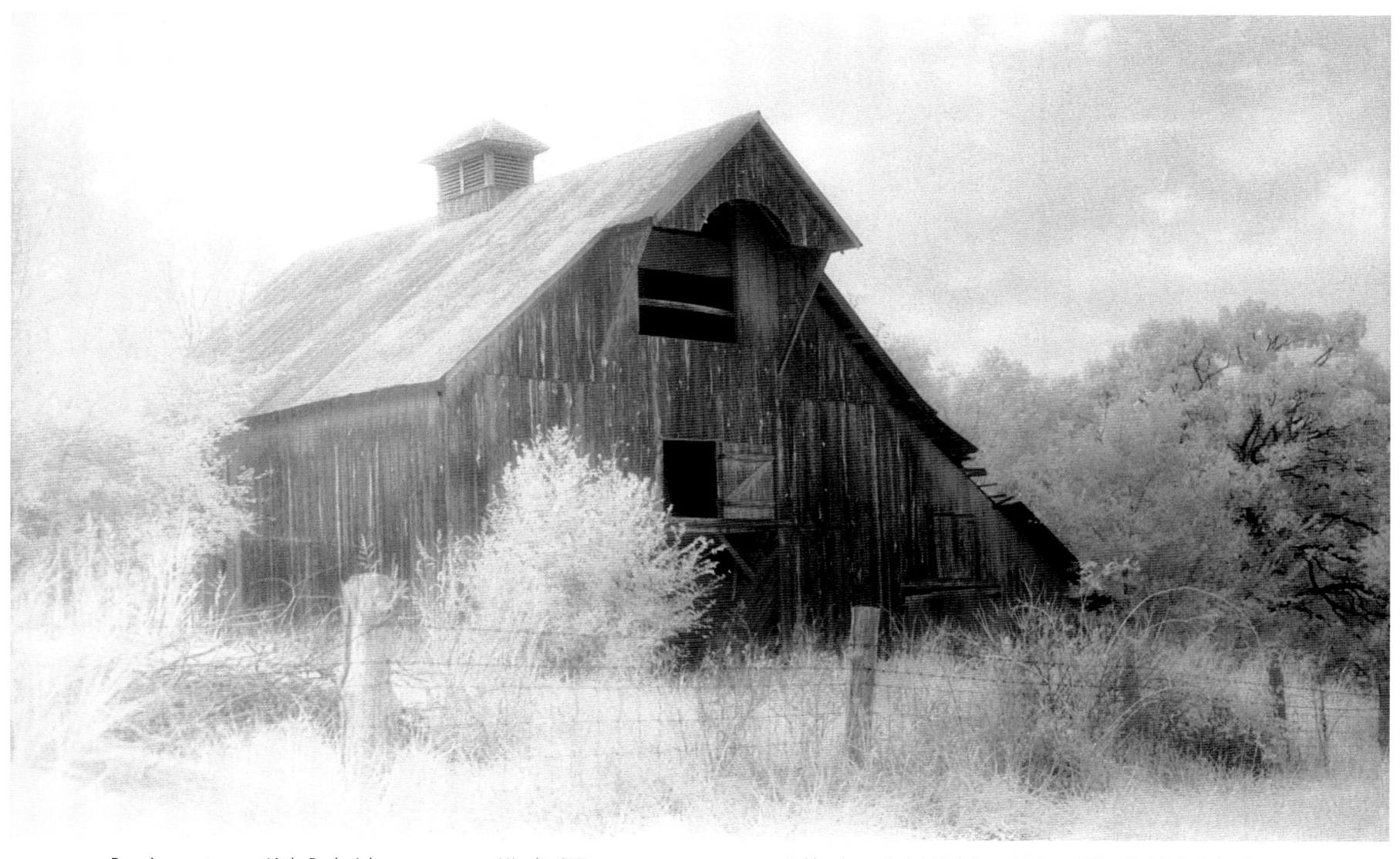

Barn in country near Little Rock, Arkansas, 10-1974; Minolta SRT 101 35mm camera; 50mm Rokkor lens; Kodak High Speed Infrared film; Kodak D76 developer.

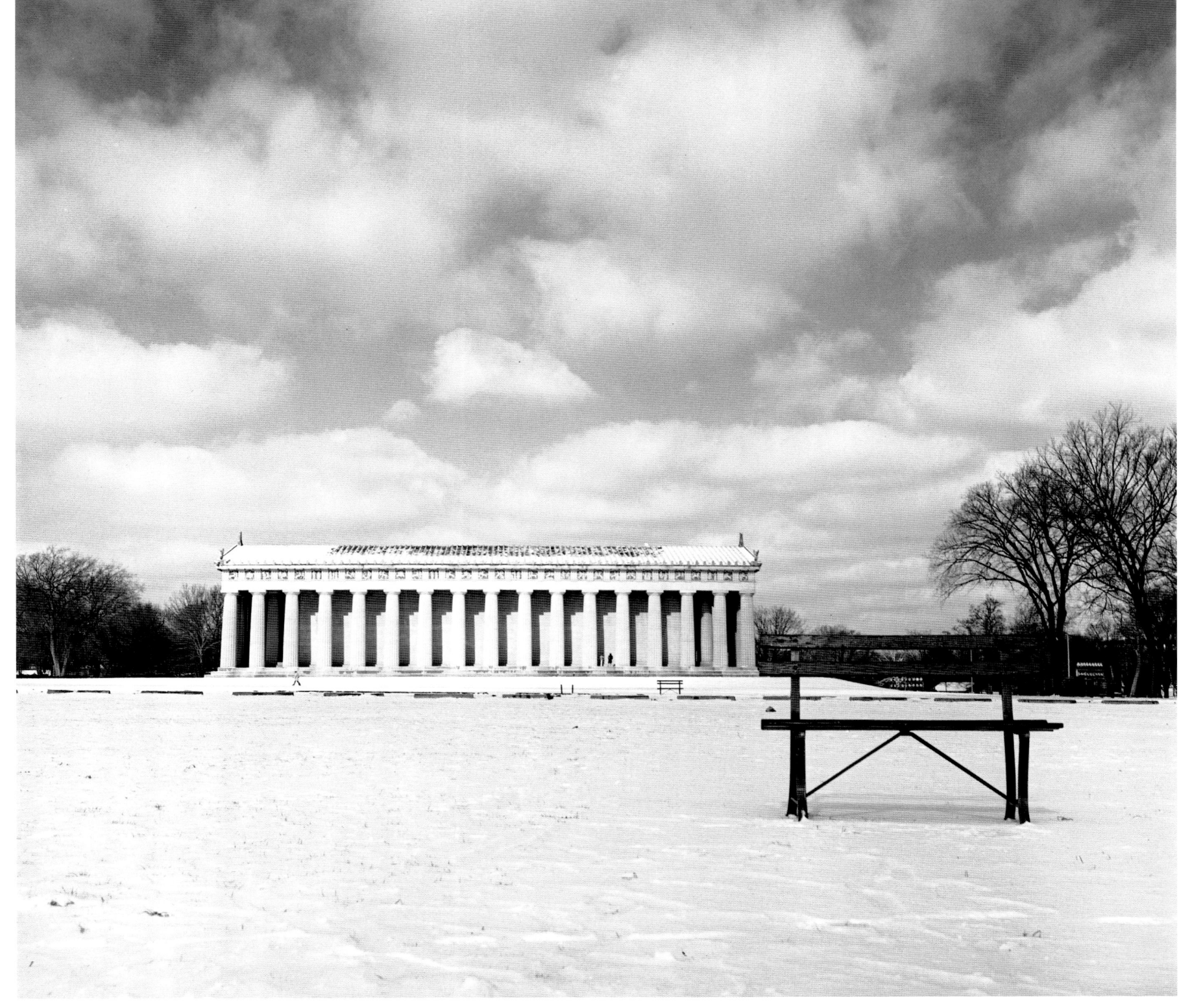

The Parthenon in Centennial Park, Nashville, Tennessee, 1-15-1978; Rolleiflex TLR camera; Zeiss Tessar lens; Ilford FP4 120 film; Ilford Perceptol developer.

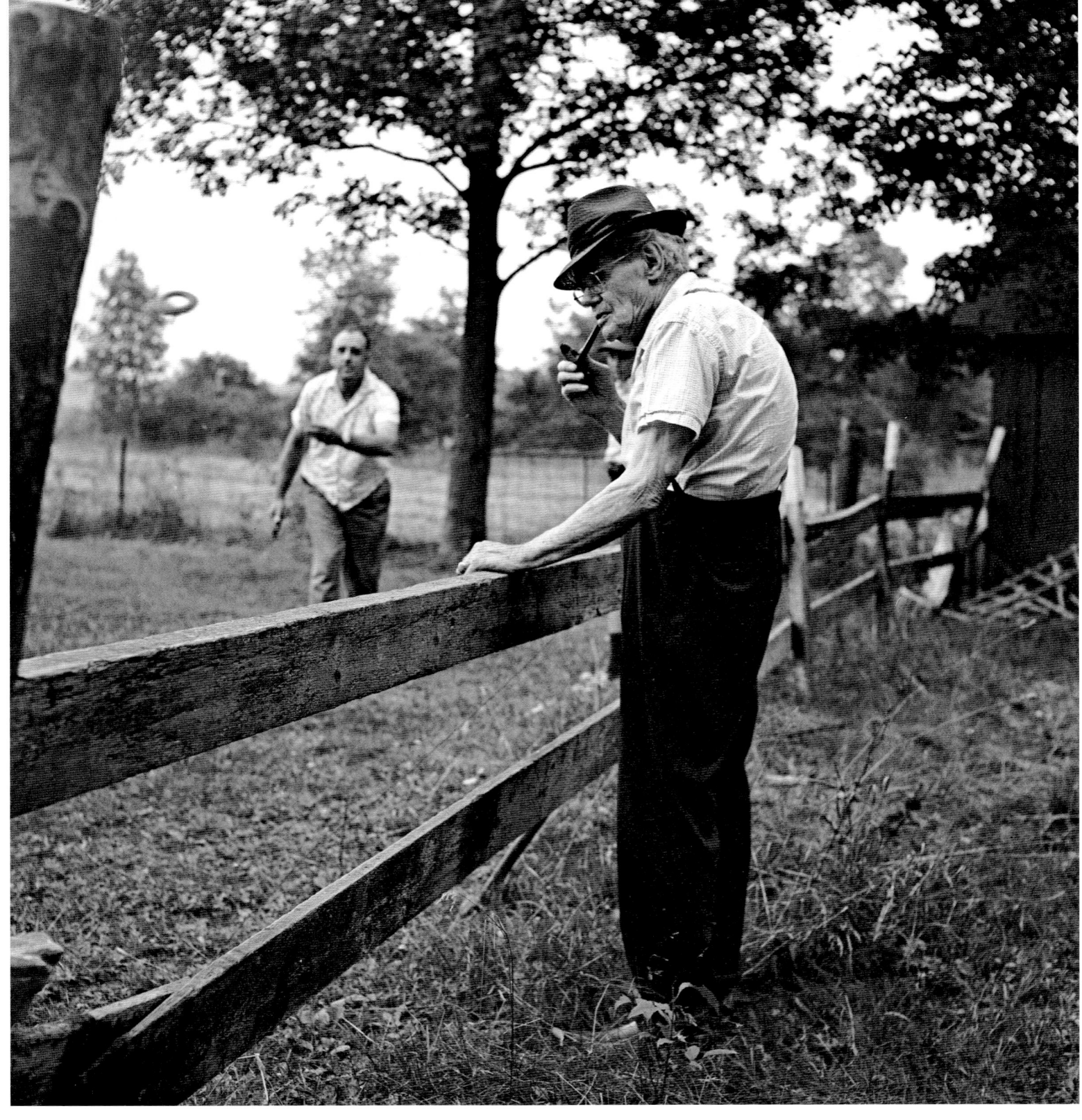

Mr. Mutschler (fence) with Dwight Shoemaker playing quoits with Clarence Shoemaker (unseen), 8-1971; Mamiya C220 TLR camera; 80mm Sekor lens; Kodak Plus X, 120 film; Edwal FG7 developer.

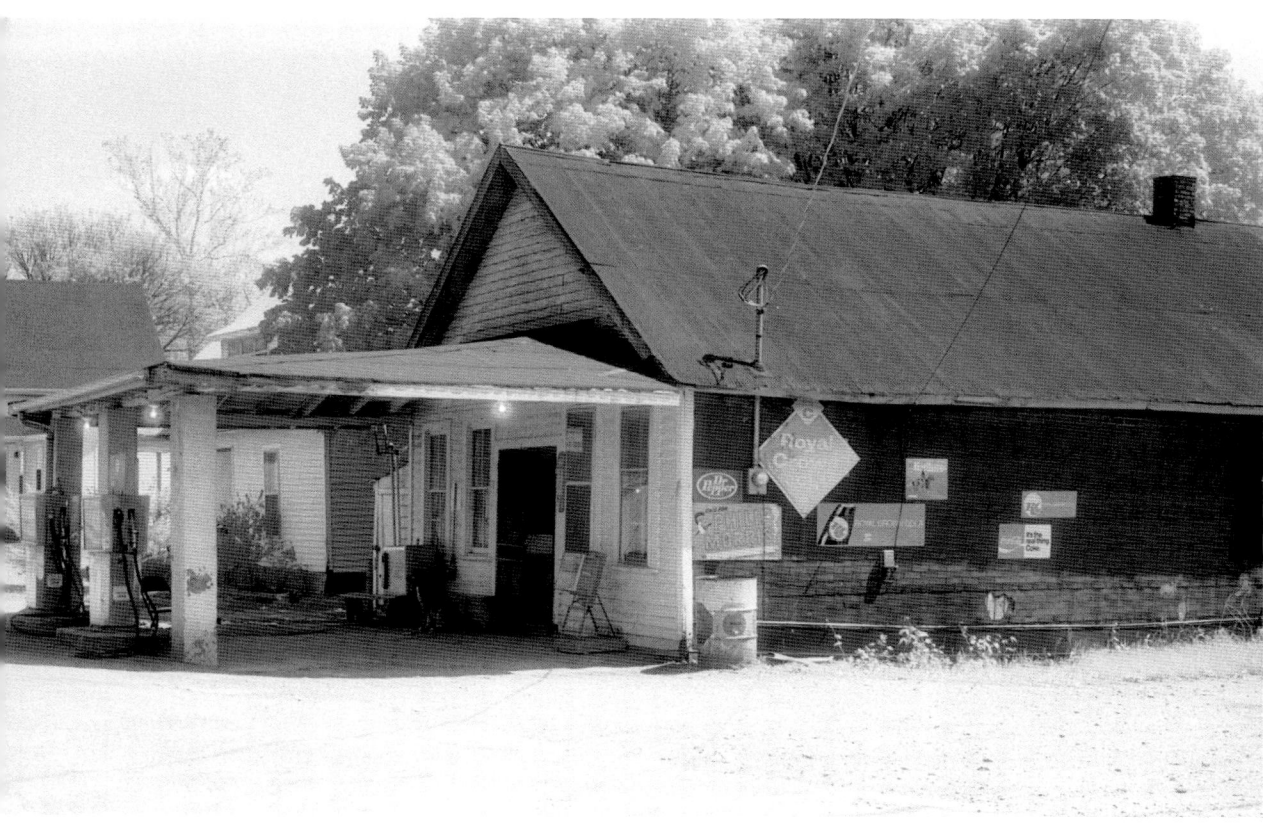 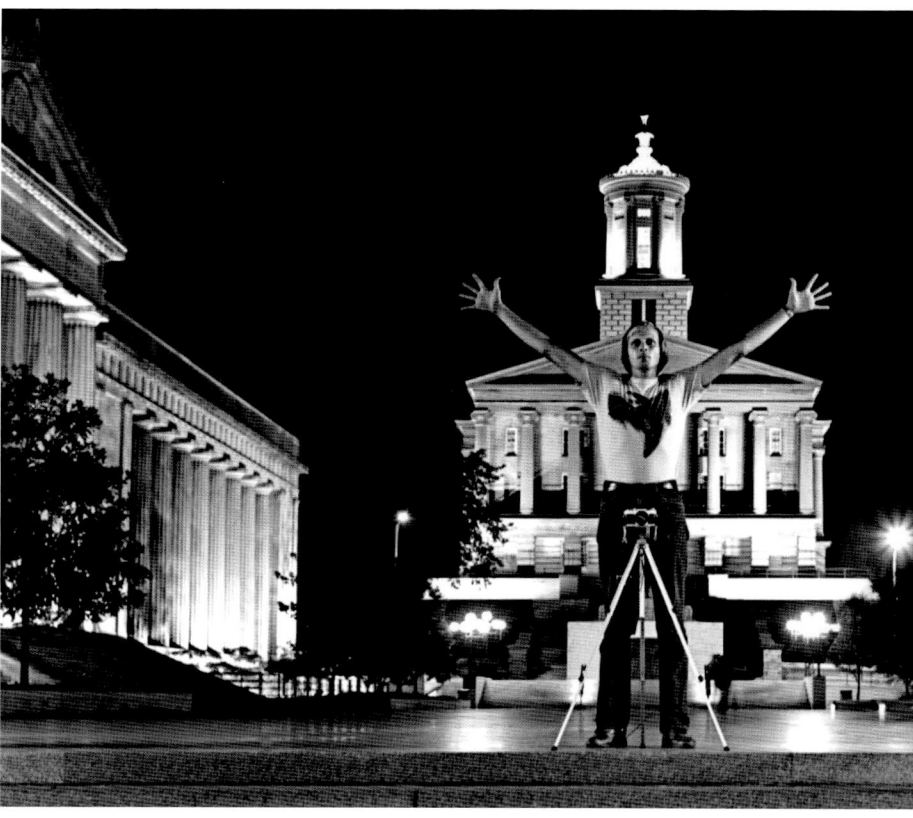

Left: Country store in Sumner County, Tennessee, 5-10-1978; Olympus OM1 35mm camera; 50mm Zuiko lens; Kodak High Speed Infrared 35mm film; Kodak D76 developer.

Right: Gary Zulauf at Legislative Plaza in front of the Tennessee Capitol, Nashville, Tennessee, 9-1-1979; Rolleiflex TLR camera;
80mm Zeiss Tessar lens; Kodak Tri X Pan, 120 film; Kodak Microdol X developer.

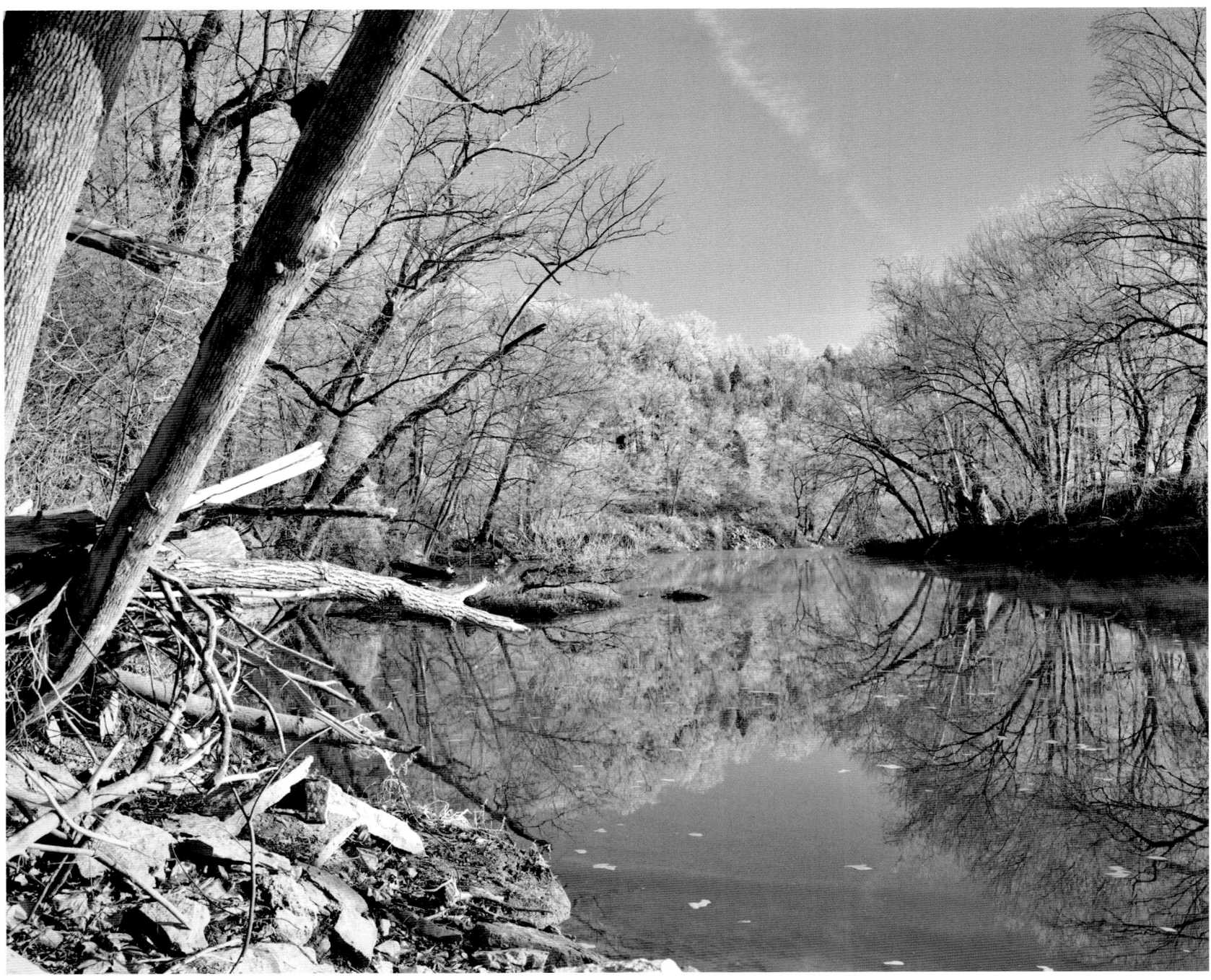

Harpeth River near Ashland, Tennessee, 12-14-1979; Toyo D45M view camera; 135mm Schneider Xenar lens; yellow K2 filter; Kodak Royal Pan 4x5 film; Edwal FG7 developer.

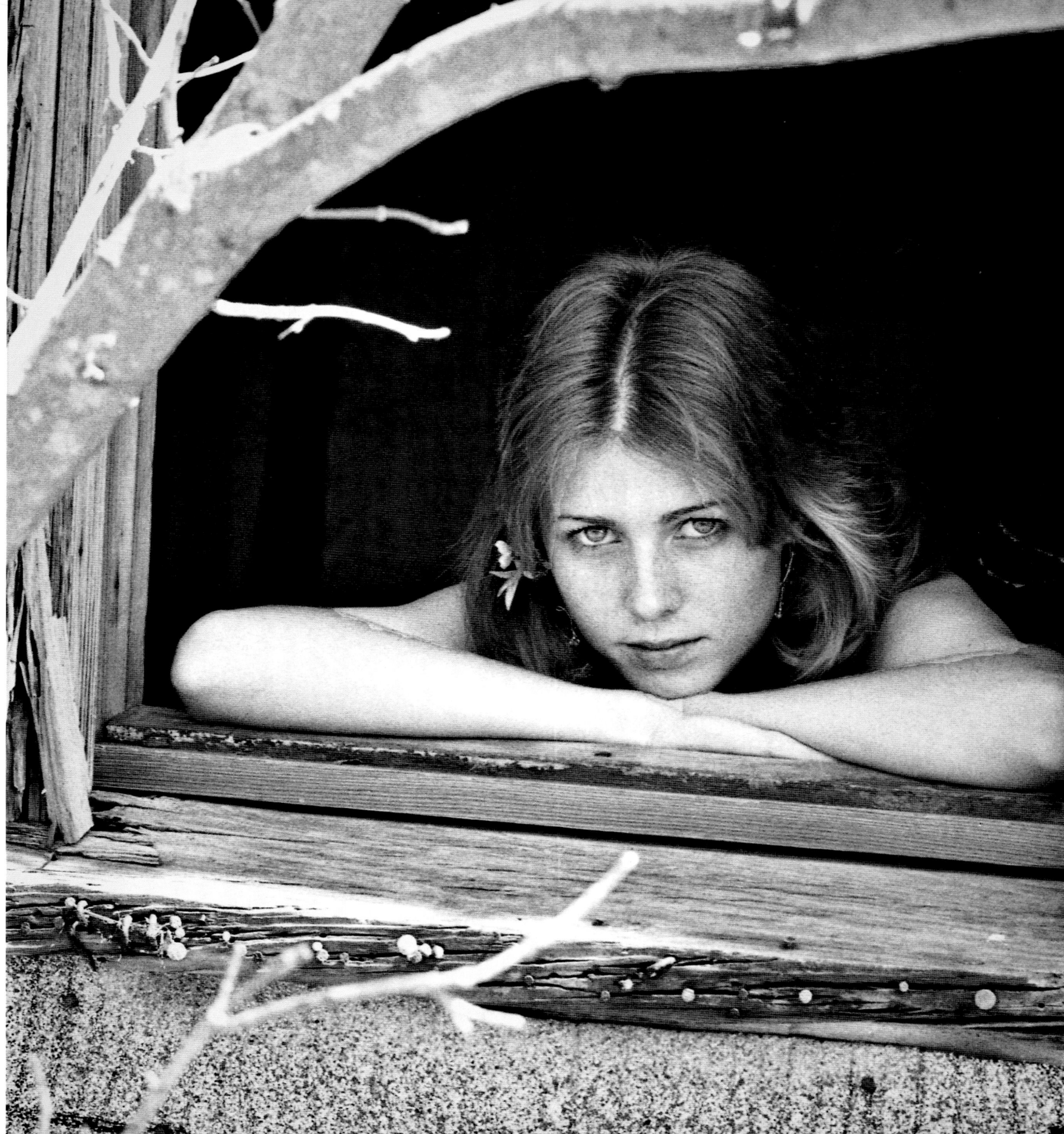

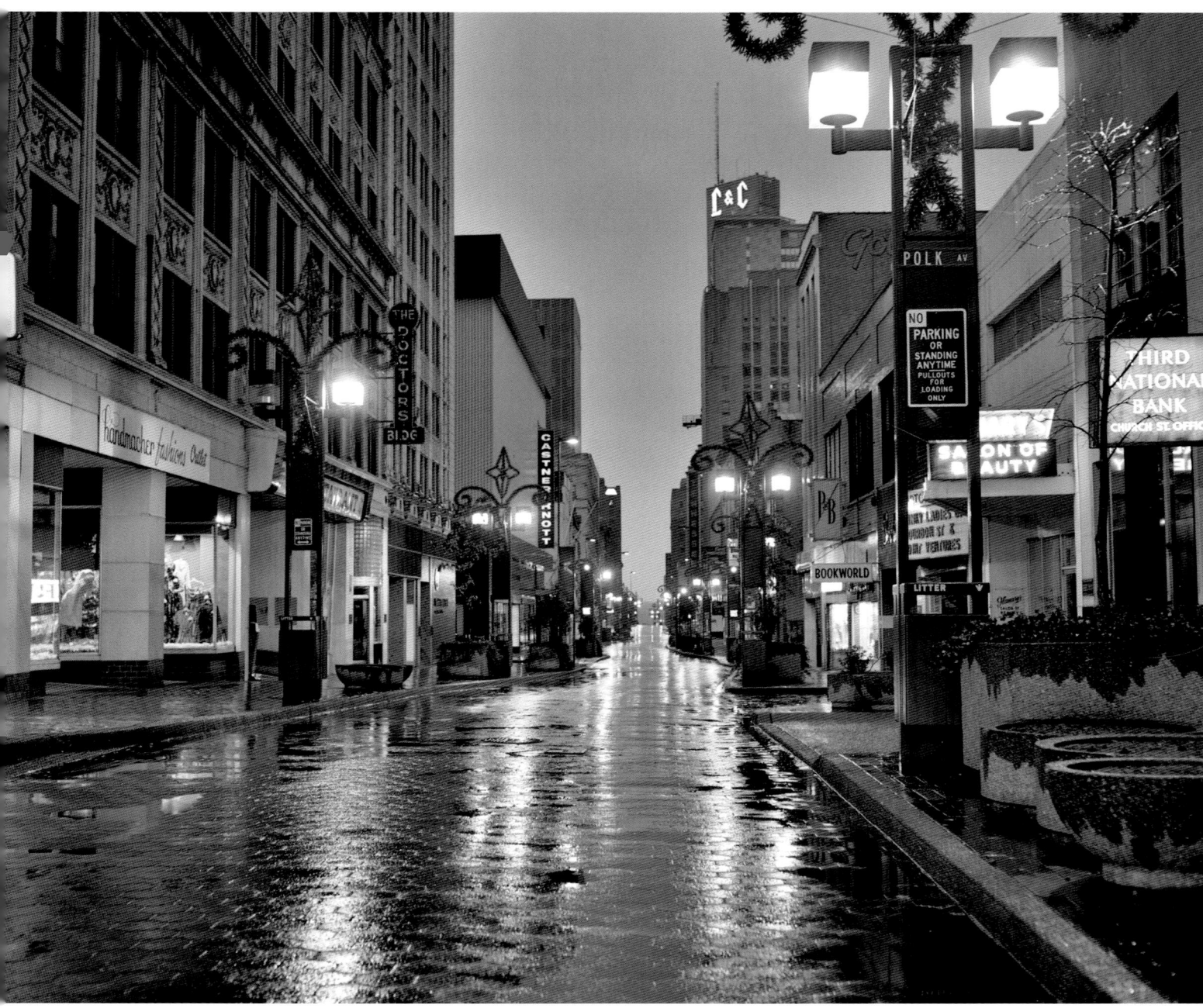

No. 12/16/79   6:00 AM   before daylight

Name Nashville on a Sunday Morning

Order It was a beautiful wet morning
Calm and quiet

Remarks looking down Church St from Eight Ave

Retouched I had to cover the top of camera
and lens to keep it dry.

Order Finished Rogen tripod
7X focus loop.

Reorder _____

Royal Pan 400 ASA, Mic. X,
Crown Graphic, Schneider Xenar 135mm
1 sec at F8

"City On A Sunday Morning"

Left and above: Nashville, a wet
Church Street in pre-daylight,
12-16-1979; Crown Graphic 4x5
camera; 135mm Schneider Xenar
lens; Kodak Royal Pan 4x5 film;
Kodak Microdol X developer.

Facing page: Susan Alpaugh near
Springfield, Tennessee, 4-1975;
Miranda Sensorex 35mm camera;
50mm lens; Kodak Plus X Pro,
35mm film; Kodak 76 developer.

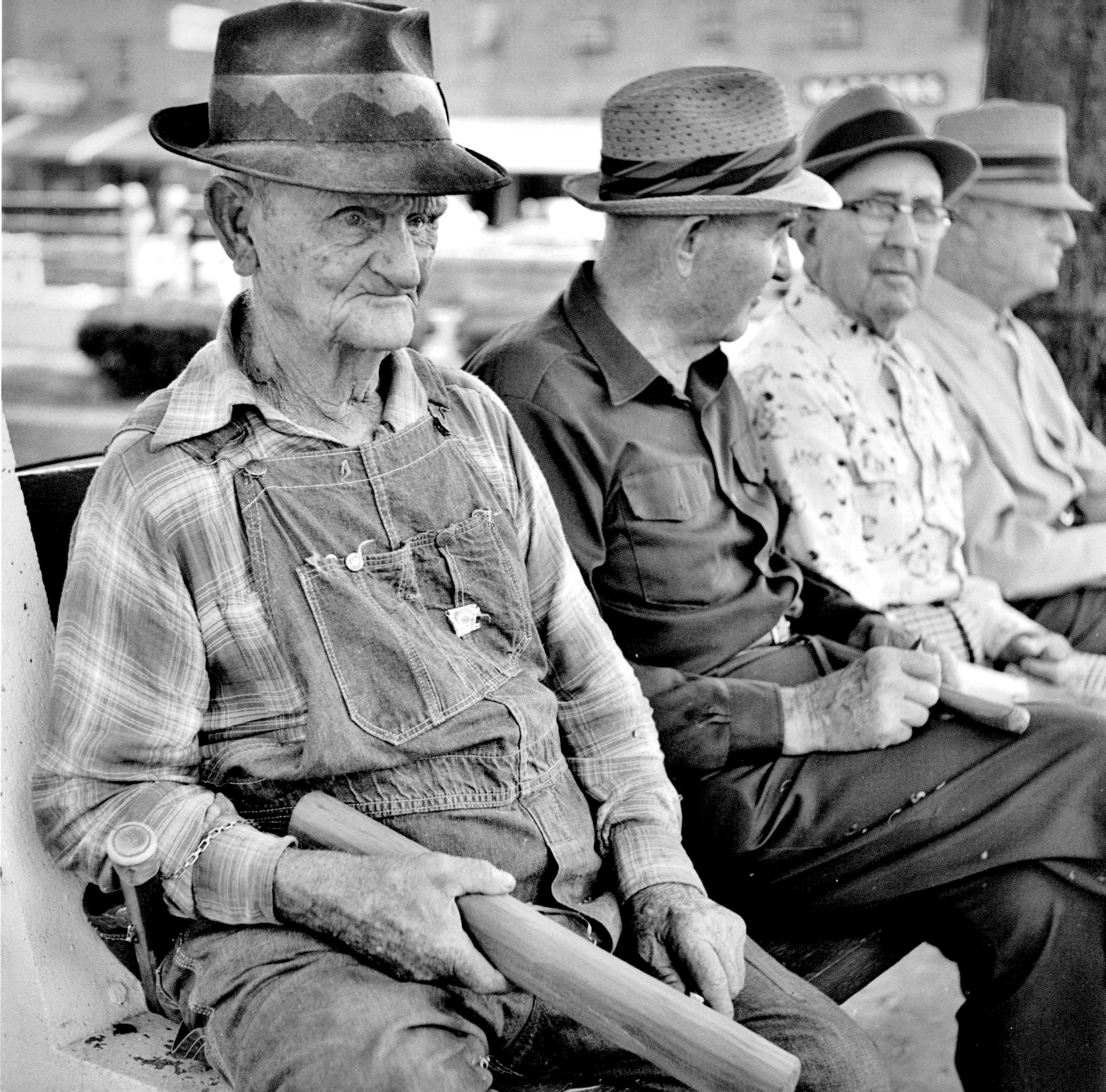

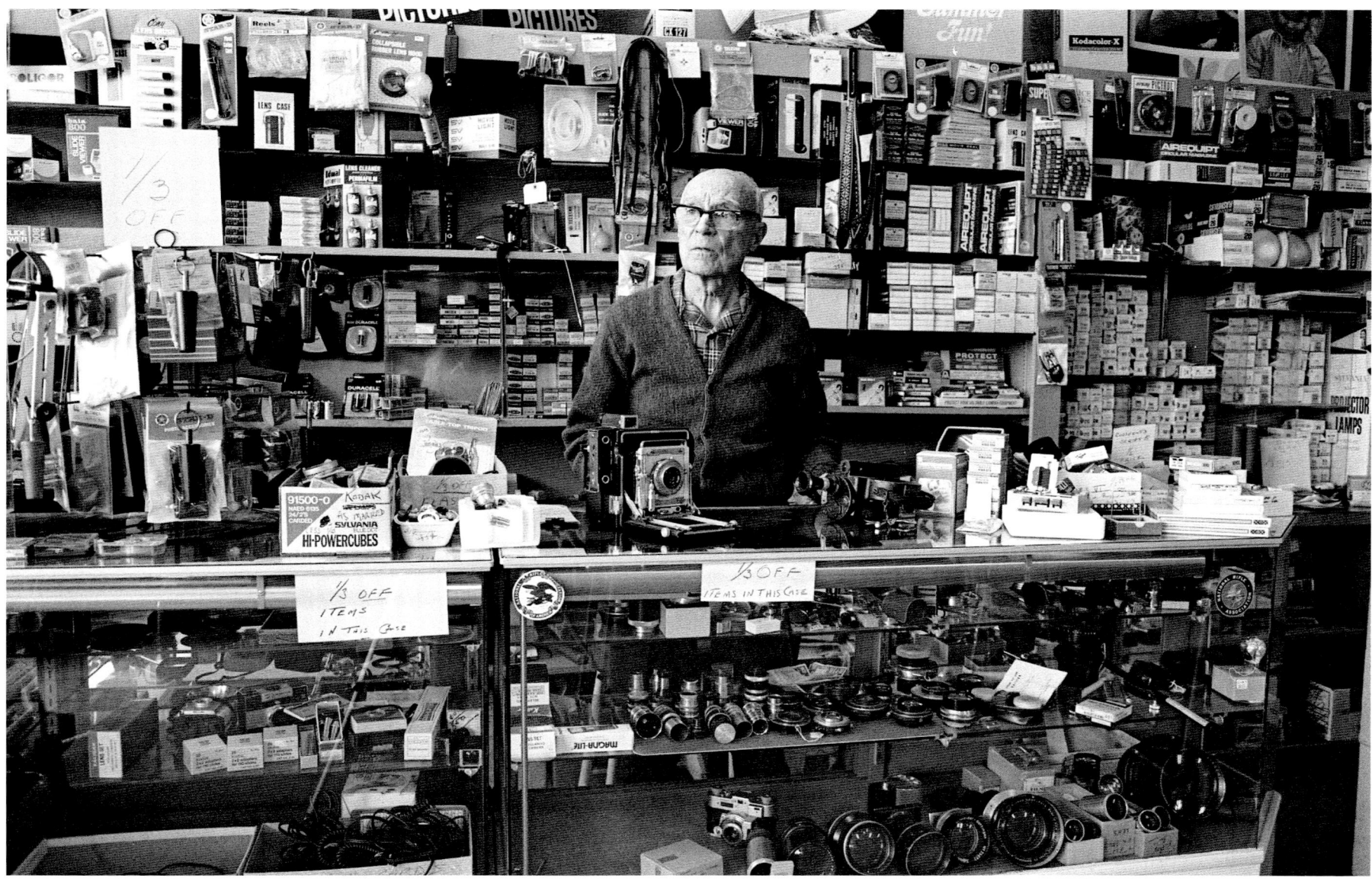

Above: Hugh Wingett, Madison Camera Shop, Madison, Tennessee, 2-24-1979; Olympus OM1 35mm camera; 28mm Chinon lens; Kodak Tri X Pan 35mm film; Edwal FG7 developer.

Facing page: Whittlers' bench at the Marshall County Courthouse, Lewisburg, Tennessee, 7-1976; Yashica 635 TLR camera; 80mm Yashinon lens; Kodak Plus X 120 film; Kodak D76 developer.

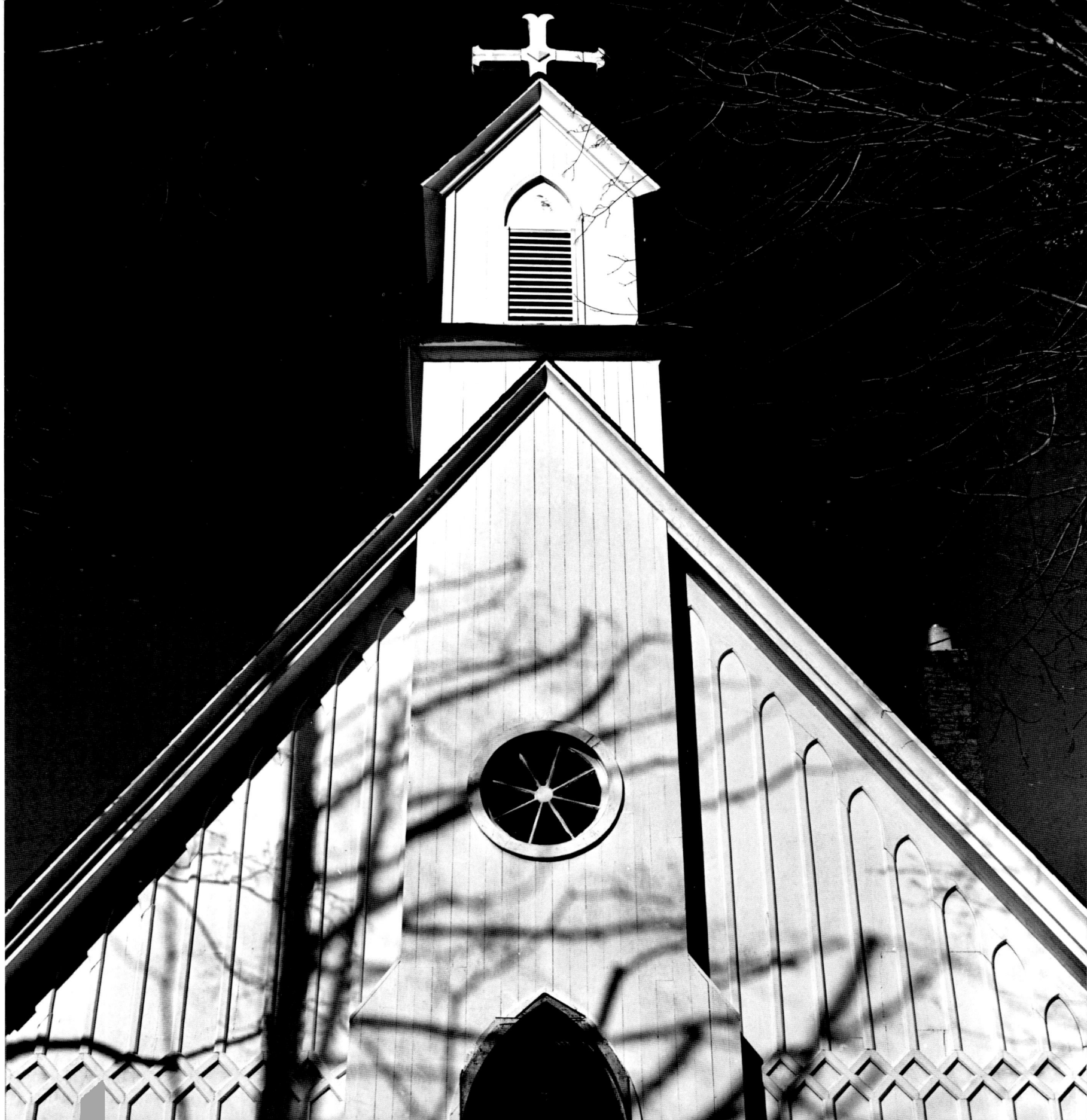

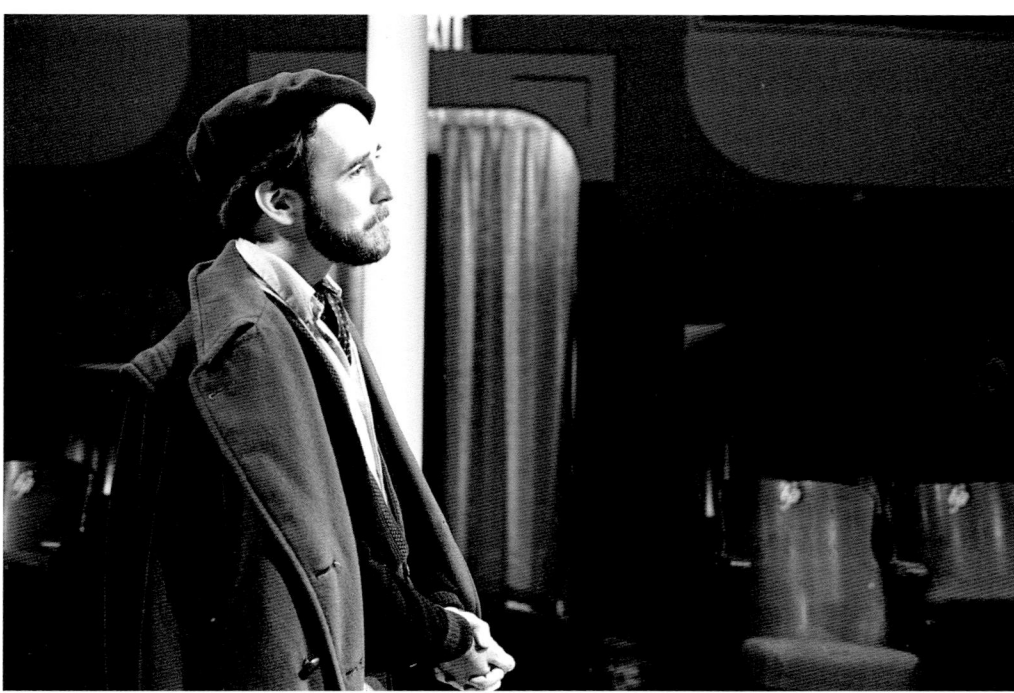

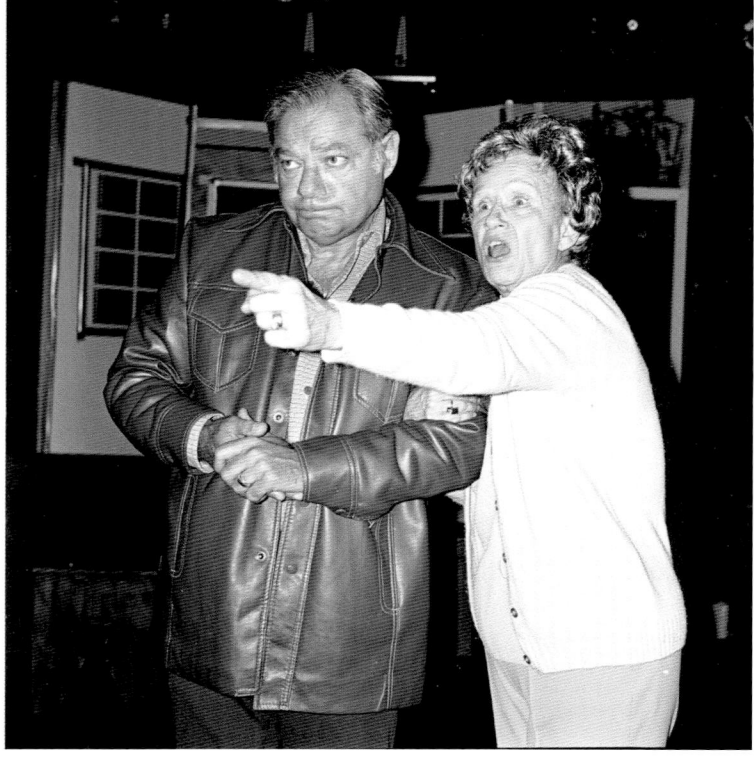

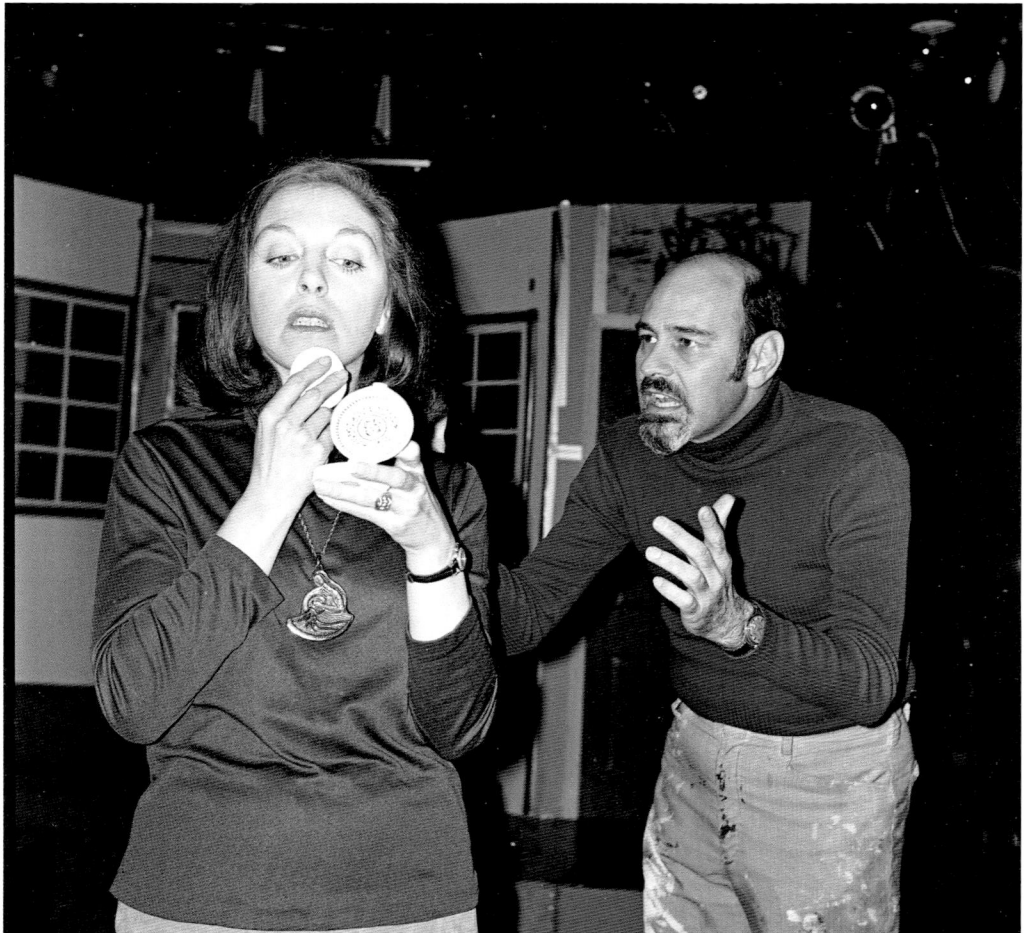

Above left: *Light up the Sky* at the Circle Theater, Nashville, Tennessee, 9-1979; Olympus OM1 35mm camera; 50mm Zuiko lens; Kodak Tri X Pan 35mm film; Kodak D76 developer.

Left and top right: *The Rainmaker* at the Circle Theater, Nashville, Tennessee, 11-1975; Yashica 635 TLR camera; 80mm Yashinon lens; Kodak Plus X Pan 120 film; Kodak D76 developer.

Facing page: Church near Gallatin, Tennessee, 1-1978; Rolleiflex TLR camera; 80mm Zeiss Tessar; red filter; Adox K17 120 film; Kodak D76 developer.

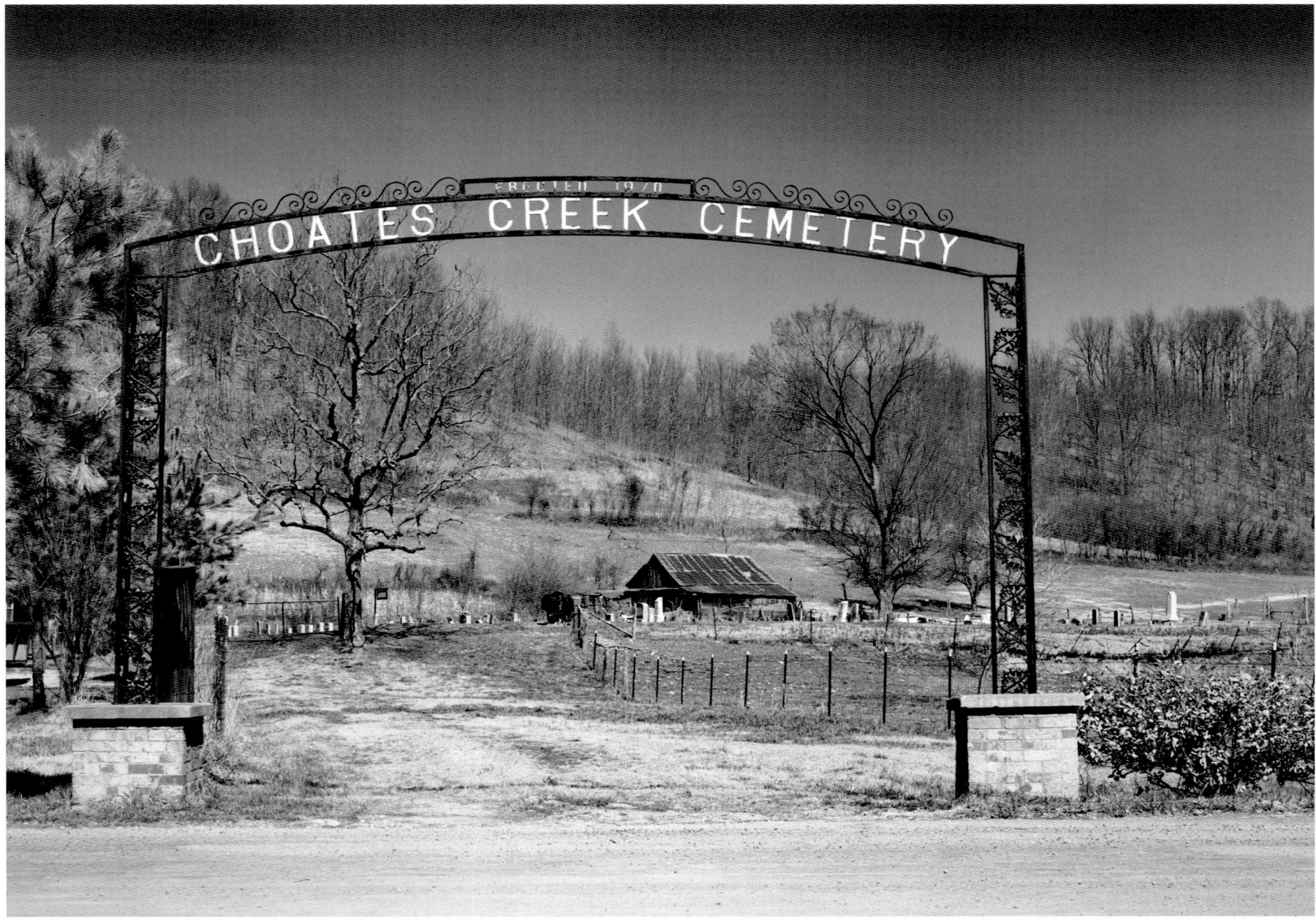

Choates Creek Cemetery, rural Tennessee, 8-1979; Crown Graphic 4x5 camera; Gundlack Korona Convertible lens; orange filter; Kodak Plus X Pan Pro, 4x5 film; Kodak D76 developer.

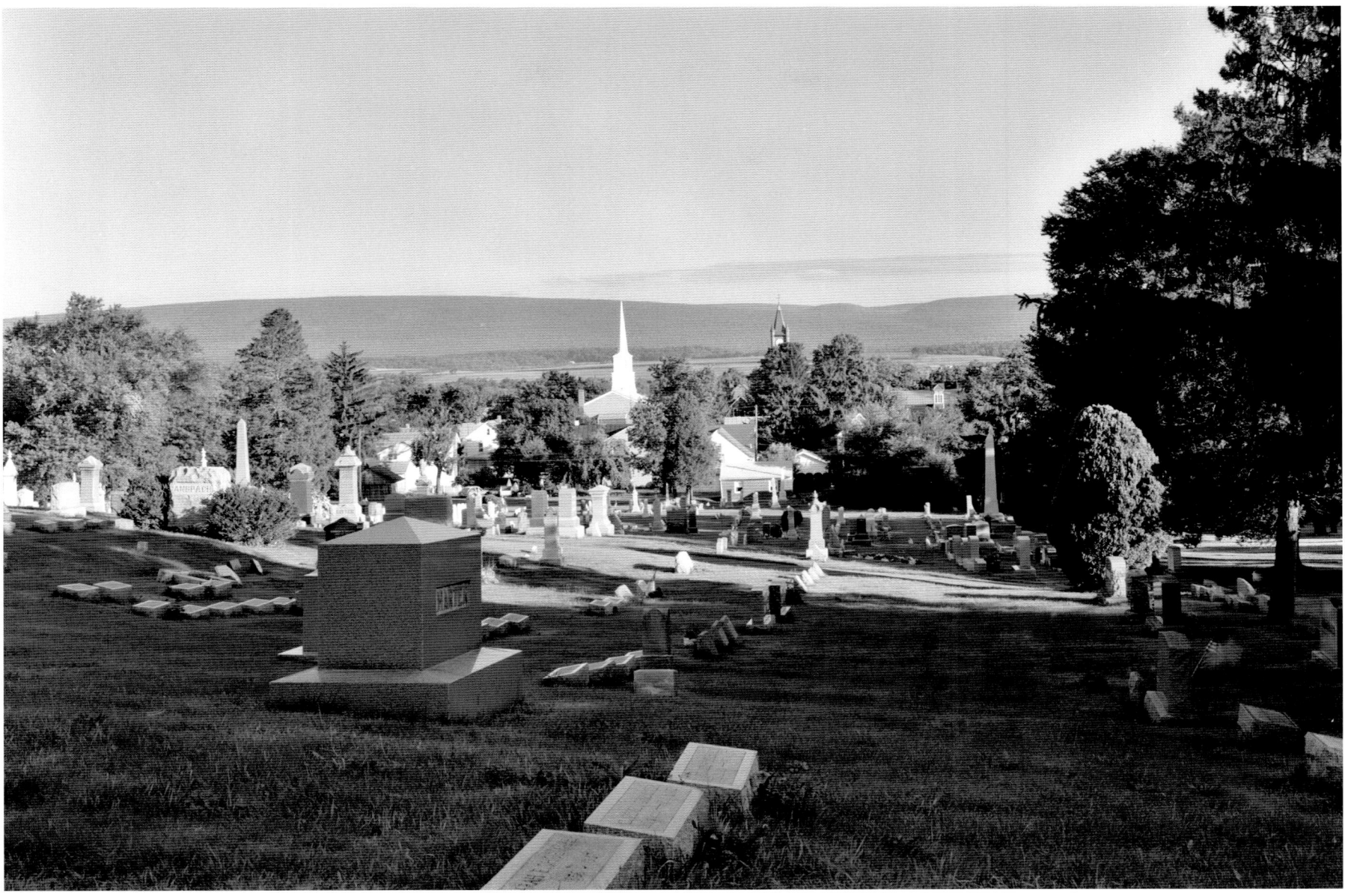

Cemetery, Mifflinburg, Pennsylvania, 8-17-1979; Crown Graphic 4x5 camera; 150mm Schneider Symmar S Lens; yellow K2 filter; Ilford FP4 4x5 film; Edwal FG7 developer.

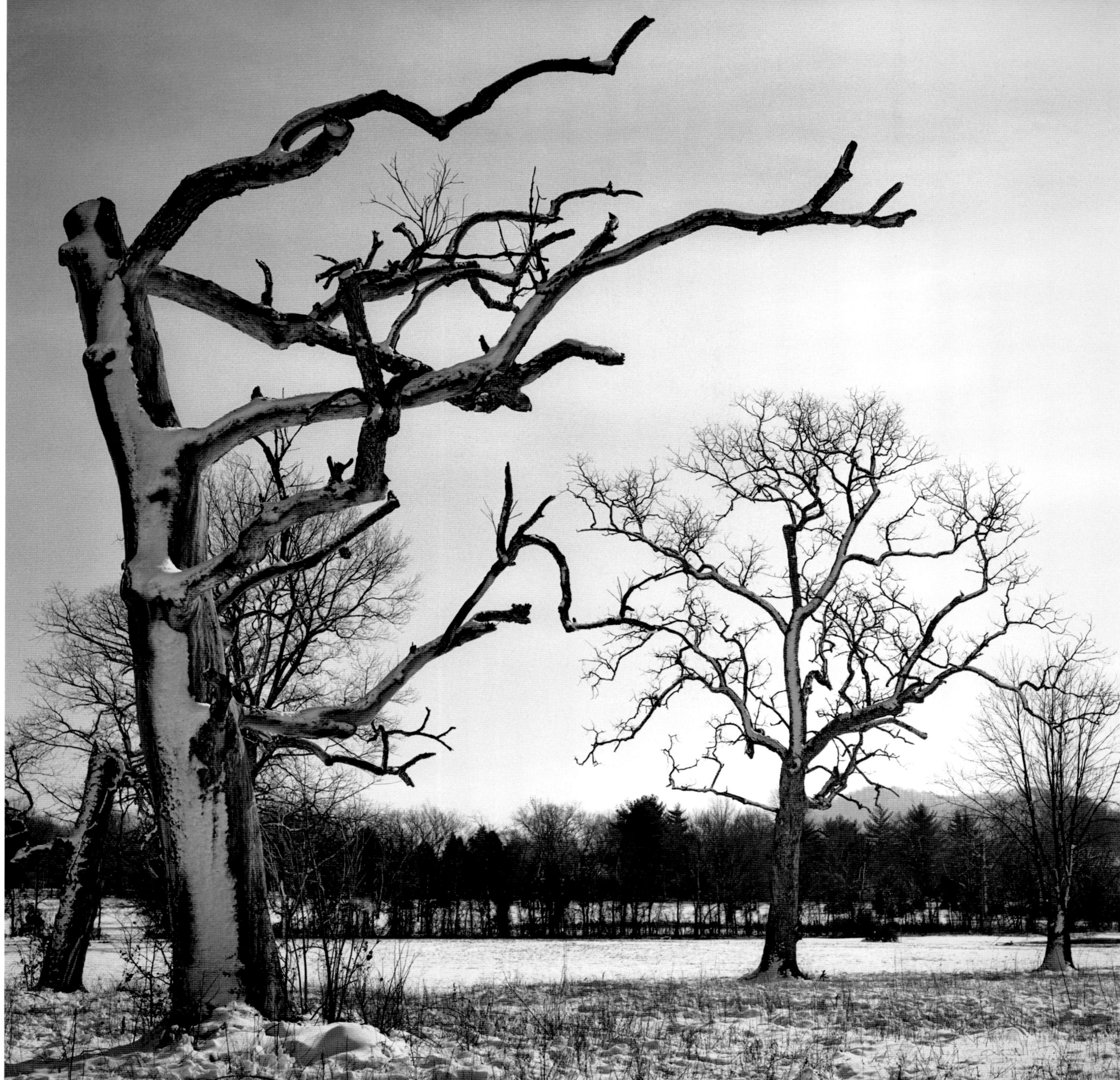

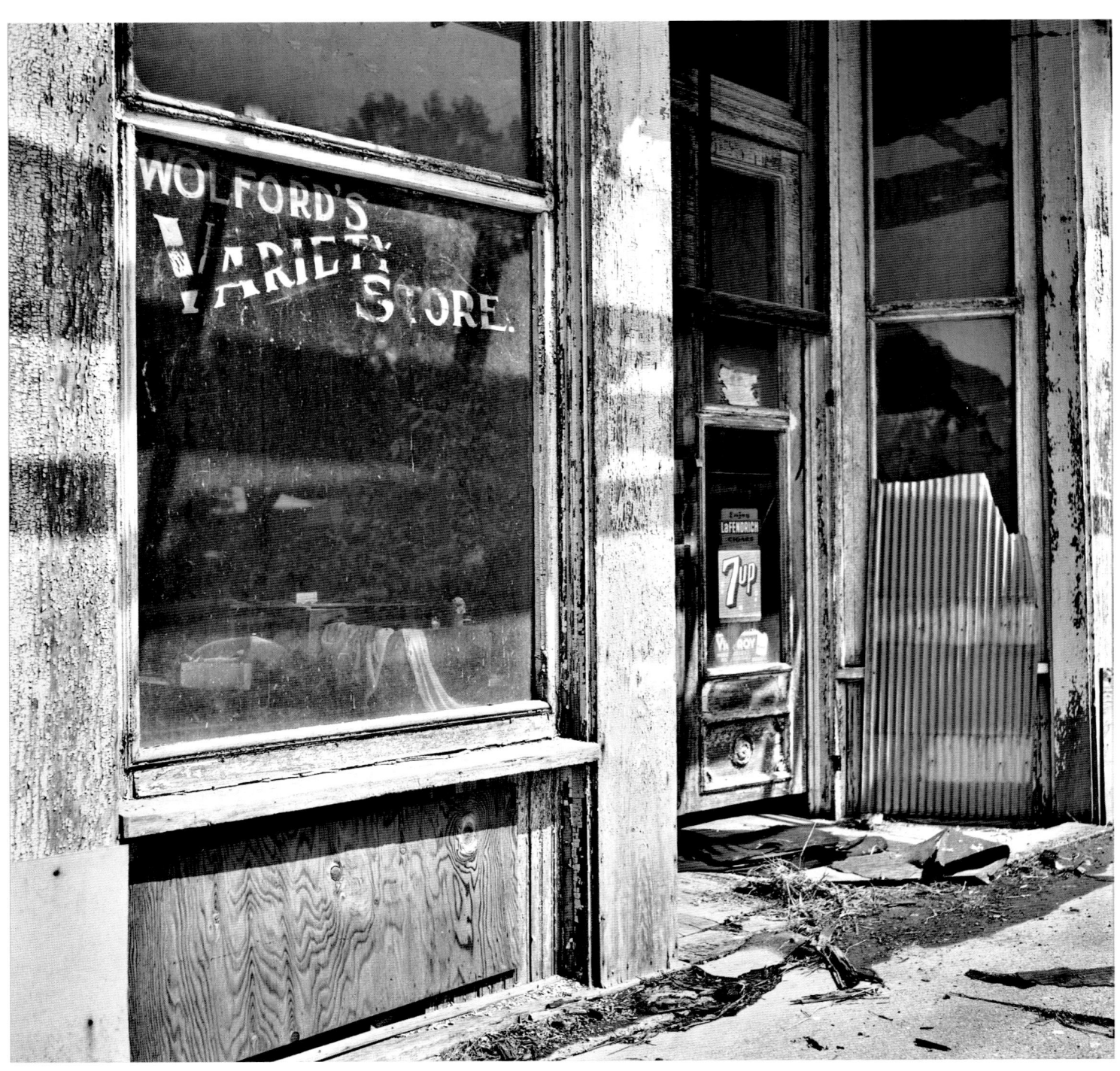

Left: Newbury, Illinois, 5-15-1979; Rolleiflex TLR camera; 80mm Zeiss Tessar lens; Ilford Pan F 120 film; Ilford Perceptol developer.

Facing page: Snow scene in rural middle Tennessee, 1-23 1979; Rolleiflex TLR camera; 80mm Zeiss Tessar lens; Ilford FP4 120 film; Ilford Perceptol developer.

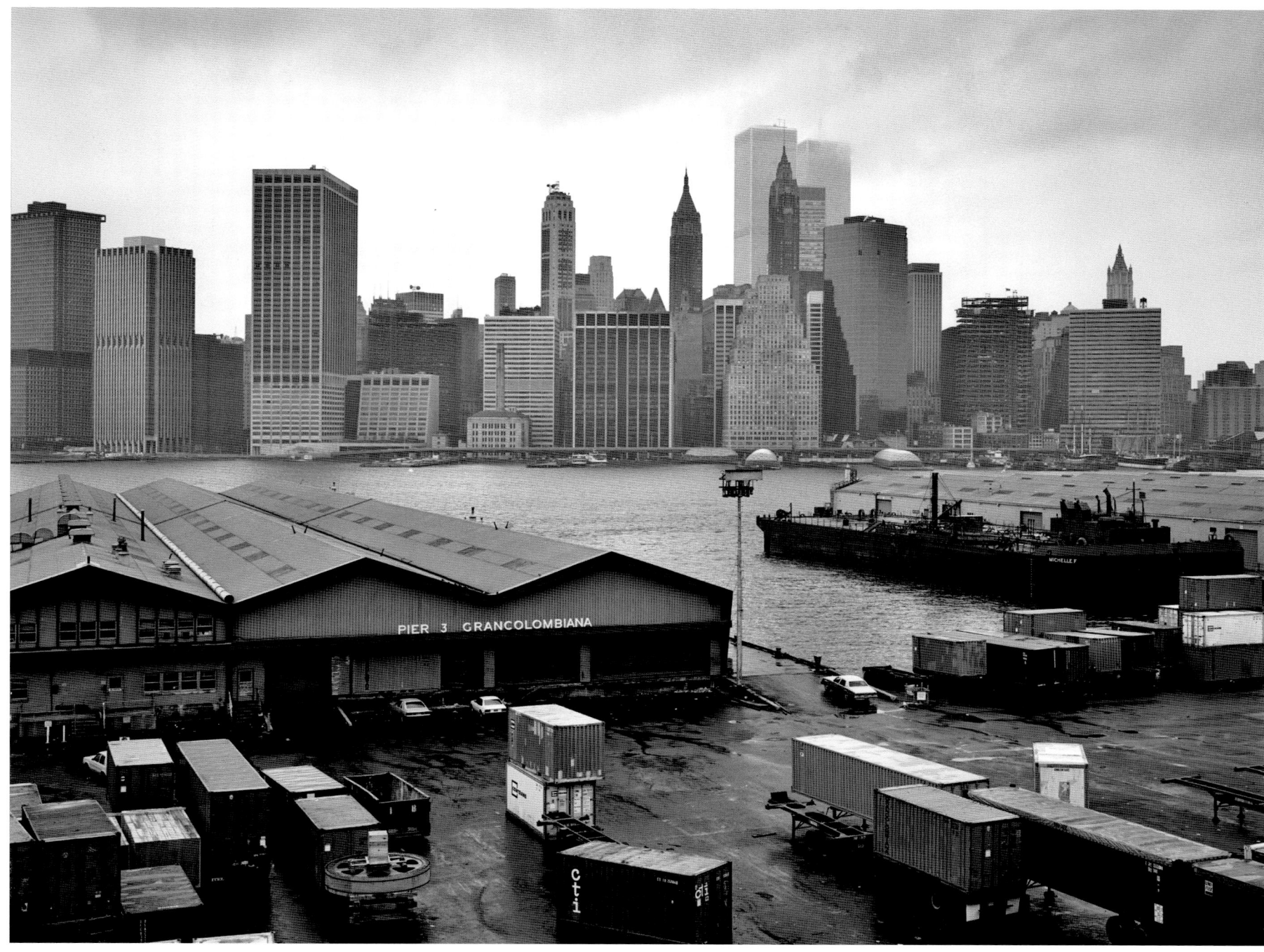

New York City from Brooklyn, 12-4-1982; Linhof Technika IV 4x5 camera; 120mm Schneider Symmar S lens; Kodak Tri X Pan Pro 4x5 film; Kodak HC110B developer.

3

The 1980s: Life in the Darkroom

The 1980s was the most significant decade for my personal photography and for my career. Both were intimately a part of each other, so it was hard to separate the photo business from my personal photography. They were useful to each other.

As I look back at the 1980s, it seems impossible that I was so engaged with my wife and children work and photography at the same time. In retrospect, it seems as if I accomplished more than what could have been done.

Colorcraft had grown to be the nation's largest wholesale photofinisher, and I now had four other people working for me in Nashville. At the same time, I made large-format photography my priority. I was shooting almost all large-format, along with some medium-format. I used 35mm for family snapshots and for color versions of my B&W work. I used Kodak Kodachrome and some Ektachrome.

In the spring of 1982, Colorcraft had acquired Snap Photo, another large wholesale photofinisher. We were growing rapidly. In May 1982, Ray Smith, the senior vice president of the Southeast, was given Philadelphia, thus adding the Mid-Atlantic region to his territory. Ray was a people person extraordinaire. Everything he

did in each of his seven divisions of the company was successful. He knew how to put the right people with each other to form a winning team.

Ray was not that happy about inheriting the Philadelphia division. It had a long history of unprofitability, severe management problems, employees that did not get along, and no positive leadership. He replaced the general manager with Rene Litalien, a young, very bright former manager of Guardian Photo in the Detroit, Michigan, area. Rene was an operations manager and experienced at running a large wholesale photofinishing lab, processing and printing thousands of rolls a film a day.

One evening in early June, Ray called me at home. Ray said they had to let their regional sales manager go. He explained it was a problematic division and had been mismanaged for years. Ray told me he thought I would be perfect for the job and a great fit for Rene Litalien. He said we would have the two top positions and together could provide the leadership necessary to be successful.

Being from Pennsylvania and still having relatives there made it sound like a great promotion. I was not sure we could afford it because up to this point we had free housing in Hendersonville due to the arrangement with my parents. The move to Philly would require rent or a mortgage and I was not sure if the income difference would cover it. Moving to Philadelphia would put my parents and Kyle's parents much further away, making our kids' visits with their grandparents less frequent. Kyle had no connection to Pennsylvania, having grown up in Overland Park, Kansas, a suburb of Kansas City, Missouri. We both loved our house and our jobs in Tennessee. But, even though I loved the joint real estate project with my parents, I felt a need to pave my own path in my career, so it seemed time for this change.

At the end of June, Kyle, the kids, and I drove to her parents' house in Greenwood, Indiana, an

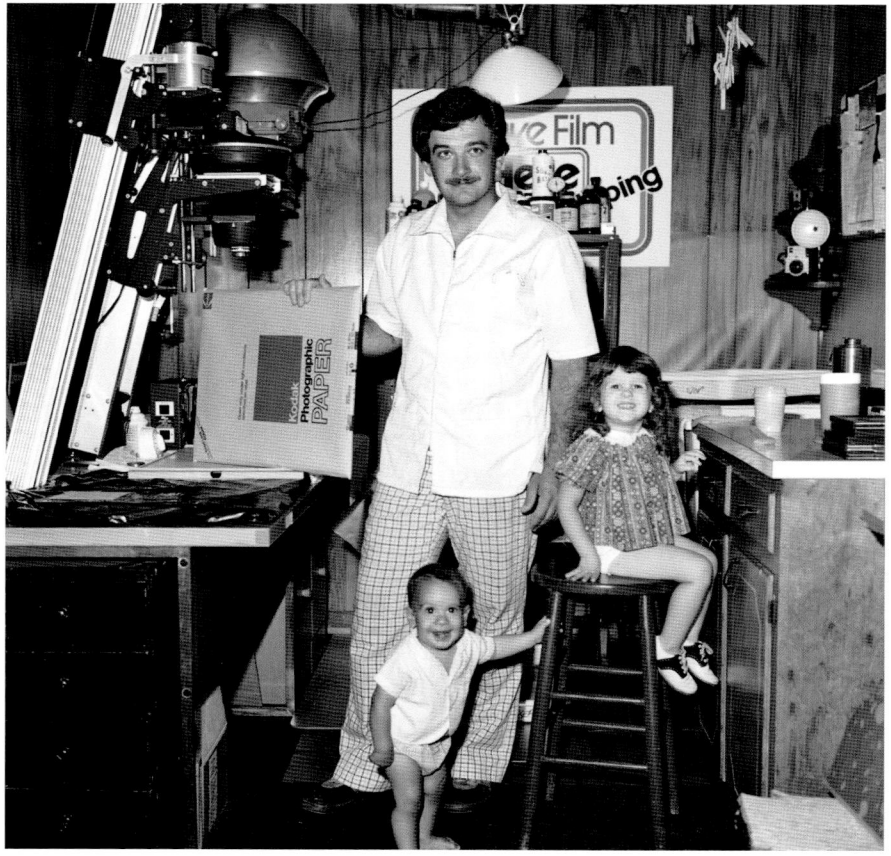

John Dersham working in his home darkroom, with children Jennifer and Jad, Hendersonville, Tennessee, 6-1981; Rolleiflex 2.8E TLR camera; 80mm Zeiss Planar lens; Ilford FP4 120 film; Edwal FG7 developer.

Indianapolis suburb. We left the kids with the grandparents as Kyle and I flew to Philadelphia so I could meet with Rene Litalien and Kyle could look at possible houses. We spent a few days in Philadelphia. Rene and I hit it off right away. Kyle found a great house to rent in Feasterville, just across the Philadelphia line in Bucks County. We would have to pay $525 a month, which sounded almost impossible, but we still said yes. The house was in a quaint, well-landscaped 1950s neighborhood a block away from a mall, restaurants, and my

favorite coffee shop . . . Dunkin Donuts.

It was a big move for our family. During the last week of July 1982, the moving van arrived and life in Philadelphia began.

MY START DATE WAS August 1. I got right to work, and Kyle stayed home with Jennifer, age four, and Jad, age two. I immediately fit in at the Philadelphia division. Rene and I worked closely with staff and plant workers who ran the large photofinishing lab where our offices were located. We had fun, and we made a significant difference in the working environment, which the employees noticed right away.

Within a few months, we were getting new business. I was hiring more territory representatives, and we were becoming profitable. Our family had a great time discovering all the fun things to do and see around Philadelphia and around Bucks County. At the same time, I joined the Focal Planes Camera Club and began making new photography friends. One was Harvey Friedman. He and I began taking Sunday morning photo trips to the Jersey Shore, central Pennsylvania (Amish country), and to the mountains in central Pennsylvania. I felt like I was back home, seeing as I was only a couple hours from our Dersham family home in Mifflinburg, where my aunt and uncle lived.

I did a lot of shooting while traveling on business trips, in which I would shoot on the way there and back. I would leave a half day early so I could shoot prior to my first scheduled event of the trip. My region included all of Pennsylvania, Maryland, Delaware, parts of West Virginia, New Jersey, and the District of Columbia. Most of my traveling was by car, making my large-format equipment easy to transport. I would always leave the house before dawn, taking pictures at daylight. I often had on a suit, but managed to make it work. I bet every passerby wondered why a guy in a suit was out taking pictures of the landscape. The focusing cloth used to see through the camera draped over my head, which would mess up my hair, but I tidied up prior to my meetings.

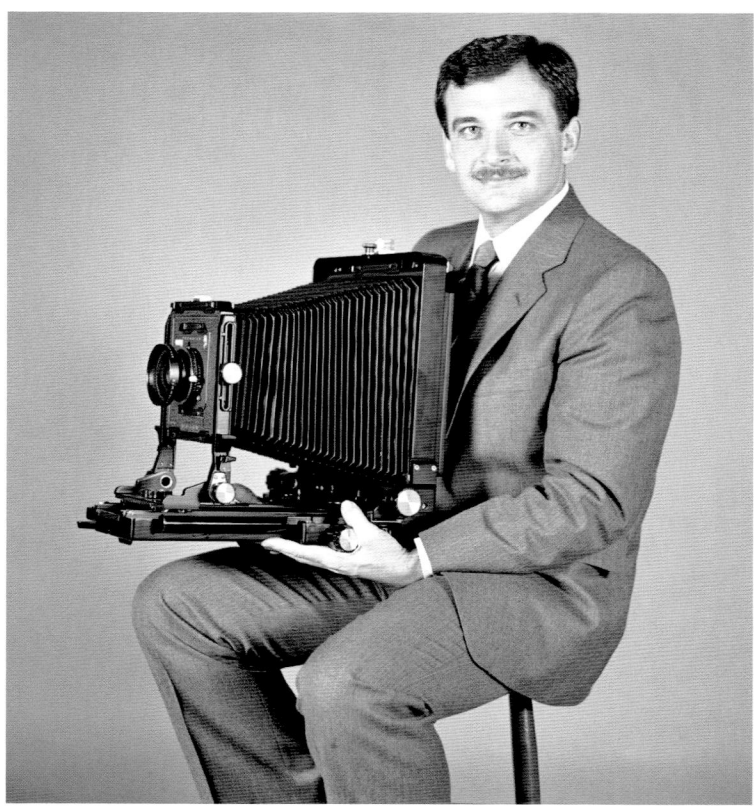

John Dersham, the day before his 34th birthday in his Philadelphia home studio, 10-30-1985; Mamiya C33 TLR camera; 105mm Sekor lens; Photogenic studio light; Kodak Plus X Pan 120 film; Kodak HC110B developer.

DURING THE 1980S, I was shooting an average of 2,000 sheets of 4x5 film a year. This is a lot, one sheet at a time. By 1985, I added 8x10 and 5x7 formats. I had been with the company long enough to get three weeks of vacation time. When flying long distances for corporate meetings, I would take a week in advance of the meetings to shoot. I would pay for a rental car and hotel rooms until the days I was assigned to be there. The company was fine with my going early

and paid the same for plane tickets as if I had left at the normal time. Over the decade, I covered the West, New England, the Midwest, and the South on business trips. It was fantastic. In turn Colorcraft, soon to be Qualex, an Eastman Kodak Company, began using my images for wall art in office buildings and factories nationwide. The company was receptive of my photography, and I even taught some photography classes to employees.

I would work in my darkroom three or more times a week. I would wait till my kids went to bed at 8 p.m. My passion for printing my latest images on 11x14 or 16x20 double-weight fine-art photographic paper was so strong in those years that I would spend three to five hours printing, washing, and getting the prints set out to dry before going to bed at 2 a.m. and getting up the next morning early for work. In those days, prior to the internet and social media, the only way to view and judge an image was the finished print or a slide on a projector. I was highly motivated by the fine-art craft of striving for perfection in the darkroom. It was an amazing feeling to work hard to get the results I wanted.

In retrospect all these many years later, I am not sure how I ever did all of that work, especially while keeping the long hours and striving to balance my home life and family. It all seemed to work out fine, and even though I remember so clearly my photo outings and darkroom marathons, I am not sure my family recalls much of it since I was usually out of their view. They have always enjoyed seeing the finished prints, and over the years my prints are hanging on all of our family members' walls; at this point some of the prints have been there for decades. This is true not just for my immediate family but for our siblings, parents, cousins, aunts, and uncles. I am honored that my pictures have been valued enough to stay permanently on my family's walls.

Kyle was very patient through all of this. We were having wonderful family times and going to a lot of new places. I have been blessed to have a spouse who tolerated the high amount of time I spent on photography and the costs associated with it.

COLORCRAFT WAS A J.B. Fuqua Company out of Atlanta. They owned Snapper lawnmowers, Martin movie theaters, Tractor Supply Company, and others. In 1985, Colorcraft purchased Berkey Photo, a large distributor of photography equipment that also had a large photofinishing division. At the time of the Colorcraft purchase, Berkey Photo was in charge of American distribution for many camera companies, including Toyo. I had wanted a Toyo 8x10 field camera, but it was $1,800 without a lens, so it was out of my price range. But after the acquisition, I was able to buy the camera as an employee for $900. I also bought an optional 5x7 back and was officially shooting 8x10 and 5x7.

Berkey was a large company in the Northeast and had a more expansive photo processing lab in Philadelphia than we did. Consolidation of people and locations began. Once again, I got a call from Ray Smith. He offered me a regional sales manager position in Hattiesburg, Mississippi. At first, I did not see how this could be a promotion. Kyle was all for it, and the kids were too young for it to matter. Kyle had never felt as comfortable in Philly as I did. I

had lived in New York and Pennsylvania as a kid, but this was her first Northeast experience. She loved the area for the scenery and the things to do, but the culture was different from what she was used to in the Midwest. In addition, despite my raise in pay, housing more expensive than where we came from, and home mortgage interest was at an all-time high of 16 percent, making many houses unaffordable.

I explained my apprehension about the move to Ray Smith. He in turn had the president of the company, Carl Hamill, call me. Carl was able to share some long-term company strategies that Ray could not. Carl explained that all the Colorcraft acquisitions would flood the company with talent in the local areas, talent that Colorcraft wanted to keep. Hattiesburg had an immediate need for a seasoned professional and a large territory that included Mississippi, Alabama, Louisiana, and the Florida panhandle. Carl explained that the move would put me in a good position for more career advancements.

IN LATE FEBRUARY 1986, being that it was cold and snowy in Philadelphia, I flew down to Hattiesburg to meet my new Regional Vice President Howard Noel, Regional General Manager Walt VanDuzer, and local General Operations Manager Don McCarthy. When I arrived, the temperature was in the sixties, and early spring flowers were blooming. I will never forget the warm feel of the sun on my face and the fragrance of spring in the air.

Don McCarthy hooked me up with real estate agent John Killen. Kyle worked with him and found a perfect house to rent. The area was quiet, pretty, and not congested. Everyone made us feel at home. In retrospect, the weather difference that time of year was wonderful.

In early March, we made the move. Both of our moves were fully paid for by Colorcraft. The moves did not cost a dime and we were given some moving allowances on top of that. The company was benefit-rich and very much focused on employee satisfaction. In those days, employee benefits, employee satisfaction, and employee retention meant everything to major companies.

Houses locally were more affordable, and interest rates had gone down to 10 percent. We felt we could buy a house. Within five months of renting our first house in Hattiesburg, John Killen found us a fantastic house that needed work. It was a foreclosure and we made an offer that was accepted. The house was in a wonderful neighborhood with good schools close by.

Kyle and I restored the interior and cleaned up the yard. When we were done, it was gorgeous. As we were working on it, we met a local handy man, John Koch, and he did what we could not do, including taking half of our two-car garage and building my darkroom. After six months without a darkroom, I was back in business.

We had three and a half great years in Hattiesburg. The kids were in elementary school and Kyle got involved in creating a Parent Teacher Organization (PTO). Kyle worked with friend Eileen McCarty to create a kid's chorus and a play; the elementary school had neither at that time. They put on several great shows over a few years. Kyle and Eileen produced them and even performed a skit called "Me and My Shadow" as they sang the classic song.

At the same time, I was taking a lot of new images in states I had not photographed before. I continued to make photography friends in retail locations and in the community. My catalog of medium- and large-format images kept growing and growing.

I began shooting with Brent Wallace, a local professional who was also a large-format photographer. He along with my friends John and Barbara Winstead at Stewart's Camera Center had a nice photo group in Hattiesburg. As home of the University of Southern Mississippi, Hattiesburg was like many college towns whose youth population brought forth a lot of energy and fun activities. At the same time, Kyle attended USM and began working as a veterinary technician for Dr. Paul Calhoun in Hattiesburg.

EASTMAN KODAK WAS THE first company to operate large photo-finishing labs. They sold only branded processing under the Kodak Processing label, mostly for camera stores and some drugstores. They were not in the wholesale market until 1986 when they acquired Fox Photo Inc., renaming it Ektra Photo. Fox at one point was the largest wholesale photofinisher. Kodak's main interest was the retention of the paper and chemical business. Competitor photofinishers used materials from Fuji, 3M, Mitsubishi, Konica, and other chemical companies; Kodak wanted to maintain the lead worldwide in the photo paper and chemical business.

In 1988, J. B. Fuqua Industries and Eastman Kodak agreed to join to form a new company called Qualex Inc. (*qual*ity and *excel*lence). Fuqua would maintain 51 percent ownership and Kodak would keep 49 percent. This move unified all former acquisitions by both companies. The consolidation of the business units and processing labs began immediately.

During the process, some labs were closed, especially if they had overlapping territory. Employee reductions also took place. Hattiesburg was part of the Florida region and Howard Noel was the vice president of the region. Florida had five labs in the state, plus Hattiesburg, New Orleans, and Baton Rouge.

The wholesale photofinishing business was gigantic. All camera stores, drugstores, mass merchants, grocery stores, and photo kiosks offered film developing and printing under their stores' names. When a customer left a roll of film at a store to be processed, it went in an envelope with that store's name on it. This consolidation meant Qualex would be processing nationwide and in Canada. Up to three million rolls of film a day were processed, most of which made it back to the originating retailer the next day. Each lab had its own routes. Company employees in logoed cars delivered yesterday's work and picked up new work each day.

In late 1988, Ray Smith, whom I no longer reported to, asked my region VP Howard Noel if he could ask me to take on the general management position of the Birmingham, Alabama, division of Qualex. Howard agreed. Once again, Smith was matching up people and locations. Birmingham was a former Fox Photo lab and was having some personnel related issues, so a change at the top was necessary.

Ray is one of those very special people everyone hopes to have at least one of in their life. Ray was a dynamic leader with a proven track record. Winning his support for the work I did early in my career proved to be the single largest contributor to my successful thirty years at Eastman Kodak. I became great friends with Ray and his family during those years. Since he retired in 1997, he calls me and his other former general managers every Christmas Eve, never missing, not even once.

ON MARCH 5, 1989, Kyle and I, on our twelfth anniversary, went to Birmingham to find a house to buy. We wanted to move from one house to the next without renting first. We found a house in the suburb of Hoover, just south of Birmingham. The schools were good, and we liked the neighborhood. We moved in on April 18, 1989 (I had been working in Birmingham since late December and going home on weekends).

Before we moved in, we had a den and a darkroom built in the basement. I was immediately able to continue my photography and darkroom work. I joined the Shades Valley Camera Club. Alabama is a photogenic state, so I shot a lot on my own and with friends. Everywhere I have lived, my photography friends have become lifelong friends.

The 1980s was a great decade for our family, my career, and my photography. From Nashville to Philadelphia to Hattiesburg, and finally to Birmingham, all in a decade. This was good for my family and my career. It also gave me a much deeper, more extensive catalog and allowed me to meet a lot of fellow photographers. Kyle once again got a job as a veterinary technician, this time for Dr. Allen Price; she would continue to work there our entire time in Birmingham. Our kids were growing up and became involved in music, sports, and scouts, all of which Kyle and I participated in and attended.

In Birmingham, I was given opportunities to show my work in galleries, libraries, camera stores, and other venues. I also began teaching weekend large-format photo workshops for the University of Alabama at Birmingham (UAB). I met great friends there. Between them and the photo club, we had a good community of people for photo shooting events.

Kodak had a mandatory continuing education mandate of forty hours per year. I was getting more than a hundred hours a year in the late 1980s. Kodak managed Kodak University which allowed me to use education hours to complete my business degree and get certified as a Master Photographer. I later qualified for Master of Arts equivalence. Kodak prioritized employee benefits and employee education. It offered multiple plans to help its employees become better educated, which in turn allowed more opportunities for advancement.

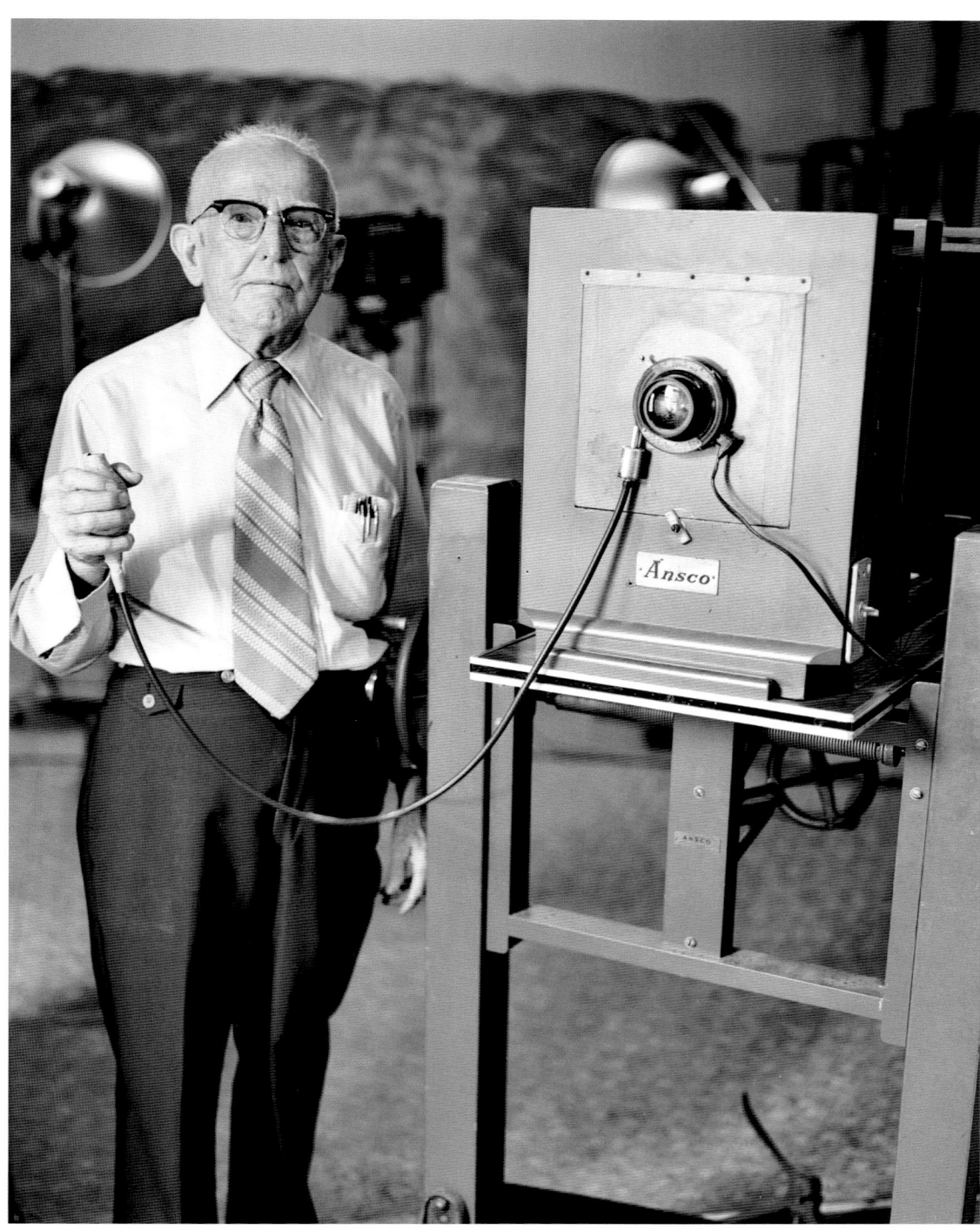

Mr. Hall at Hall's Studio, Manchester, Tennessee; he had used the same camera in the same studio for fifty years; 5-17-1982; Linhof Technika V 4x5 camera; 150mm Schneider Symmar S lens; Ilford FP4 4x5 film; Kodak HC110B developer.

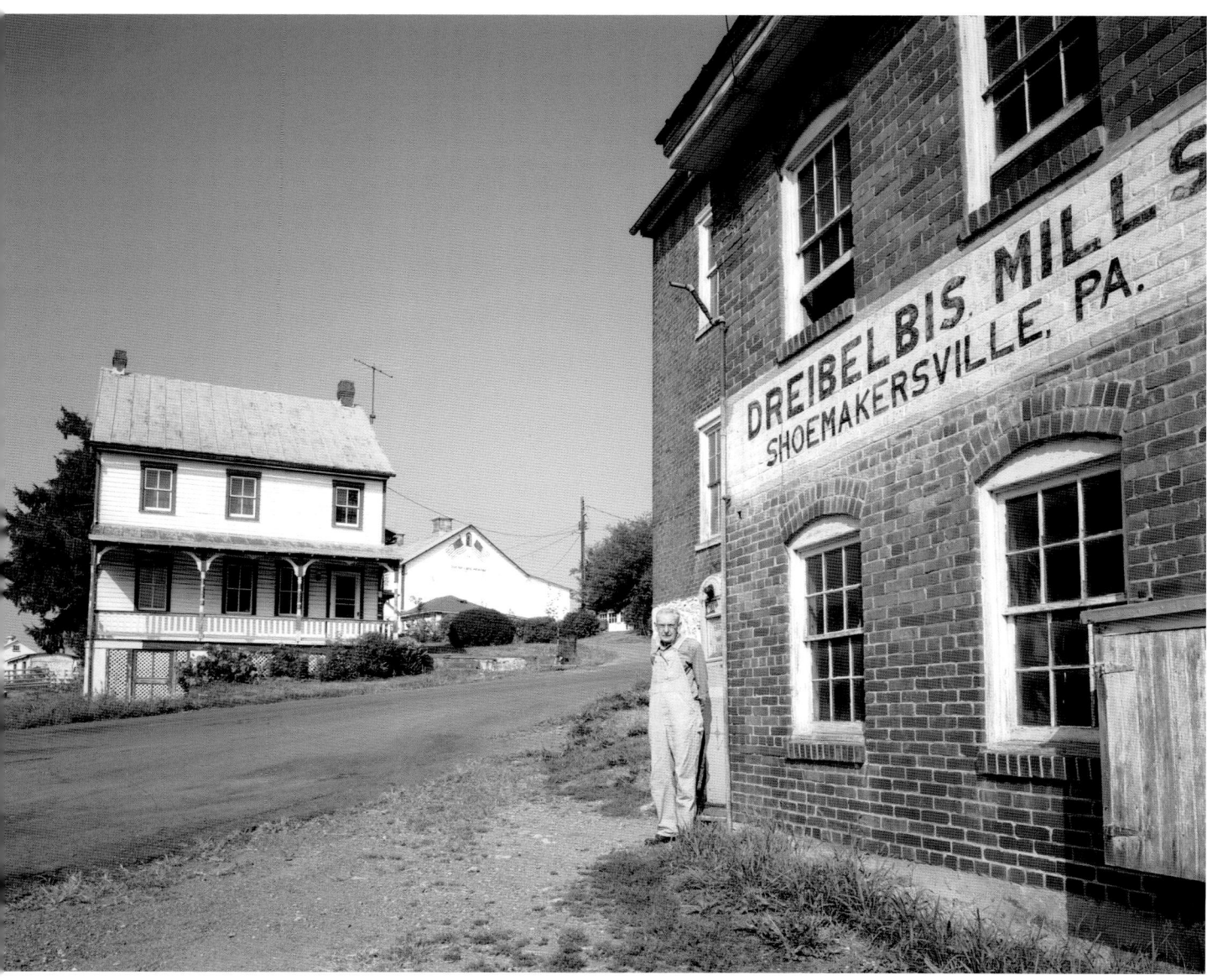

Mr. Dreibelbis of Dreibelbis Mills farm, established 1765, Shoemakersville, Pennsylvania, 8-17-1983; Cambo Super view camera; 90mm Schneider Super Angulon lens; yellow G filter; Ilford FP4 4x5 film; Kodak HC110B developer.

Print info
on back

No. 8/17/83   8:45 AM   Sunny summer morning

Name Earl J Dreibelbis (at his Farm)
Shoemakersville, Pa. (Est 1765)

Order 90 mm F9 Schneider Super Angulon

Remarks Yellow G filter

Retouched Camera tilted up slightly

Order Finished slight rear swing for focus on near Mill

Reorder Earl is 4th generation at this farm

FP-4 4X5   64 EI
HC 110 1:7 (N)
F 45 at 1/4
Cambo SC

Nikon 7X

Neg#1 Galerie #2 11X14
F16 15 secs. burn in
barn and house very slightly
burn in sky slightly
8/21/83 Zone II light + Dev.

Neg#1 Galerie #2 8X10
F16 10½ secs.
burn in barn + house slightly
burn in sky slightly
Selectol soft + Zone II Dev.
Old light
9/17/83

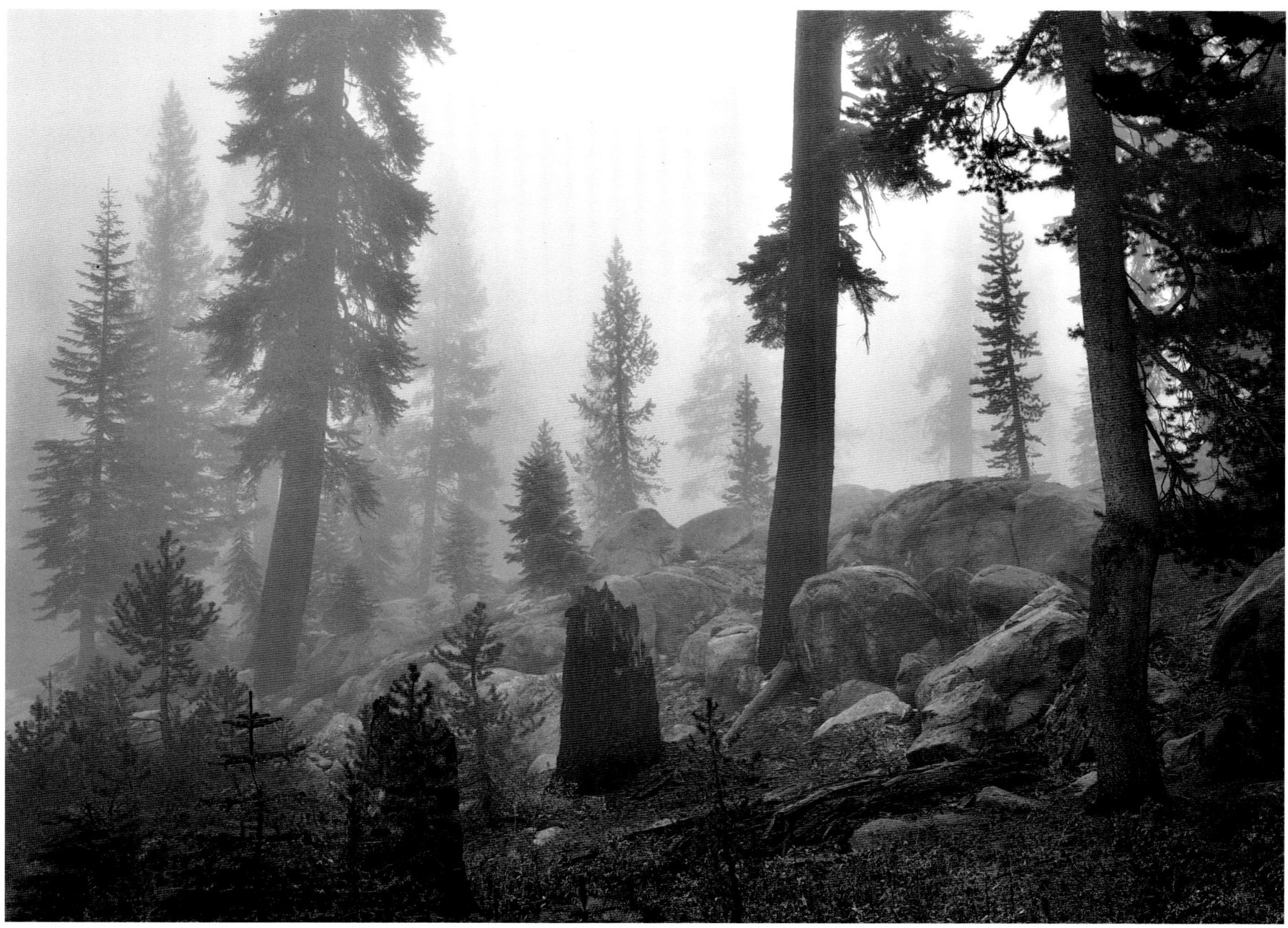

Yosemite National Park, fog and rain at 5,000 feet, 9-29-1984; Linhof Technika V 4x5 camera; 90mm Schneider Super Angulon lens; Kodak Tri X Pan Professional film; Kodak HC110B developer. The cool wet fog of an early morning is invigorating, fresh, and moody. It serves as a quiet silencer for the sounds of the woodlands, deadening the sounds of the woodland creatures stirring in the forest. I am alone in the forest, trying to keep my camera and lens dry to capture in black and white that which even in color appears nearly black and white.

Foggy Daybreak at Yosemite Valley

The night before my morning shoot in Yosemite National Park, I stayed at a small, rustic motel about fifty miles away. I cleaned and loaded my film holders before going to sleep. I left the room at 3 a.m. The drive in the dark was beautiful in itself—no lights anywhere and wildlife in the road along the way, including a black bear and a moose.

I arrived at Yosemite Valley overlook in total darkness. The October weather was crisp but comfortable, with lots of fog. I used my car lights to get my 4x5 Linhof Technika positioned on its tripod. I set my camera case with lenses and film holders next to the tripod, waiting for first daylight to see well enough to focus. The scene that gradually came into view was breathtaking, with patches of landscape showing through the fog. It would still be most of an hour before the sun rose over the mountains above Yosemite Falls.

As soon as I could see through my 210mm Schneider Symmar S lens—opened wide at F5.6—I began focusing, using an 8x loupe on the ground glass. Just as daylight was taking hold, I took light-meter readings and began to shoot.

Over the next hour and a half, I exposed thirty sheets of 4x5 film, changing lenses and angles throughout.

After the sun was up, the fog was gone, and the sky was blue, I was done there. I loaded up my equipment to move to another site in the park. I had been alone until then, but as I was leaving a sixteen-passenger van drove up and came to a stop.

The side door slid open and a guy with a 4x5 camera in his arms stepped out. He looked at me and said "Perfect!"

I said, "No, you missed it"

He was part of a large-format workshop that included breakfast before going out to shoot. They had no idea the fog had even been there.

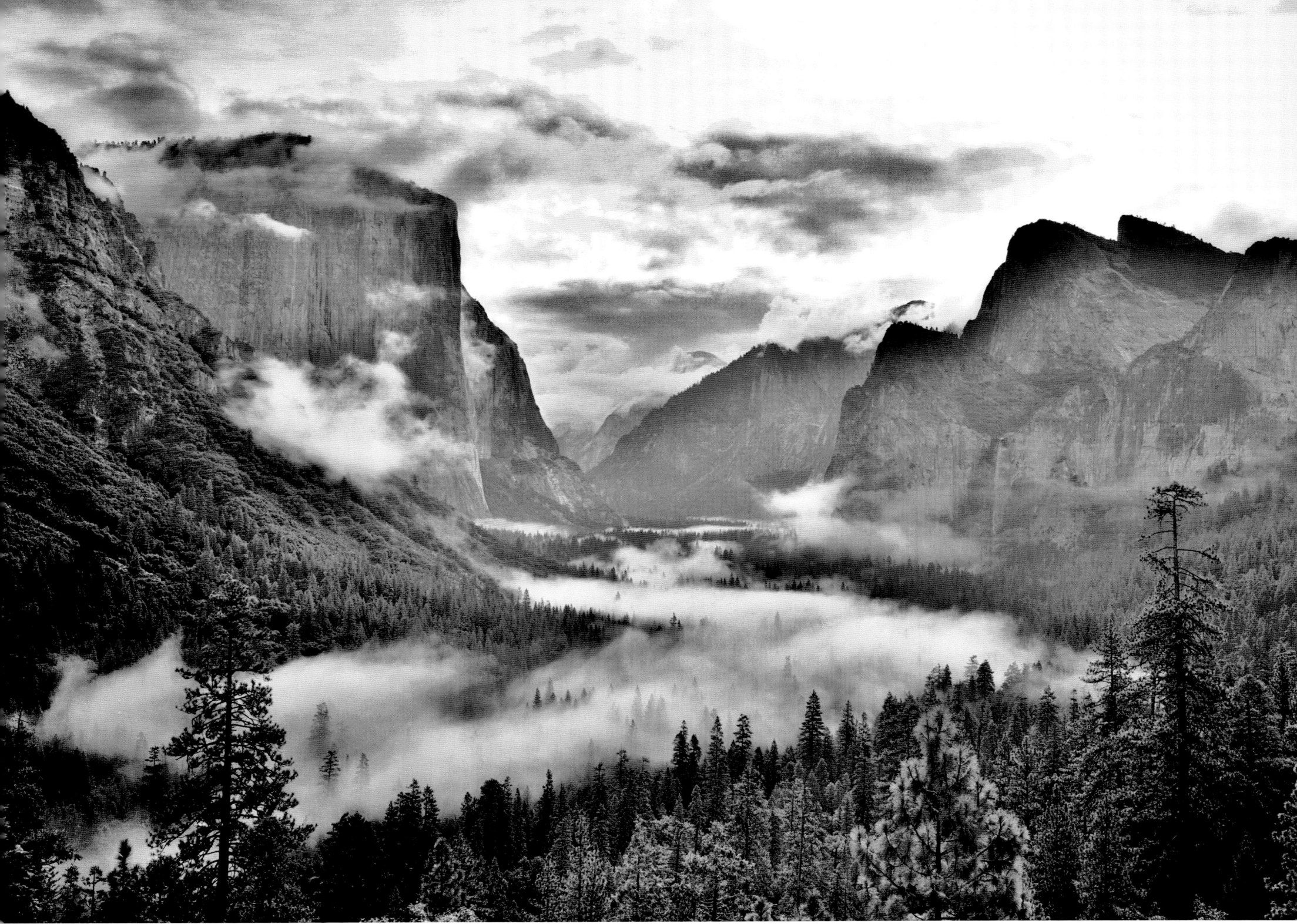

Fog at daybreak, Yosemite National Park, California, 10-1-1984; Linhof Technika V camera; 120mm Schneider Symmar S lens; yellow K2 filter; Ilford FP4 4x5 film; Kodak HC110B developer.

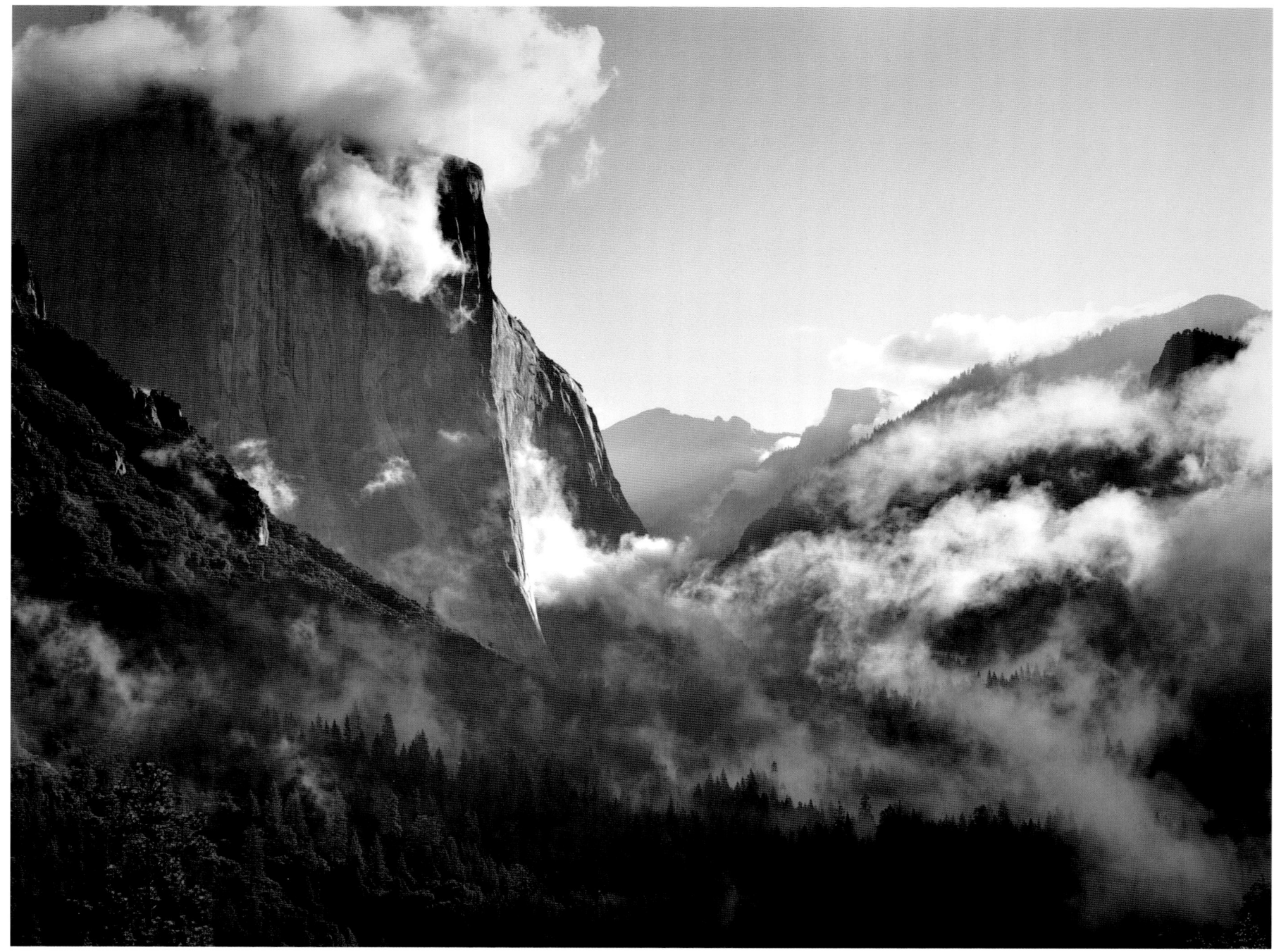

Yosemite National Park, California, 10-1-1984; Linhof Technika V camera; 210mm Schneider Symmar S lens; yellow K2 filter; Ilford FP4 4x5 film; Kodak HC110B developer.

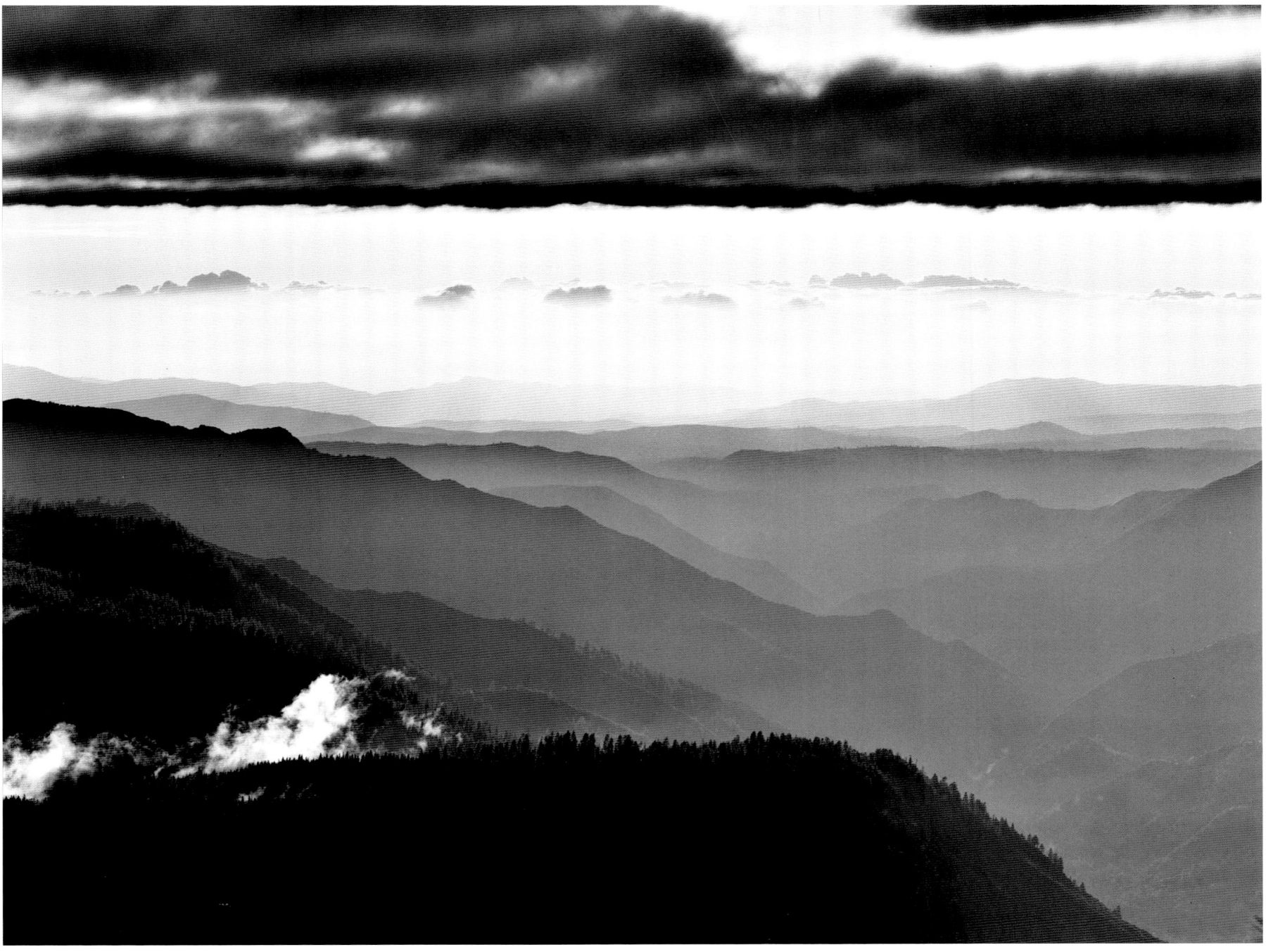

Clearing storm at Yosemite National Park, 9-30-1984; Linhof Technika V camera; 300mm Schneider Xenar lens; yellow G filter; Kodak Tri X Pan Pro 4x5 film; Kodak HC110B developer.

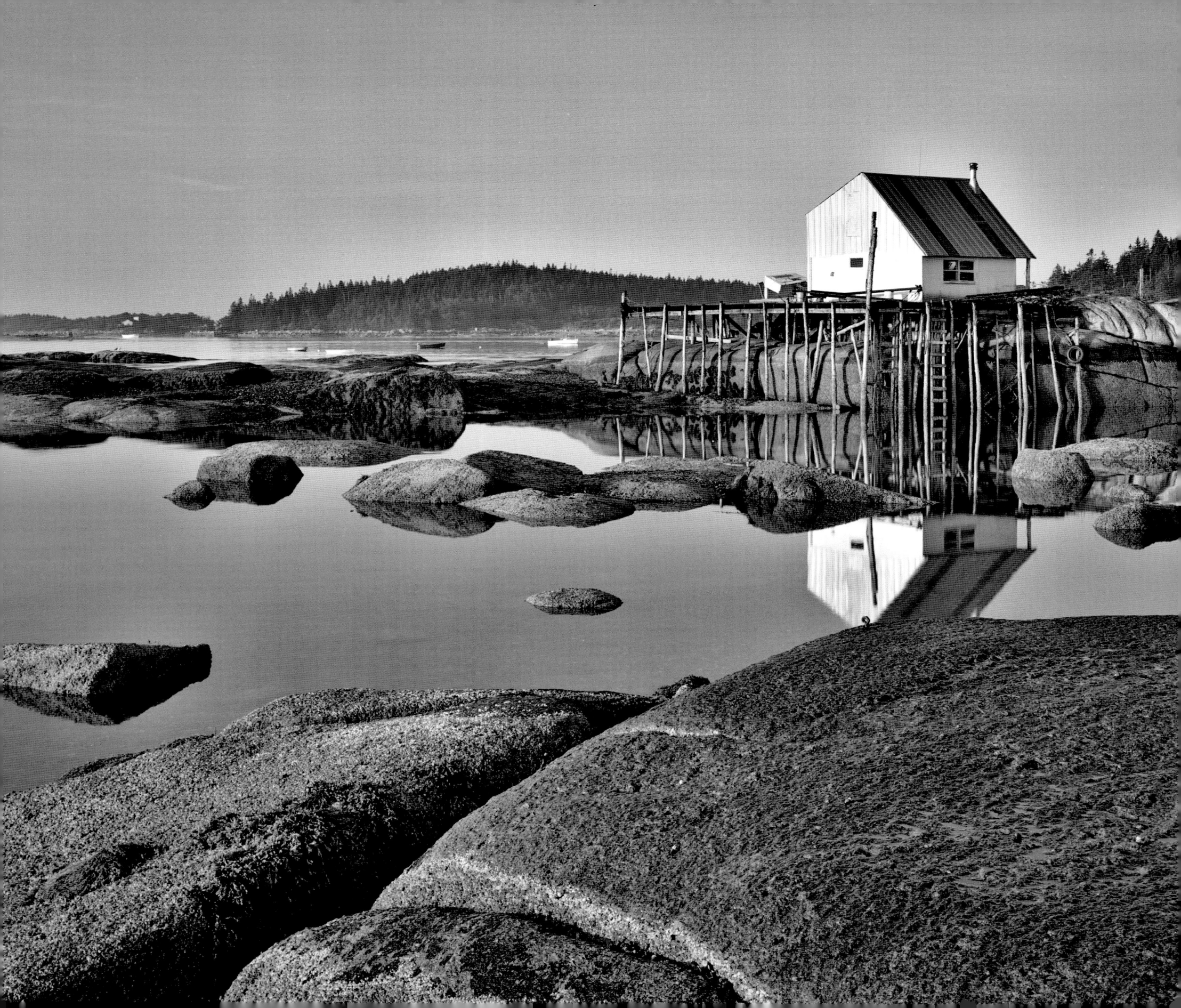

Reflected Boat House

When using a large-format camera, depth of field becomes a science. Large format requires longer lenses to have an image circle large enough to cover the larger film size.

The longer the focal length, the narrower is the depth of field at any given aperture. This means the lens must be stopped down more to a smaller aperture, and the shutter speed must be slowed to expose properly the film.

Large-format lenses stop down to F45 or F64 as opposed to F22 on a digital, 35mm, or medium-format camera. Some lenses for 8x10 negatives, and larger, stop down to F64, F90, and even F128. Since my large-format cameras are always used on a tripod, holding them still during exposure is not a problem but movement in the scene, such as wind, is. This means I often wait for the wind to stop blowing so the leaves and grass do not become blurred due to the long exposure.

In these particular images the wind was blowing ripples in the water harming my perfect mirror effect of the boat house in the water I was looking for. As I often do, I waited for the wind to die so I could achieve the look I wanted.

Everything about large-format photography is more difficult: cameras are heavier, must be used on tripod, allow only two pictures per film holder, and challenge with issues of depth of field and camera movements which must be correct to prevent image distortion.

Facing page: Stonington, Maine, 9-10-1986; Linhof Technika V 4x5 camera; 210mm Schneider Symmar S lens; yellow K2 filter; Kodak Tri X Pan Pro 4x5 film; Kodak HC110C developer.

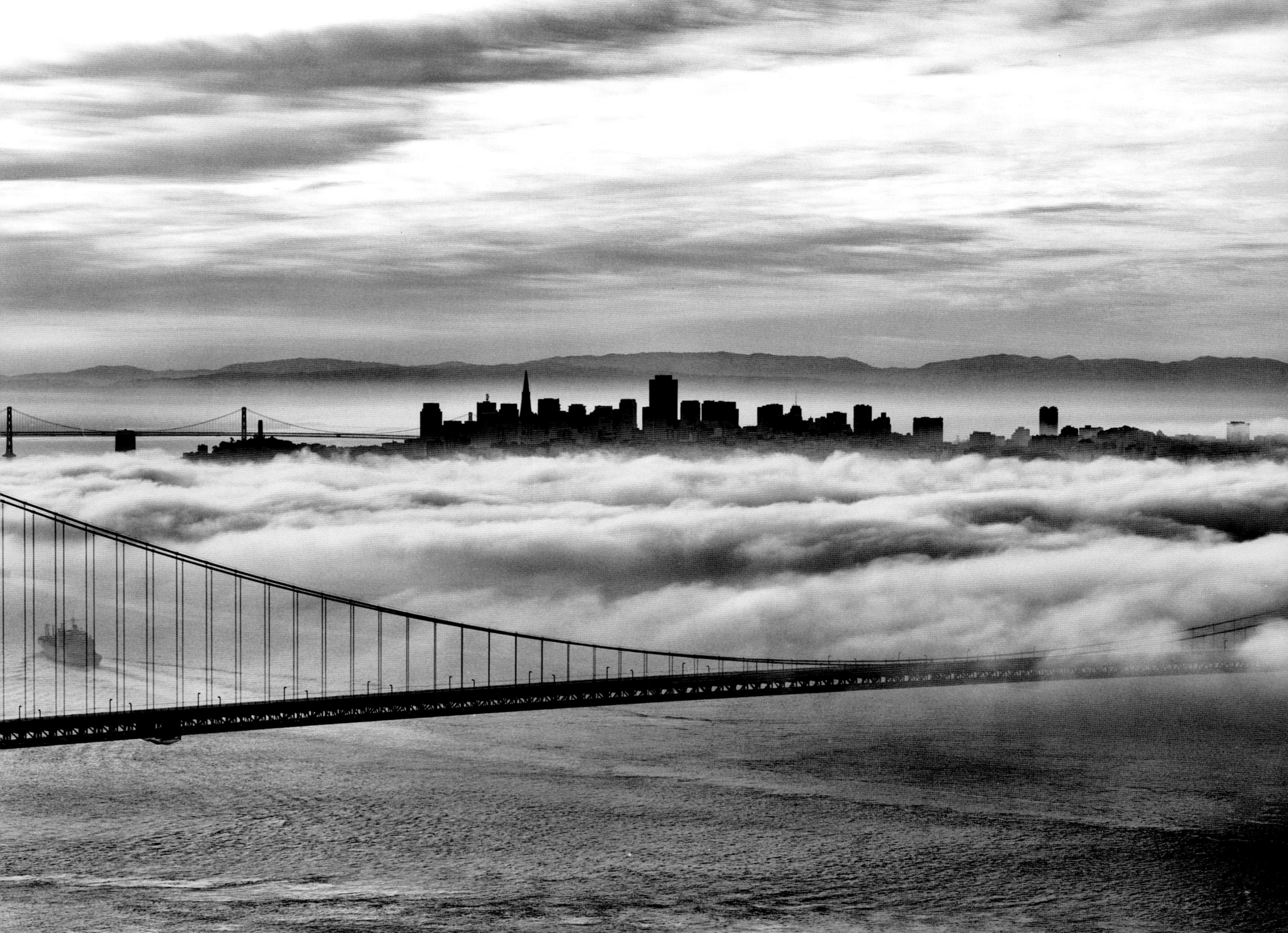

Golden Gate Series

September 28, 1984, I arrived in San Francisco on a flight from Philadelphia at midnight. I was so excited about this photo trip that I made no arrangement to sleep. I rented a car at the airport and went downtown San Fran to take night shots. After a few hours, I drove to Sausalito to sit in my car overlooking the Golden Gate Bridge. It was about 2:30 a.m. when I parked the car at just the right spot overlooking the bay and the bridge.

I may have dozed off for a few minutes, but the sound of foghorns from the ships below rose up the canyon and seemed to amplify much like using a megaphone. I loved the sound; it had a mournful tone, lonely yet somehow peaceful as it cut through the night fog.

The view of the San Francisco skyline was beautiful and still undisturbed by the sounds and sights of humanity trying to get to work.

Before daylight I set up my 4x5 Linhof Technika camera on its tripod, carefully positioning it for my first shot. I would watch closely as the sky slowly began to lighten along the eastern horizon, still dark, but gradually bright enough to reveal that the bay and the bridge had a fog layer just above the bridge roadway but lower than the San Francisco skyline.

I began shooting prior to daylight and shot picture after picture, one film holder at a time, for the next two and a half hours. Then the scene was in full daylight, the fog was gone, and the most dramatic images had passed.

Facing page: The Golden Gate Bridge in the pre-dawn fog, from Sausalito, California, 9-29-1984; Linhnof Technika V camera; 300mm Schneider Xenar lens; yellow K2 filter; Ilford FP4 4x5 film; Kodak HC110B developer.

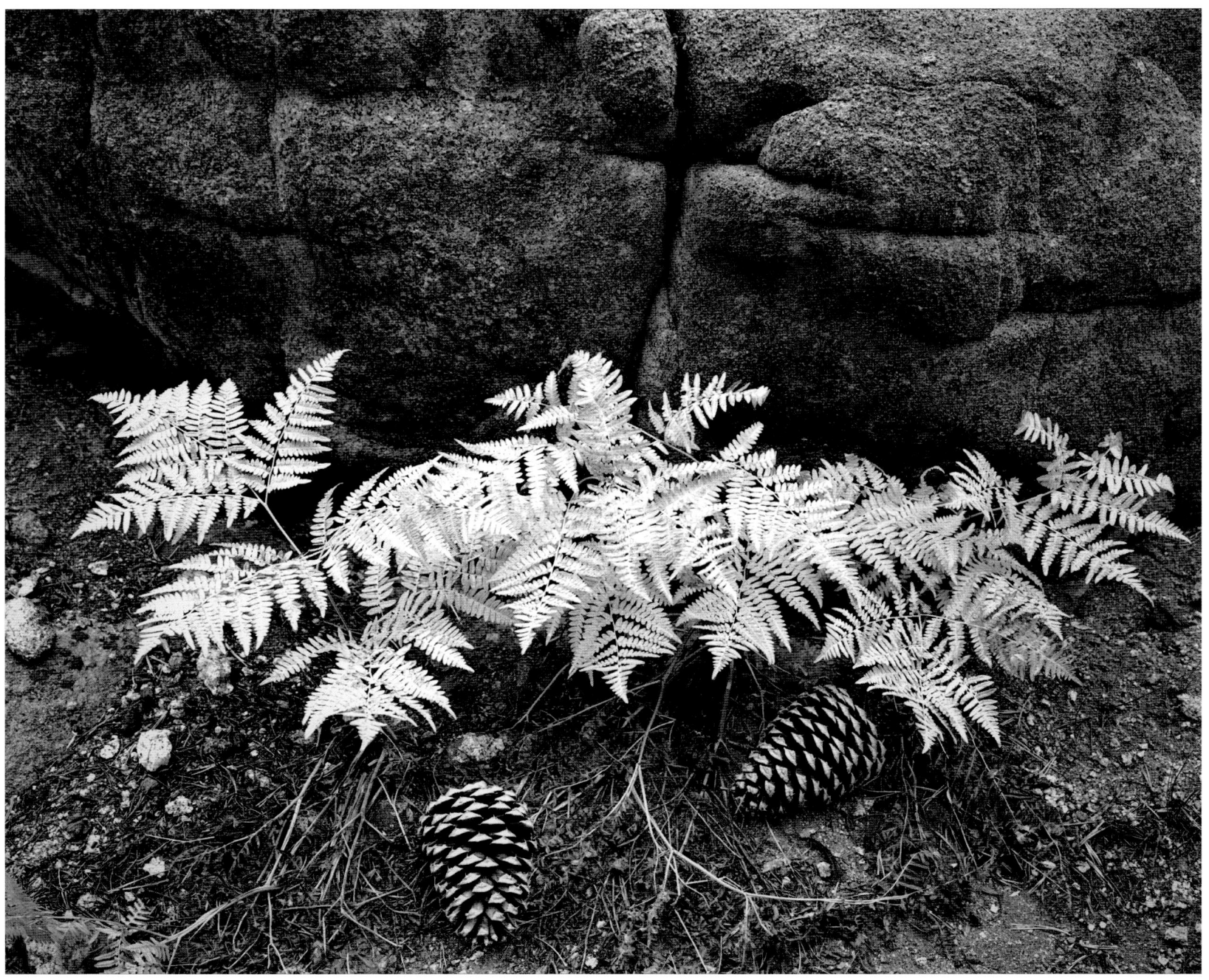

Fall yellow ferns at 5,000 feet, Yosemite National Park, California, 9-30-1984; Linhof Technika V camera; 120mm Schneider Symmar
S lens; Kodak Tri X Pan Pro 4x5 film; Kodak HC110B developer.

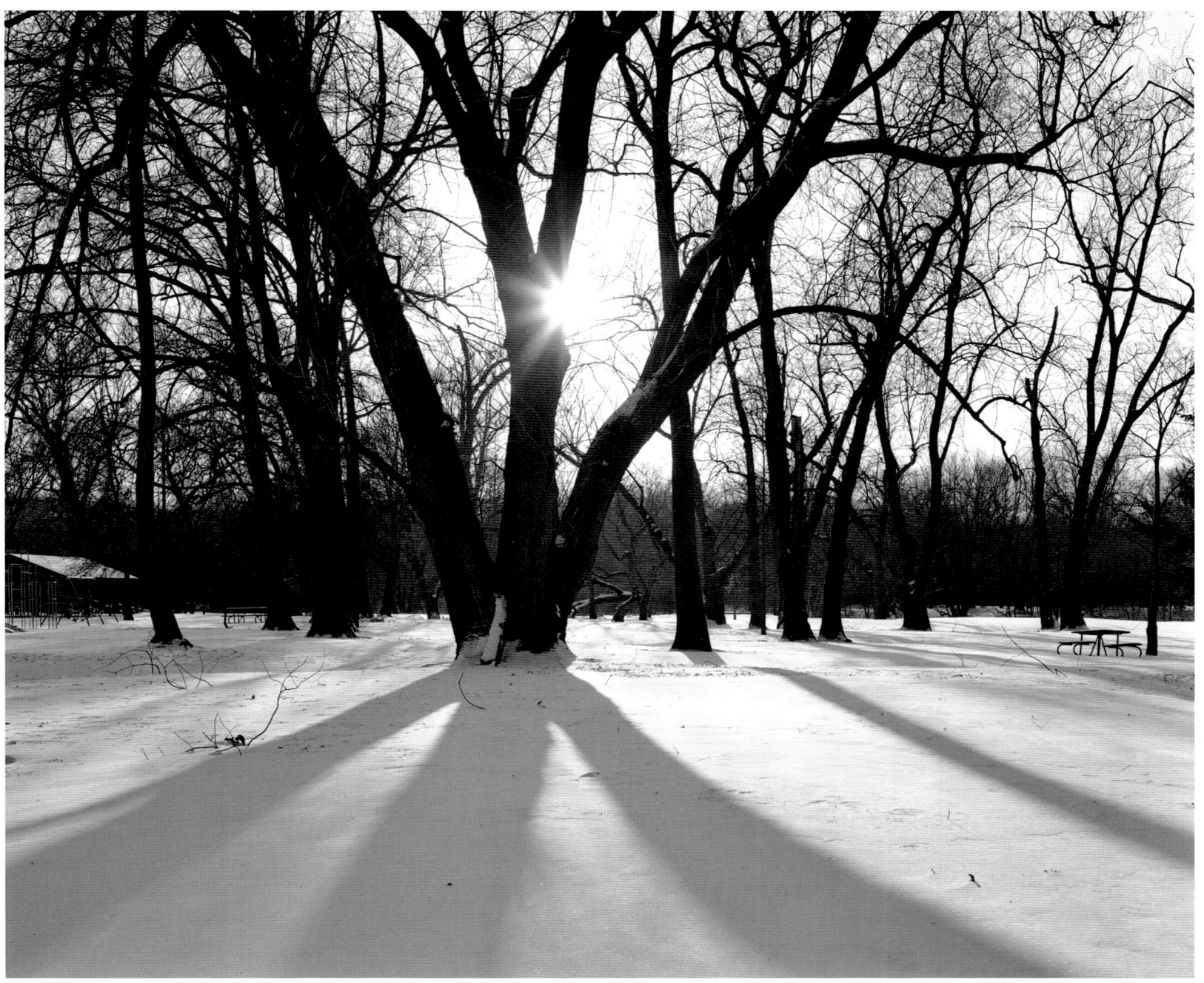

Sunrise at Playwicki Park, Bucks County, Pennsylvania, 1-19-1985; Linhof Technika V 4x5 camera; 120mm Schneider Symmar S Lens;
yellow K2 filter; Kodak Tri X Pan Pro 4x5 film; Kodak HC110B developer.

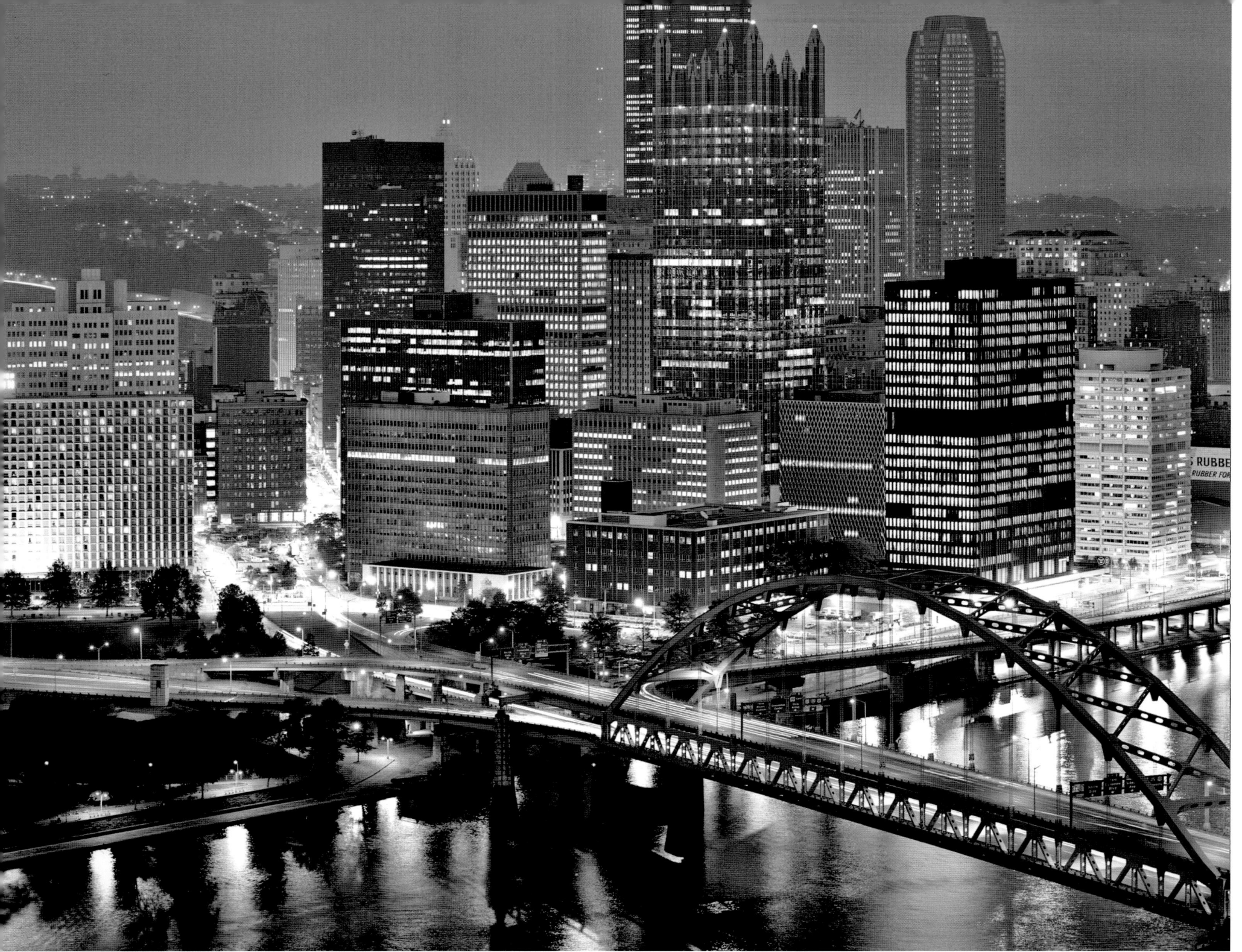

Pittsburgh, Pennsylvania, just prior to total darkness, 10-30-1983; Cambo Super View 4x5 camera; 300mm Schneider Xenar lens; Kodak Tri X Pan Pro 4x5 film; Kodak HC110B developer.

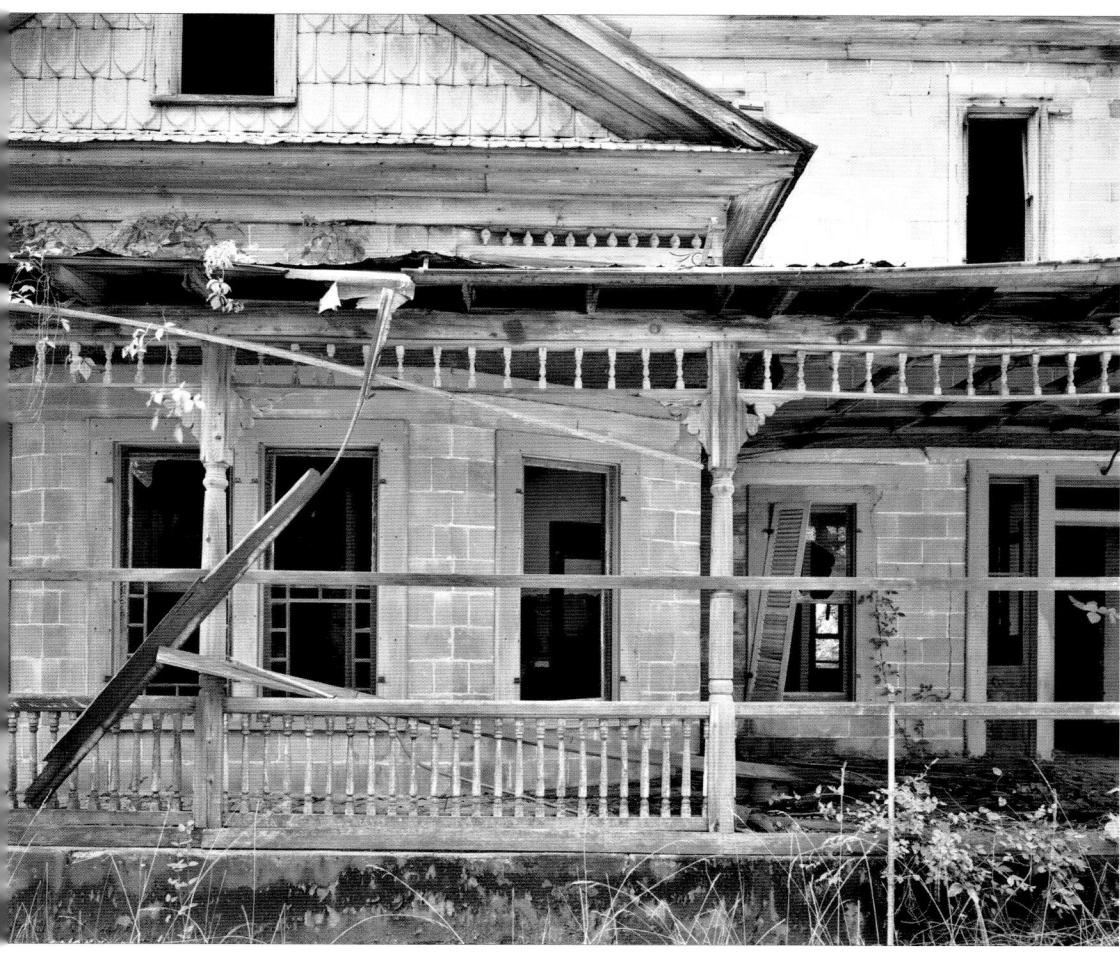

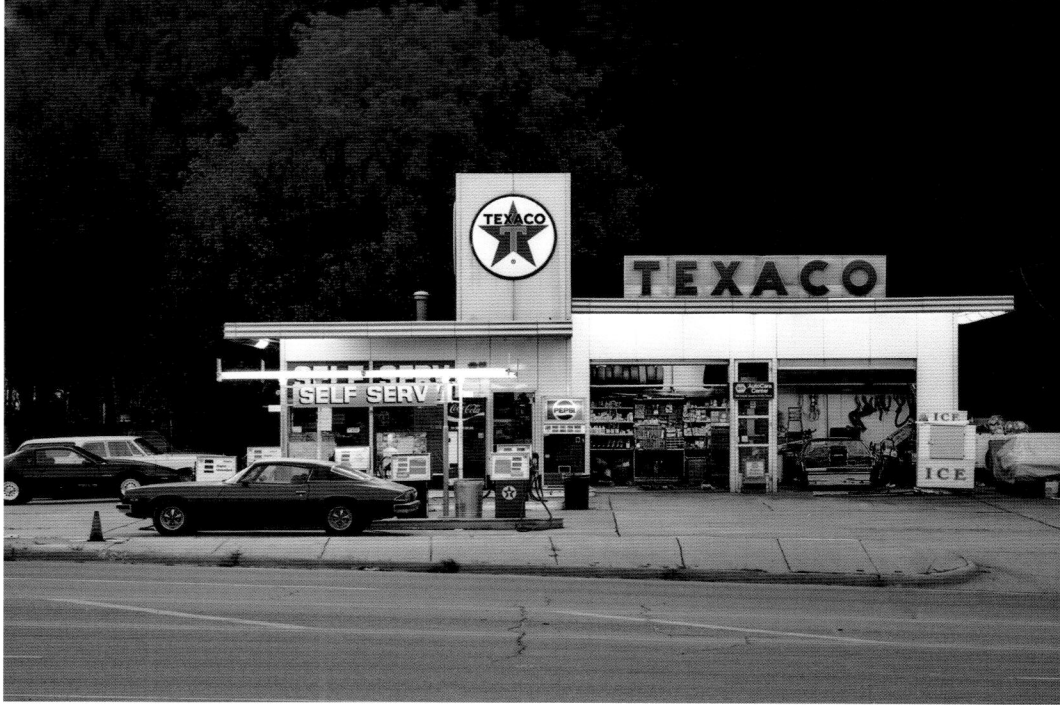

Left: 1912 Bassfield Mansion, near Columbia, Mississippi, 8-8-1987; Linhof Technika V 4x5 camera; 150mm Nikkor lens; Kodak Tmax 100 4x5 film; Kodak HC110B developer.

Above: Texaco station, Meridian, Mississippi, 10-4-1988; Linhof Technika V 4x5 camera; 300mm Schneider Xenar lens; Kodak Tmax 100 4x5 film; Kodak HC110B developer.

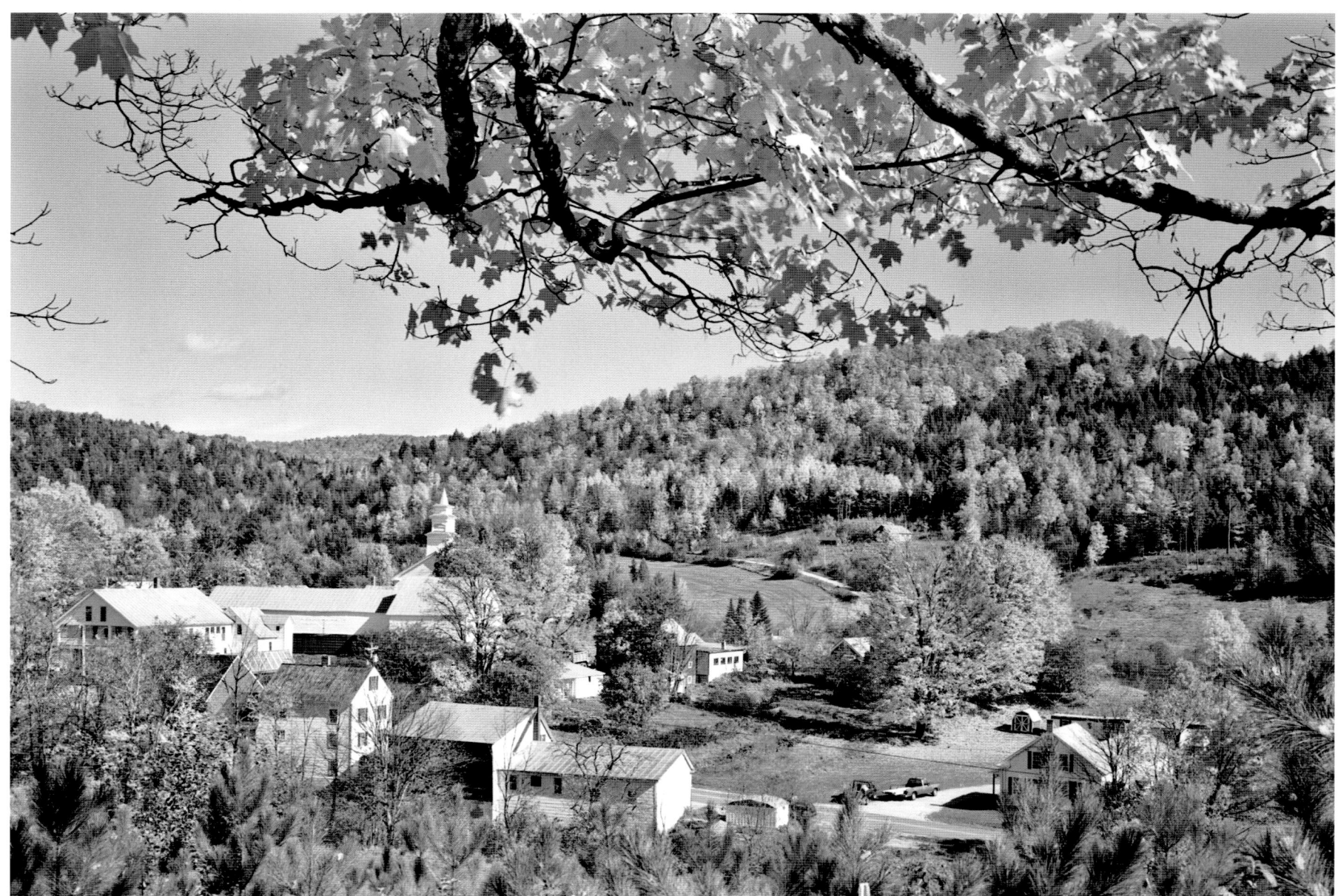

Above: East Topsham, Vermont, 10-12-1985; Toyo 8x10M camera, 5x7 back; 210mm Schneider Symmar S Lens; yellow K2 filter; Kodak Tri X Pan Pro 5x7 film; Kodak HC110B developer.

Facing page: Waits River, Vermont, 10-12-1985; Toyo 8x10m camera; 300mm Schneider Xenar lens; yellow K2 filter; Kodak Tri X Pan Pro 8x10 film; Kodak HC110B developer.

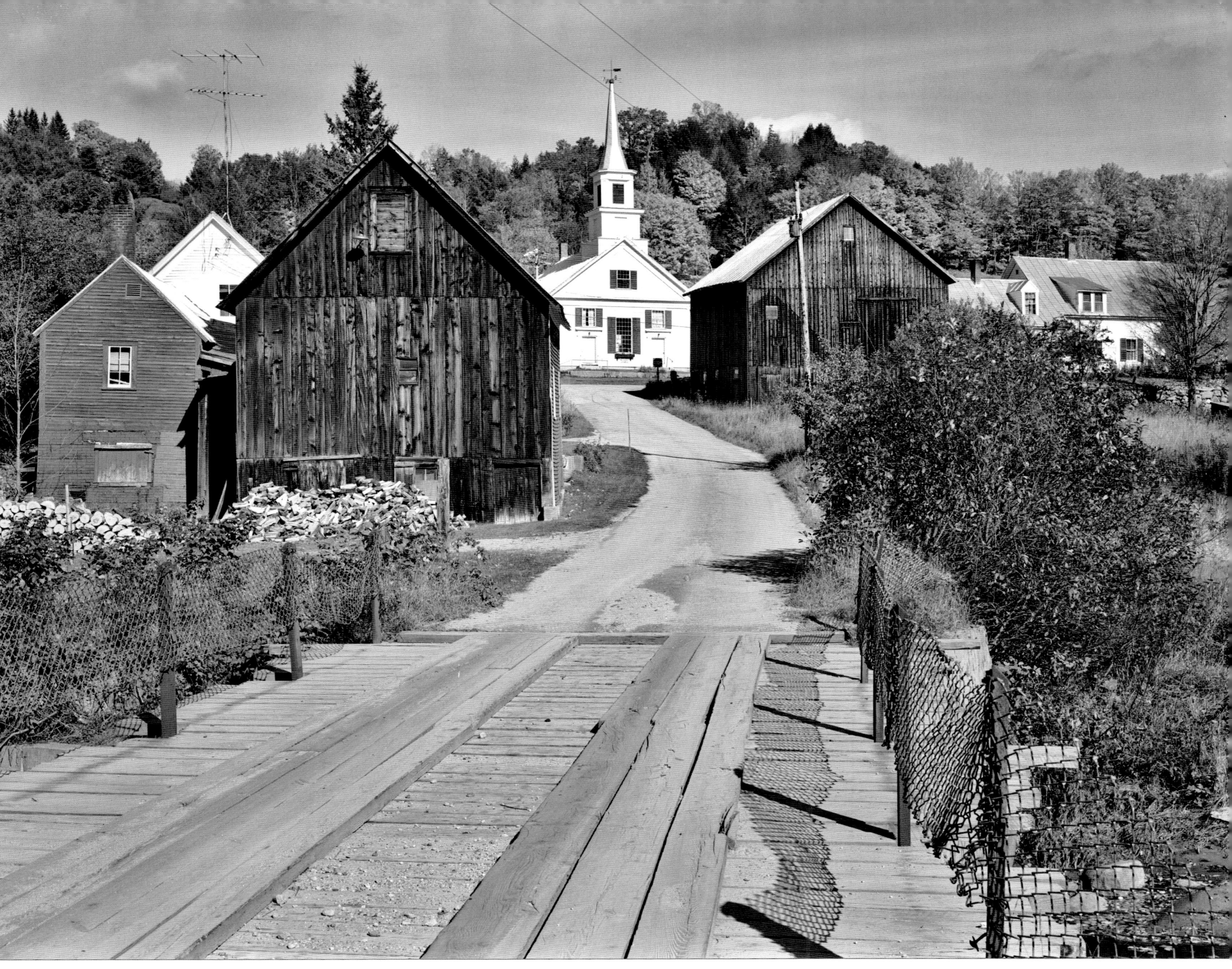

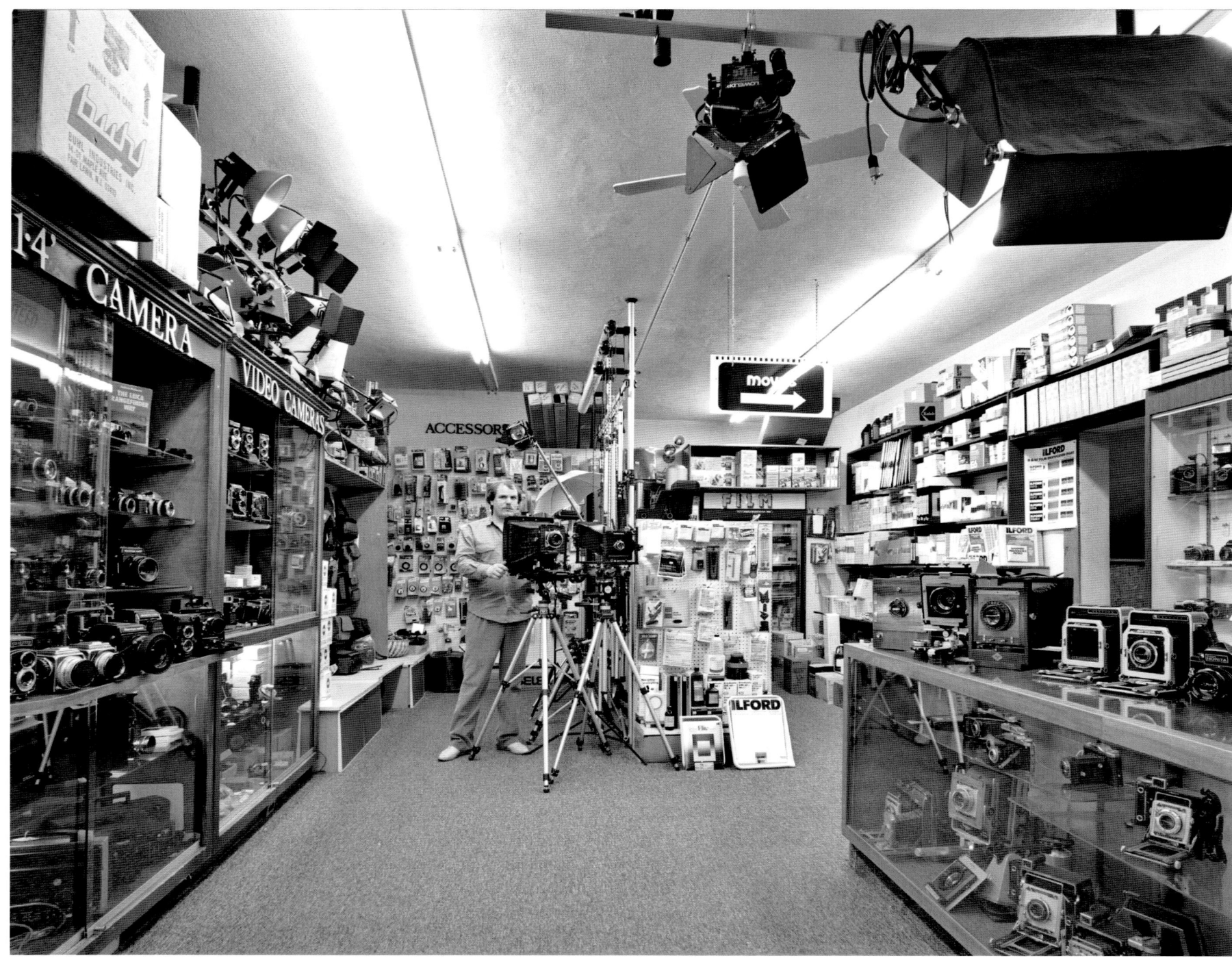

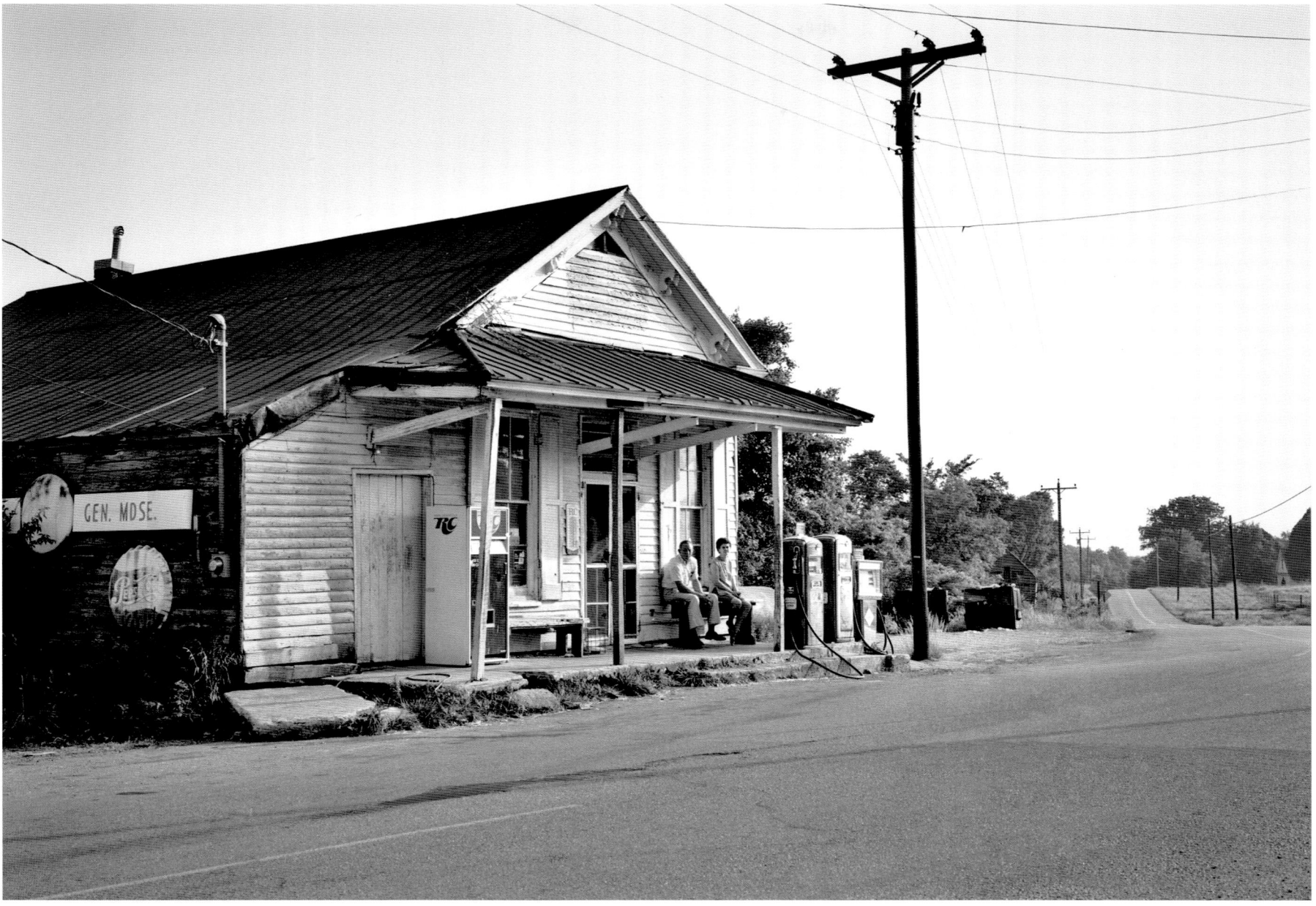

Above: Mr. and Mrs. Windrow in front of Windrow's General Store, Rockvale, Tennessee, 6-22-1980; Crown Graphic 4x5 camera; 150mm Schneider Symmar S Lens; yellow K2 filter; Kodak Plus X Pan Pro 4x5 film; Edwal FG7 developer.

Facing page: Owner Frank Cundari at New York Camera and Video, Feasterville, Pennsylvania, 1-25-1986; Linhof Technika V camera; 90mm Schneider Super Angulon lens; Kodak Tri X Pan Pro 4x5 film; Kodak HC110B developer.

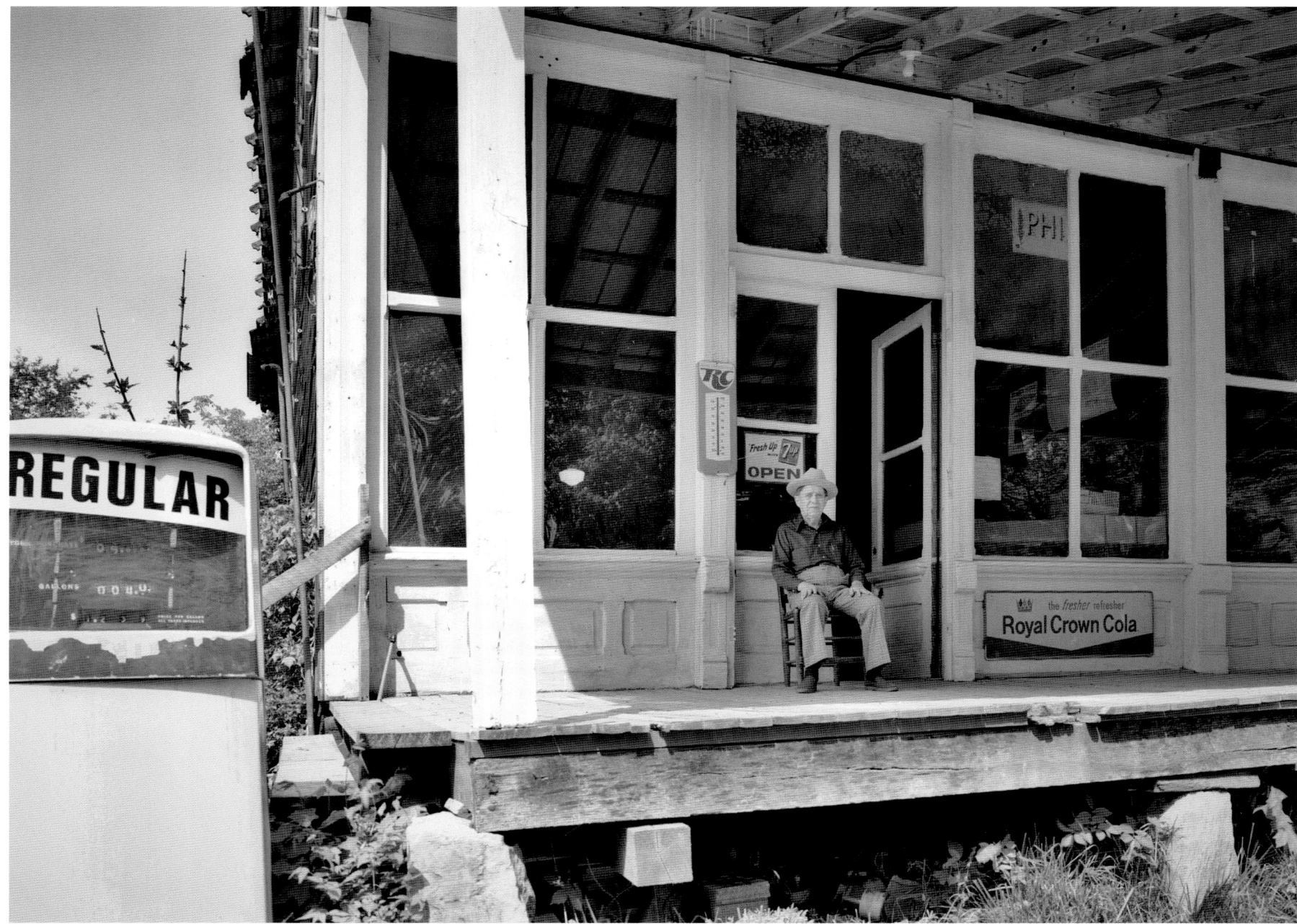

Pleasant View, Tennessee, hardware and general store, 5-10-1982; Linhof Technika V camera; 90mm Schneider Super Angulon lens; Ilford FP4 4x5 film; Kodak HC110B developer.

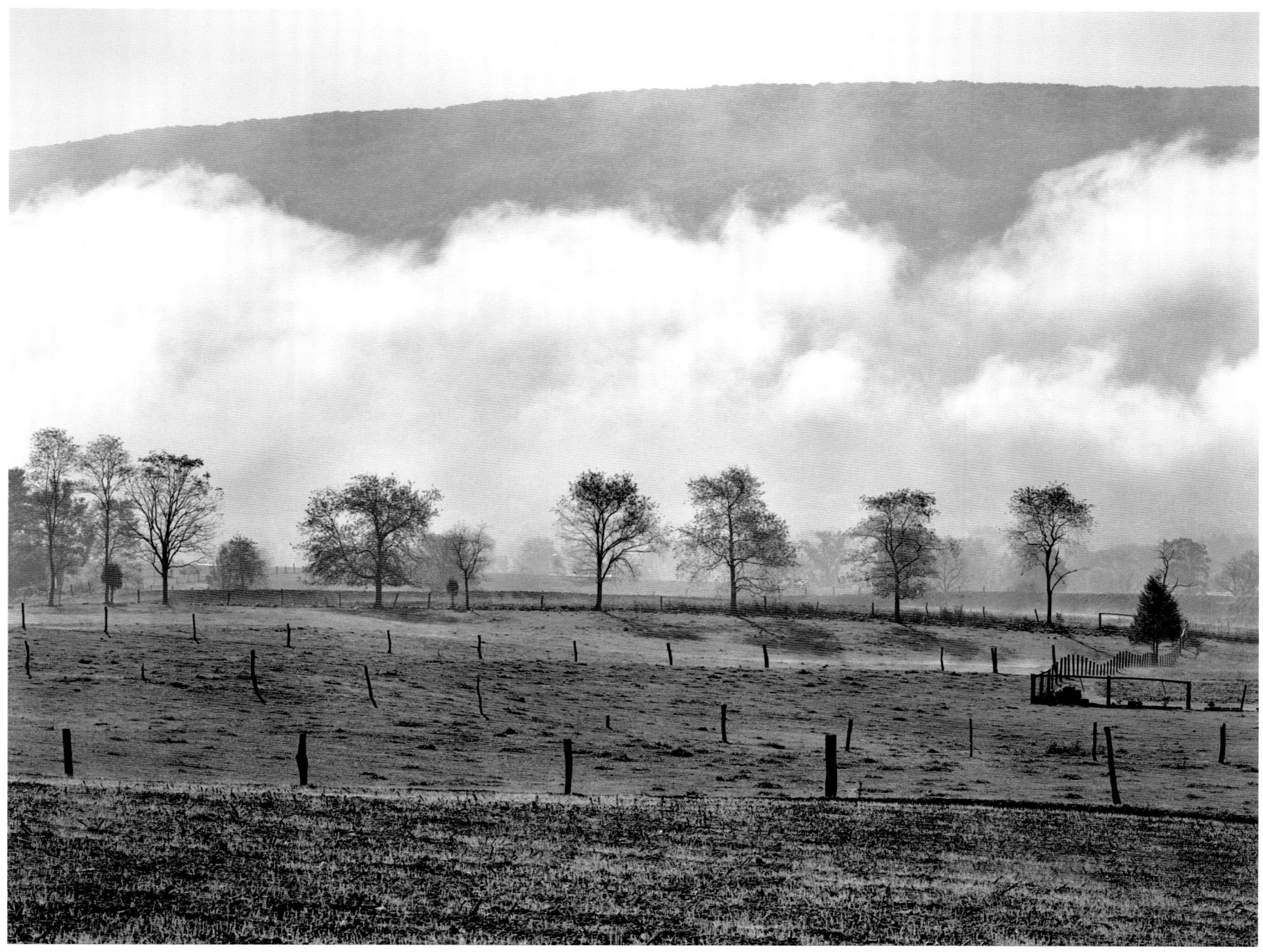

Foggy sunrise near Lewistown, Pennsylvania, 10-16-1983; Cambo Super View 4x5 camera; 300mm Schneider Xenar lens; yellow G filter; Kodak Tri X Pan Pro 4x5 film; Kodak HC110B developer.

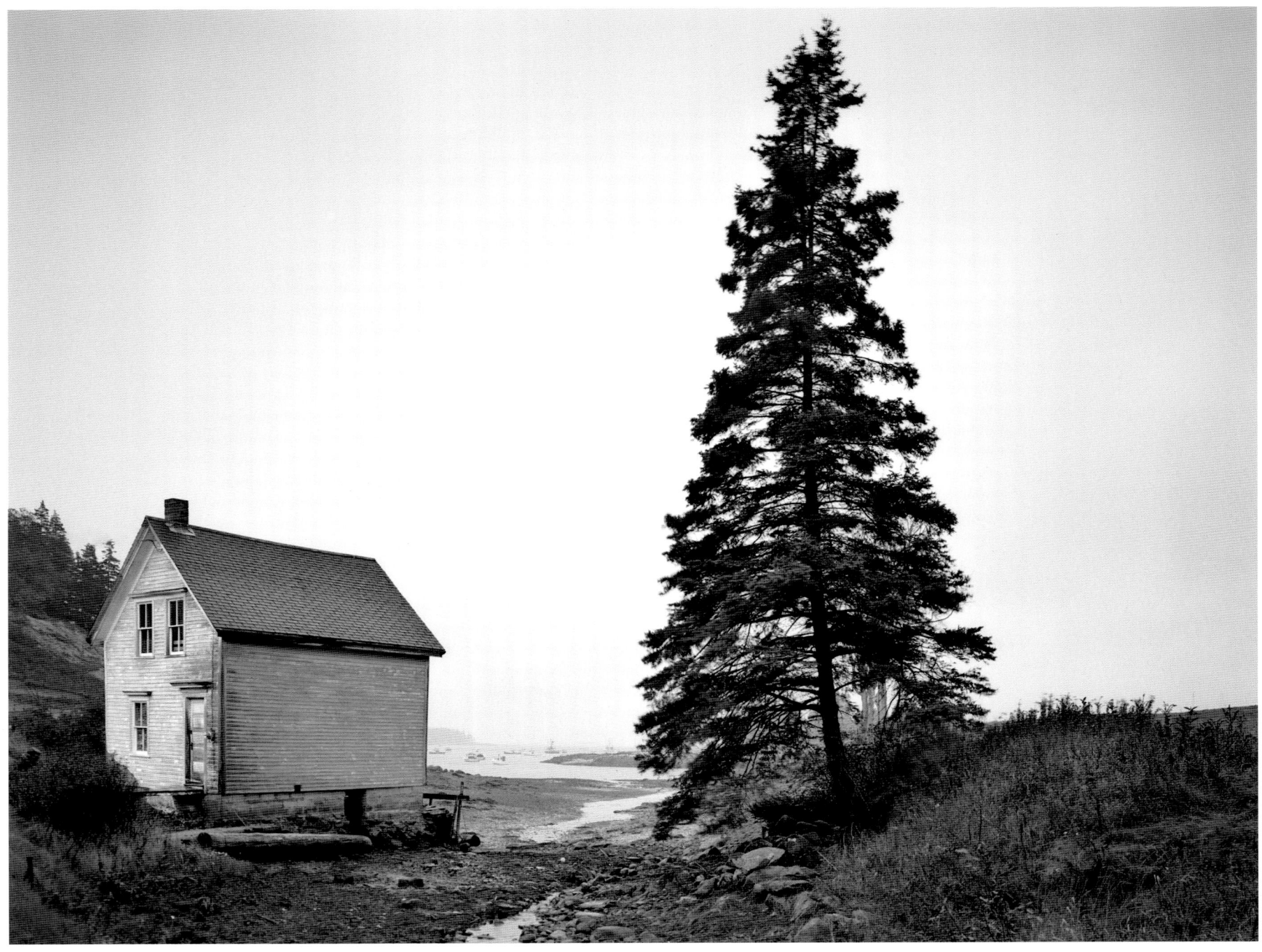

Above and facing page: Port Clyde, Maine, 10-14-1985; Linhof Technika V 4x5 camera; 90mm Schneider Super Angulon lens; Kodak Tri X Pan Pro 4x5 film; Kodak HC110B developer.

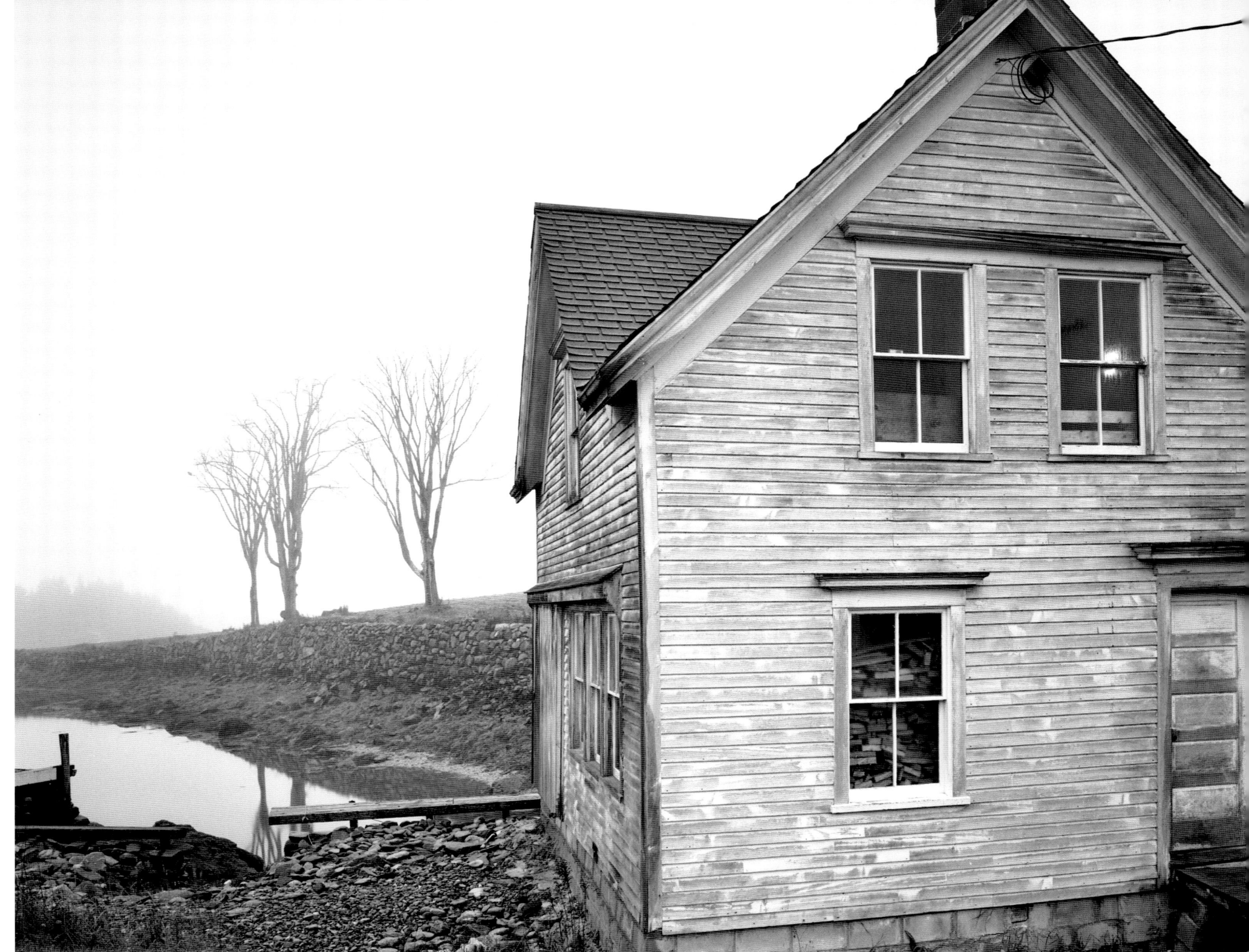

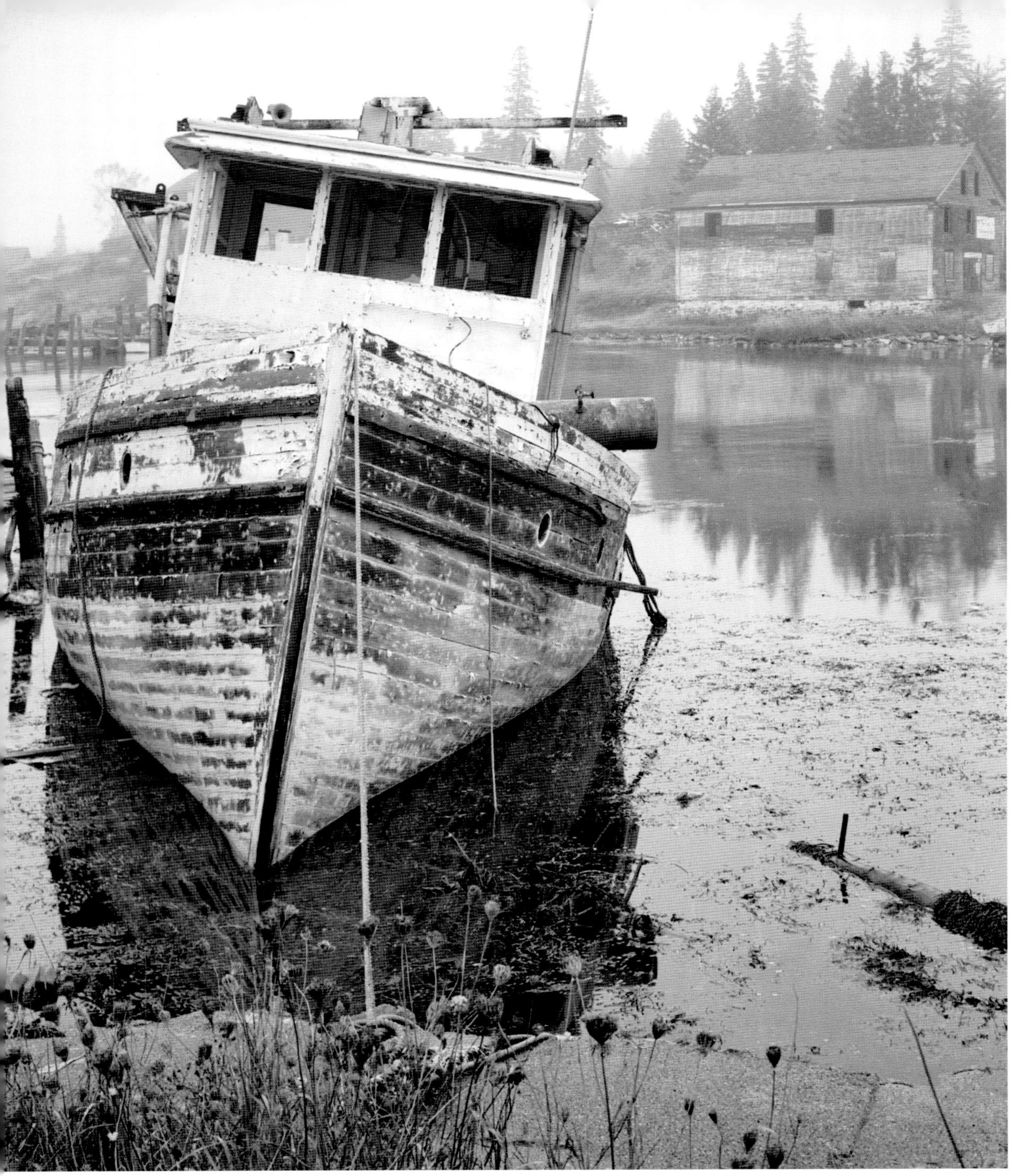

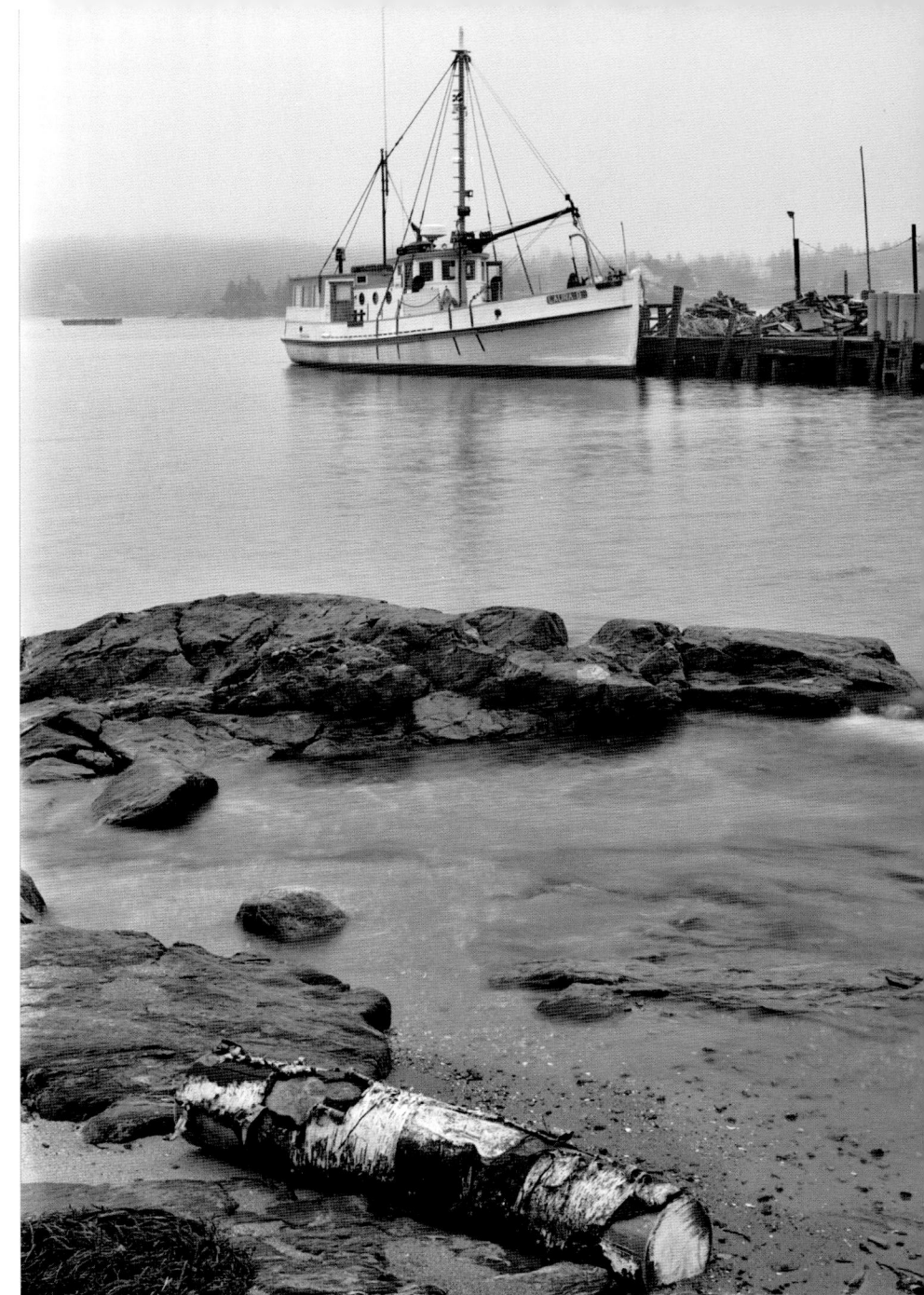

Above left and right, and facing page: Port Clyde, Maine, 10-14-1985; Toyo 8x10M with 5x7 back; 210mm Symmar S lens; Kodak Tri X Pan Pro 5x7 film; Kodak HC110B developer.

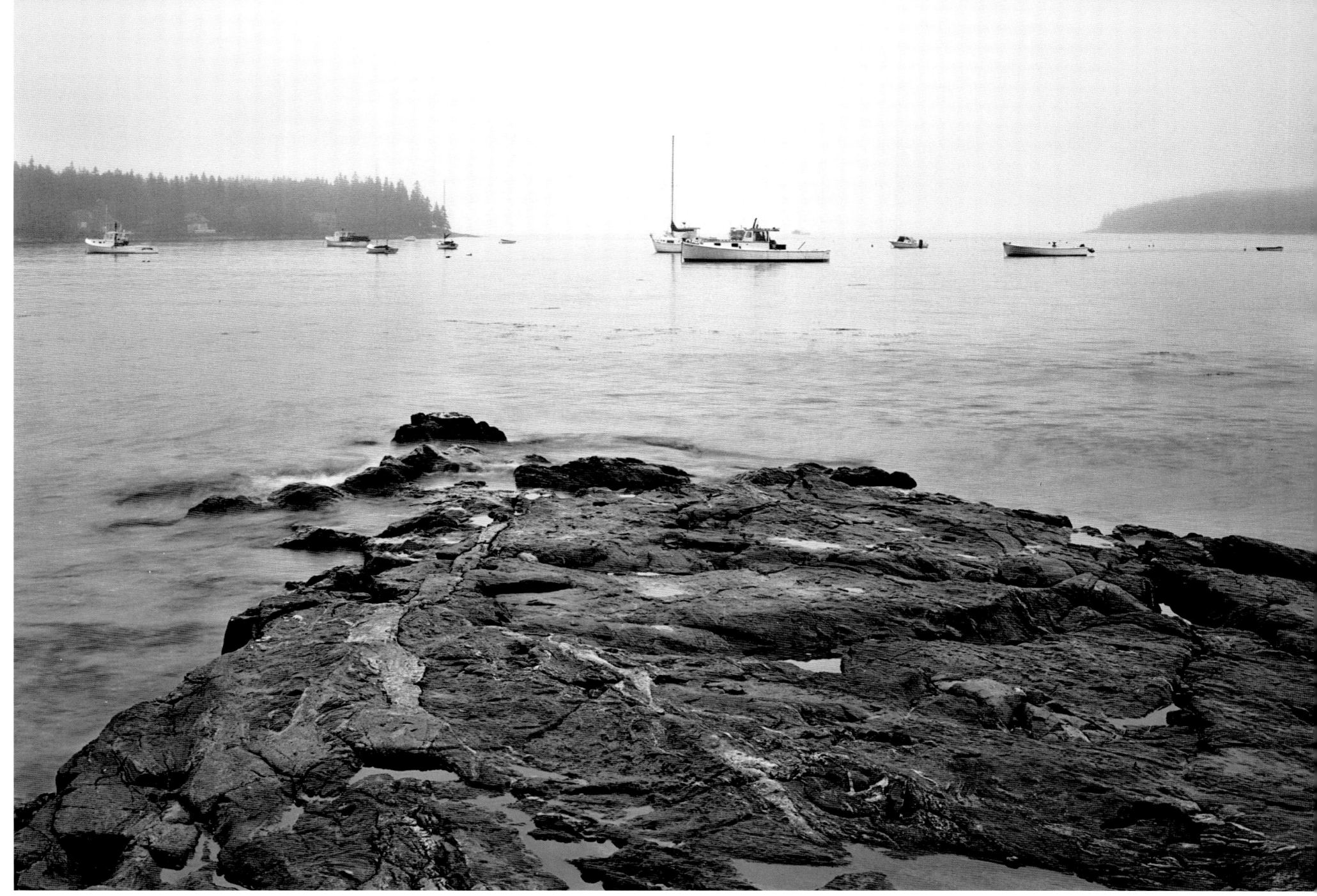

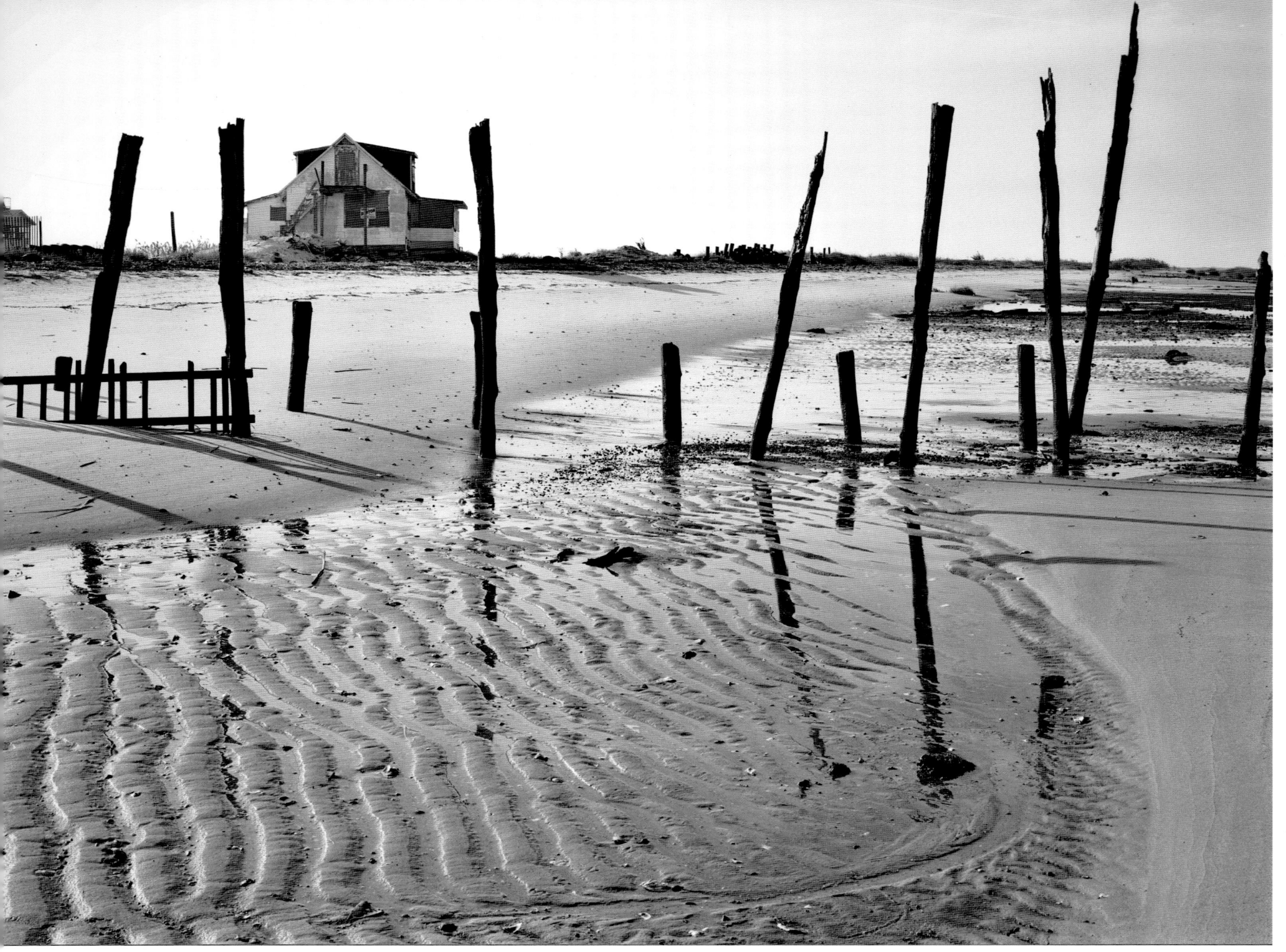

Fortescue, New Jersey, at daylight, 9-21-1985; Toyo 8x10M camera; 300mm Schneider Xenar lens; yellow K2 filter; Kodak Tri X Pan Pro 8x10 film; Kodak HC110B developer.

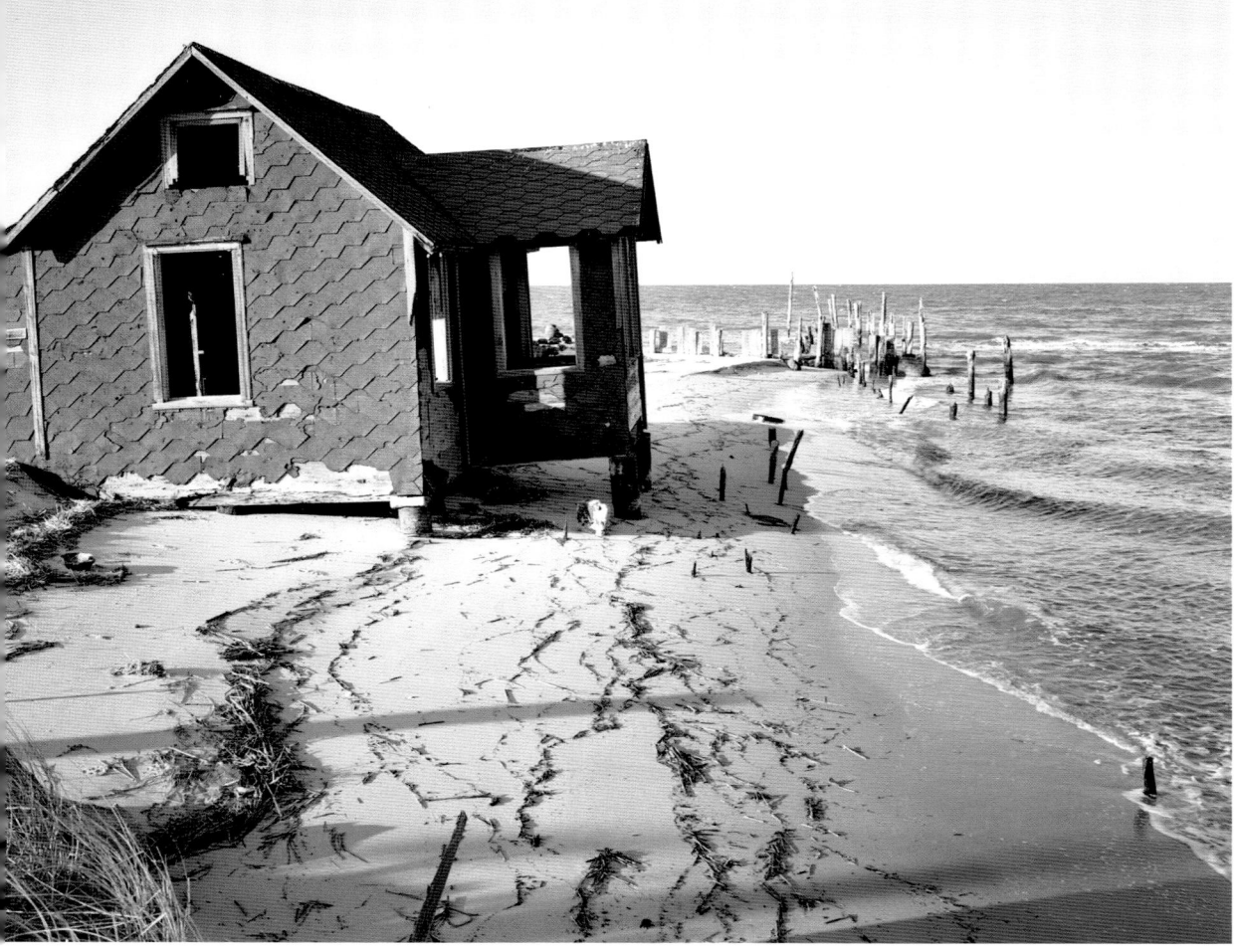

A Large-Format Beach Ghost Town

Fortescue, New Jersey, became one of my favorite locations for photo shoots while I was living in Philadelphia. My great friend Harvey Friedman also loved to shoot along coastlines, especially in fishing villages. We were both in the Focal Planes Photography Club. On some Sunday mornings, I would leave my house a few hours before daylight to pick up Harvey. The drive from Philly was about two hours, and we would arrive just before daylight.

Fortescue was on the southern west coast of New Jersey on the shores of Delaware Bay. It looked like the ocean to me. Before 1970, it was the best place to catch weakfish, a member of the drum family. By the time we were going there, weakfish were mostly fished out, and Fortescue was nearly a ghost town, with many abandoned fishing cabins that were really cool to photograph, especially in black and white. In my mind, Fortescue itself was black and white—the white/gray sand, gray water, gray deteriorating buildings, and what seemed to be a gray sky on most trips. I think we loved it because of that. Harvey and I would shoot three or four hours, then drive home. I could then spend the rest of the day with my wife and young family.

In the fall of 1985 and 1986 we took photo trips to New England and New York City, only ninety miles from Philly. I was also able to shoot while on business trips.

During my Philadelphia years, I amassed my largest body of large-format work in the least amount of time.

All this page: Fortescue, New Jersey, 2-16-1985; Cambo Super View 4x5 camera; 120mm left, 150mm right top, 210mm right bottom Schneider Symmar S Lenses; yellow K2 filter; Kodak Tri X Pan Pro 4x5 film; Kodak HC110B developer.

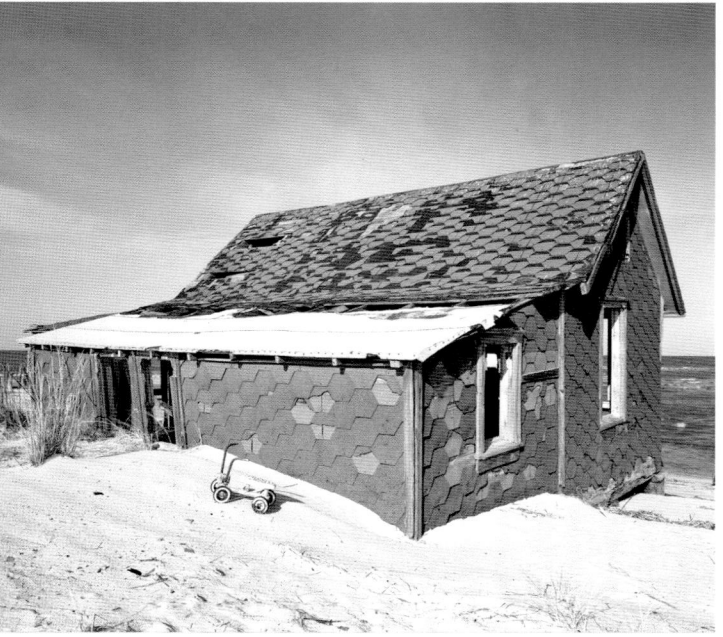

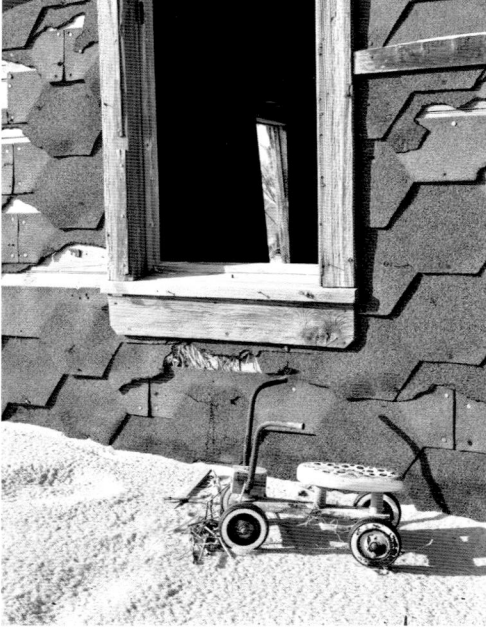

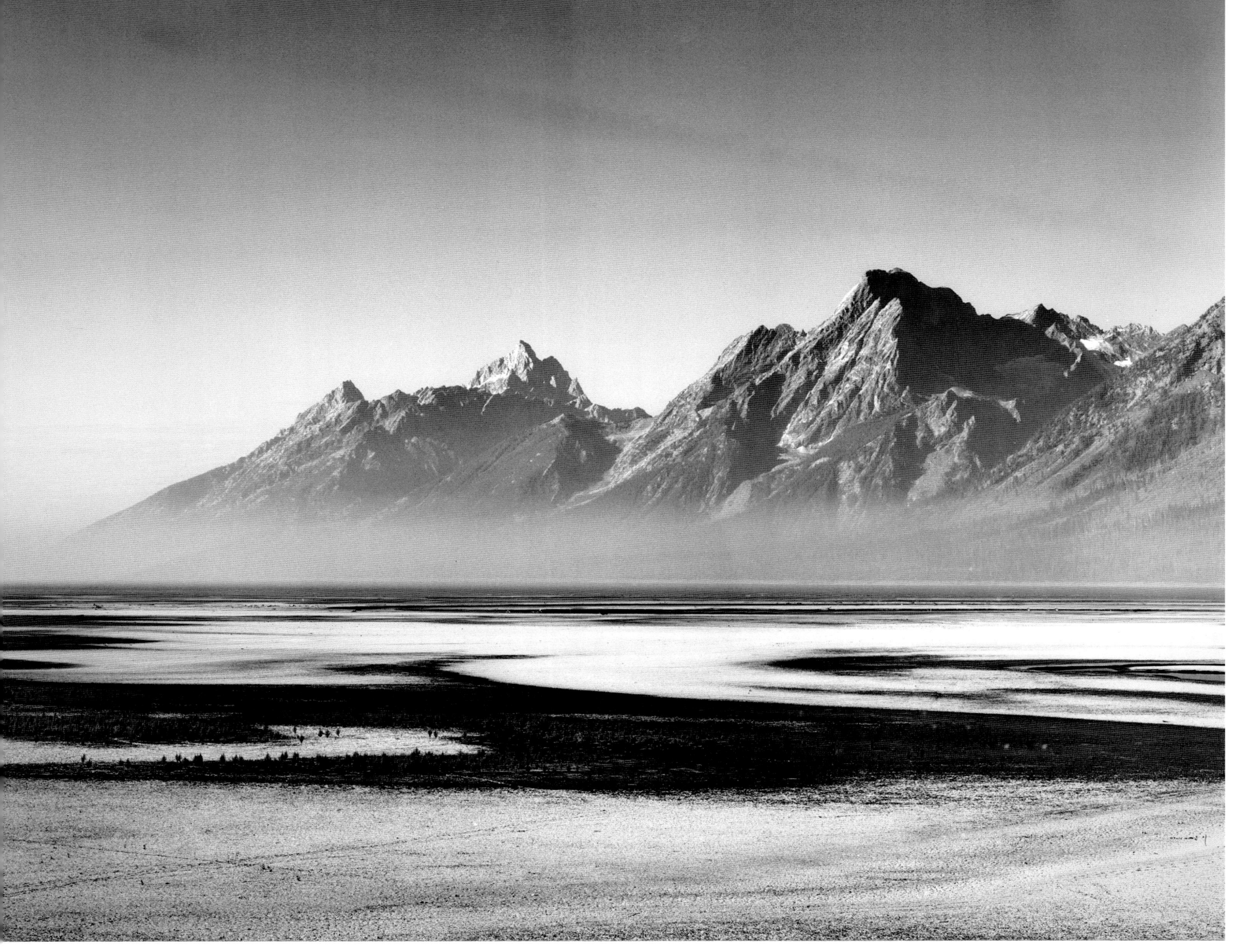

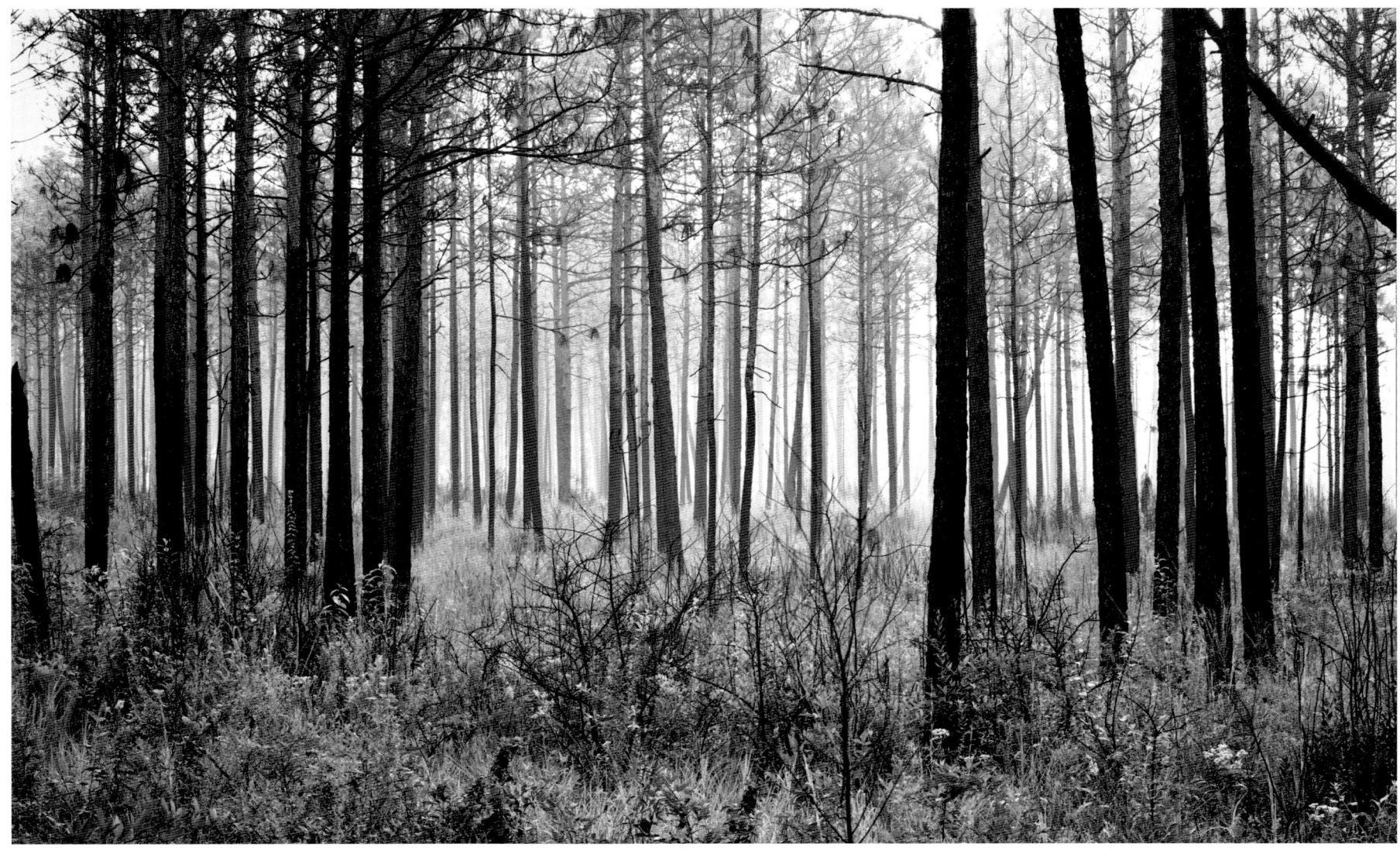

Above: Longleaf pines in fog, Oak Grove, Mississippi, 8-4-1988; Linhof Technika V 4x5 camera; 210mm Schneider Symmar S lens; Kodak Tmax 100 4x5 film; Kodak HC110B developer.

Facing page: Dried-up Jackson Lake with fog at Grand Teton National Park, Wyoming, 8-19-1988; Linhof Technika V 4x5 camera; 300mm Schneider Xenar lens; yellow G filter; Kodak Tmax 100 film; Kodak HC110B developer.

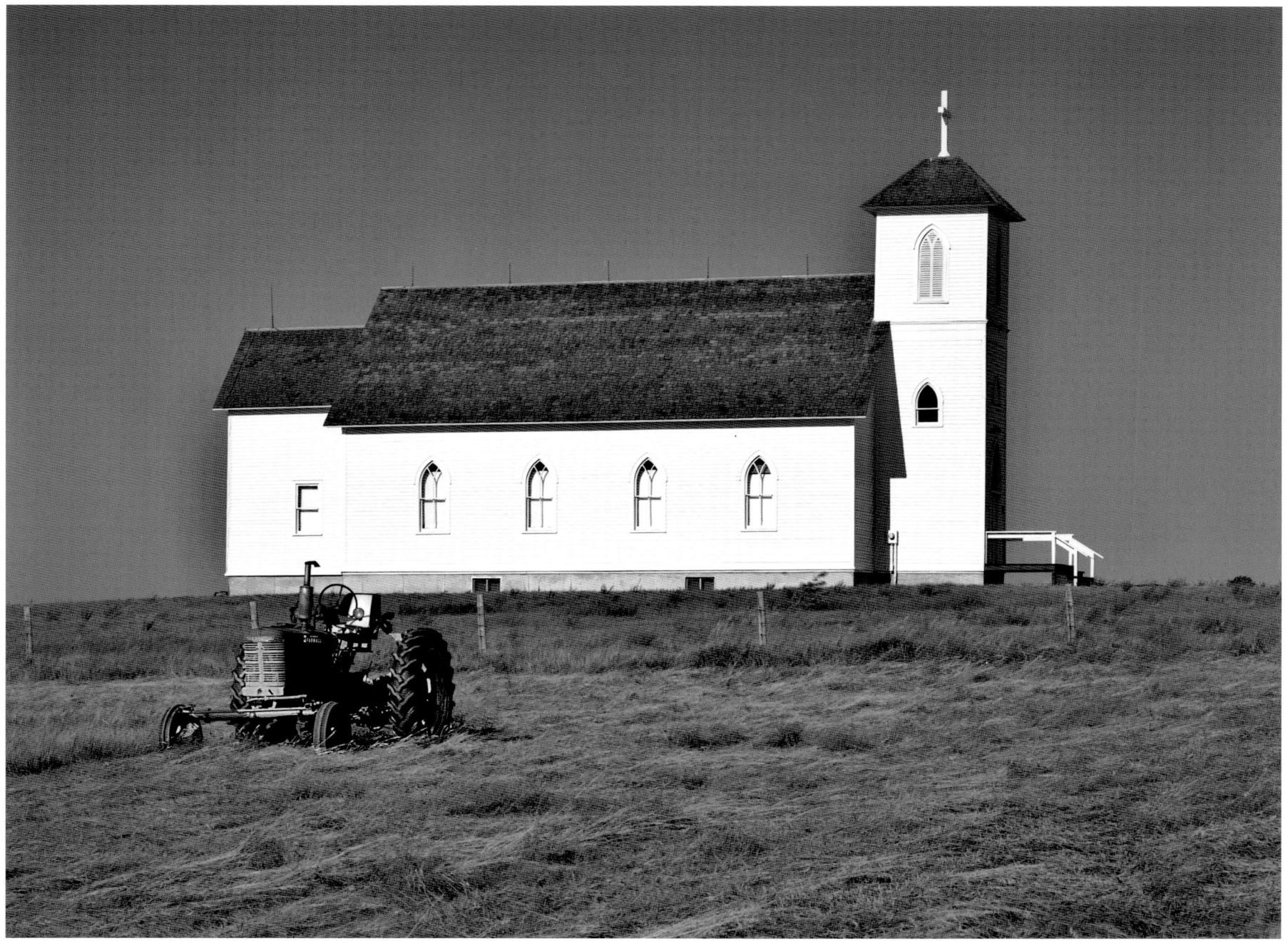

Church with Farmall tractor near Chamberland, South Dakota, 8-16-1988; Linhof Technika V 4x5 camera; 300mm Schneider Xenar lens;
yellow G filter; Kodak Tmax 100 4x5 film; Kodak HC110B developer.

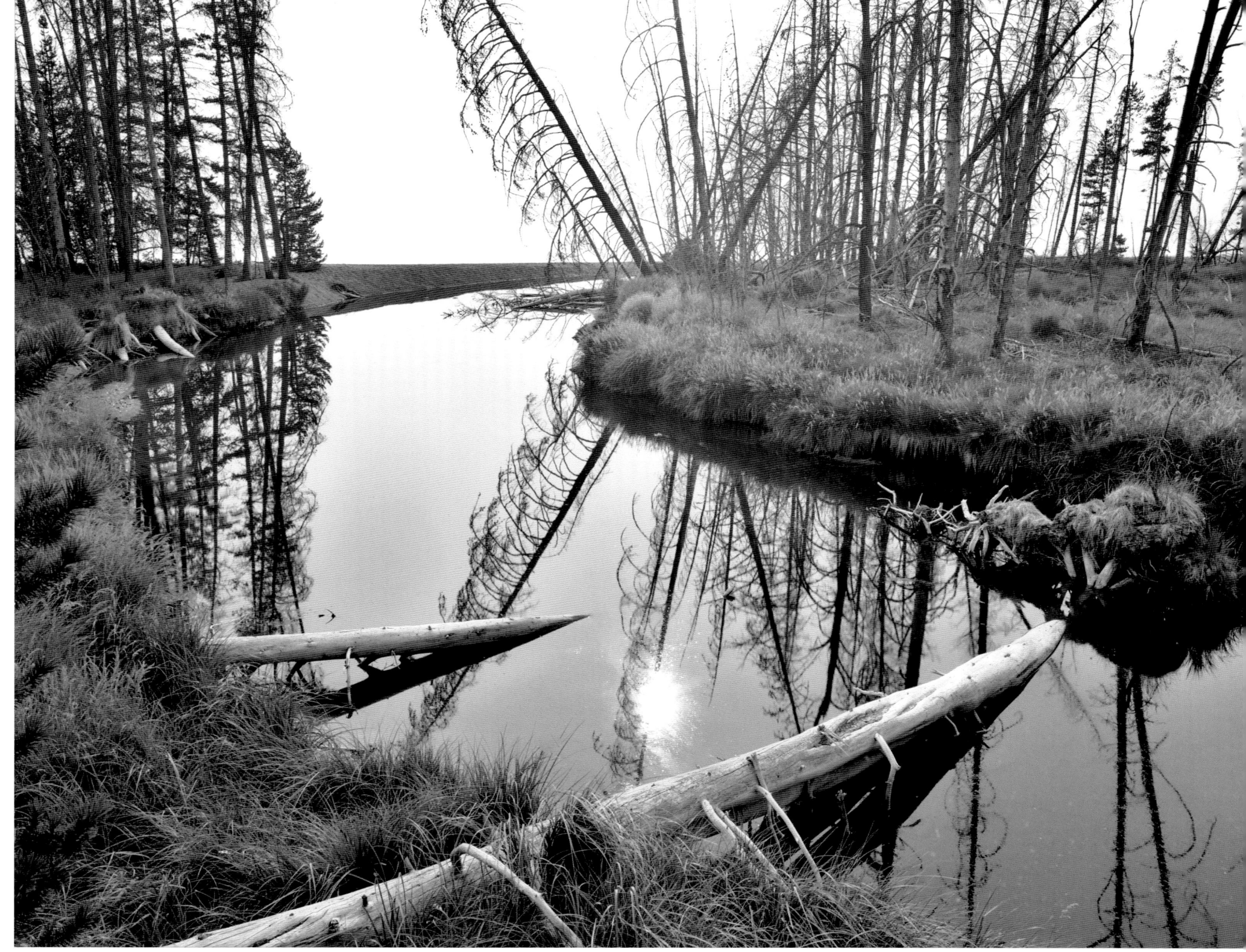

Yellowstone National Park, Wyoming, 8-17-1988; Linhof Technika V 4x5 camera; 90mm Schneider Super Angulon lens; Kodak Tmax 100 4x5 film; Kodak HC110B developer.

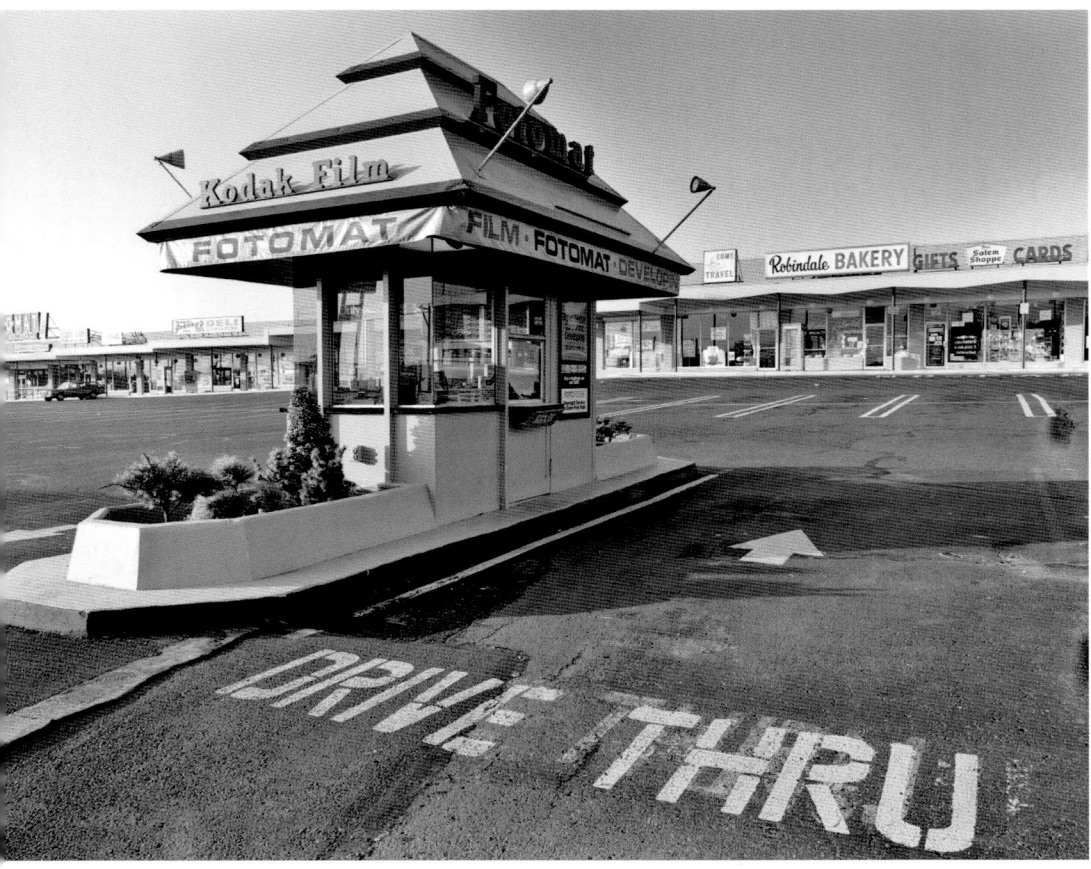 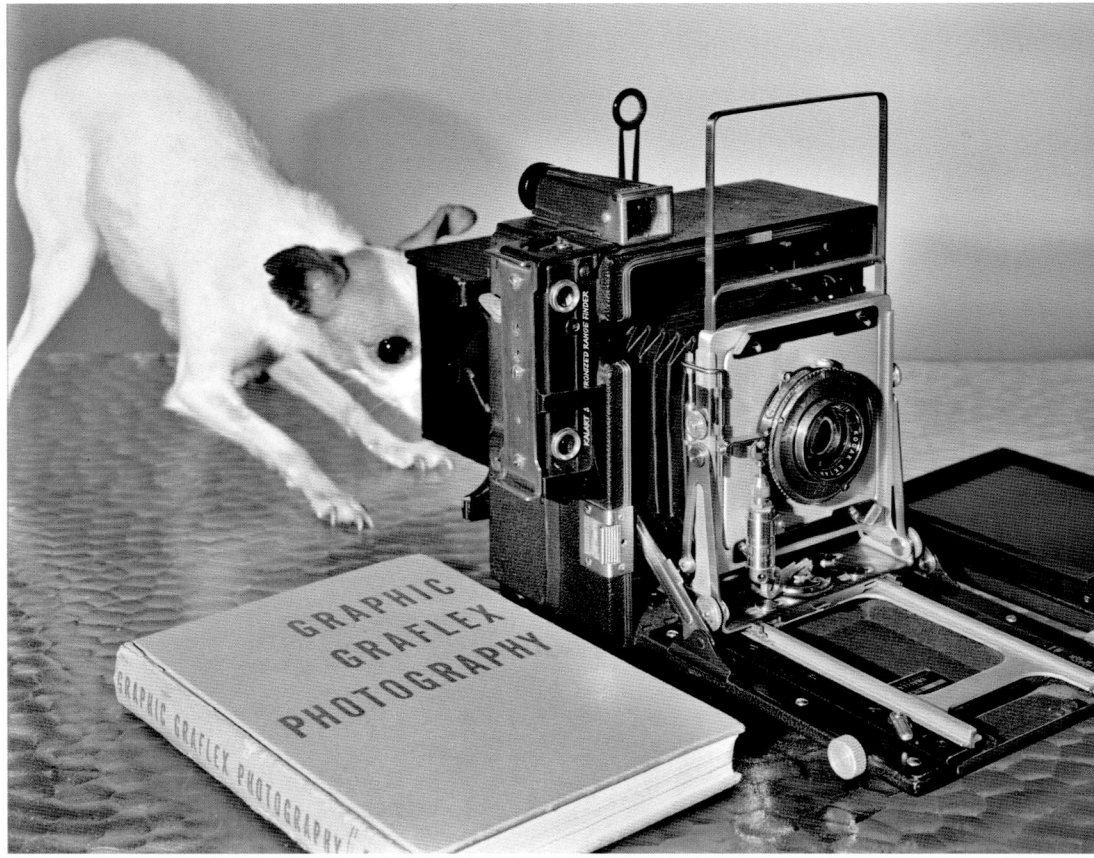

Left: Fotomat drive thru film developing drop off, Bensalem, Pennsylvania, 11-7-1982; Linhof Technika IV 4x5 camera; 90mm Schneider Super Angulon lens; yellow G filter; Kodak Trii X Pan Pro 4x5 film; Kodak HC110B developer.

Right: Dog Photography Student, Hendersonville, Tennessee, 2-14-1981; Burke and James Saturn 75 view camera with 4x5 back; 12-inch Gundlack Radar lens; Kodak Royal Pan 4x5 film; Edwal FG7 developer.

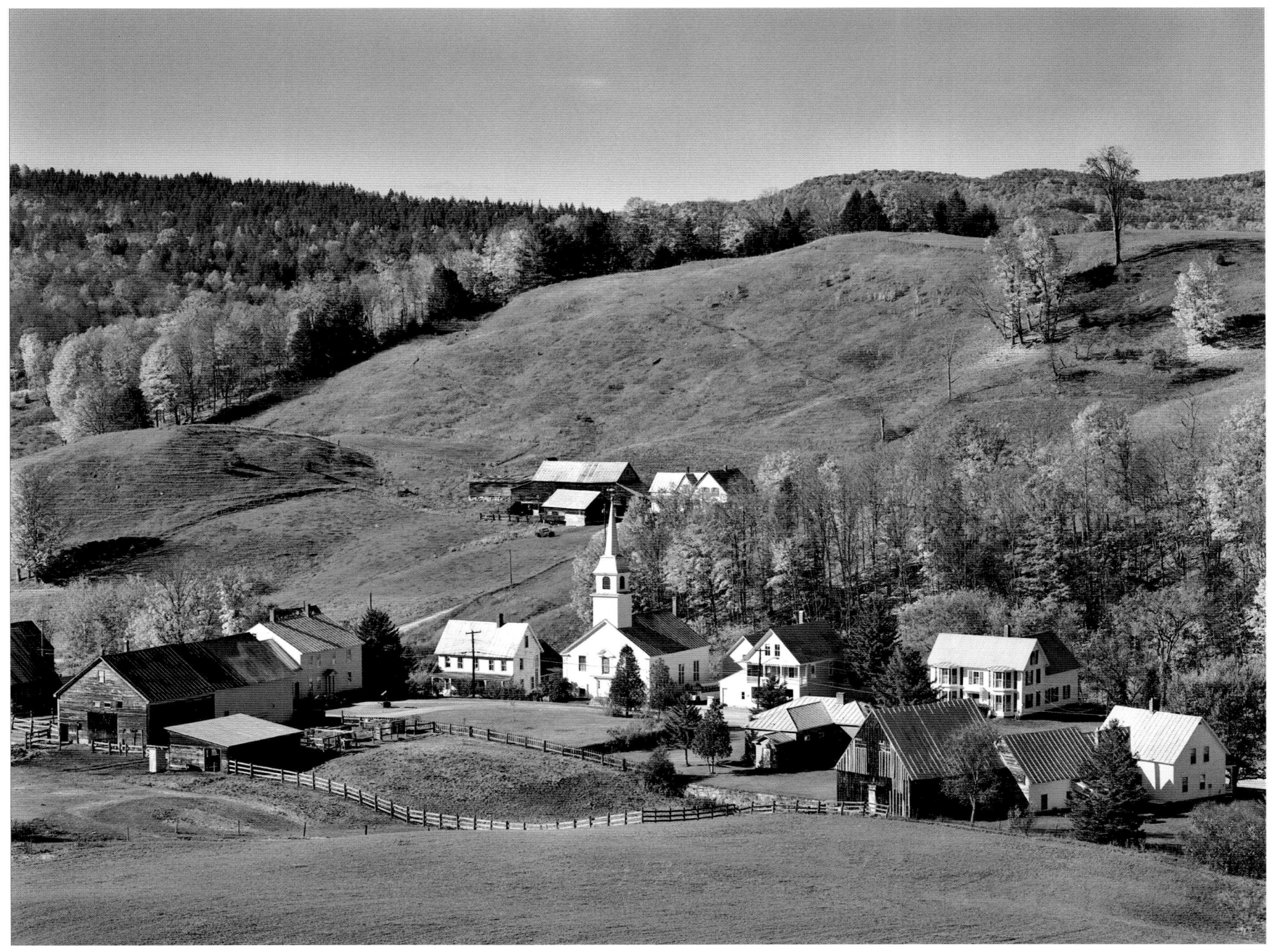

Morning in East Corinth, Vermont, 10-12-1985; Linhof Technika V 4x5 camera; 300mm Schneider Xenar lens; yellow K2 filter; Kodak Tri X Pan Pro 4x5 film; Kodak HC110B developer.

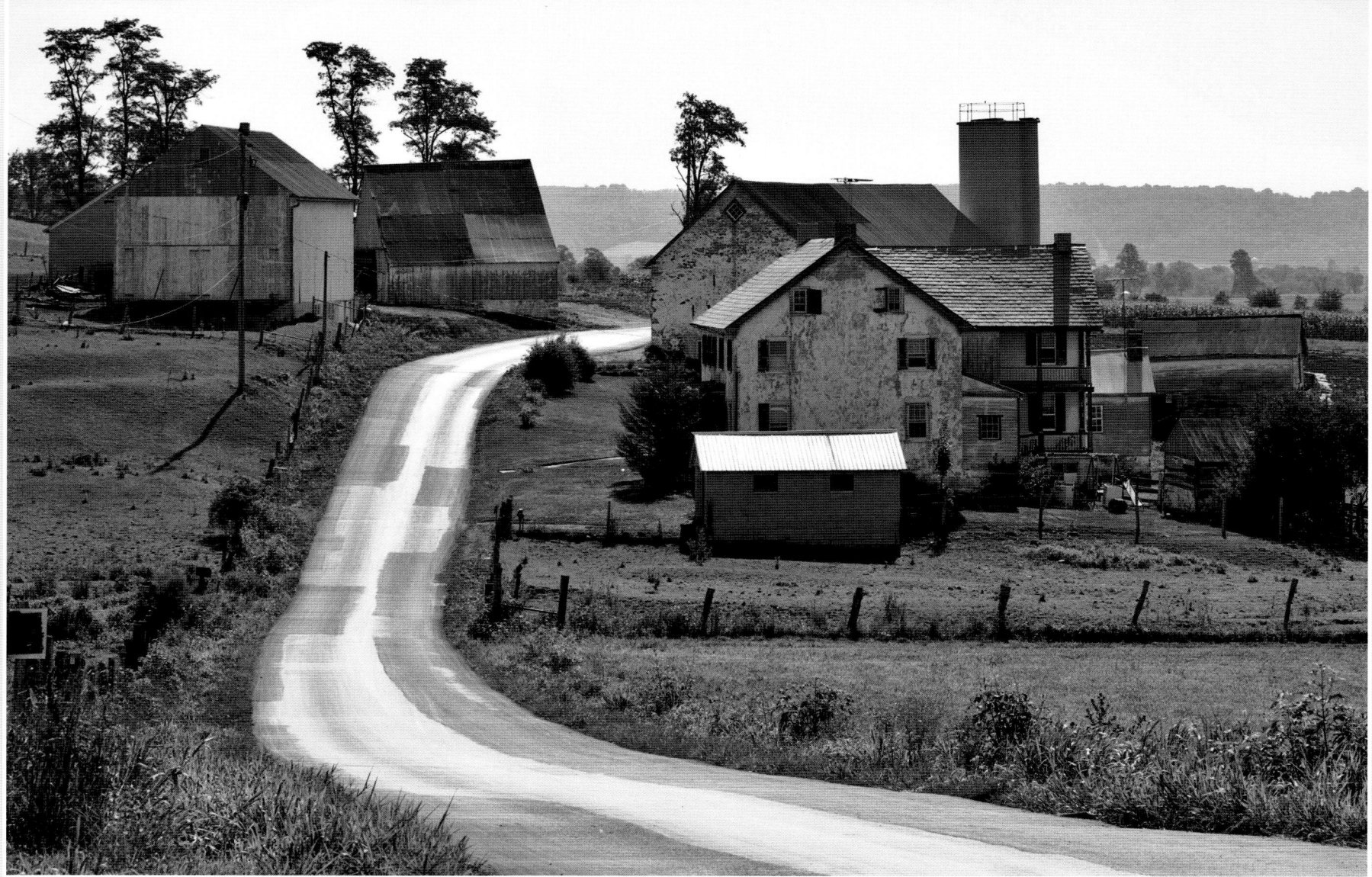

Image Impact

Basic guidelines of photography, as with all two-dimensional visual arts, lay the groundwork for visual appeal: composition, lighting, and impact. If all three are achieved, then it is likely viewers will be pleased.

Understanding basics like the rule of thirds, line, form, contrast, and tonal depth or, if in color, color depth will help an artist or a photographer. This image is a good example of using the brightly sunlit road to draw the viewer into the scene. The viewer can inherently understand the scene and determine without analyzing whether the image is pleasingly composed, well balanced, well lit, and has visual impact.

When I began photography in the 1960s, I joined a camera club. Each meeting was about taking and making better pictures. The print was king, and craftsmanship in the darkroom was critical to make a piece of art that would deliver the photographer's vision equal to the factors of the composition itself.

When I first started taking pictures and making my own darkroom prints, I felt an explanation of my vision and purpose was necessary. But I learned quickly that viewers do not need or want an explanation; they decide on their own, usually in a glance, whether they like a picture, and no explanation is likely to improve or diminish their appraisal.

Farm scene in Lancaster County, Pennsylvania, with reflection in road from melting oil in the macadam road surface, 8-14-1983; Cambo Super View 4x5 camera; 300mm Schneider Xenar lens; yellow K2 filter; Kodak Tri X Pan Pro 4x5 film; Kodak HC110B developer.

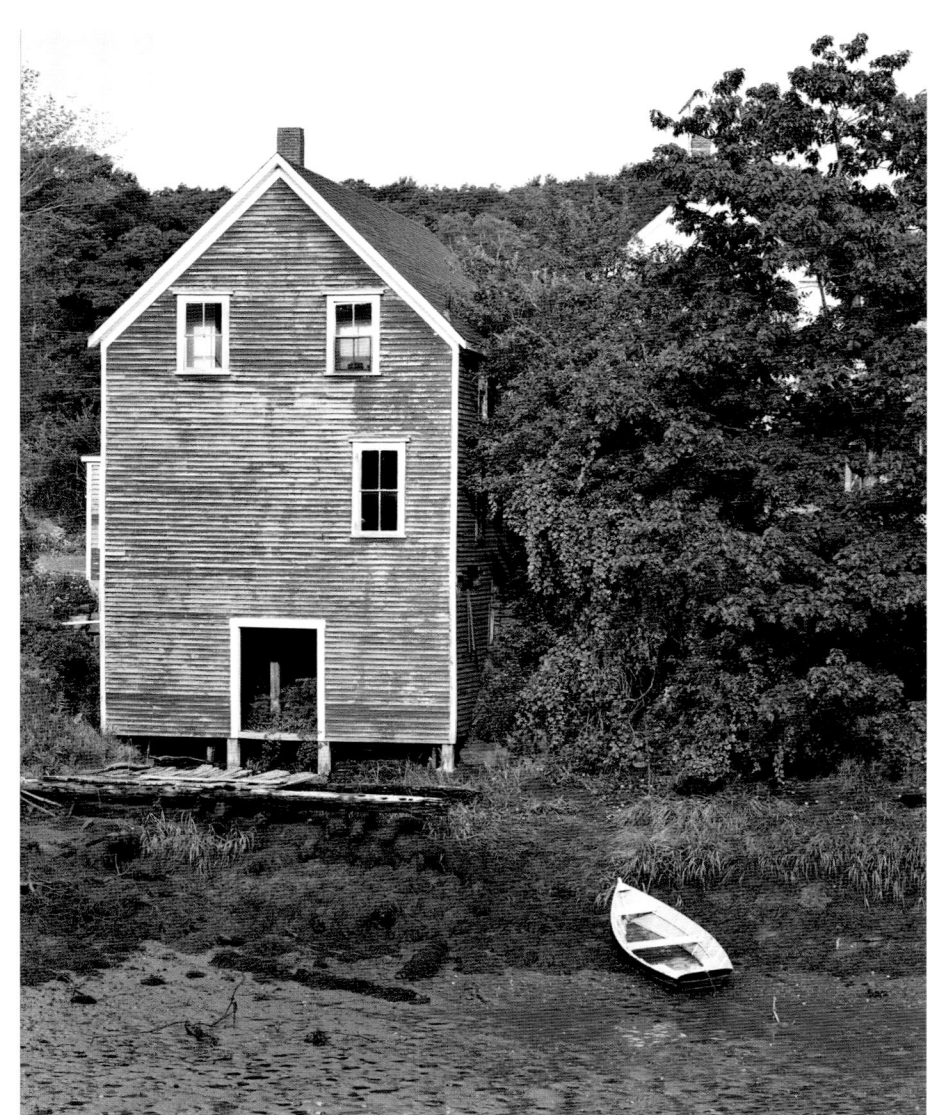

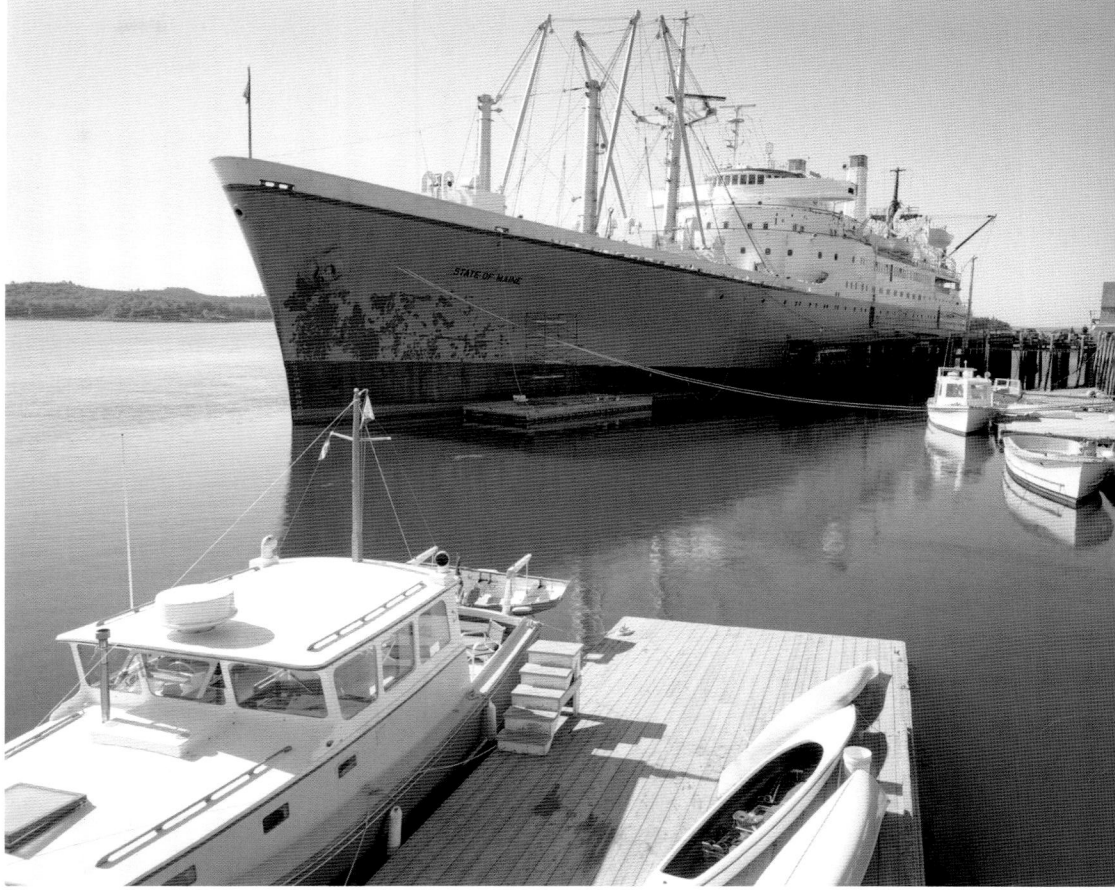

Left: Boathouse, coastal Maine, 9-11-1986; Linhof Technika V 4x5 camera; 300mm Schneider Xenar lens; Kodak Tri X Pan Pro 4x5 film; Kodak HC110C developer.

Above: *State of Maine* ship and dock, Castine Maine, 9-9-1986; Linhof Technika V 4x5 camera; 120mm Schneider Symmar S lens; yellow K2 filter; Kodak Tri X Pan Pro 4x5 film; Kodak HC110C developer.

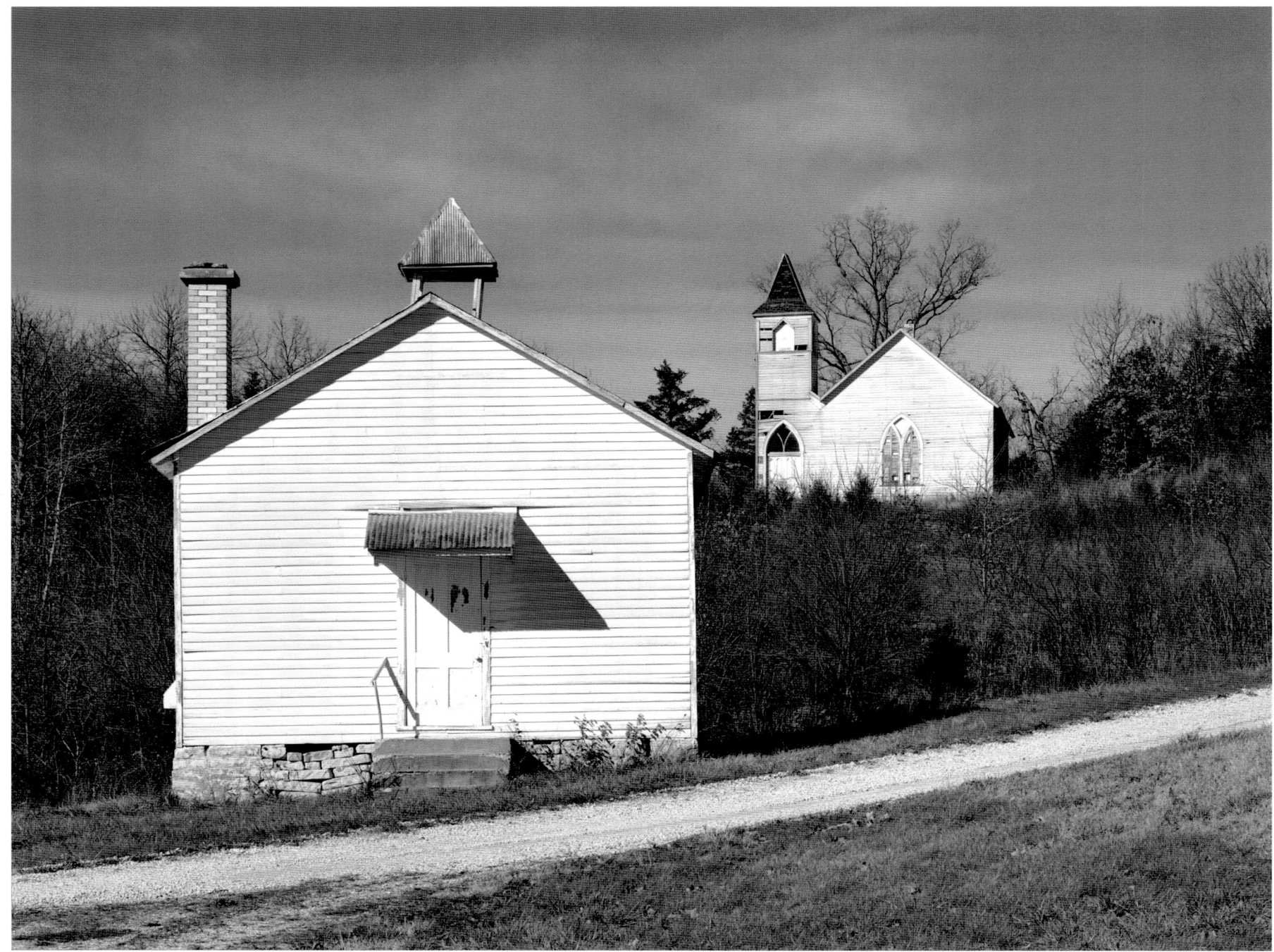

Abandoned school, church near Linn, Missouri, 11-19-1987; Linhof Technika V 4x5 camera; 300mm Schneider Xenar lens; yellow G filter; Kodak Tmax 400 4x5 film; Kodak HC110 developer.

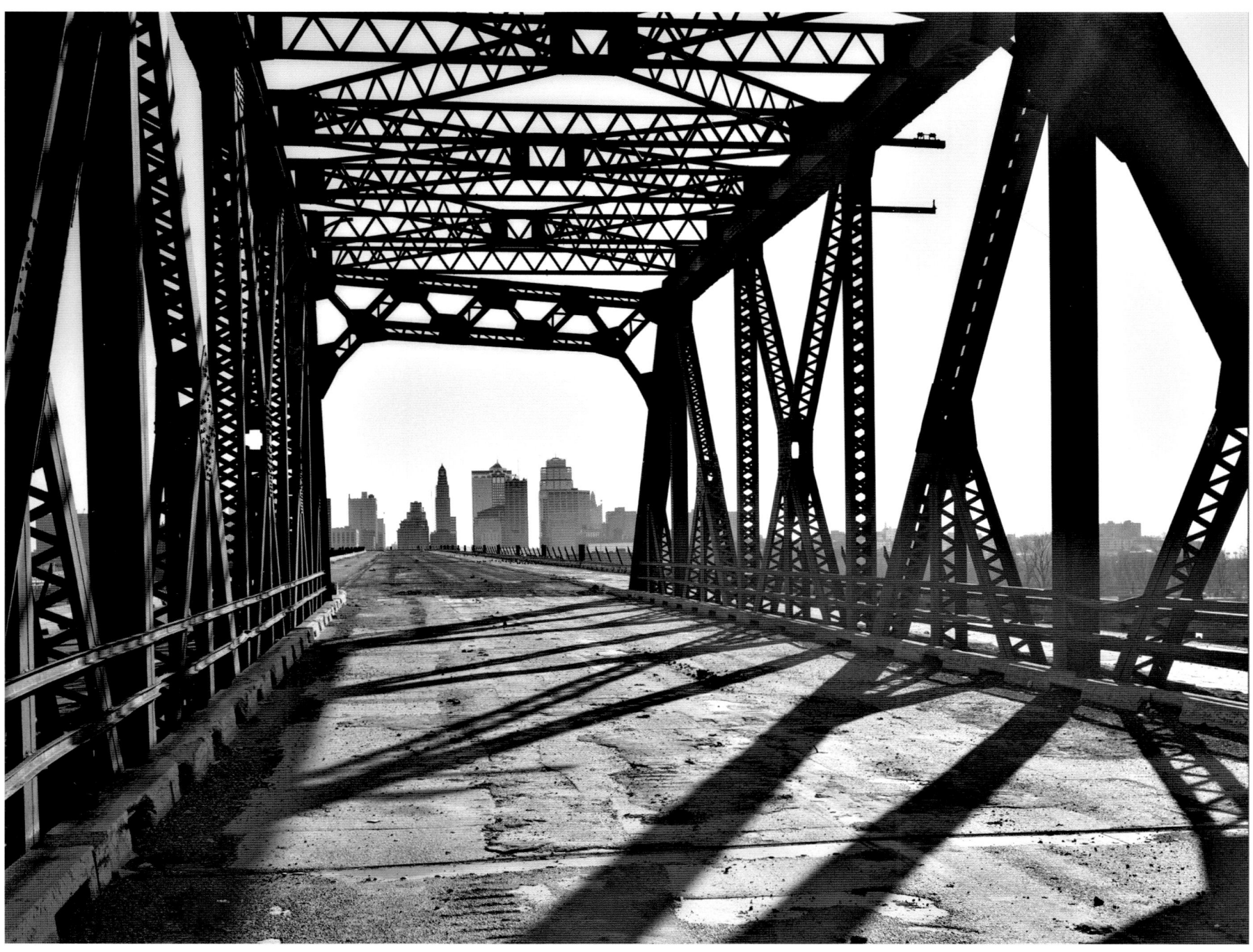

Retired Broad Street Bridge, Kansas City, Missouri, 11-21-1987; Linhof Technika V 4x5 camera; 150mm Schneider Symmar S Lens; yellow K2 filter; Kodak Tmax 400 4x5 film; HC110B developer.

Right: Foggy sunrise near Newtown, Bucks County, Pennsylvania, 9-5-1983; Cambo Super View 4x5 camera; 300mm Schneider Xenar lens; yellow K 2 filter; Ilford FP4 4x5 film; Kodak HC110B developer.

Facing page: Provincetown, Cape Cod, Massachusetts, 8-4-1985; Linhof Technika V 4x5 camera; 90mm Schneider Super Angulon lens; yellow K2 filter; Kodak Tri X Pan Pro 4x5 film; Kodak HC110B developer.

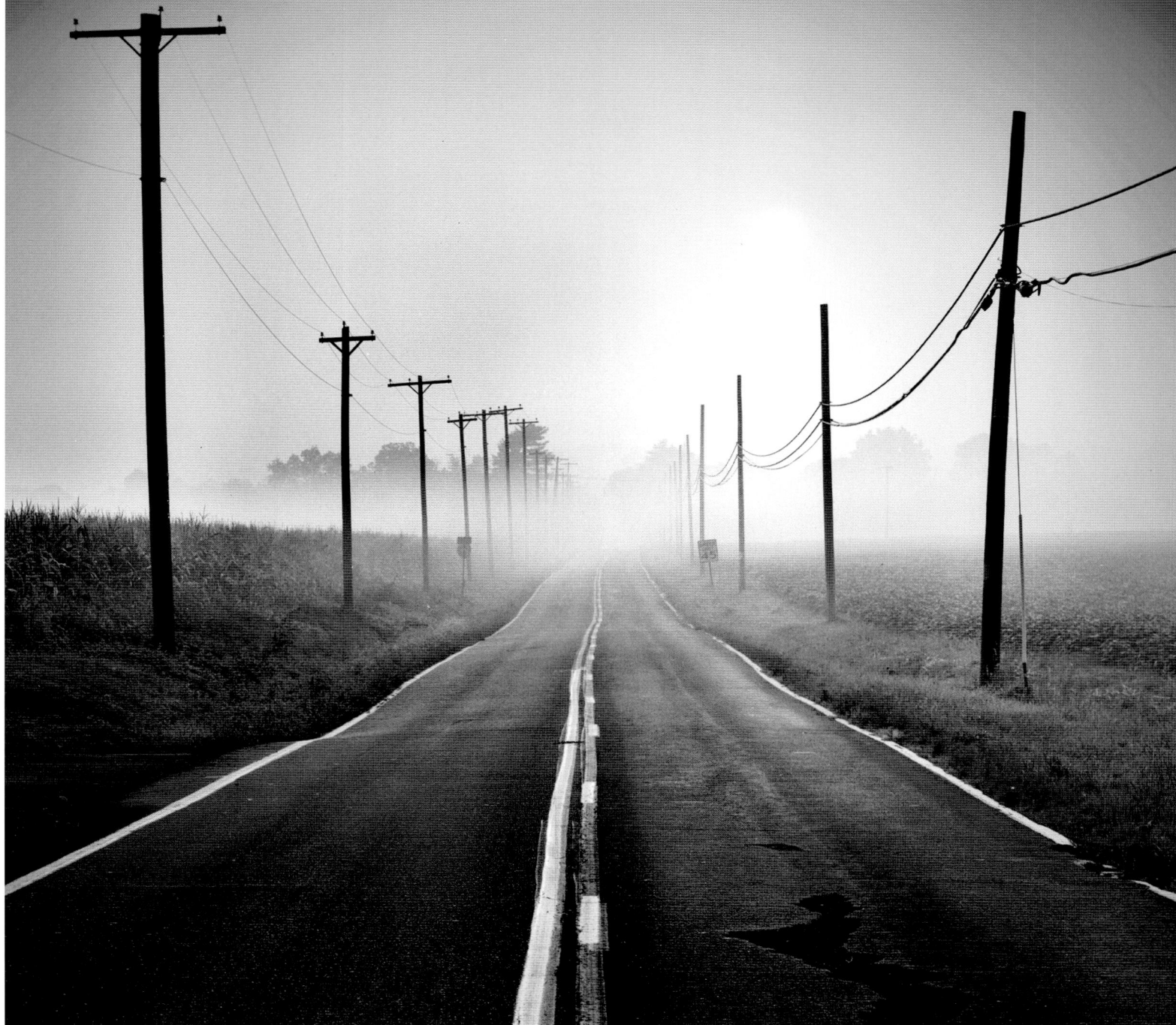

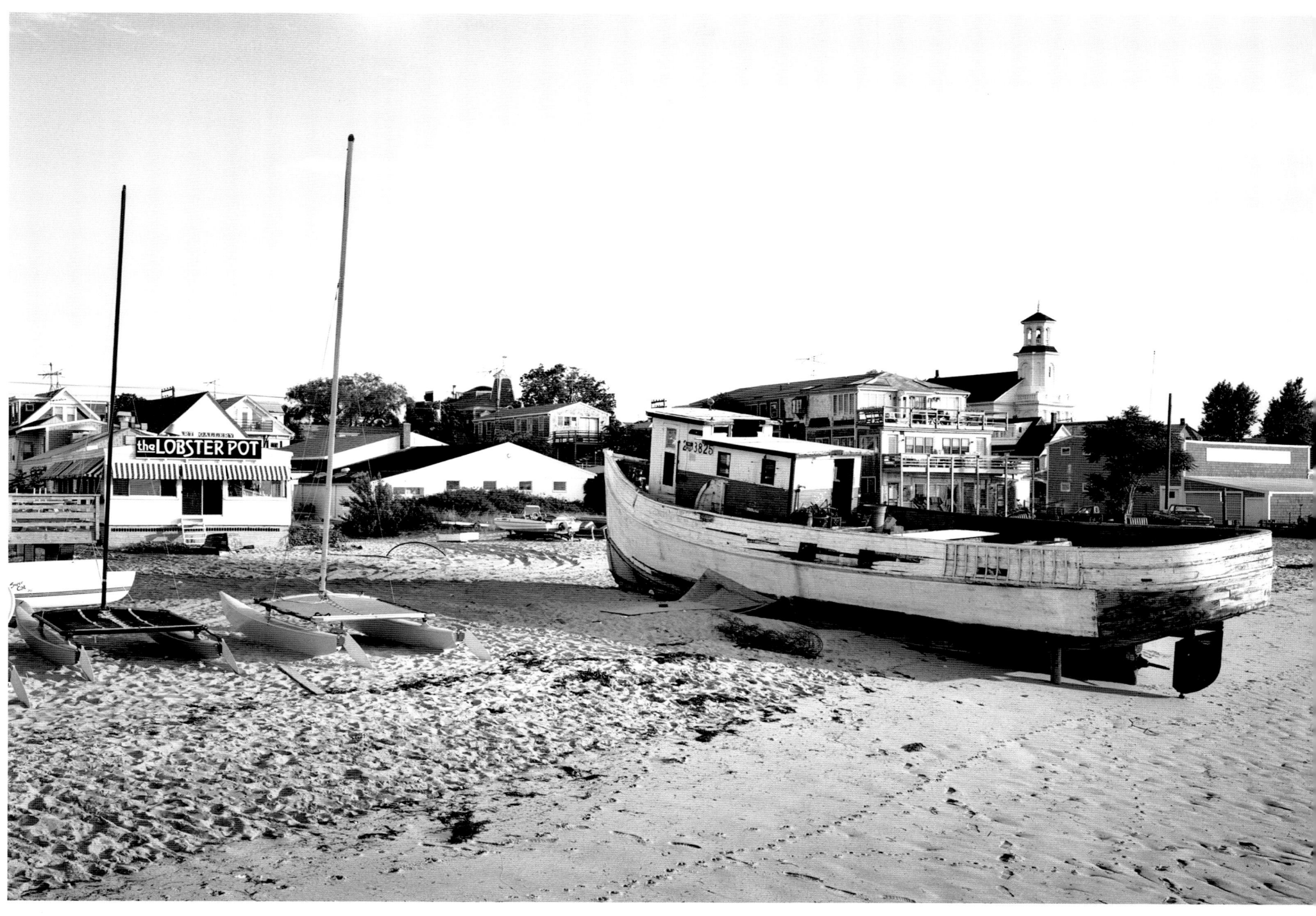

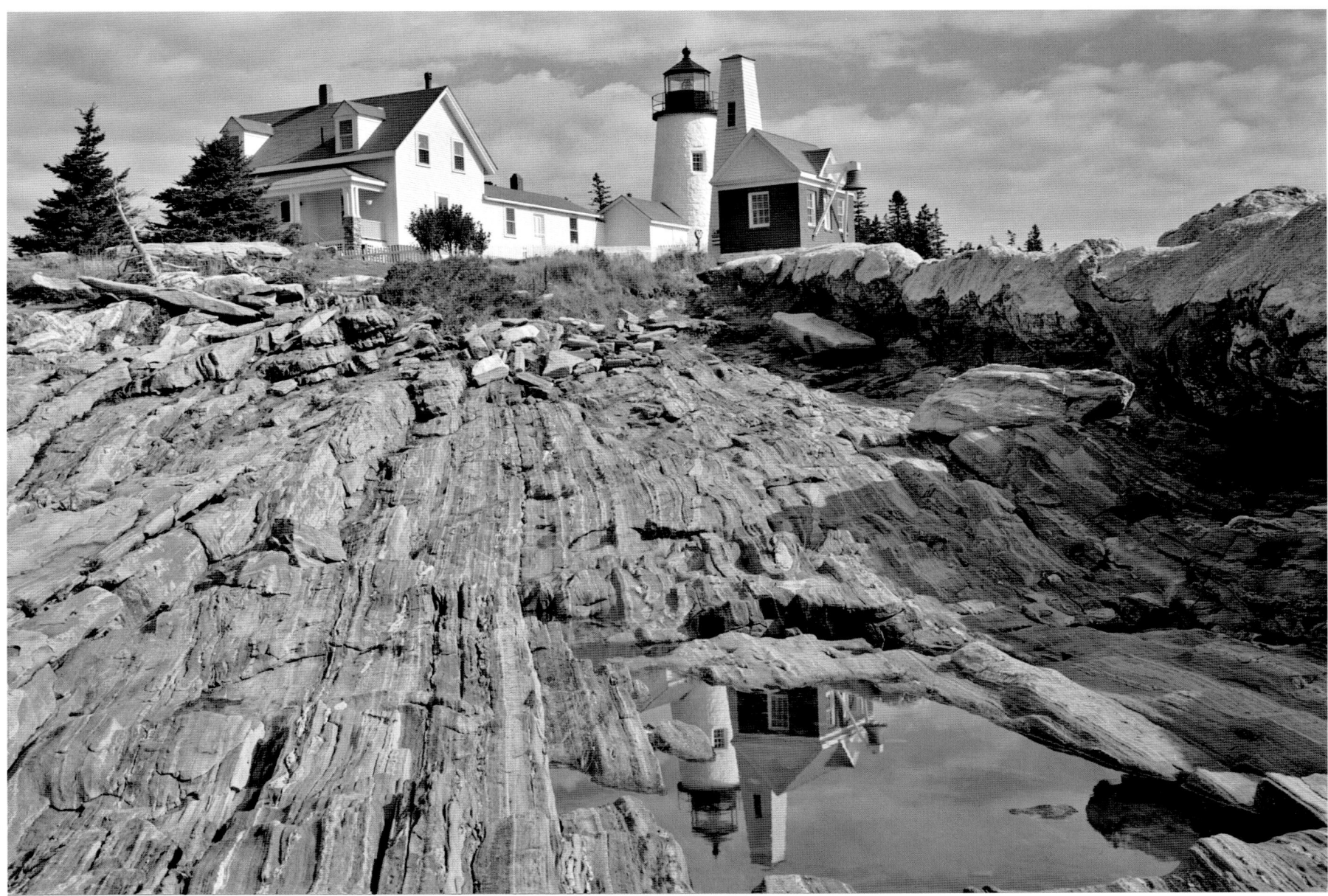

Pemaquid Point Light, Bristol, Maine, 9-8-1986; Toyo 8x10M camera with 5x7 back; 210mm Schneider Symmar S lens; yellow K2 filter; Kodak Tri X Pan Pro 5x7 film; HC110C developer.

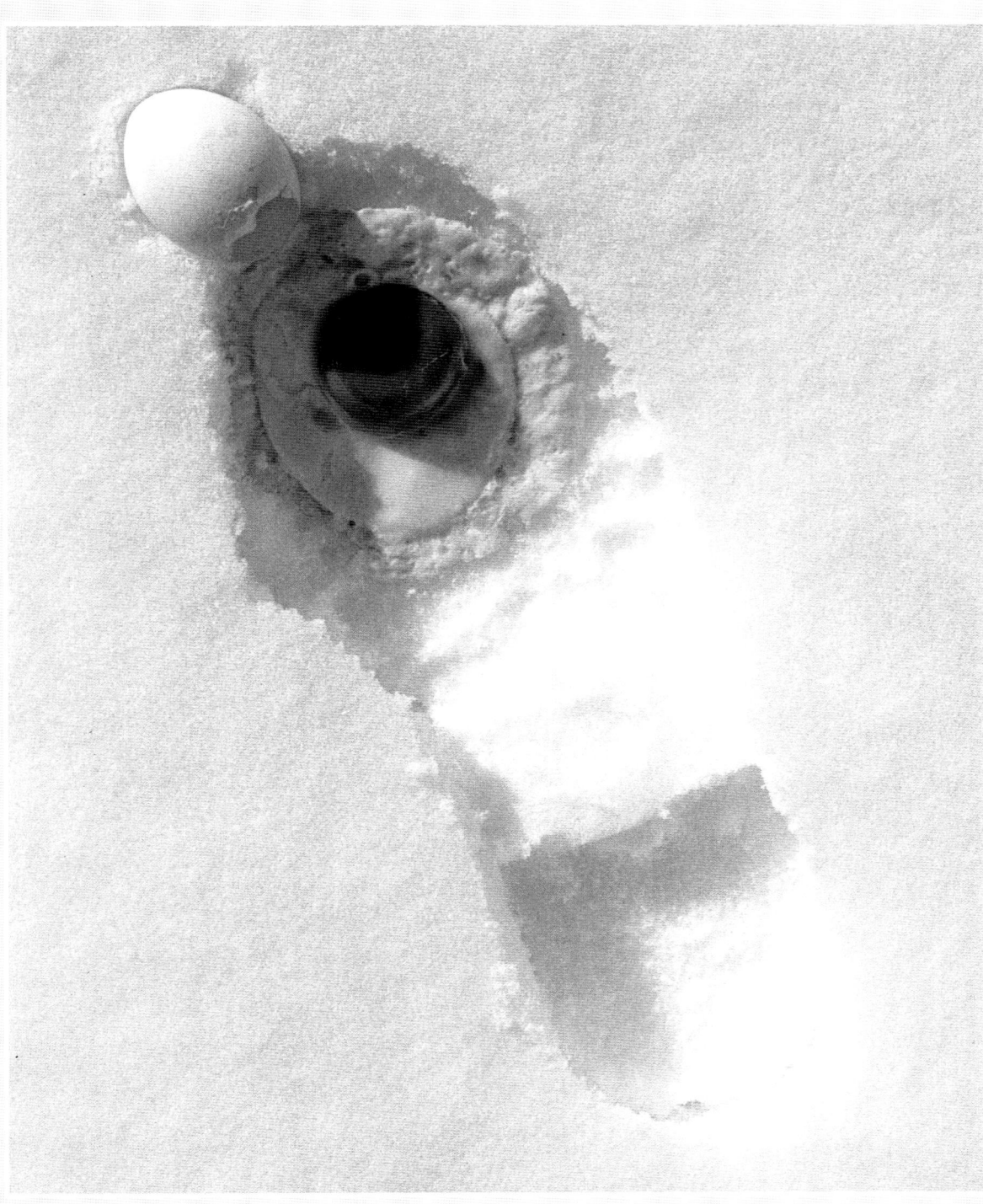

Cold Enough to Fry an Egg

My family and I were visiting my wife's family in Indianapolis in the winter of 1983. It was an especially cold, snowy time in the area and had been for our entire drive from Philadelphia. I always bring plenty of camera equipment regardless of the occasion. In the case of this shot, we were stuck in the house, roads were bad, and there was a minus-zero wind-chill factor. By afternoon, after a lot of eating events and fun in the house with family (my kids were young at the time), I began to get restless. The sun was out and the snow was beautiful so I felt somehow I needed to take some pictures. My kids tried to play outside for awhile and when my son came back in the house he said, "It's so cold it burns."

That concept inspired this still life out in the snow. I asked my mother-in-law if she could fry a really pretty egg—not burnt and the yoke just right (I told her I'd mess it up). She fried the egg and I went out to an unblemished area of fresh white snow and put one foot print in the snow and carefully placed the egg in it. With the camera on a tripod, I shot several frames. I liked this one the best.

I have shown this print in galleries over the years and just call it "Tell Me the Meaning." I have gotten some interesting interpretations over the years.

Indianapolis, Indiana, 2-14-1982; Mamiya C33 TLR camera; 105mm Sekor lens; Kodak Plus X Pan Pro 120 film; Kodak HC110B developer.

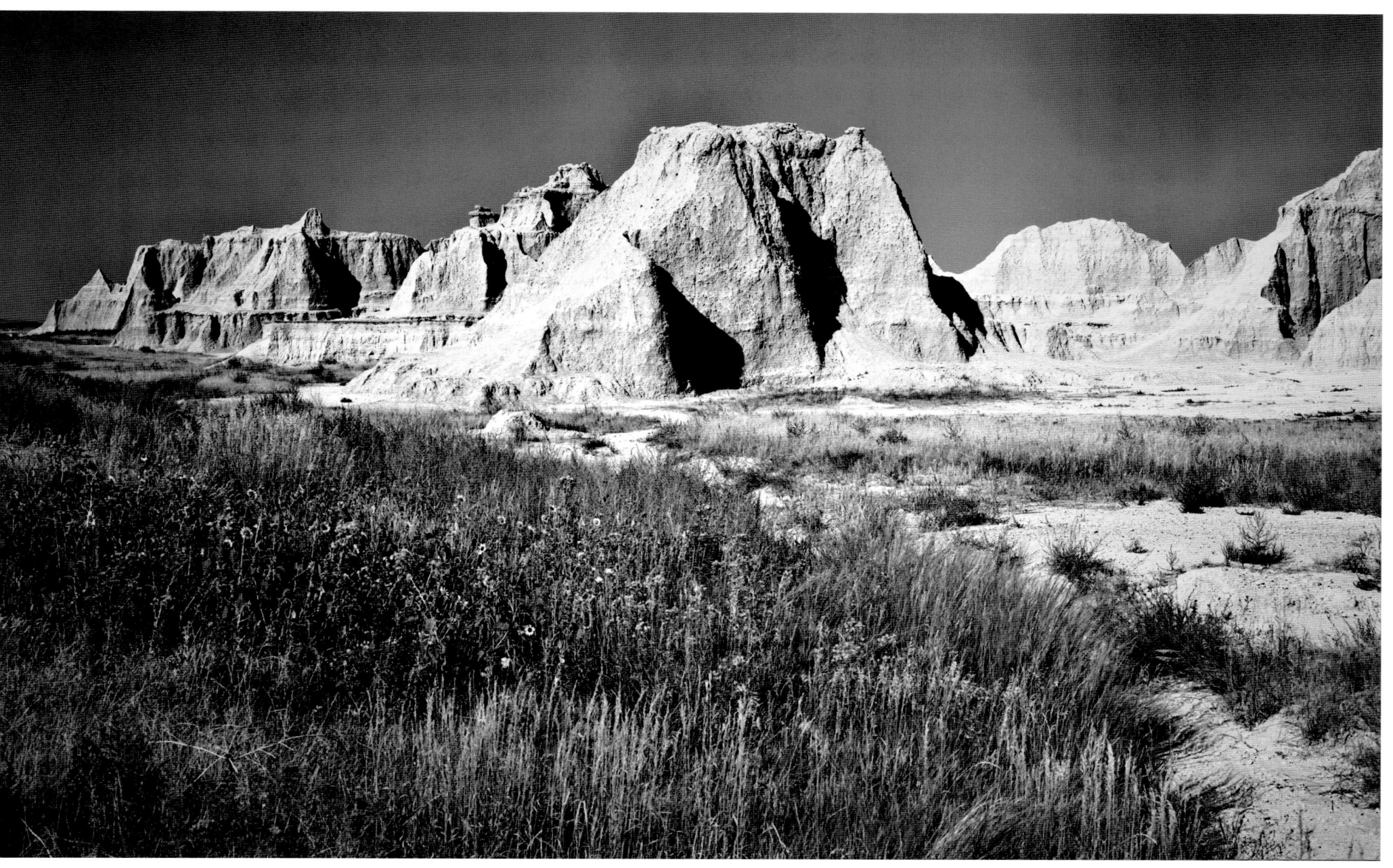

Above: Badlands of South Dakota, 6-23-1988; Toyo 8x10M camera; 300mm Schneider Xenar lens; yellow G filter; Kodak Tmax 100 8x10 film; Kodak HC110B developer.

Facing page: Amish buggy coming and Amish farm scene, Lancaster County, Pennsylvania, 8-14-1983; Cambo Super View 4x5 camera; 300MM Schneider Xenar lens; yellow K2 filter; Ilford FP4 4x5 film; Kodak HC110B developer.

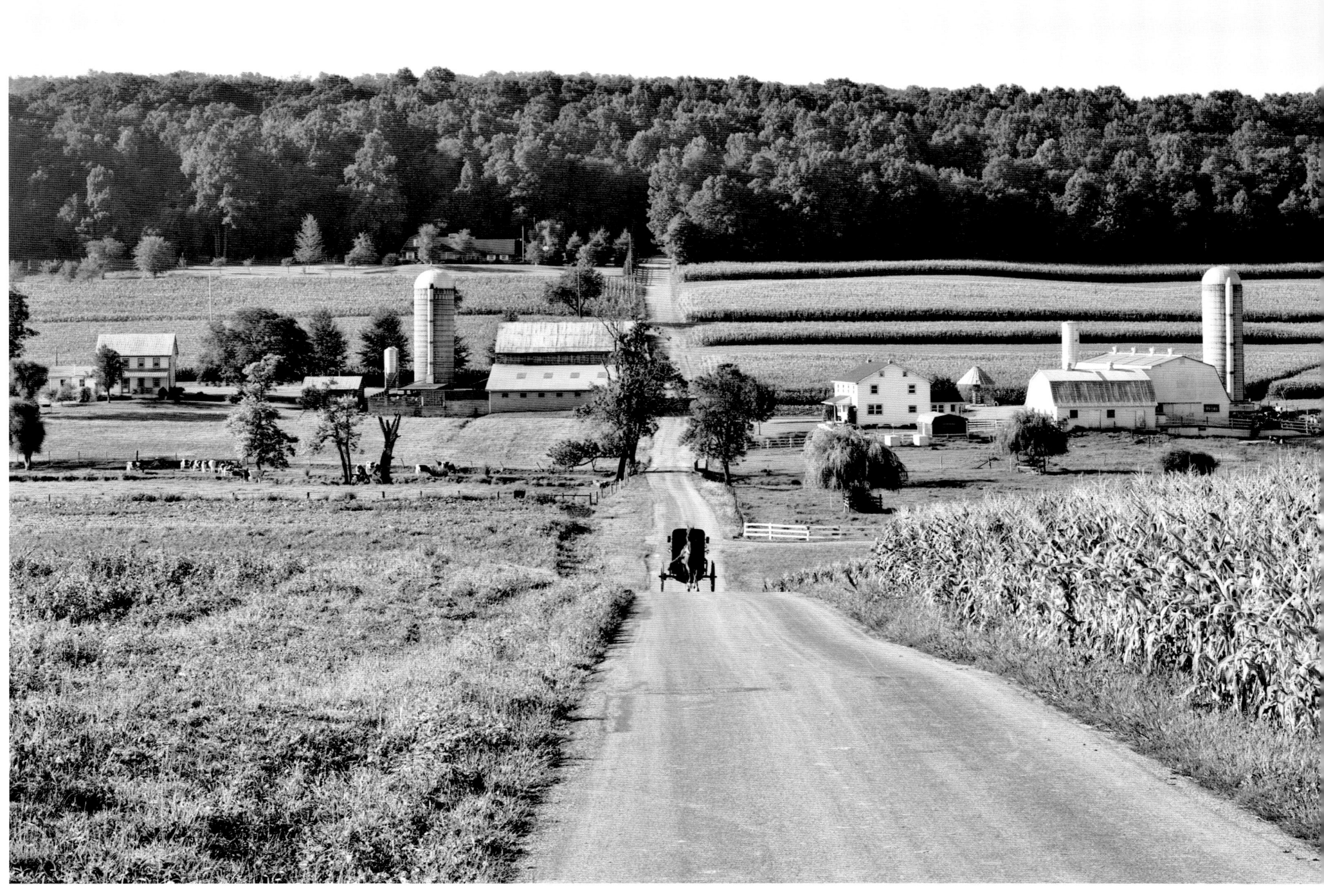

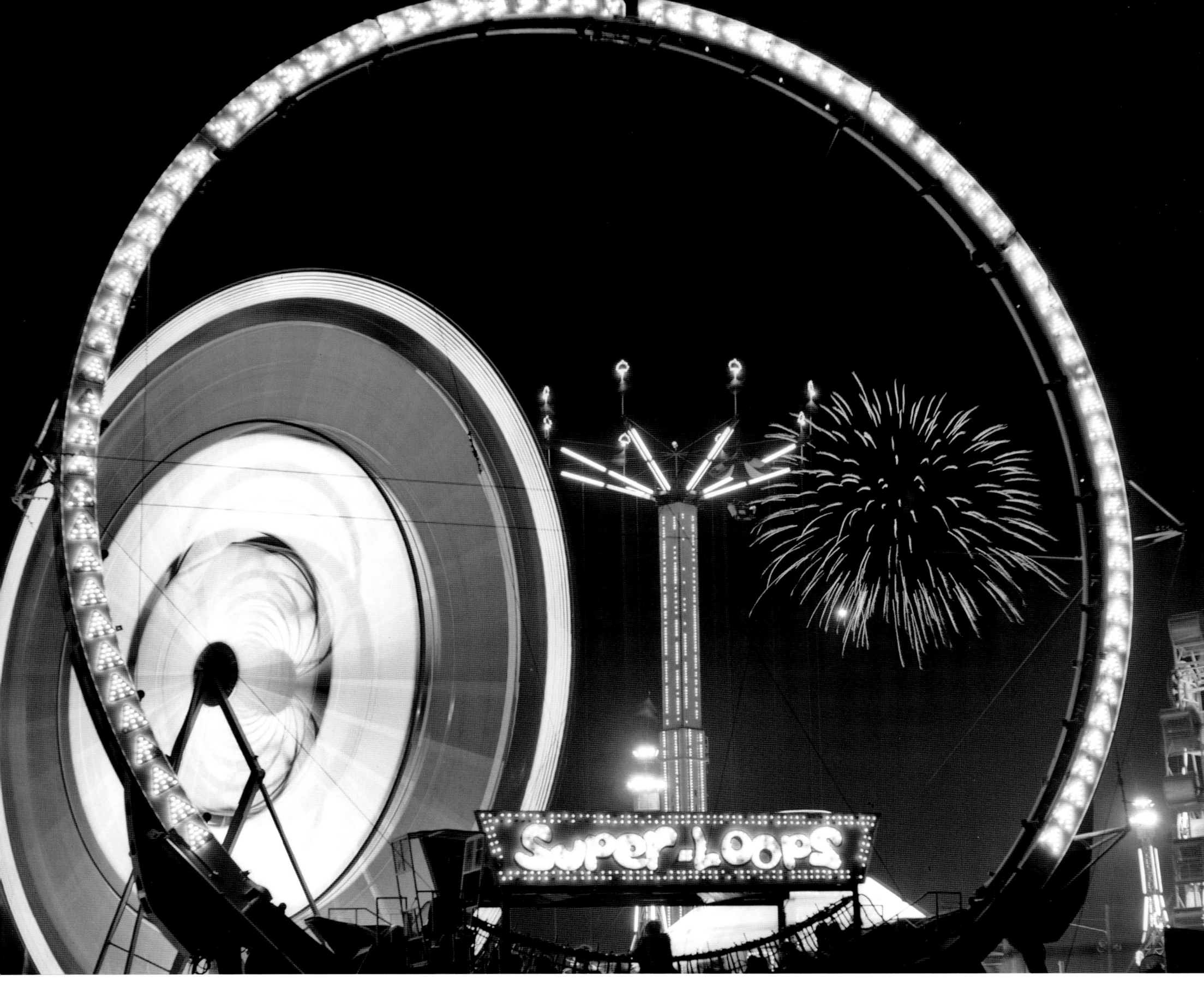

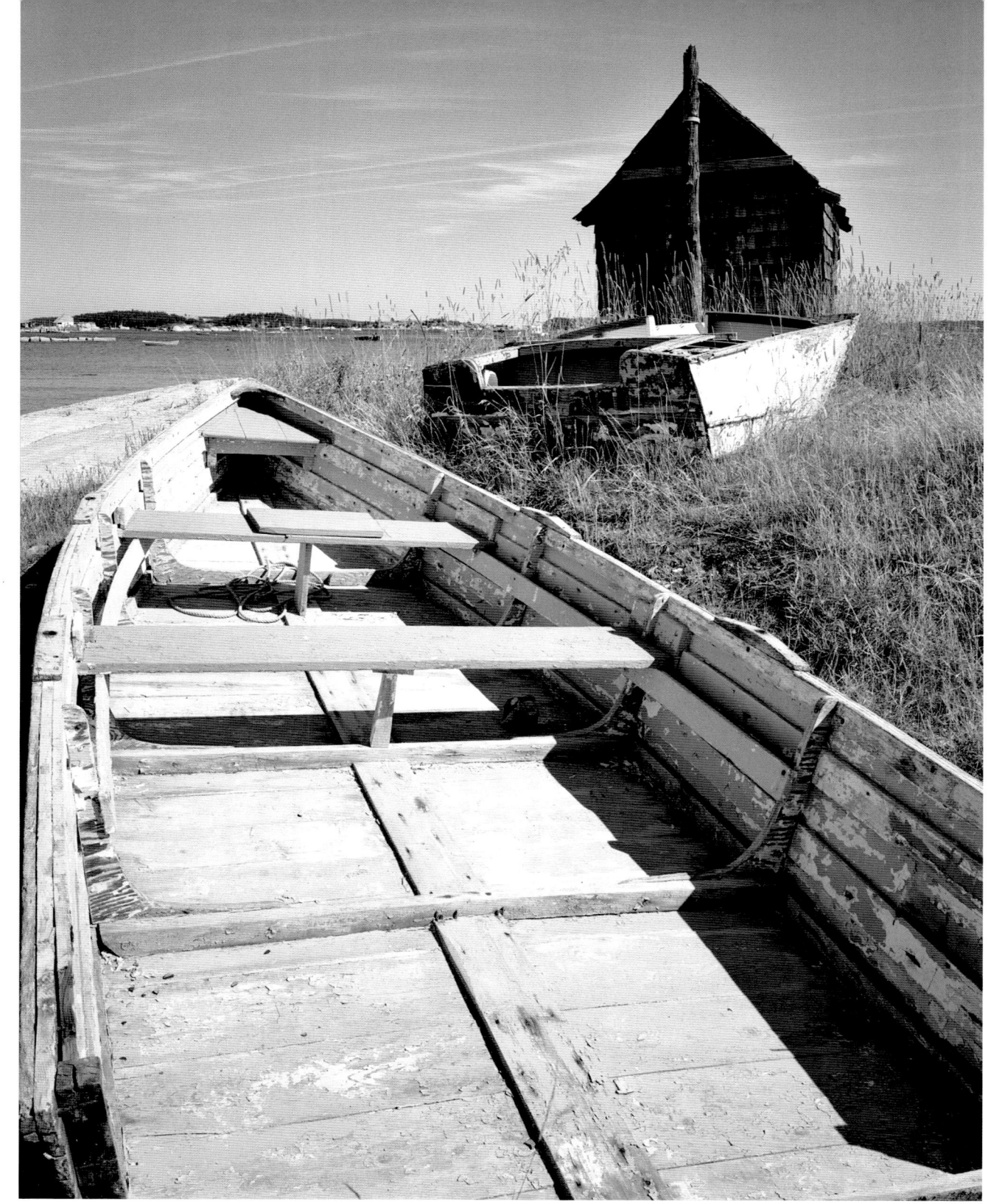

Left: Stonington, Maine,
9-9-1986; Linhof Technika V
4x5 camera; 90mm Schneider
Super Angulon lens; Kodak Tri X
Pan Pro 4x5 film; Kodak HC110B
developer.

Facing page: Tennessee State
Fair, Nashville, Tennessee,
9-1981; Crown Graphic 4x5
camera; 90mm Ilex Super
Veriwide lens; Kodak Plus X
Pan Pro 4x5 film; Edwal FG7
developer.

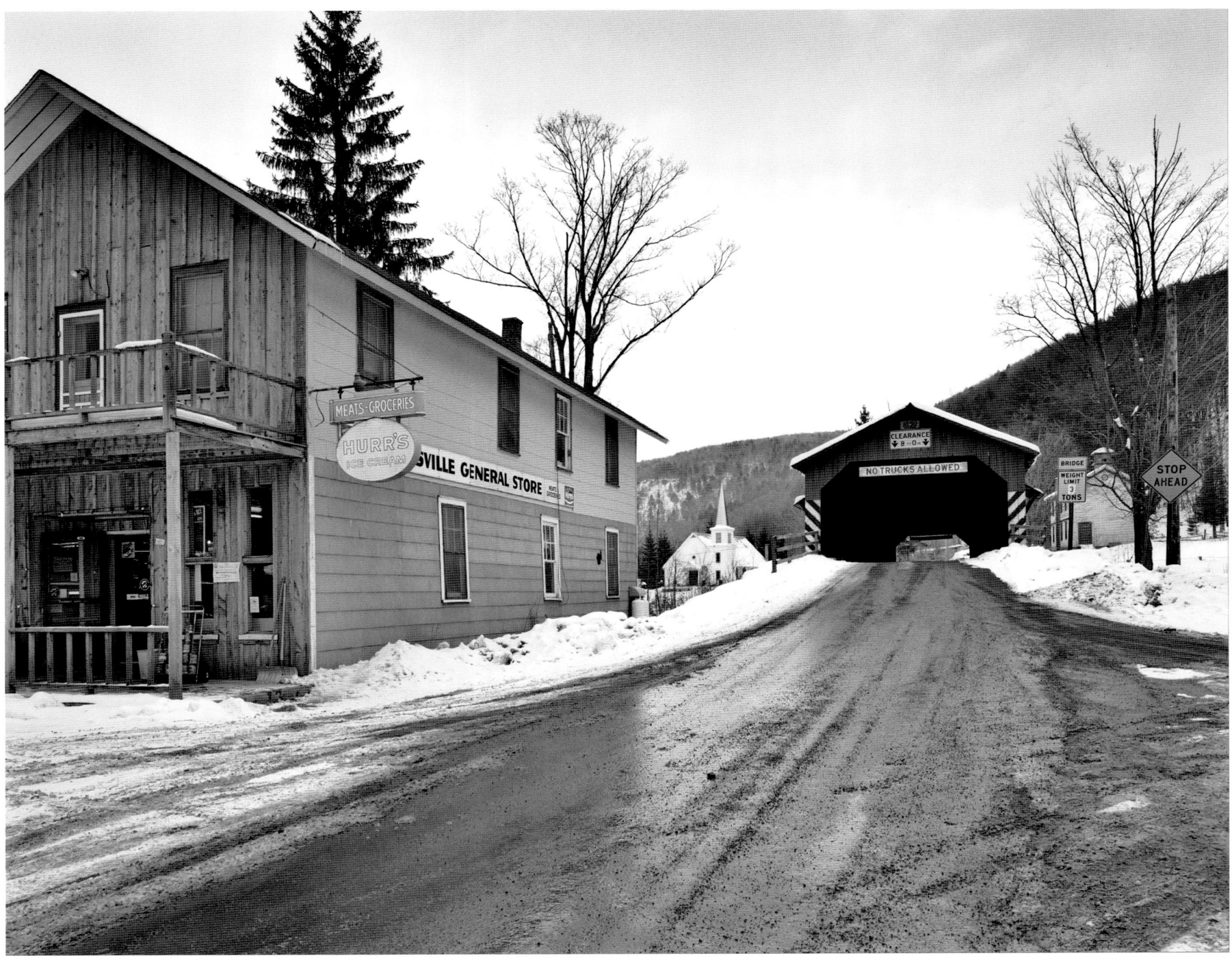

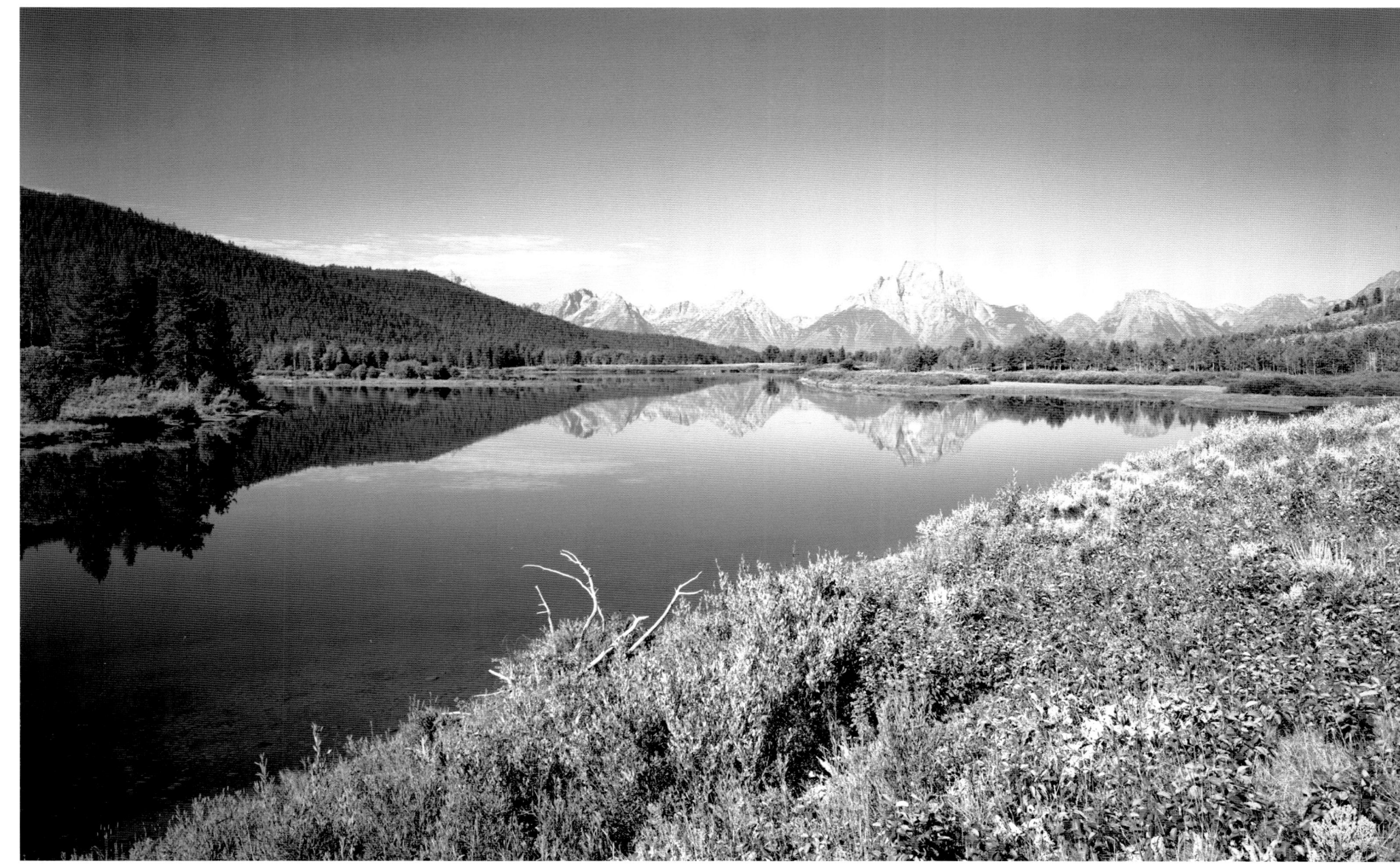

Above: Oxbow Bend, Grand Tetons National Park, Wyoming, 8-18-1988; Linhof Technika V 4x5 camera; 90mm Schneider Super Angulon lens; yellow G filter; Kodak Tmax 100 4x5 film; Kodak HC110B developer.

Facing page: Forksville, Pennsylvania, 2-15-1986; Linhof Technika V 4x5 camera; 90mm Schneider Super Angulon lens; Kodak Tri X Pan Pro 4x5 film; Kodak HC110B developer.

Right: Last sunlight on
hillside near Fresno,
California, 10-1-1984;
Mamiya C33 TLR camera;
105mm Sekor lens; Kodak
Plus X Pan Pro 120 film;
Kodak HC110B developer.

Facing page: Lonely road
through the Badlands of
South Dakota, 8-21-1988;
Linhof Technika V 4x5
camera; 210mm Schneider
Symmar S Lens; yellow
k2 filter; Kodak Tmax 100
4x5 film; Kodak HC110B
developer.

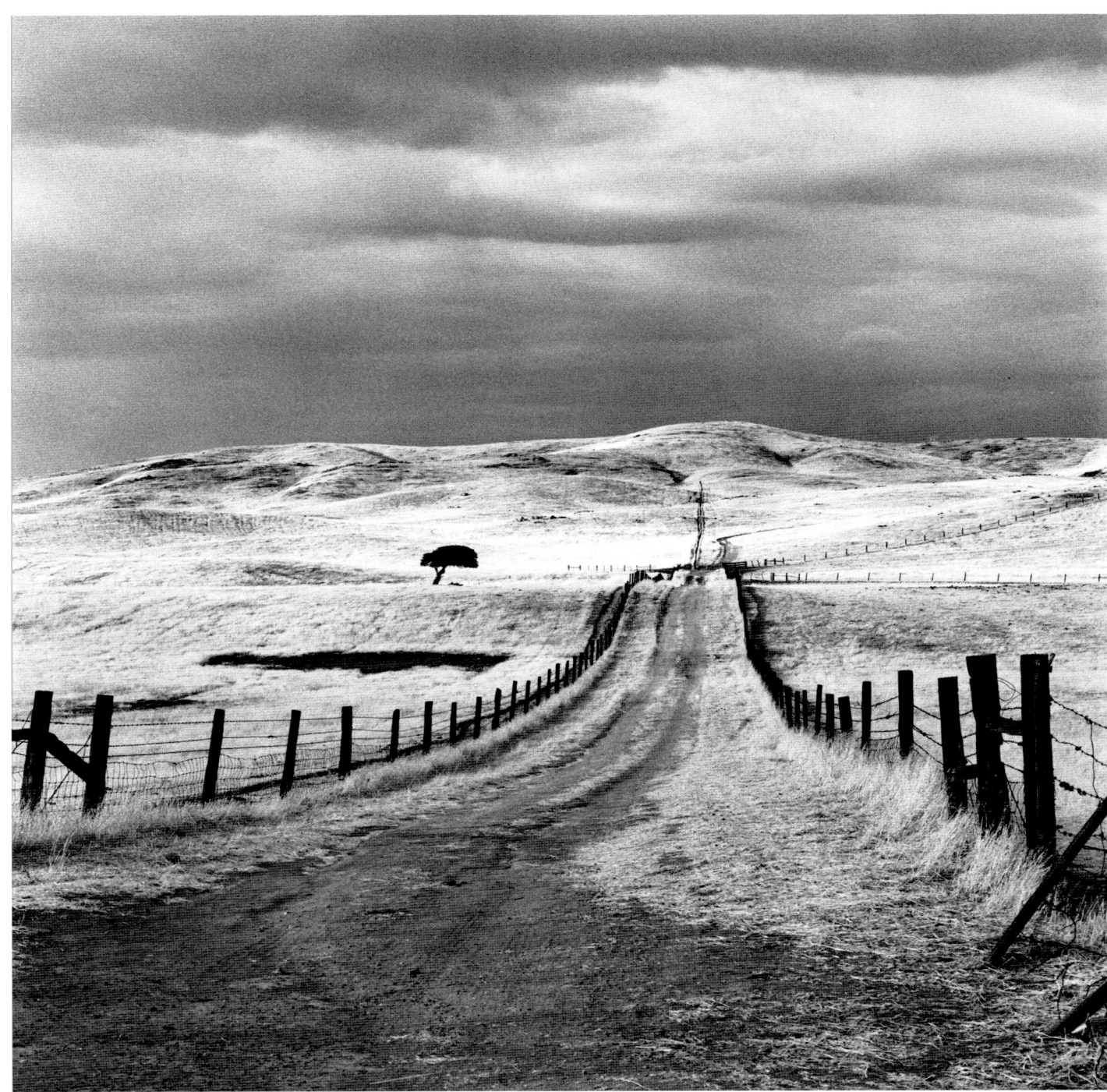

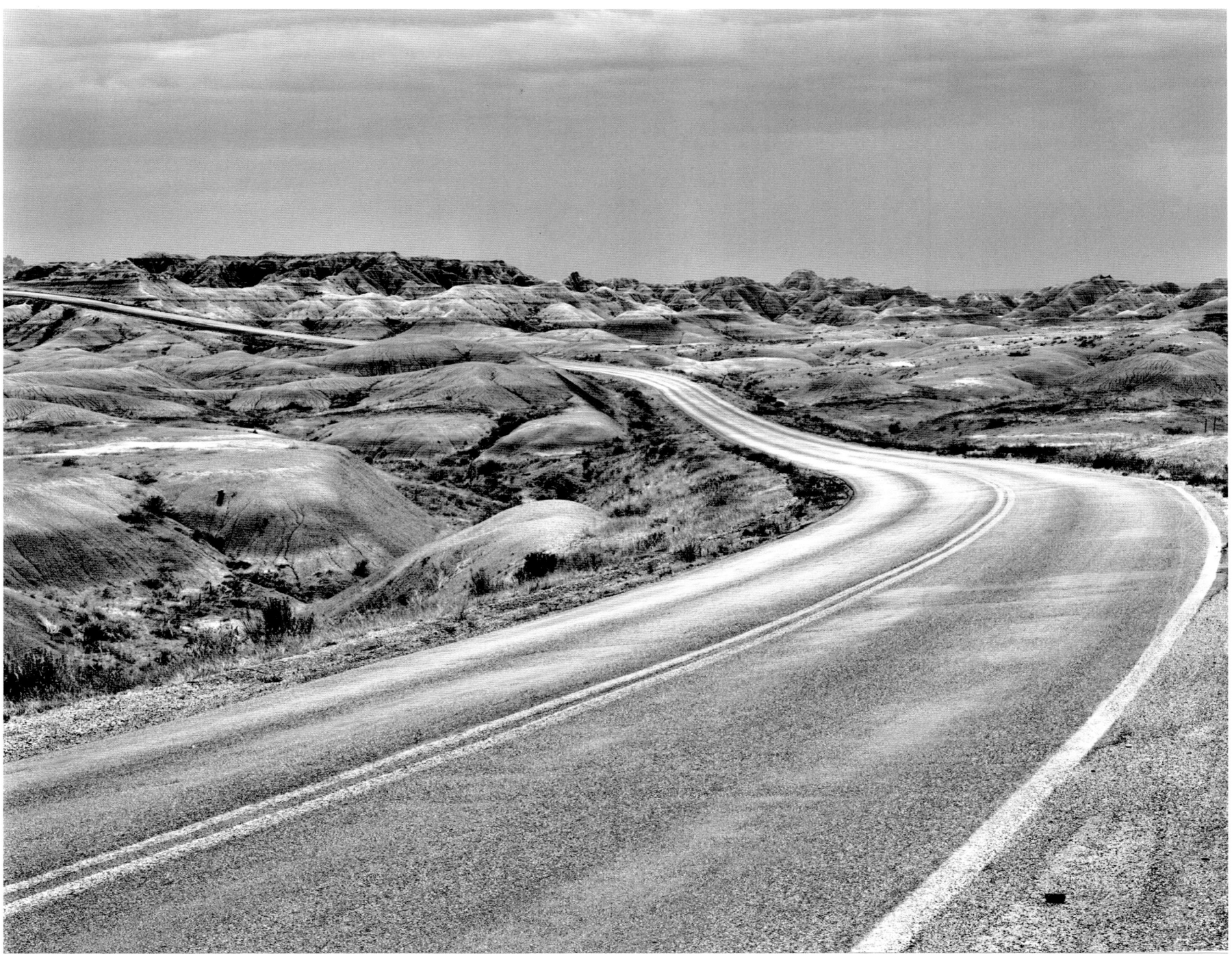

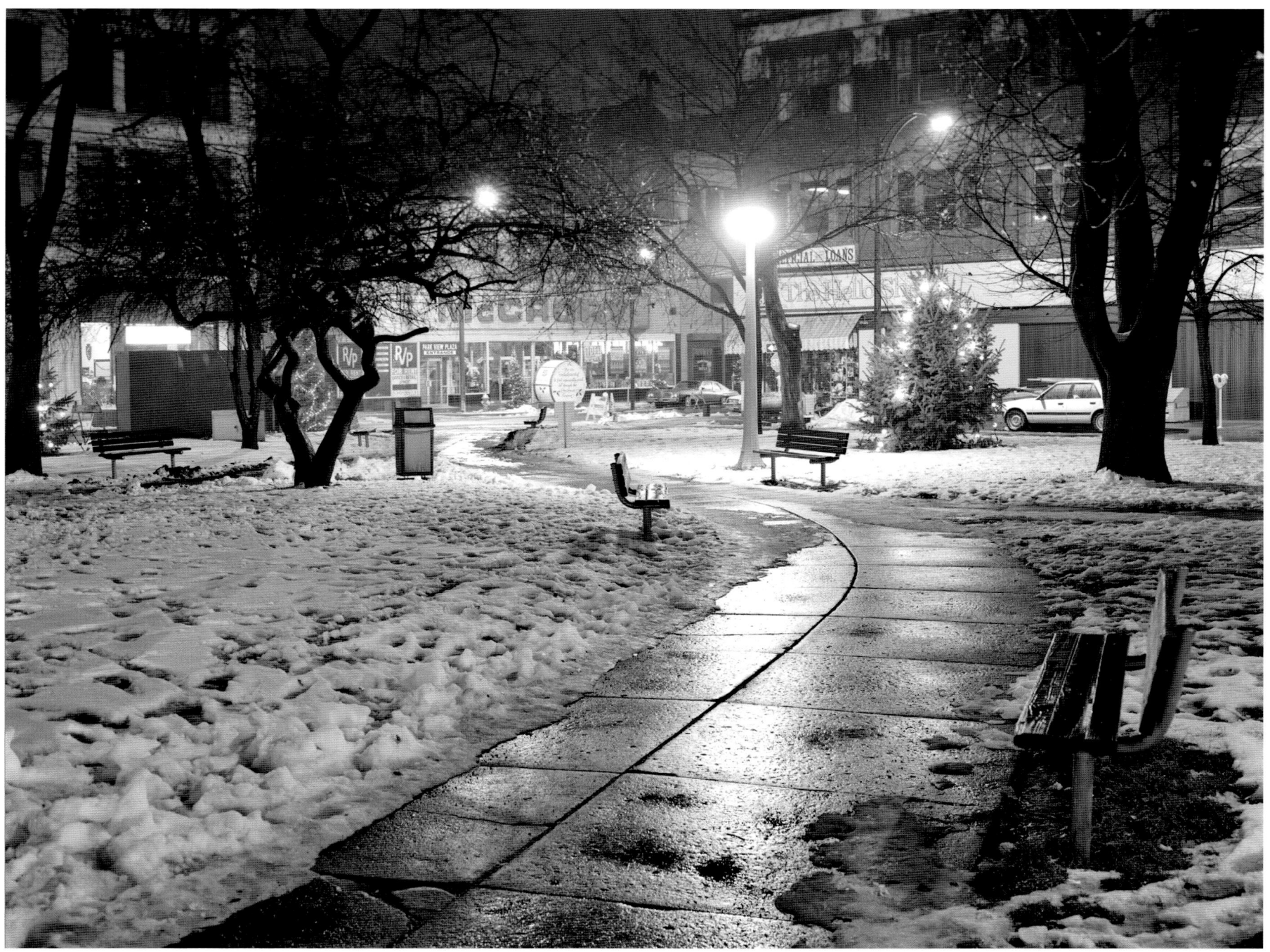

10 degrees on square, Johnstown, Pennsylvania, 12-19-1984; Linhof Technika V 4x5 camera; 150mm Schneider Symmar S lens; Kodak Plus X Pan Pro 4x5 film; Kodak HC110B developer.

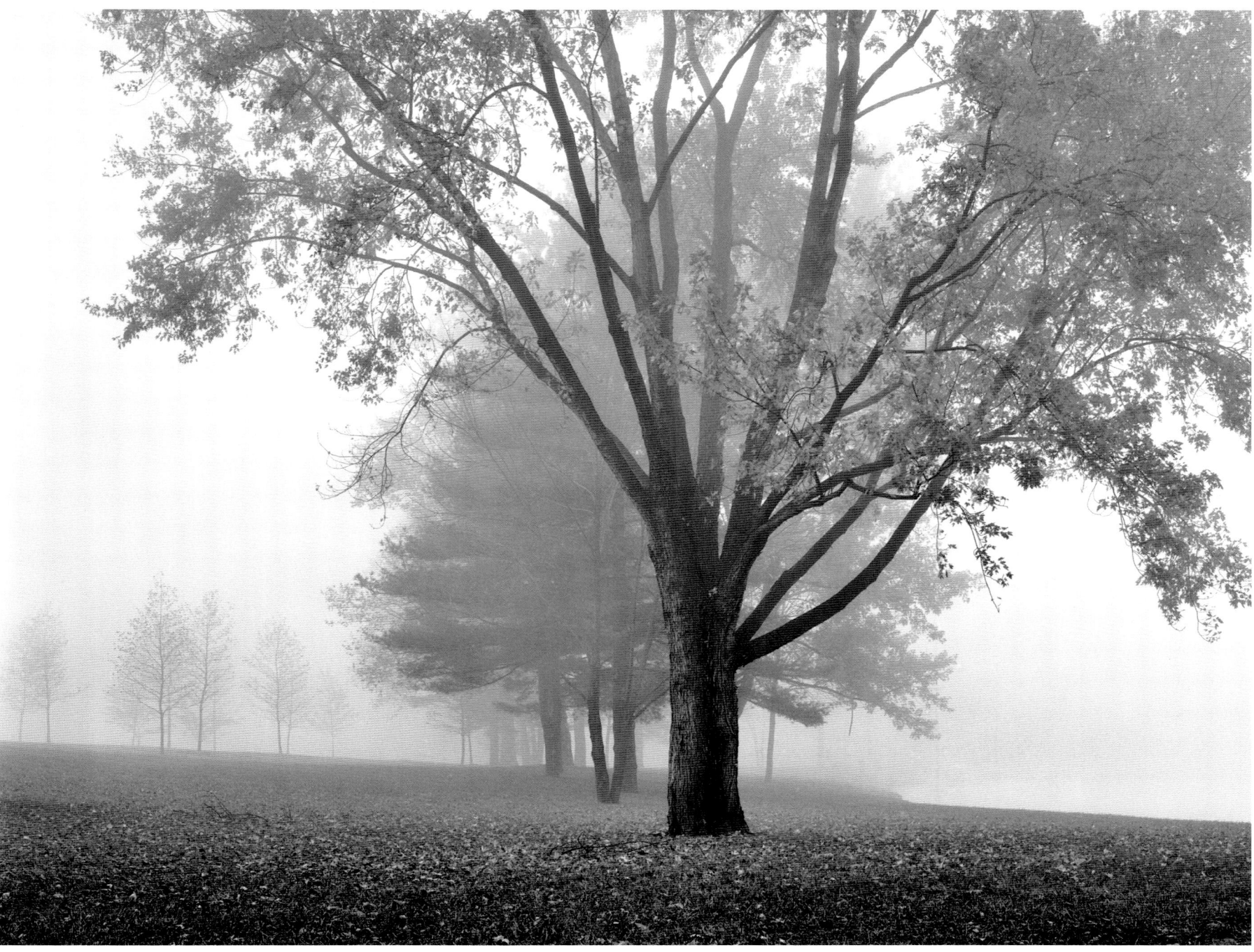

Trees in fog, Silver Lake, near Newtown, Pennsylvania, 10-30-1982; Linhof Technika IV 4x5 camera; 150mm Schneider Symmar S lens; Kodak Tri X Pan 4x5 film; Kodak HC110B developer.

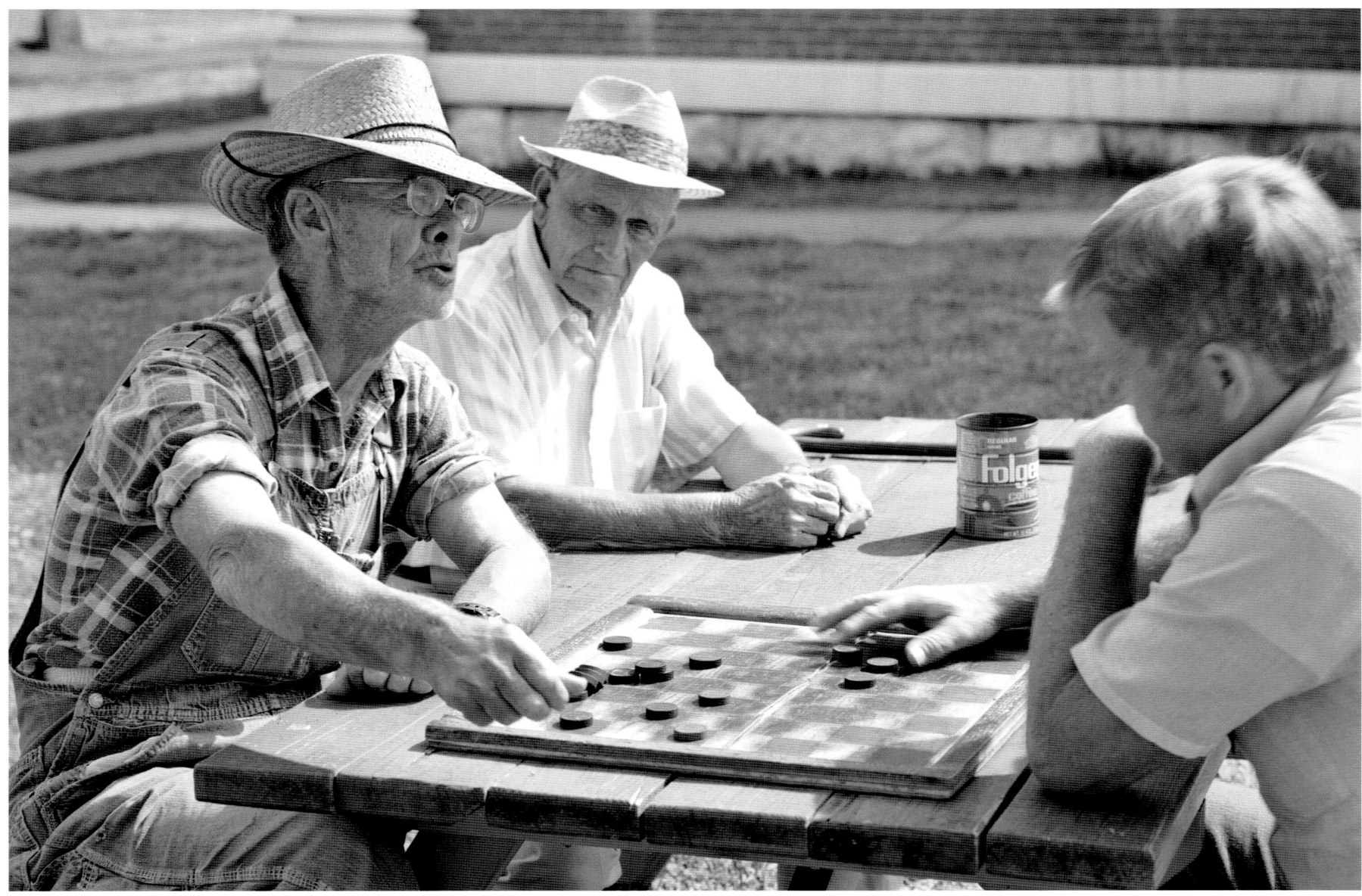

Above: Cheatham County Courthouse, Ashland, Tennessee, 5-10-1982; Linhof Technika V 4x5 camera; 210 Schneider Symmar S lens; Ilford FP4 4x5 film; HC110B developer.

Facing page: Daily men's gathering at the Post Office, Frankewing, Tennessee, 5-17-1982; Linhof Technika V 4x5 camera; 150mm Schneider Symmar S lens; Ilford FP4 4x5 film; Kodak HC110B developer.

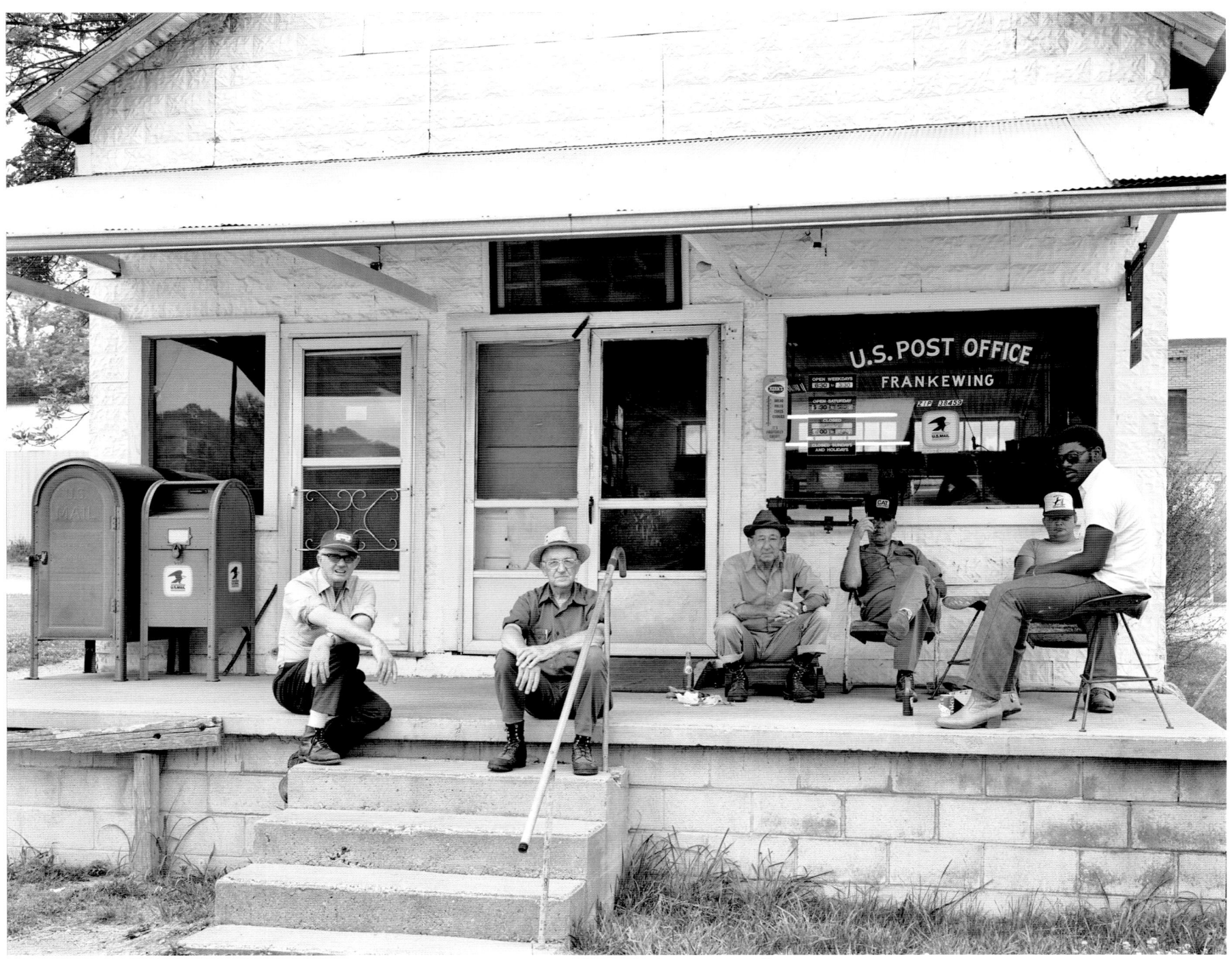

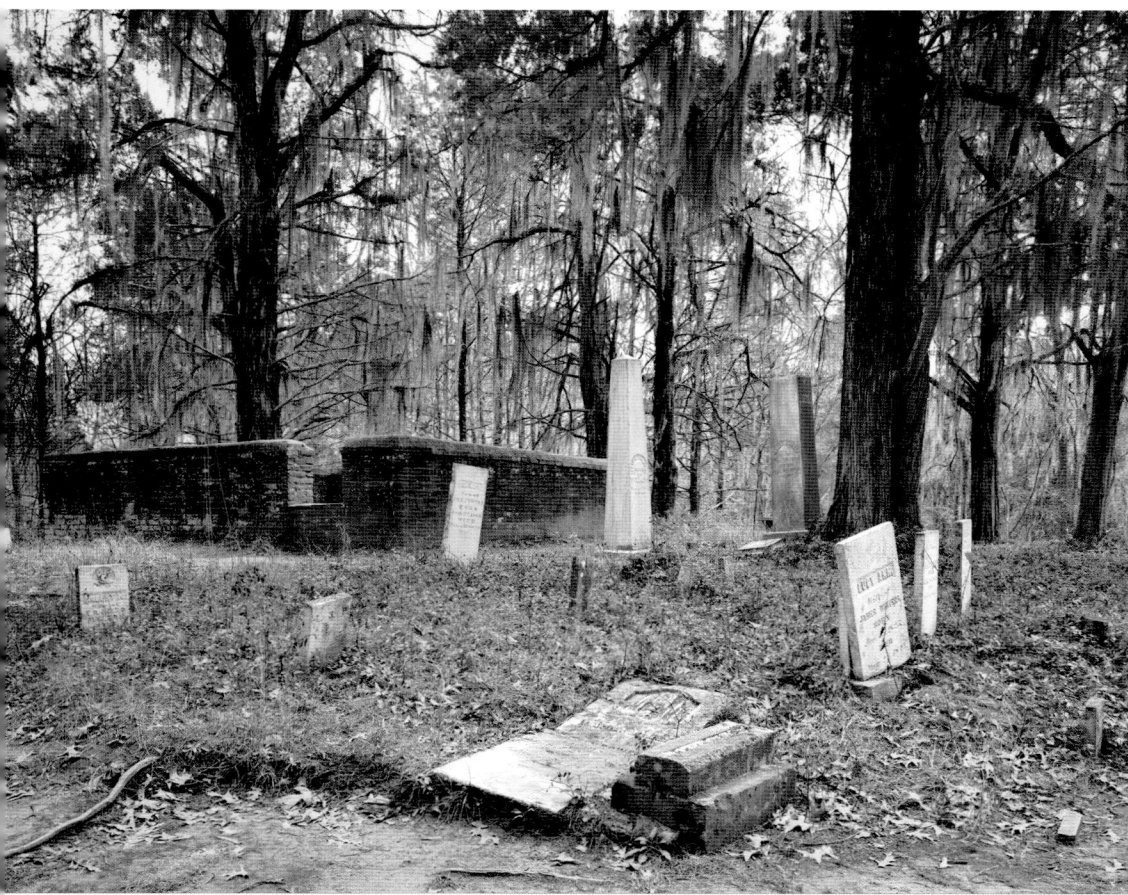 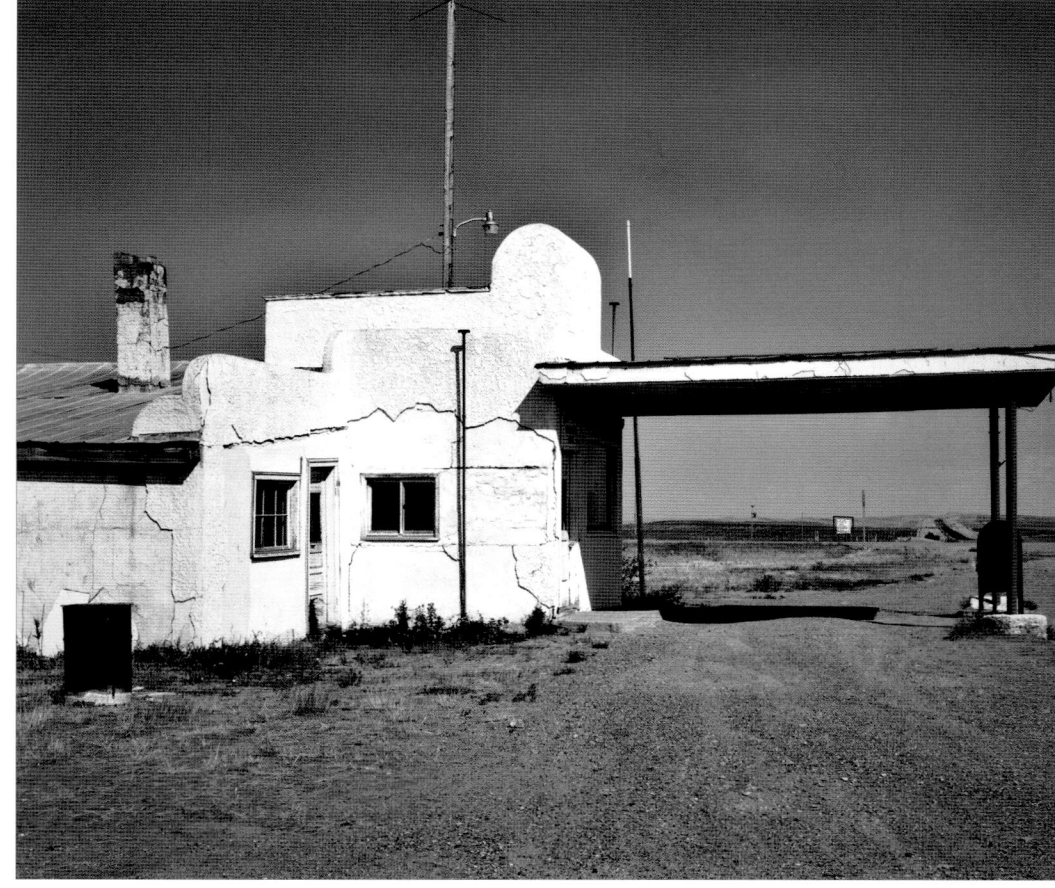

Left: Rocky Springs Methodist Church cemetery, Natchez Trace Parkway, Mississippi, 2-17-1988; Linhof Technika V 4x5 camera; 90mm Schneider
Super Angulon lens; Kodak Tmax 400 4x5 film; Kodak HC110B developer.

Right: Post Office, Hammond, Montana, 8-19-1988; Linhof Technika V 4x5 camera; 150mm Schneider Symmar S Lens; yellow K2 filter; Kodak Tmax 100 4x5 film; Kodak HC110B developer.

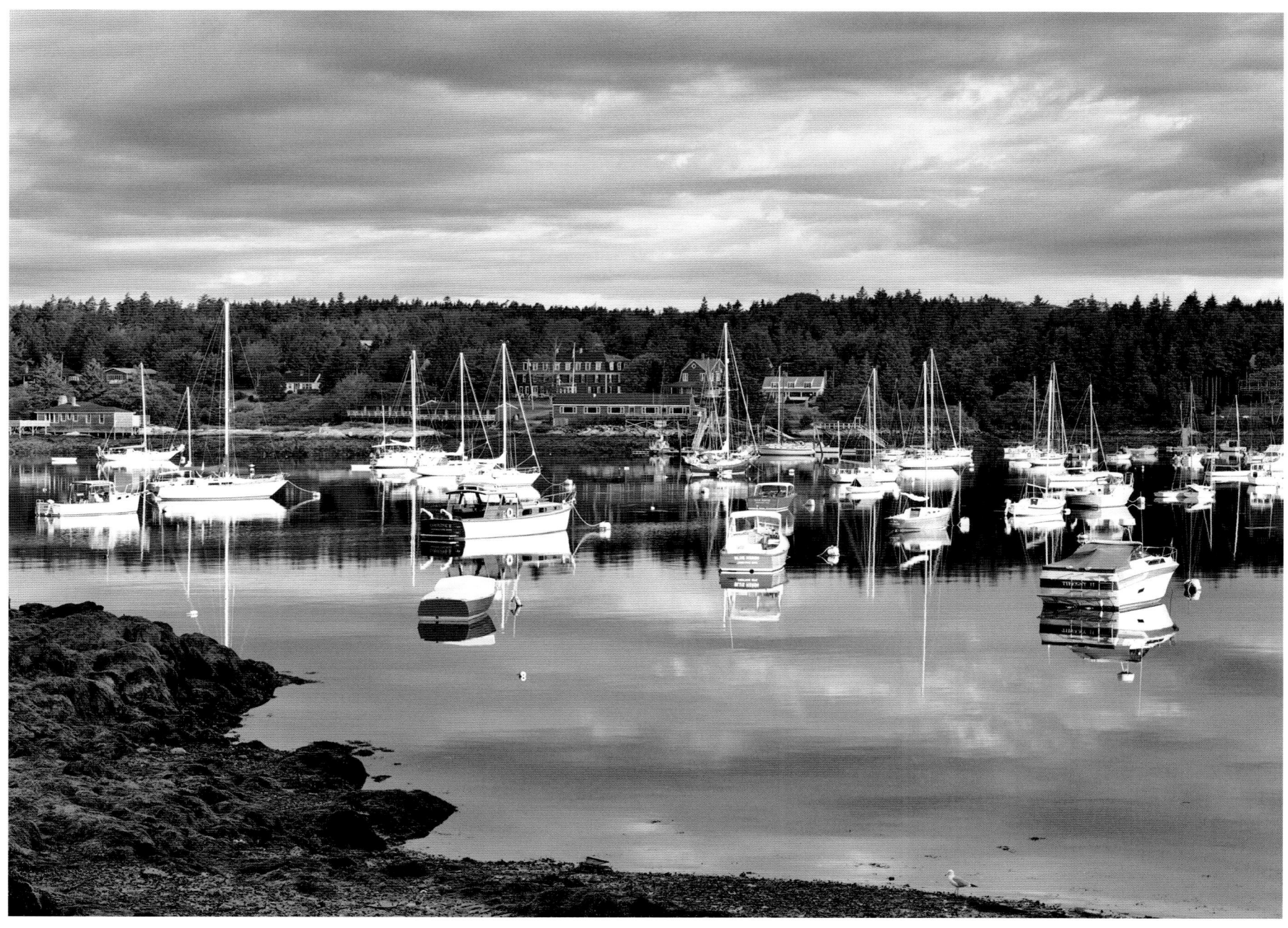

Christmas Cove, Maine, at sunrise, 9-8-1986; Linhof Technika V 4x5 camera; 150mm Schneider Symmar S lens; Kodak Tri X Pan Pro 4x5 film; Kodak HC110C developer.

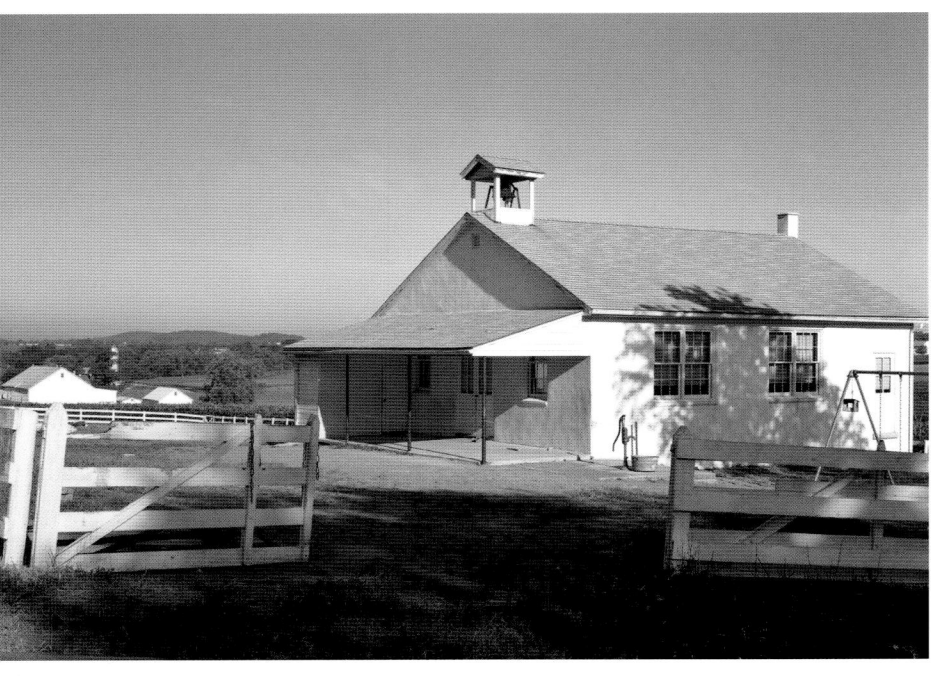

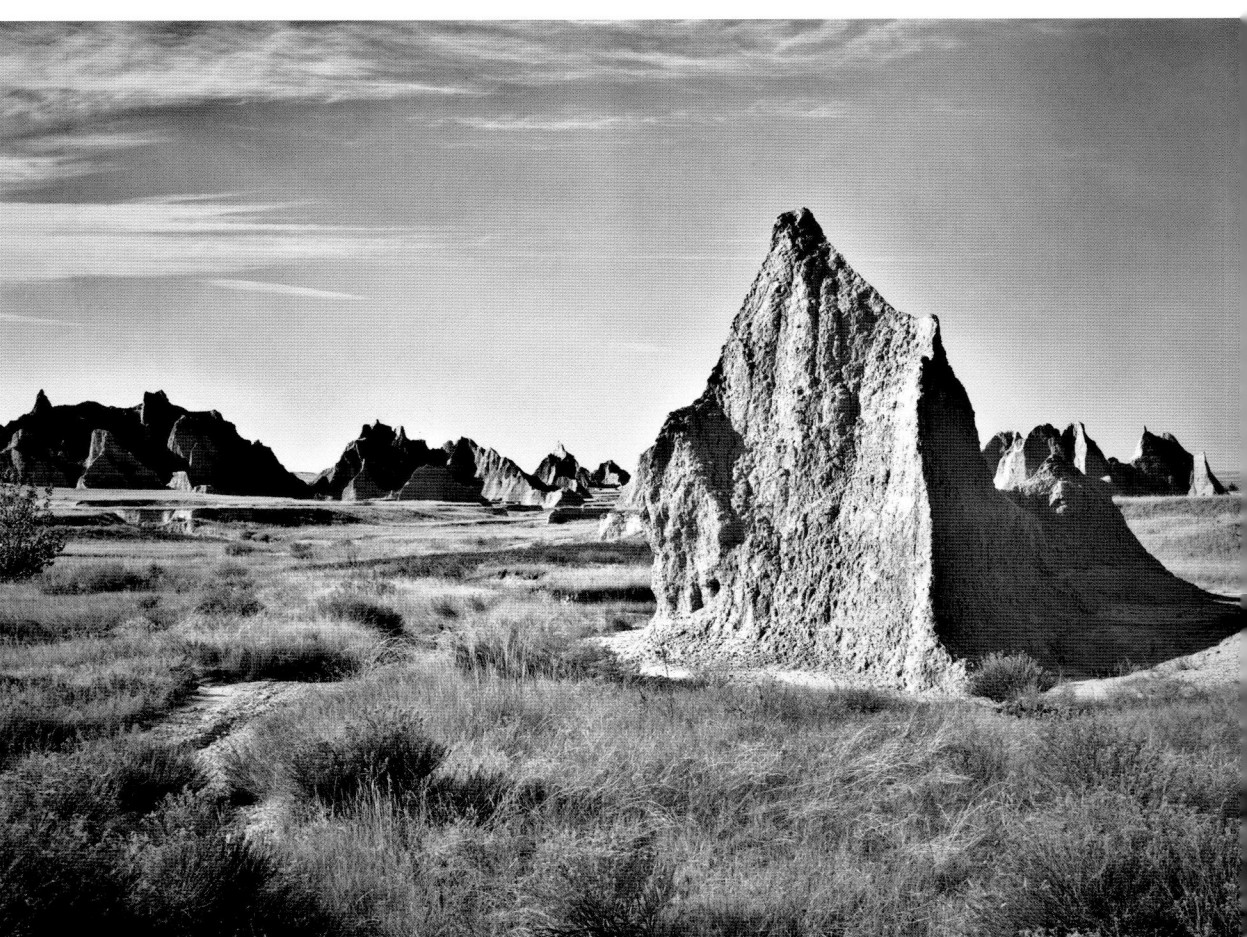

Above: Amish School in Lancaster County, Pennsylvania,
7-23-1983; Cambo Super View 4x5 camera; 150mm
Schneider Symmar S lens; Ilford FP4 4x5 film; Kodak HC110B
developer.

Right: Badlands of South Dakota, 8-1988; Toyo 8x10M
camera; 355mm Schneider Gold Dot Dagor; yellow K2 filter;
Kodak Tmax 100 8x10 film; Kodak HC110B developer.

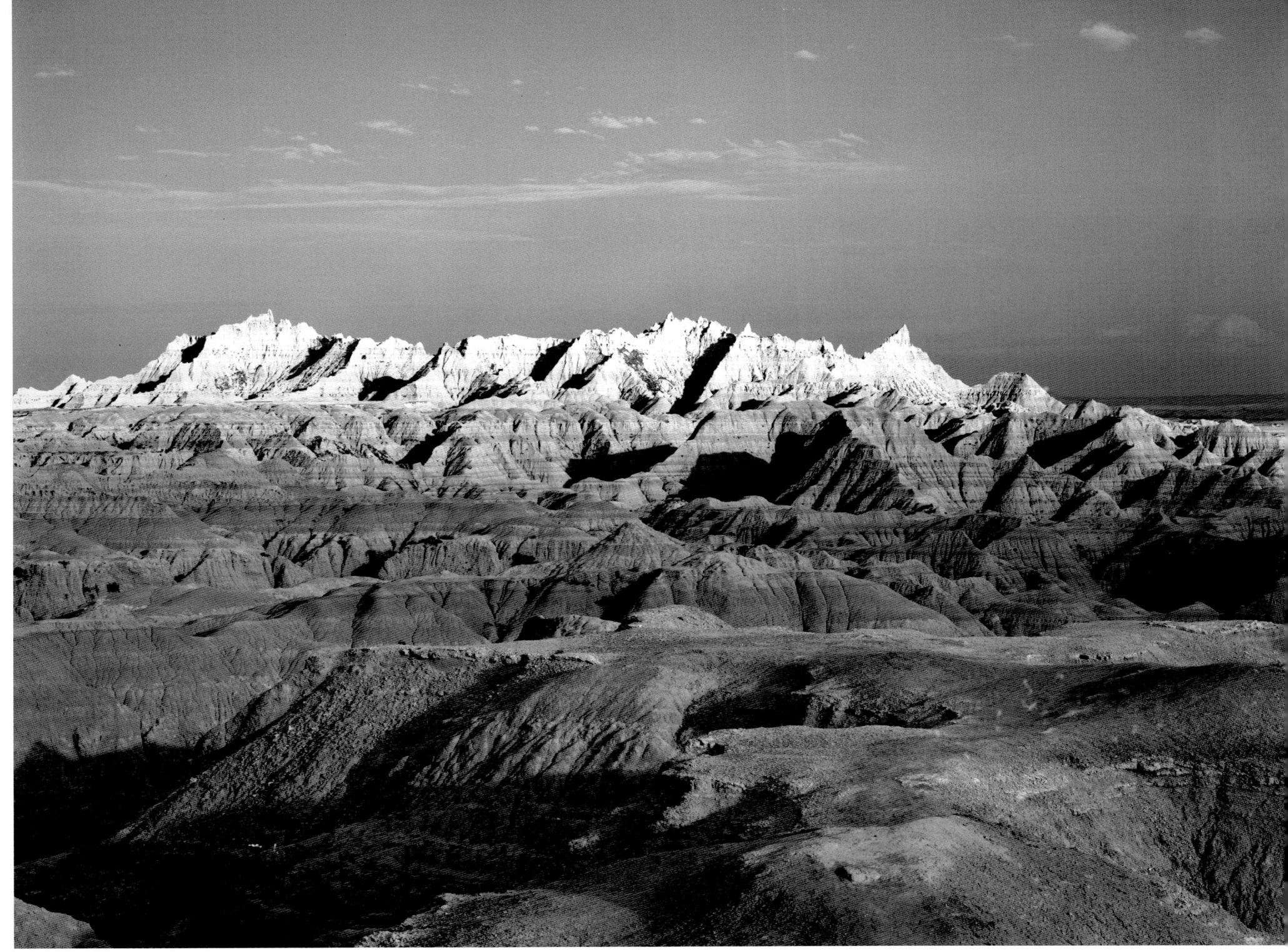

Badlands at sunset, South Dakota, 8-21-1988; Linhof Technika V 4x5 camera; 210mm Schneider Symmar S lens; yellow K2 filter; Kodak Tmax 100 4x5 film; Kodak HC110C developer.

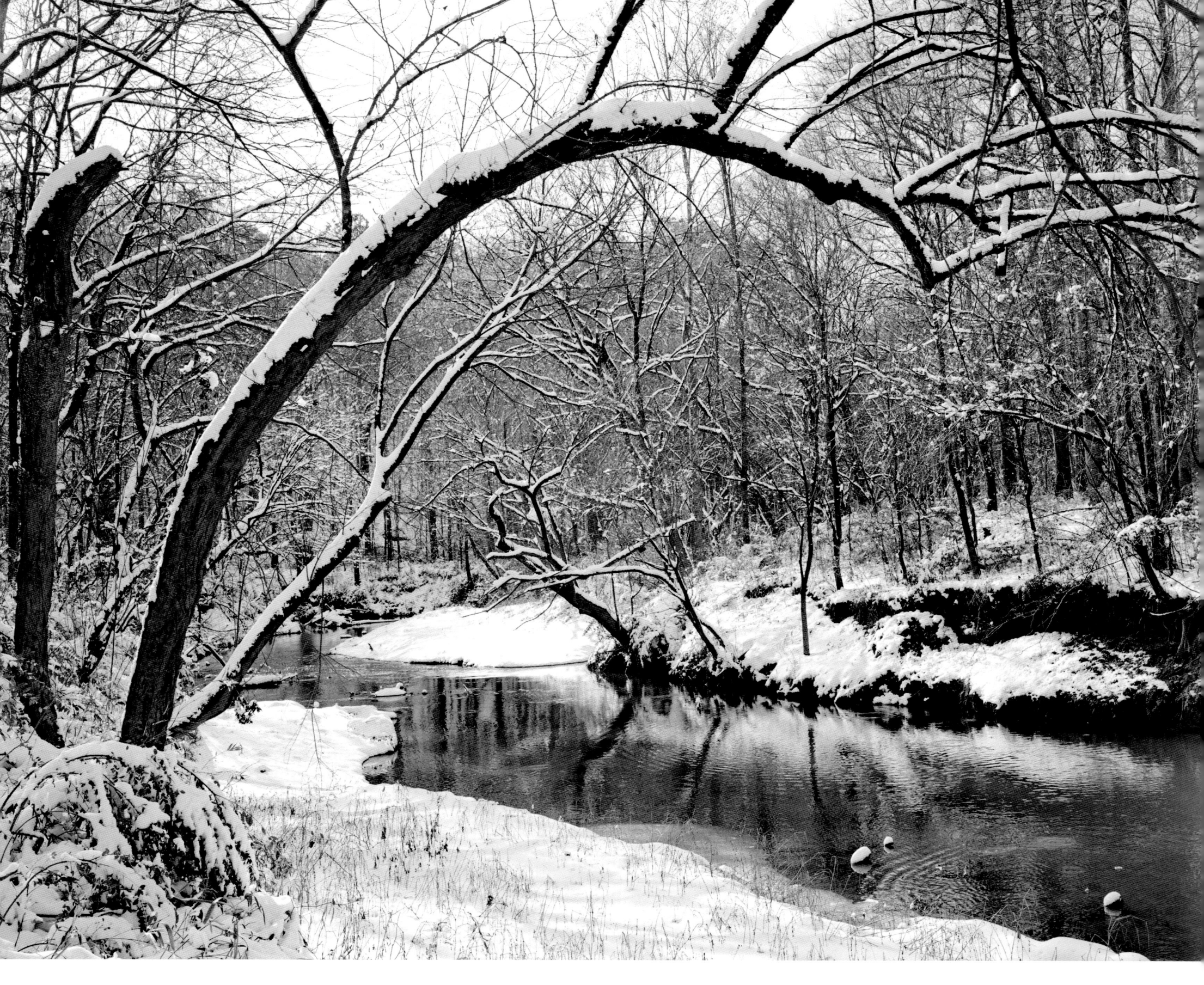

4

The 1990s: Sharing and Teaching

Our family spent this entire decade and our kids went from elementary school through high school in Hoover, Alabama, a suburb of Birmingham. Kyle continued working at Vestridge Animal Clinic in Vestavia for Dr. Allen Price. In addition, Kyle went to massage therapy school, graduating in May 1995. She worked at several massage therapy locations, adjusting her schedule so she could continue at Vestridge Animal Clinic.

I started in Birmingham as division general manager, holding that position through 1993, when the company replaced the position with two separate positions: operations manager and sales manager. I then became regional sales manager, covering the entire Southeast—Alabama, Mississippi, Louisiana, Georgia, Florida, North Carolina, South Carolina, and Tennessee. It was my largest territory and my most satisfying job. At one point, I had eight major processing labs in my region, along with forty-five area sales representatives reporting to me. The sales offices for each were located in the labs.

Throughout the 1990s, I kept the same job, but the parameters changed. The coverage area changed, as did the regional vice president. My long-term friend and mentor Ray Smith retired in 1997. I began reporting to Bill Villines, the eastern region operations vice president. There were several more changes up until January 1, 1998, when our division, which was called Kodak Retail Services but reported through Qualex, became Kodak representatives, calling on all Kodak accounts, handling all of Kodak's consumer imaging products: including cameras, film, photofinishing, batteries, and videotapes. Along with the size of the regions, my sales representatives were gradually reduced to twelve in Alabama, Tennessee, Georgia, Mississippi, and Louisiana.

During my career, quality, customer service, and employee satisfaction were everything. As division general manager in Birmingham I had to send in test photo processing each month. Corporate did blind quality tests of the fifty-eight nationwide mega labs; these tests were ranked. The personnel manager for each region visited each lab once a year to interview all employees. They were asked to rank their employee satisfaction with a questionnaire that covered everything from benefits, workplace environment, and how they felt about the

Facing page: Snowy creek, Hoover, Alabama, 1-9-1982; Linhof Technika V 4x5 camera; 120mm Schneider Super Symmar HM lens; Kodak Tmax 100 4x5 film; Kodak Tmax RS developer.

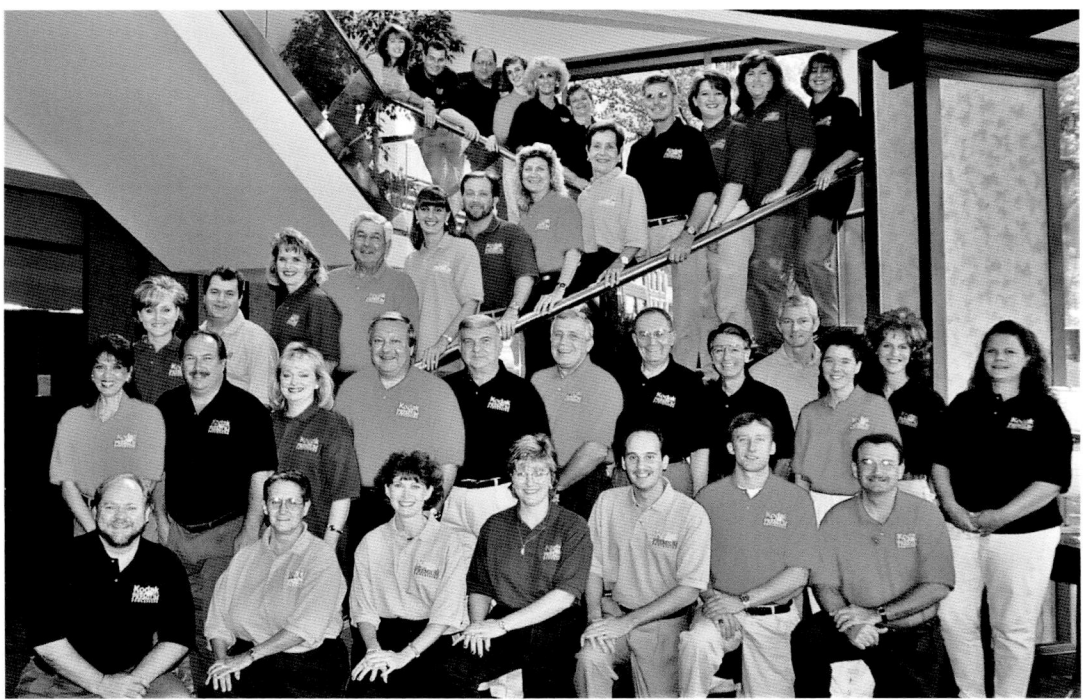

District/Region Manager John Dersham (front row, seated far right) with Kodak Retail Services representatives, annual meeting, New Orleans, 1997.

enough, digital photography was invented by a Kodak research and development person, Steven Sasson, to fulfill a request in the middle of the 1970s by Steve Jobs of Apple. Jobs asked Kodak to find a way to put pictures on his computer screens. The technology was low-quality until the early 2000s, when all the major camera companies came out with cameras in the eight to ten megapixel range.

Kodak knew there was no money to be made in digital. The business of film, chemicals, and paper was bound to diminish and would no longer be a renewable business,. In the years that followed, this proved true.

MY PERSONAL PHOTOGRAPHY ALSO thrived during these years. I was on the road a lot, so I had a variety of states to photograph. A majority of my photography in the 1990s was done on large-format, 4x5, 5x7, and 8x10 film. I continued doing studio work and some landscape on medium-format. I kept studio backdrop paper hanging from the ceiling that could be pulled down and rolled across the floor. I had portable but professional studio lighting. A lot of my studio work has been of my wife and kids, friends, models for portfolio shots, product shots, still lifes, and fine-art nudes.

By October 1993, I was well known at Kodak for my personal photography, and it was used heavily in advertising and for wall art in office buildings and factories. The president of the photofinishing division, whom I reported to at the time, was Peter Fitzgerald. He asked if I would represent Kodak as the host on a photography excursion to the Southwest for winners of a nationwide Kodak photo contest in the summer of 1993. The workshop instructor was famed

performance of their superiors. This took place at all levels. In my career, I am perhaps most proud of my high employee satisfaction levels and high employee retention rates. It meant everything to me that people were happy in their workplace. I also found that our high employee satisfaction rates matched our being at the top in product quality rankings. It is easy to understand that satisfied employees will try harder to produce a quality product.

I remained in this position for the remainder of my career with Eastman Kodak, even though the job itself changed in scope every so often. The company finished the decade with growing pressure and concern over the improved quality of digital photography and the increase in the number of people buying digital cameras. Funnily

Sports Illustrated Swimsuit Issue photographer Robert Huntzinger. The motivation was to get people shooting Kodachrome again. Kodachrome became available in 1935 and was the most used color film for home movies and slides for decades. *National Geographic* and many other major magazines insisted their photographers use Kodachrome for all their color work.

But Kodachrome had lost sales due to the long processing times for amateur and professional photographers' film. There was never a way to process Kodachrome in a home darkroom. The equipment was too large and the chemical processes too complex. Kodak invented a K-lab Kodachrome minilab to be scattered across the country in their large labs, making processing available in more locations.

Each contest winner was given fifty rolls of Kodachrome or Ektachrome, or a mix of the two and would get free processing for it at the end of the contest trip. It was a great trip. We went to Lake Powell, Monument Valley, and several other nearby national parks. I was the only one who shot 4x5 film on the trip, in addition to my fifty rolls of Kodachrome.

Unfortunately, the Kodachrome minilab project came to a sudden halt. The renewed focus on the recovery of the world's most beloved color film was short-lived. Kodak continued to make Kodachrome through 2009 and continued processing it until the end of 2010.

IN THE 1990S, THERE were quite a few large-format shooters around. We were all friends and would regularly go out shooting together, in addition to our personal shooting trips. By this time, I had large-format photography friends from all my former locations. I was still in touch with on a regular basis, so I would also get together to shoot with them in Nashville, Philadelphia, or Hattiesburg.

In Birmingham, I immediately got opportunities to show my work in galleries, libraries, camera stores and other venues. I also began teaching weekend large-format photo workshops for UAB (the University of Alabama Birmingham). I met great friends there, and between them and the Shades Valley Camera Club, we had a good community of people to attend photo shooting events. While teaching large-format classes, I befriended a number of people who I would shoot with on outings. We would then meet to show our finished prints. They included David Haynes, Will Varnell, Jerry and Carolyn Jackson, David McKaig, Ken Boyd, Robert Falls, David Elder, Don Harbor, John Craner, Mark Gooch, Ron Bowen, Howard Bond, Randal Crow, Mike Mills, Steve Higginbotham, Lewis Kennedy, Chris Boswell, Sarah Jones, David Black, and Dan and Lisa Clark. It was a fun and rewarding network.

I taught workshops not only at UAB, but also at camera clubs and camera stores. These workshops always included a day of shooting at various locations. The real fun was in bonding with the classmates. It creates relationships when people with a common interest are spending time together on their shared passion. For many years, I have used the term "perpetuating the craft" when discussing my photo outings.

Throughout the years I have maintained photography friends from camera clubs, workshops, and camera stores. This is a wonderful blessing that has come out of my lifelong hobby.

I continued in the 1990s taking photography trip vacations in conjunction with my travel for Kodak business meetings throughout the United States.

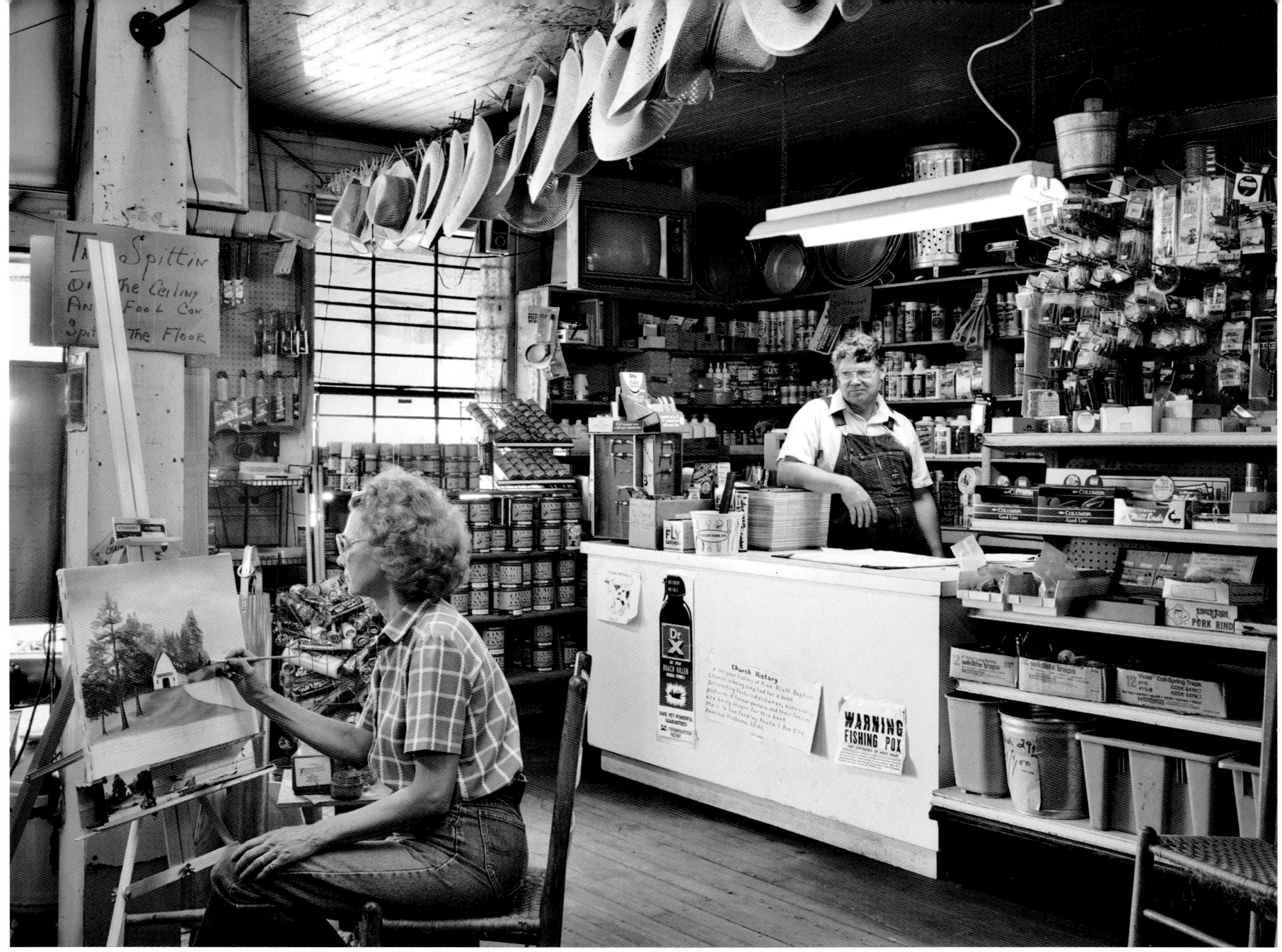

Above: Dan and Nila Marsh, Paul C. Marsh and Son General Store, Locust Fork, Alabama, 7-31-1991; Toyo 8x10M camera; 250mm Fujinon WS lens; Kodak Tmax 400 8x10 film; Kodak Tmax RS developer.

Facing page: Negative sleeve for 1991 shoot.

Facing page, top right: 2014 reunion with Dan Marsh at my exhibit at Little River Canyon National Preserve, Jacksonville State University Canyon Center. Propped against Dan's leg is the painting his now-deceased wife was working on when I took my photograph, and he is holding a painting she later made from my photograph.

Facing page, bottom right: Paul C. Marsh in front of Paul C. Marsh and Son General Store, Locust Fork, Alabama, 6-9-1991; Toyo 8x10M camera; 355mm Schneider Gold Dot Dagor camera; Kodak Tmax 400 8x10 film; Kodak Tmax RS developer.

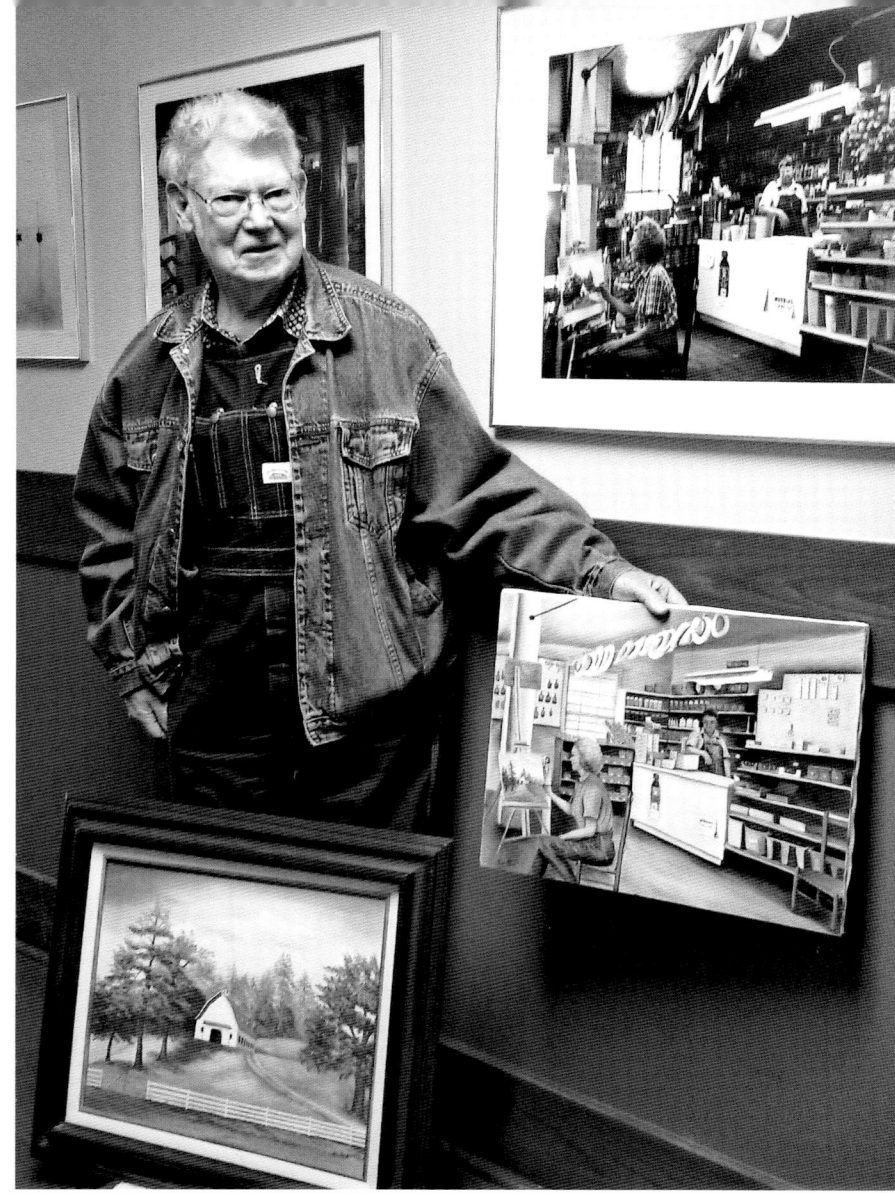

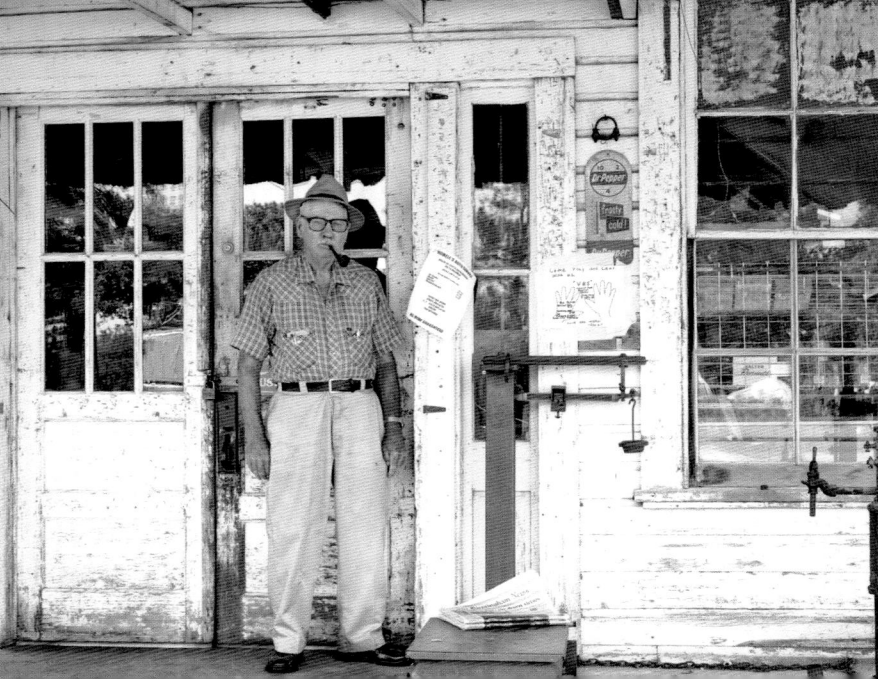

8/1/91   Contact print - Galerie E2 Dektol

4/10/94   Portriga Rapid 118 #2   20x24
F16   20 secs - burn in window
hots and ceiling highlight. dodge
right side shadowed Shelves & ceiling
dodge mrs. Marsh sl.
Sel. soft 20% LPD 1:3 80% of time

1/18/93 - Printed for David Haynie and one
extra copy - Multigrade II # 1½ filter
F16   7 secs - burn in ceiling + under sl.
dodge right side sl. - Dektol

8-3-2012 #1   16x20 Emaks #3
F11-16   14 Secs.
LPD 1:2½

Weds 7/31/1991   Noon hr.

Paul C Marsh and son General Merchandise - Locust Fork, Alabama
Dan marsh with wife Nila Cornelius Marsh
This was my first visit here when the store was open. I've always been there
on Sunday mornings before. Today I visited with Mr. and Mrs. Marsh that operate
the store. Mr. Marsh is the son of Paul C Marsh whom I photographed
already in front of the store when he dropped by while David McKaig and I
were shooting there one Sunday morning. I had a nice conversation today
with the Marsh's. Mrs. Marsh is a painter, she shows her work various places.
They had already seen the picture I did of Paul C Marsh, in fact they had
it to get it framed, so they know who I was when I introduced myself.
The picture enclosed is pretty much as it looked when I walked in. Mrs.
Marsh was busy painting and Mr. Marsh was waiting on a few customers. I met
several nice people while I was standing there with my camera. A couple of
men where just looking at the old store because they had heard about it, one
of them owns and 8X10 so we talked, then a young man walked up that
just graduated from Montevallo with a degree in Art & Photography so
we talked awhile. I gave him my card. He asked if I show my work
and I told him that I had a show at Joe Bar right now and he
said "I can't believe it, I was there last night and looked at
your show -- I loved it" .... Small world
    I promised to bring the Marsh's a contact print of this shot

Toyo 8X10 M
250 mm Fujinon W   * Front swing used for proper focus
F 64   3 secs.
T-max 400 (800 EI) I developed negs +20% over normal 400 times
T-max RS dev.   even though instructions do not call for increased time
7X Tri   when shooting at 800

Why Large Format?

Shooting large-format film is challenging, rewarding, disappointing at times, and it takes a sincere amount of dedication and discipline to get what you seek. Many people struggle to achieve acceptable results and end up quitting prior to mastering the craft. Do not give up. It takes time.

Large-format equipment is heavy, cumbersome, and must be used on a tripod. To control image distortion and depth of field requires an understanding of the camera movements. On top of this, the image on the ground glass is dim and requires a focusing loupe. If that's not hard enough, the image is upside down and in reverse. You must compose with your eyes then match the composition on your ground glass.

There is magic in large-format photography because you can perfect your image by getting any and all the depth of field you want, and you can correct for vertical and horizontal distortion. Only large-format cameras can do this. There is a reason to have camera movements. The longer the focal length of the lens, the less depth of field you can get at any given aperture. The normal lens for a full-frame DSLR is 45–50mm; on an 8x10 camera, the normal focal length is 300mm. Normal means you see the subject through the camera at about the same size as your eyes. Controlling depth of field with 300mm and it being a standard, not telephoto lens is challenging. With proper understanding of a large-format camera, you can adjust the camera movements to attain any depth of field you desire. In addition, large-format lenses stop down to F45, F64, and, in some cases for 8x10 lenses, F90 and F128.

Then there is handling the sheet film. The film holders have to be loaded in total darkness and have to be precisely put in the holder with the emulsion side up and with caution not to bend, touch, or scratch the sensitive emulsion getting the holder loaded. Processing took the same great care not to damage the exposed film A film holder takes two sheets of film. You will need multiple film holders to have enough to shoot on a photo outing. For example, six film holders lets you take twelve pictures. This means you will learn to compose more carefully and view your subject very carefully to make sure the composition is perfect before taking the picture. This discipline will improve your photography.

Once you set up your camera, you will open the lens to its widest aperture to focus through it using a focusing cloth and a focusing loupe. You will carefully take manual light readings with a handheld meter. You will adjust your camera movements to correct for distortion and to achieve the desired depth of field at the aperture you have selected.

Once your shots are taken, you will head back to a darkroom to unload your exposed film and put it in a light-tight package to send for processing—or, if you are like me, you will head straight to the darkroom to process it yourself.

It is so exciting to see your finished results on a sheet of 4x5 or 8x10 film. It is tangible, viewable. You really feel you have worked hard to achieve these results and you will be proud to stand there staring at your negatives on a light box.

Okay, so why large-format film? In addition to being razor sharp, the image size allows for wonderful enlargements without loss of quality. Here is the real reason. Film, especially in large format, delivers a tonality, contrast, and depth of tone unequaled by digital images. The feel, character, life, and emotion conveys mood. It is rich and gorgeous. It is analog and earthy. It is human, not sterile or perfect like digital. One of my digital cameras now is a 51-megapixel full-frame digital SLR, and, yes, it is sharp, but sharp is not the whole story. Film conveys humanity at its best and worst in a permanent, tangible record. Prints from large-format negatives are so rich in tone and depth that you almost feel you can walk into the scene.

With all this said, large-format photography is a discipline, a craft, an art form of its own. It is also more fun. The effort required to shoot large format is rewarded in the results and in the effort it took to produce, and it is so much fun. Composing the images, setting up the camera, processing the film, and then printing it, for me, is a lot more fun than sitting at a computer on Photoshop.

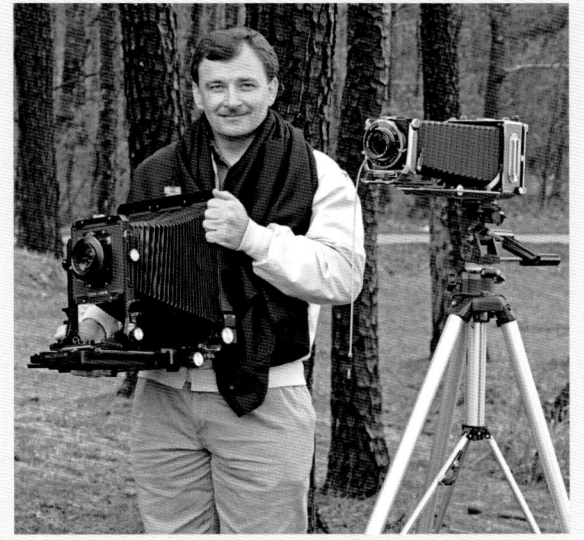

John Dersham holding Toyo 8x10M camera, with Linhof Super Technika V on tripod; photo by David McKaig.

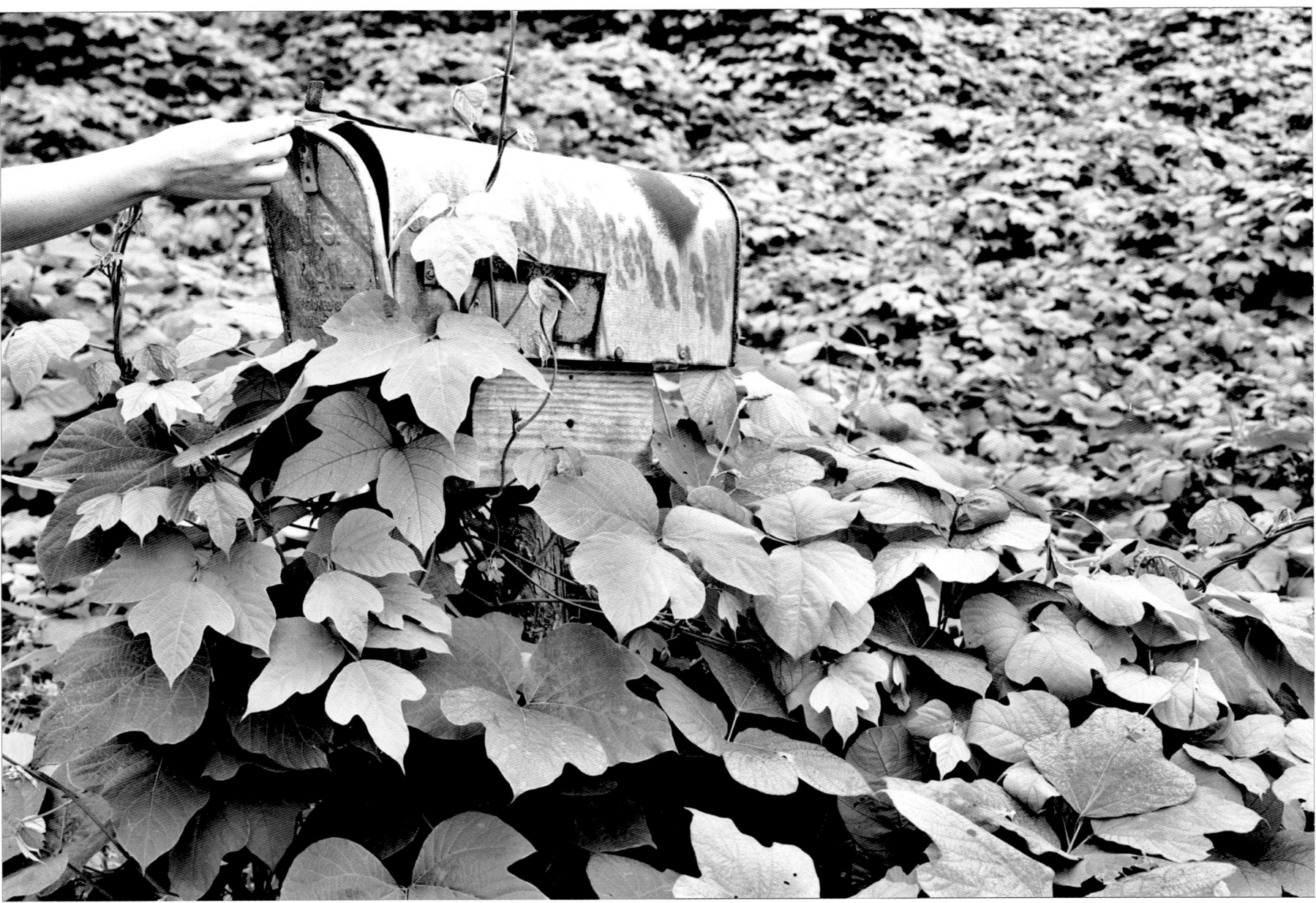

Kudzu mailbox, 8-14-1994; Toyo 8x10M camera with 5x7 back; 21 Schneider Apo Symmar lens; Kodak Tmax 400 5x7 film; Kodak Tmax RS developer.

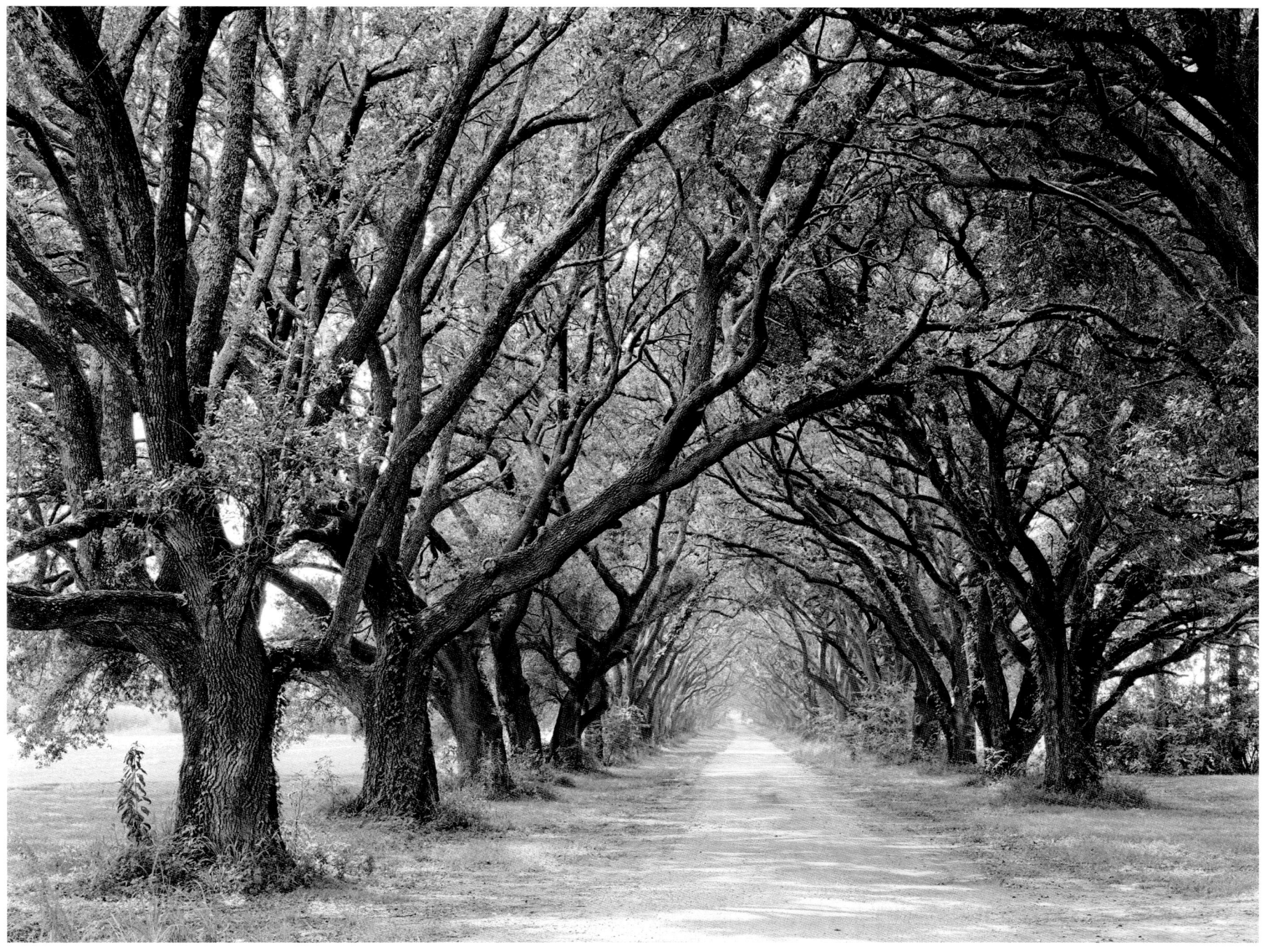

Evergreen Plantation with live oaks, Vacherie, Louisiana, 9-8-1994; Linhof Technika 4x5 camera; 120mm Schneider Super Symmar HM lens; Ilford HP5+ 4x5 film; PMK Pyro developer.

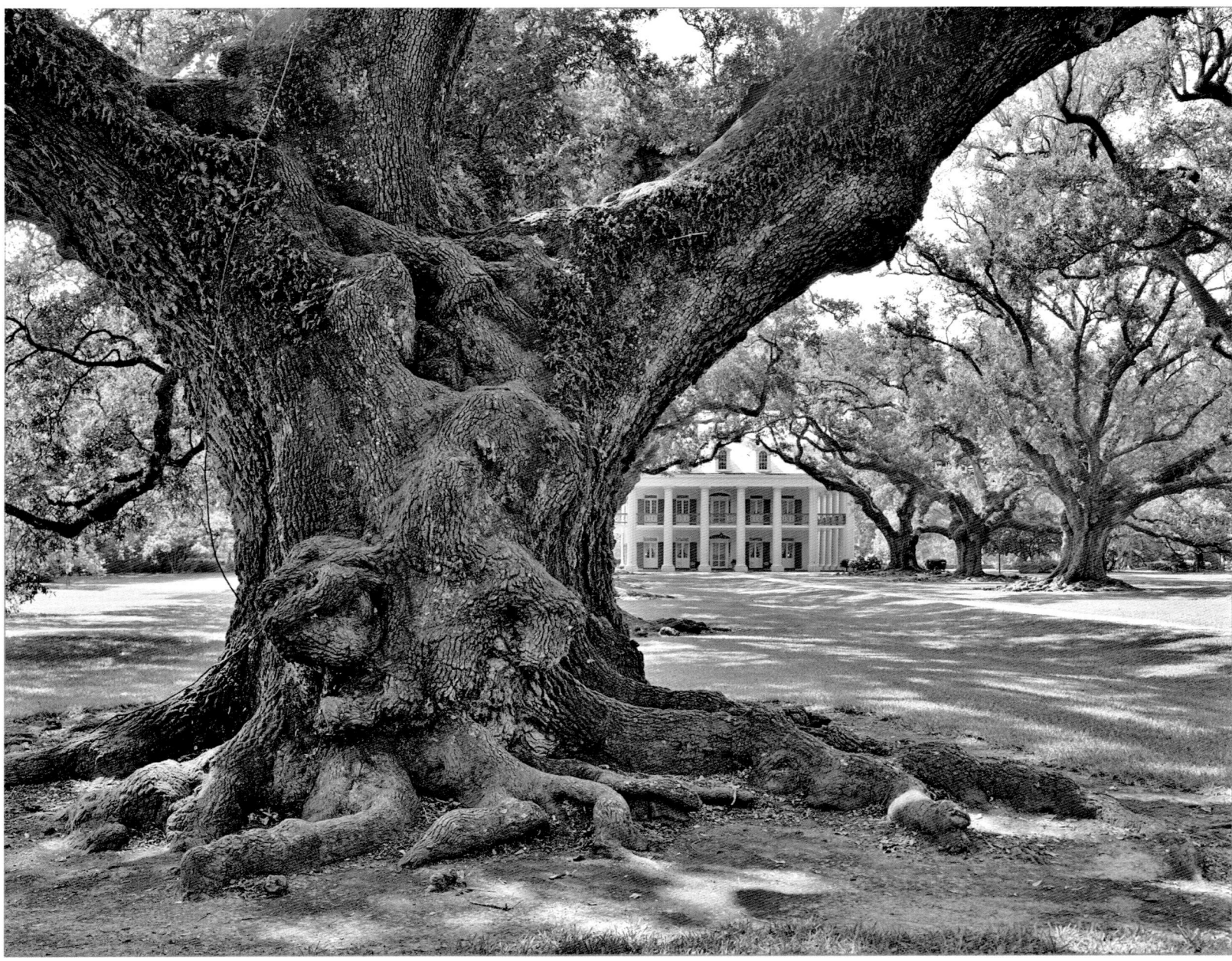

Oak Alley Plantation with 1790 live oak tree, 9-8-1994; Linhof Technika V 4x5 camera; 120mm Schneider Super Symmar HM lens; Kodak Super XX 4x5 film; PMK Pyro developer.

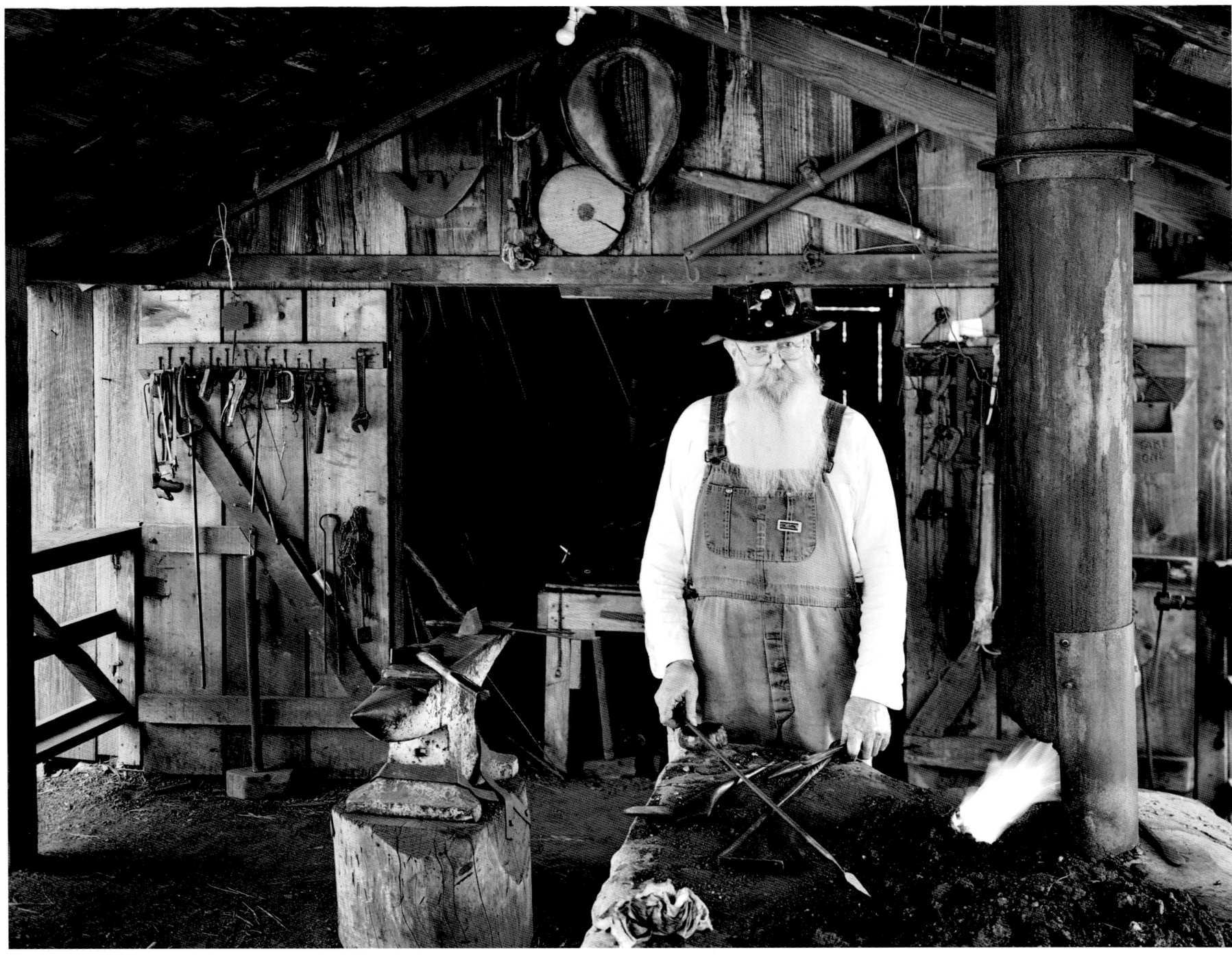

TANNEHILL

11/13/93 Galerie #2 11×14 f/6
7 secs, dodge dark areas 5/.
Sel Soft 75° Dektol 250
2 prints made one for Bill Shoemaker

7/31/93   8:00 AM hr.

Bill Shoemaker - Blacksmith
at Tannehill State Historical Park - Alabama
Bill has been a life long Blacksmith. He's been at
Tannehill on weekends for 15 years.
He is a computer programer for a medical supply
company in Tusc for a living ... What a
Contrast !!

Toyo 8×10 m

250 Fujinon WS
T-max 100   100 EI
N/E

F 22 ^ 32   3 secs.

Pyro PMK dev.

7X Tripod 3051

❋ Bill made me a nice metal leaf
    I'll make him a print

    Base   0.12
    Fix   1.89
    board   1.22
    Shirt   1.43

❋ Interesting story. I first printed negative 1 in 1993 thinking
it was the best of the two negatives. The exposure was 3 sec. and the
image was not perfect due to Bill shoemaker moving a little. I never
showed this print because it was not razor sharp. Now 21 years
later I scanned negative #2 and it is perfect giving me an
image I always wanted but did not think I got. I will now
print #2 and start showing it.
2-16-2014
                                                    John Dewbar

Facing page, and negative sleeve, this page: Bill Shoemaker,
blacksmith at Tannehill State Park, Alabama, 7-31-1993; Toyo 8x10M
camera; 250mm Fujinon WS lens; Kodak Tmax 100 8x10 film; PMK Pyro
developer.

#1,2
2-16-2014 32000 16 B&C

#2 Scanned 9-23-2020 Tiff 24000 48 B&C

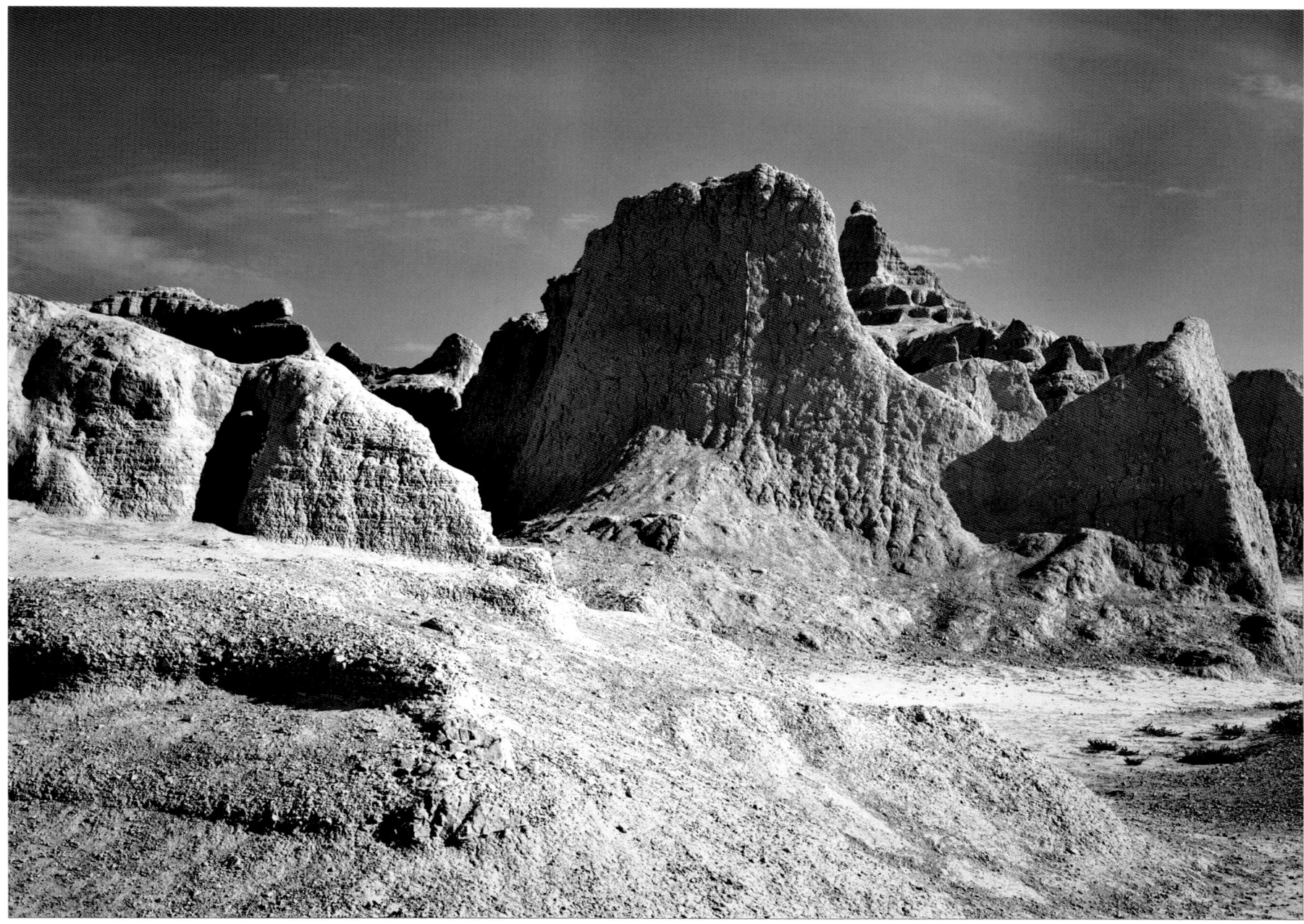

Above: Badlands of South Dakota, 6-1990; Toyo 8x10M camera; 300mm Schneider Xenar lens; yellow K2 filter; Kodak Tmax 100 8x10 film; Kodak Tmax RS developer.

Facing page: Mussels, Locust Fork of the Black Warrior River, Alabama, 8-25-1991; Linhof Technika V 4x5 camera; 210mm Schneider Apo Symmar lens; Kodak Tmax 100 4x5 film; Kodak Tmax RS developer.

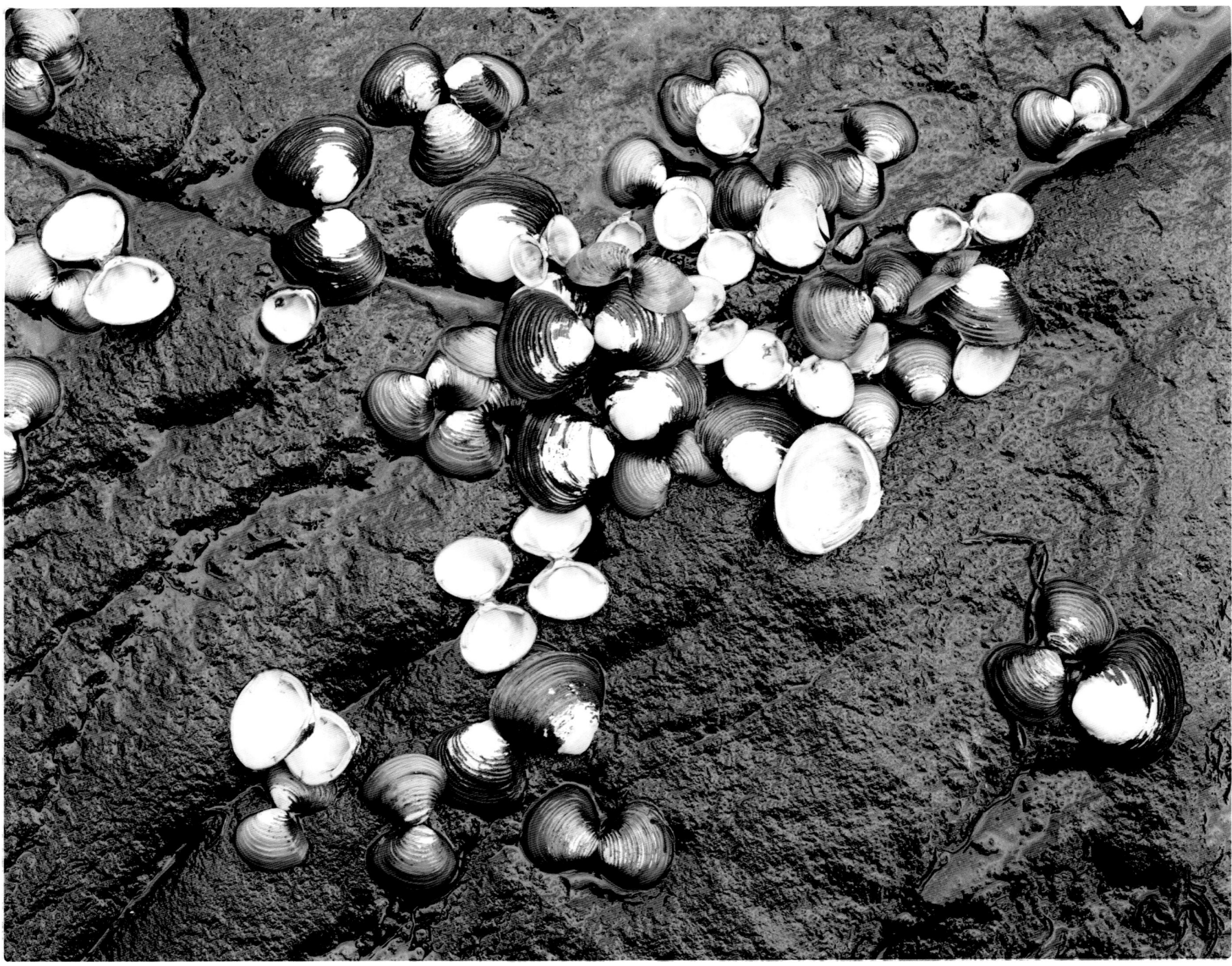

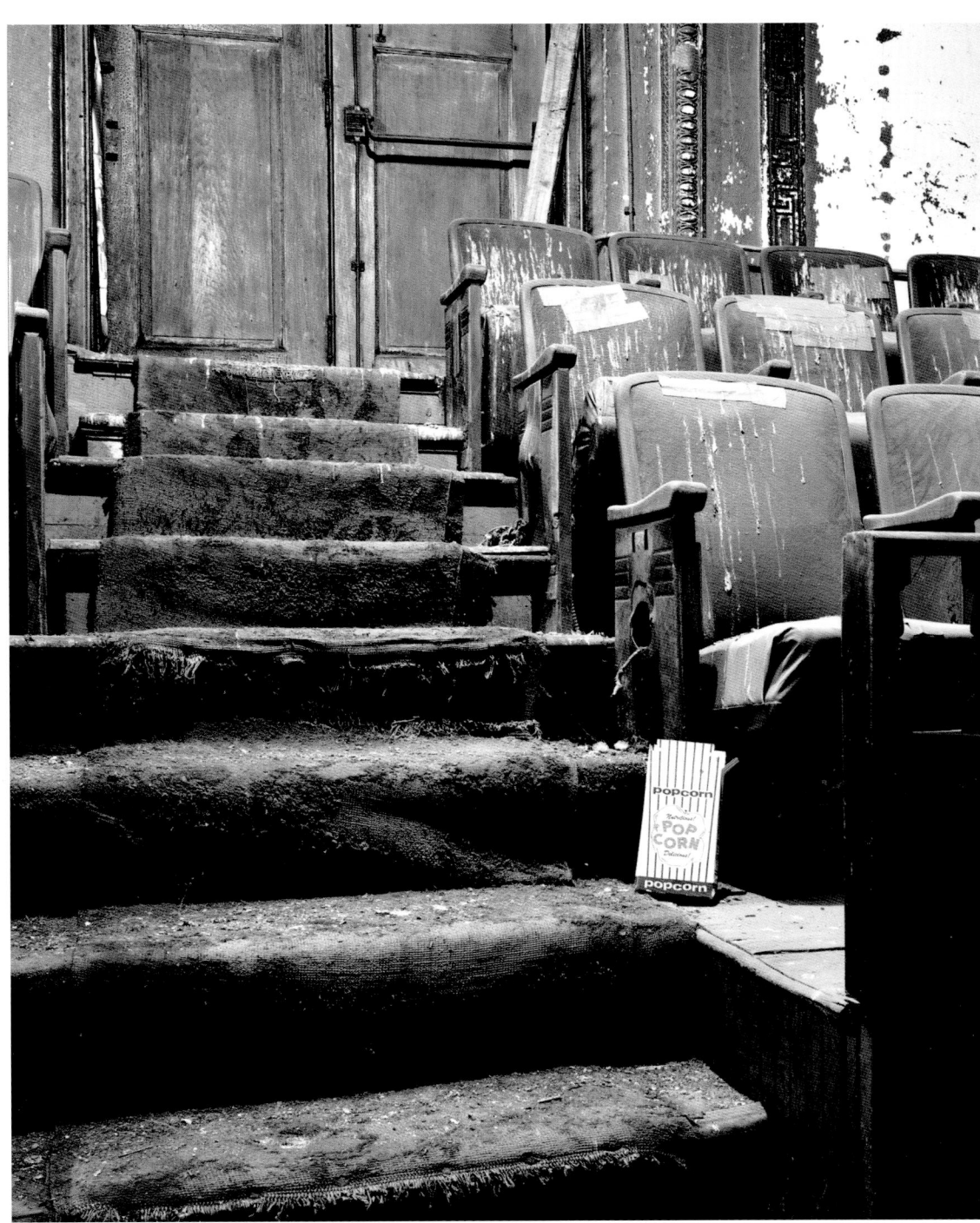

Right: Lyric Theatre, Birmingham, Alabama, 7-10-1993; Linhof Technika V camera; 120mm Schneider Super Symmar HM lens; Kodak Tmax 100 4x5 film; PMK Pyro developer.

Facing page: Lyric Theater, 7-10-1993; Toyo 8x10M camera; 250mm Fujinon WS lens; Ilford HP5+ 8x10 film; PMK Pyro developer

(The 1914 Lyric has since been restored.)

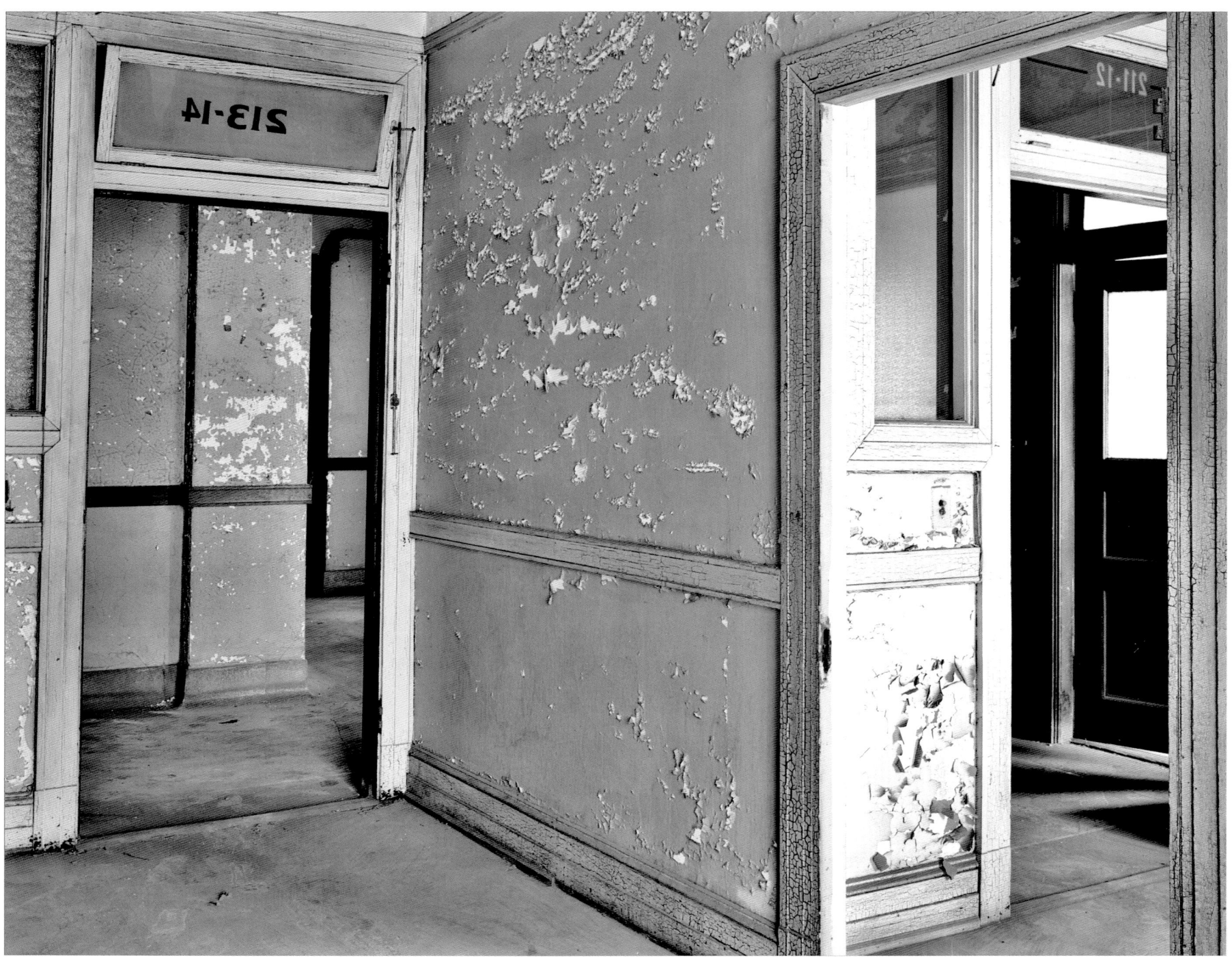

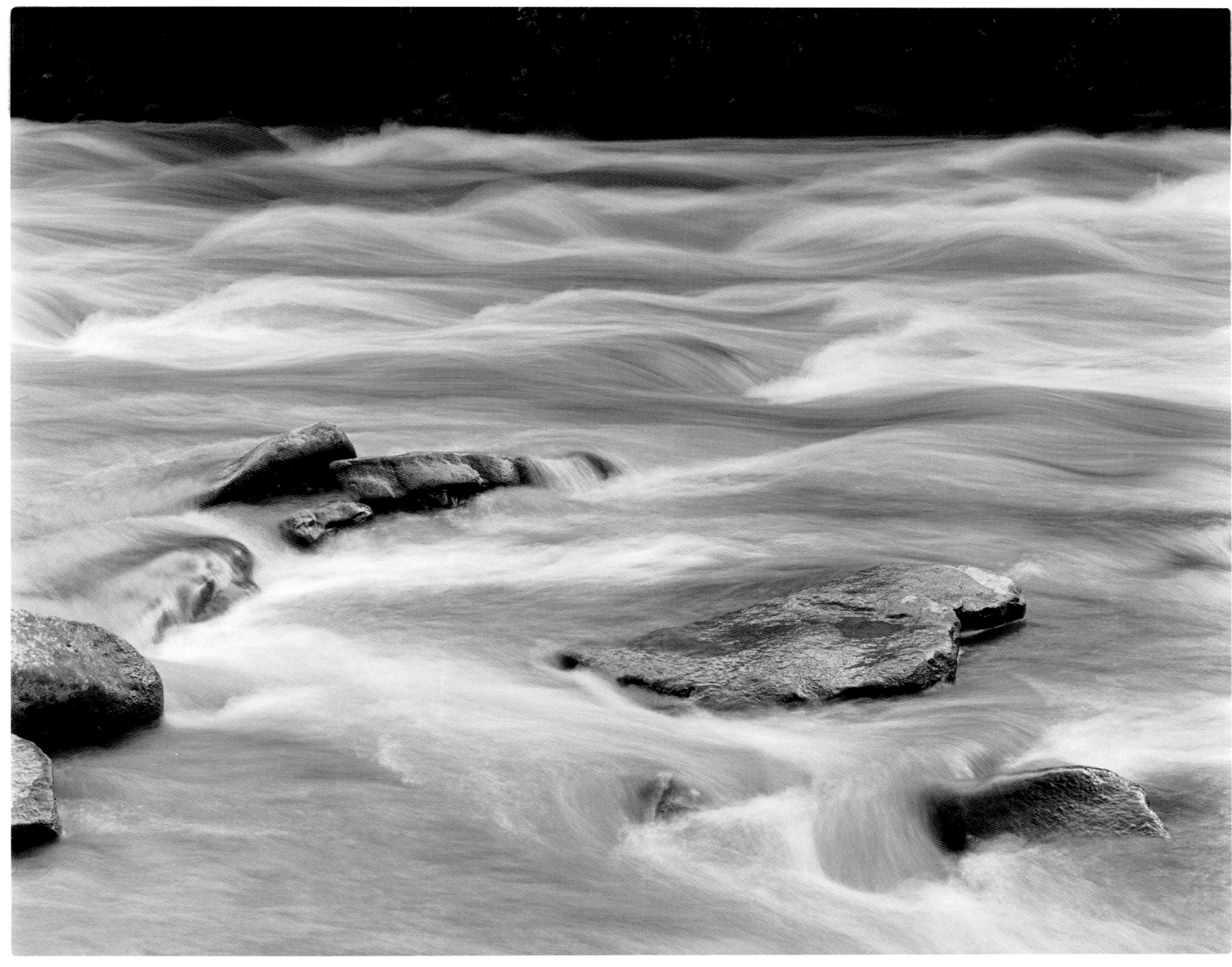

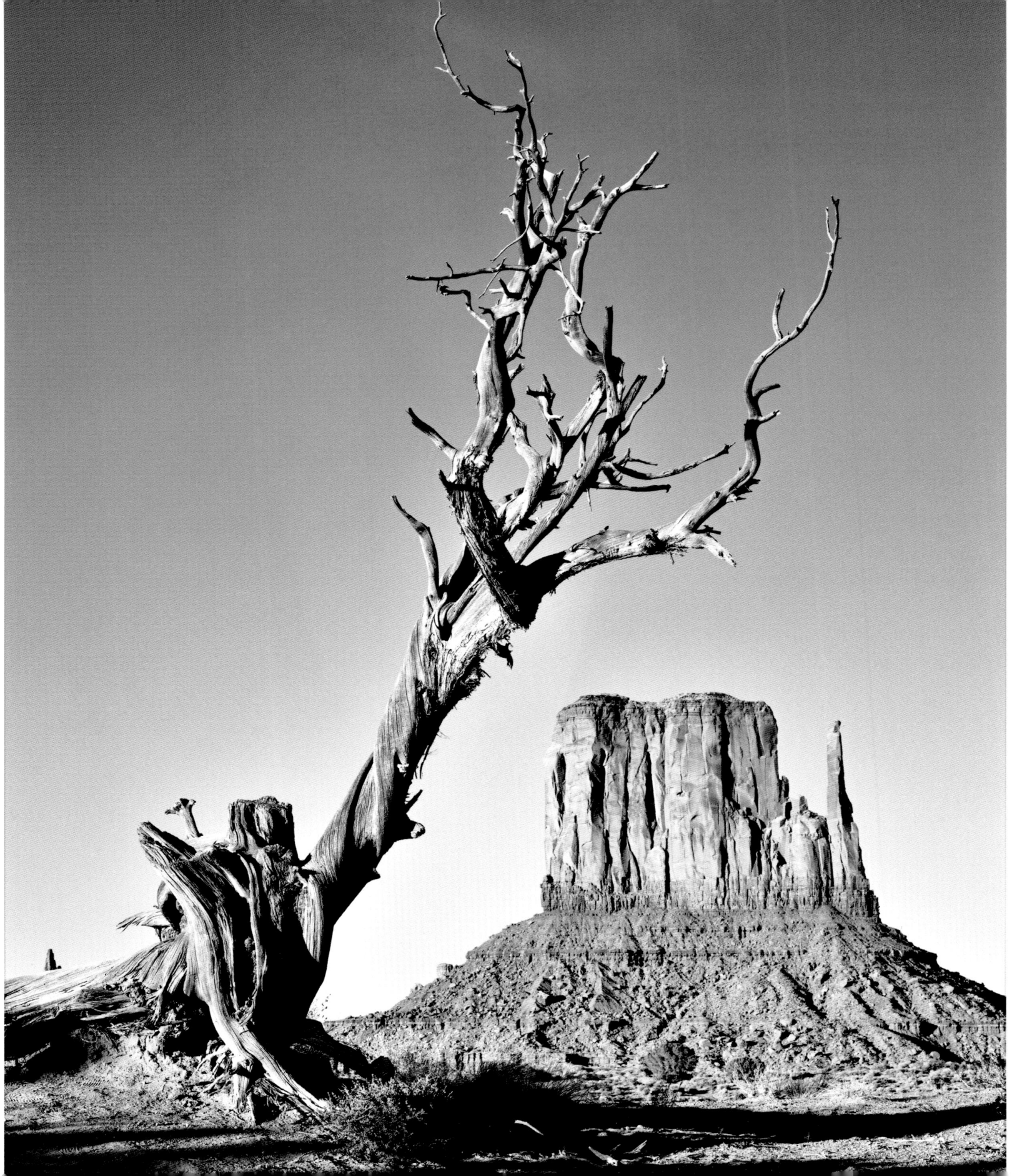

Left: Dead juniper at Monument Valley, Utah, 10-5-1993; Linhof Technika V 4x5 camera; 150mm Nikkor lens; yellow G filter; Kodak Tmax 100 4x5 film; PMK Pyro developer.

Facing page: Locust Fork of the Black Warrior River, Alabama; 5-7-1994; Linhof Technika V 4x5 camera; 120mm Schneider Super Symmar HM lens; Kodak Tmax 100 4x5. film; PMK Pyro developer.

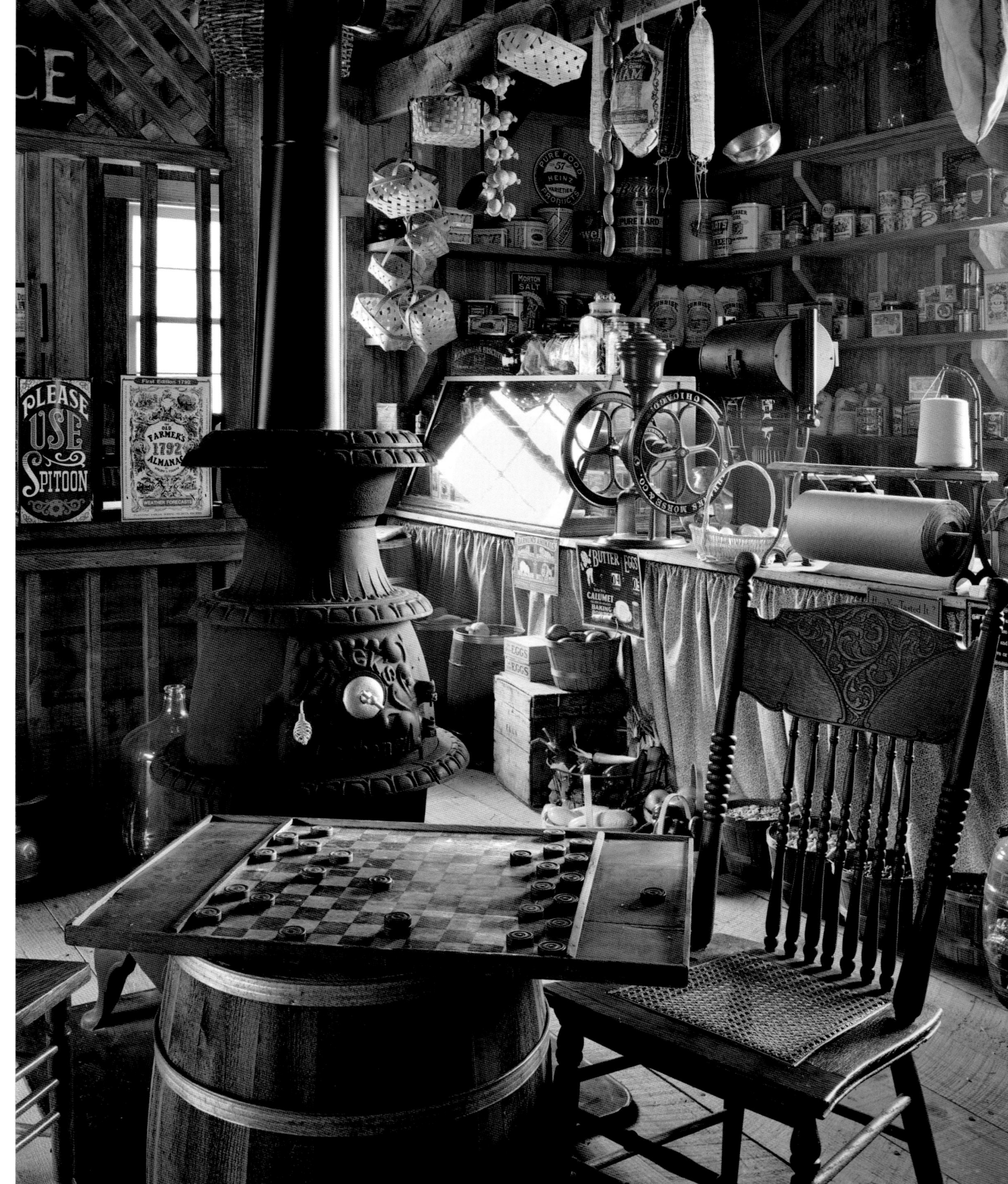

Kimberly Clarke,
Old Alabama Town,
Childersburg,
Alabama, 2-2-1992;
Linhof Technika
V 4x5 camera;
120mm Schneider
Super Symmar HM
lens; Kodak Tmax
100 4x5 film; Kodak
Tmax RS developer.

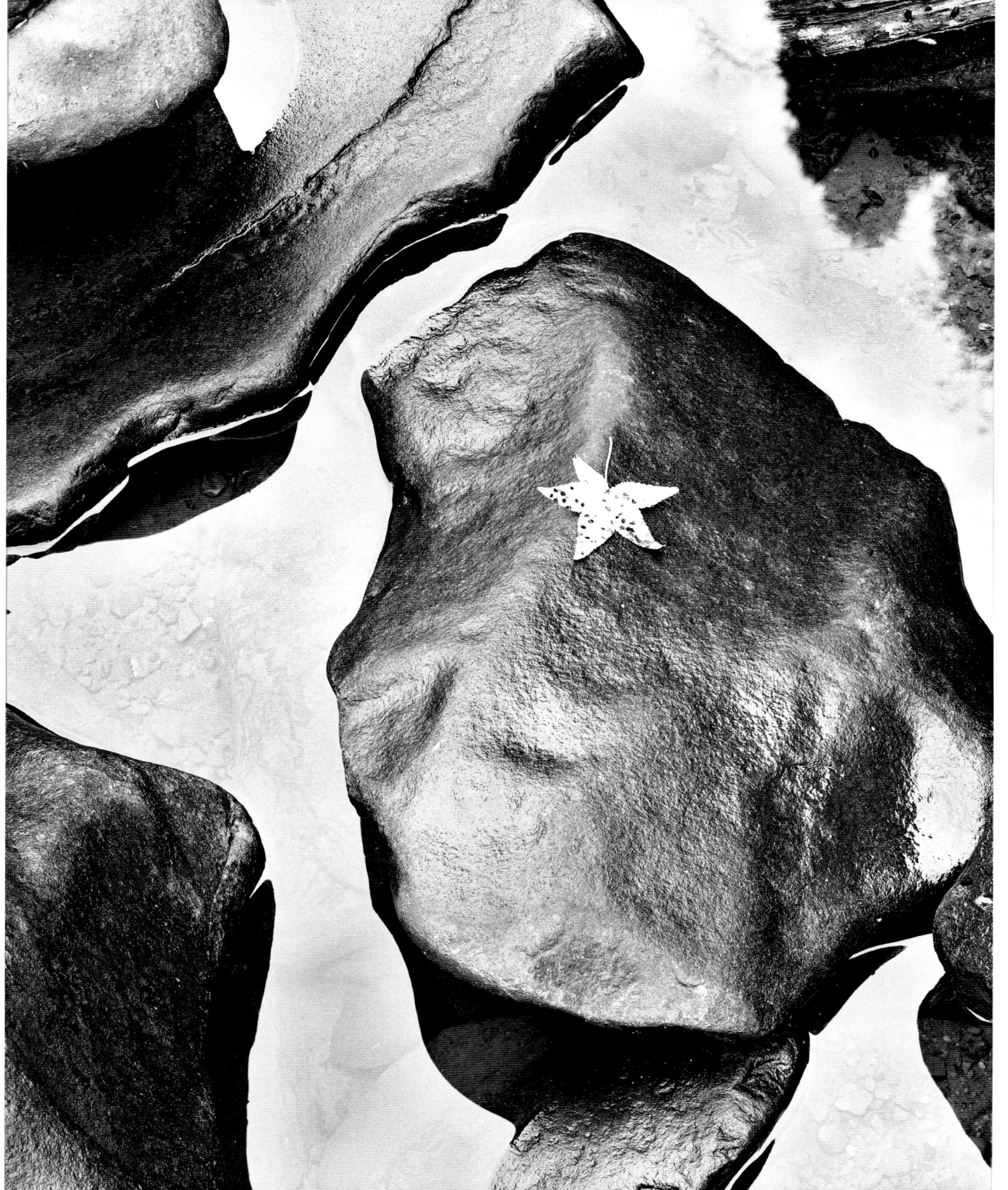

Yellow fall sweet
gum leaf on wet rock
in the Locust Fork
of the Black Warrior
River, Locust Fork,
Alabama, 9-16-1995;
Linhof Technika 4x5
camera; 210mm
Schneider Apo
Symmar lens;
Kodak Tmax 100
film; Kodak Tmax RS
developer.

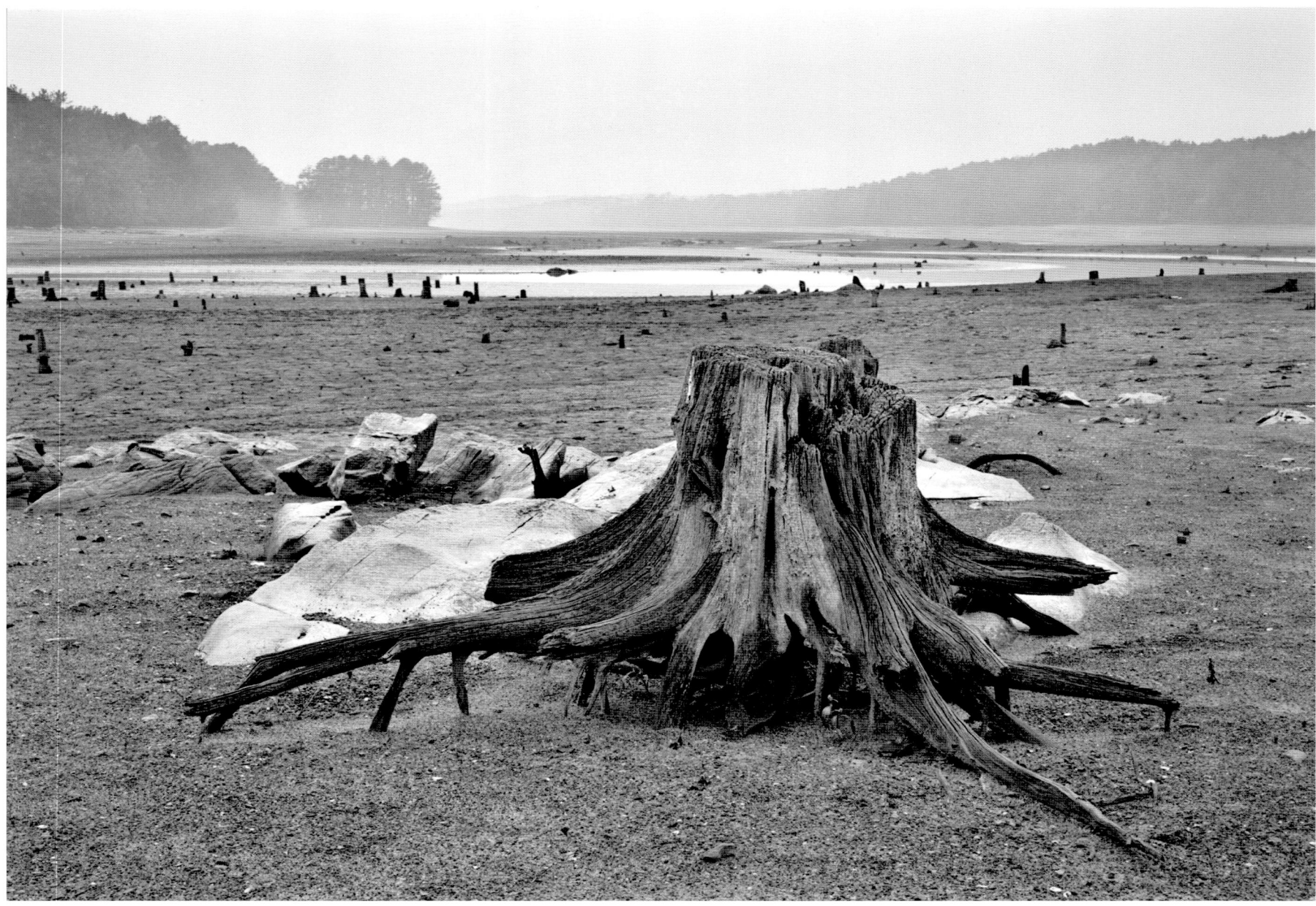

Above: Lake Purdy, Birmingham, Alabama, 11-3-1993; Toyo 8x10M camera with 5x7 back; 210mm Schneider Apo Symmar lens; Kodak Tmax 400 5x7 film; PMK Pyro developer.

Facing page: River bottom next to Missouri River, near Jefferson City, Missouri, 11-1994; Toyo 8x10M camera with 5x7 back; 210mm Schneider Apo Symmar lens; Kodak Tmax 400 5x7 film; PMK Pyro developer.

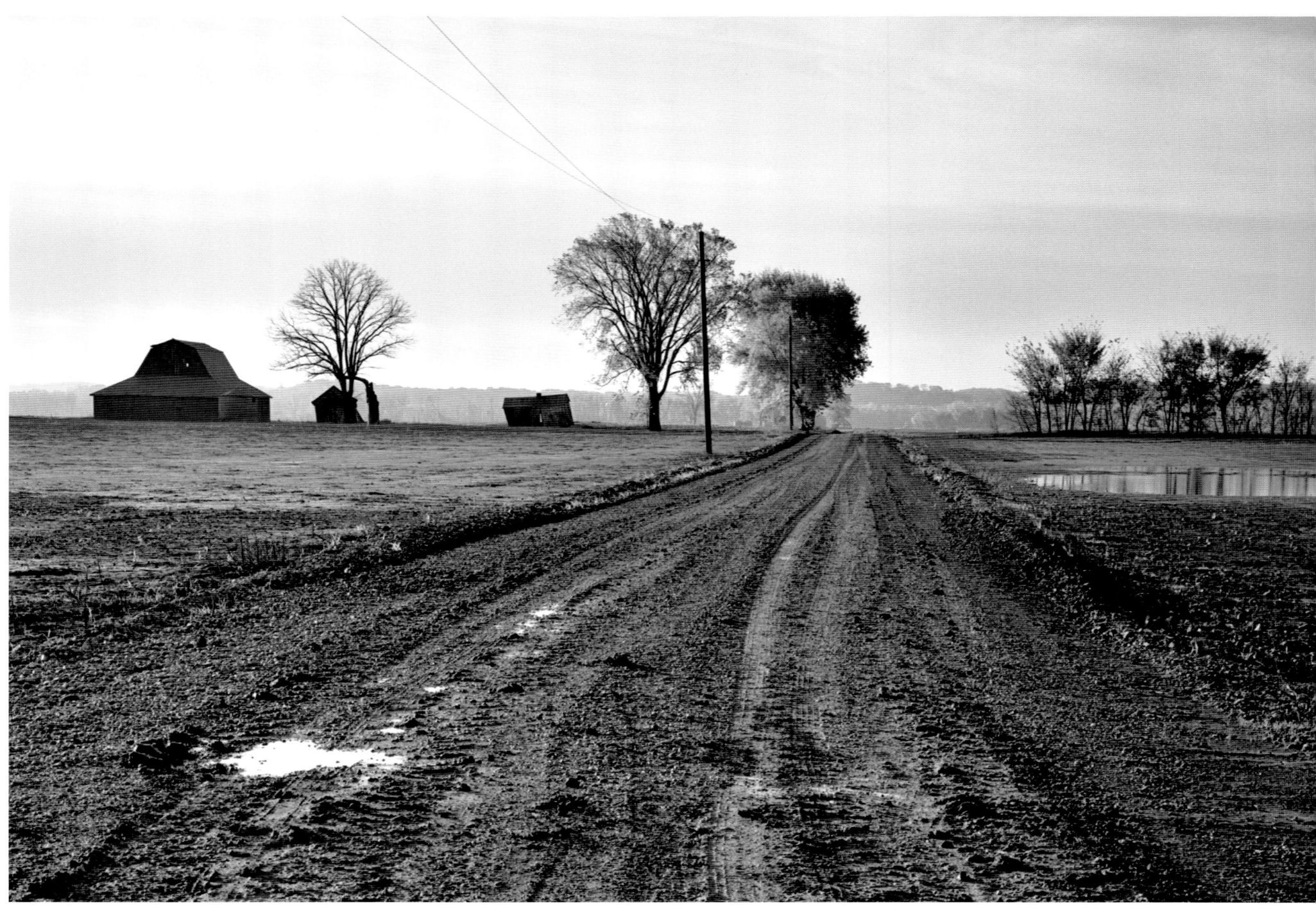

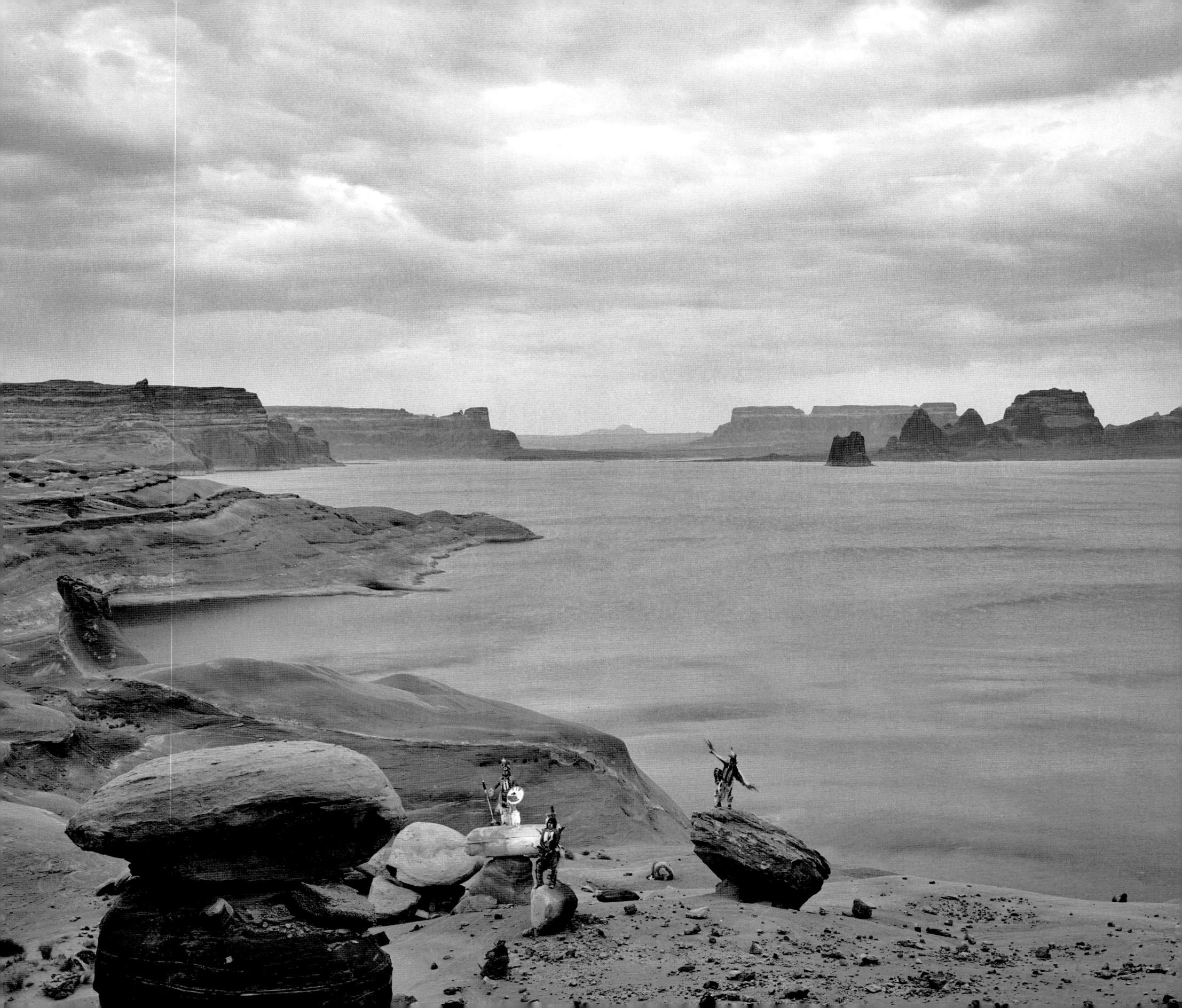

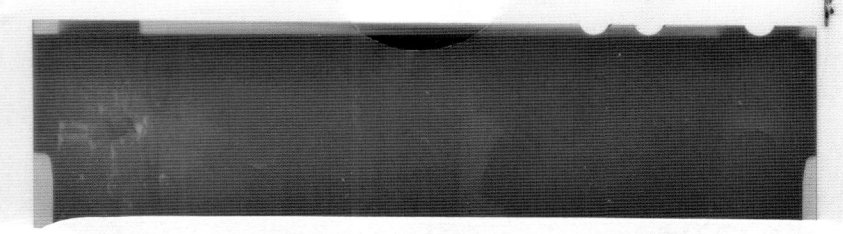

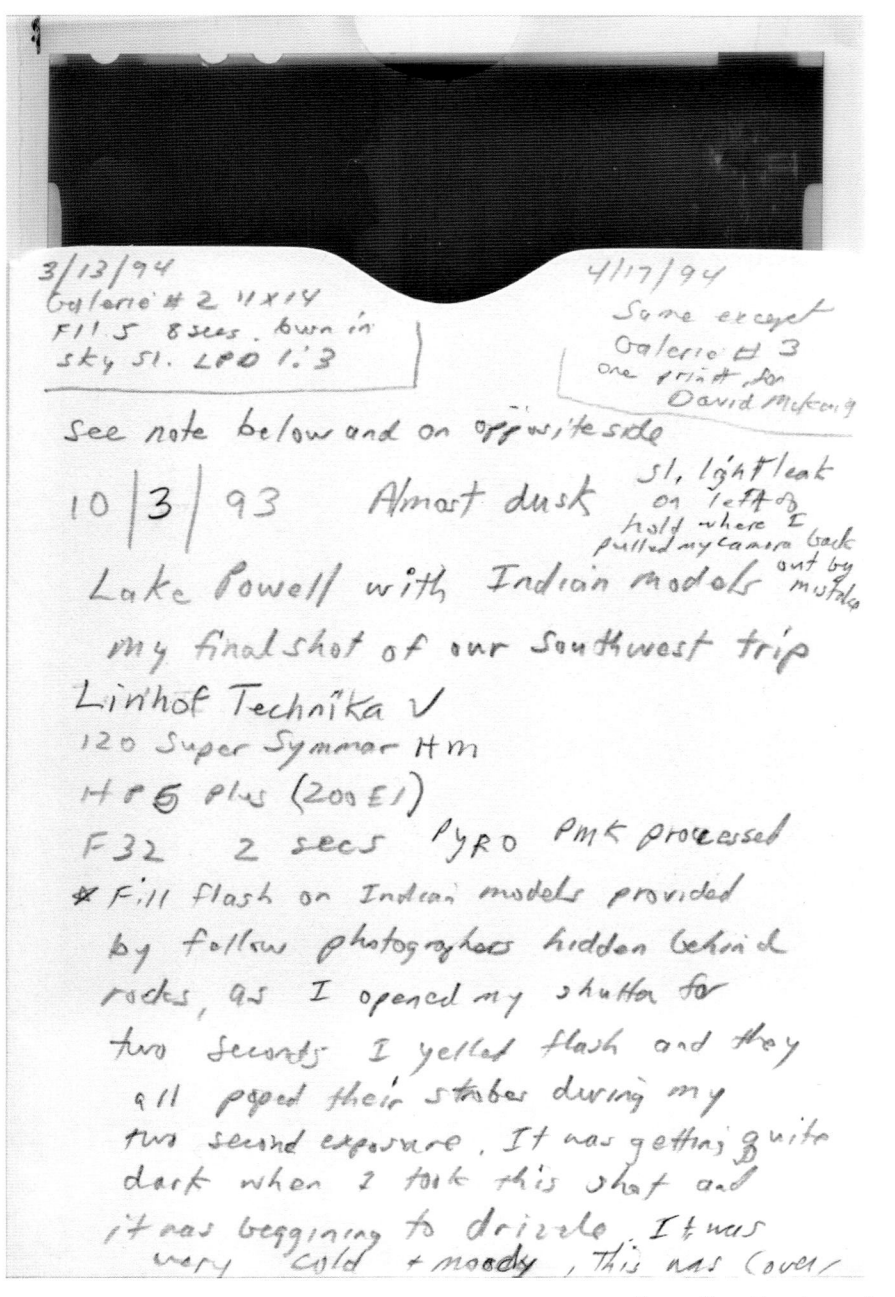

3/13/94
Galerie # 2 11x14
F11 5 8 secs. burn in
sky, sl. LBD 1.3

4/17/94
Same except
Galerie # 3
one print for
David McKenng

See note below and on opposite side

10/3/93   Almost dusk   sl. light leak
on left of
hold where I
pulled my camera back
out by
mistake

Lake Powell with Indian models

my final shot of our Southwest trip

Linhof Technika V
120 Super Symmar HM
HP5 plus (200 EI)
F32   2 secs   Pyro PMK processed

*Fill flash on Indian models provided
by fellow photographers hidden behind
rocks, as I opened my shutter for
two seconds I yelled flash and they
all popped their strobes during my
two second exposure. It was getting quite
dark when I took this shot and
it was beginning to drizzle. It was
very cold + moody, this was (over

4/18/98 # 2 ex. Boy and a man in out photo of the neg.
Multigrade # 3 11x14 # 4. F11 8 sec - burn in sky, sl
Dektol

Scanned 12-1-2010 16.6:t -3200 Opt
Scanned 5-5-2020 Tiff 6400.11 4813 B+W
48 B+W Color

The only cloudy cold weather on
the whole trip and it came just
in time for this moody shot.

This sheet of film was not
processed until yesterday 3/12/94.
I had stuck it away and
had assumed it to be blank
because the other side of the
holder that I processed the day
after I returned from the trip appeared
double exposed. I was very
disappointed because I felt this
was one of my better shots on
the trip, the other people
commented that they thought
this shot was going to be fantastic!
They loved my fill flash idea on
the Indians. Yesterday I spent
some time processing some odds +
ends that I already had a good
negative of, I decided to do this one
& I got a big SURPRISE!!

Above: Negative sleeve, front and back, for Lake Powell.

Facing Page: Lake Powell with Navajo Indian models for Kodak Photography workshop with Robert Huntzinger (I served as the Kodak host), 10-3-1993; Linhof Technika V 4x5 camera; 120mm Schneider Super Symmar HM lens; Ilford HP5+ 4x5 film; PMK Pyro developer.

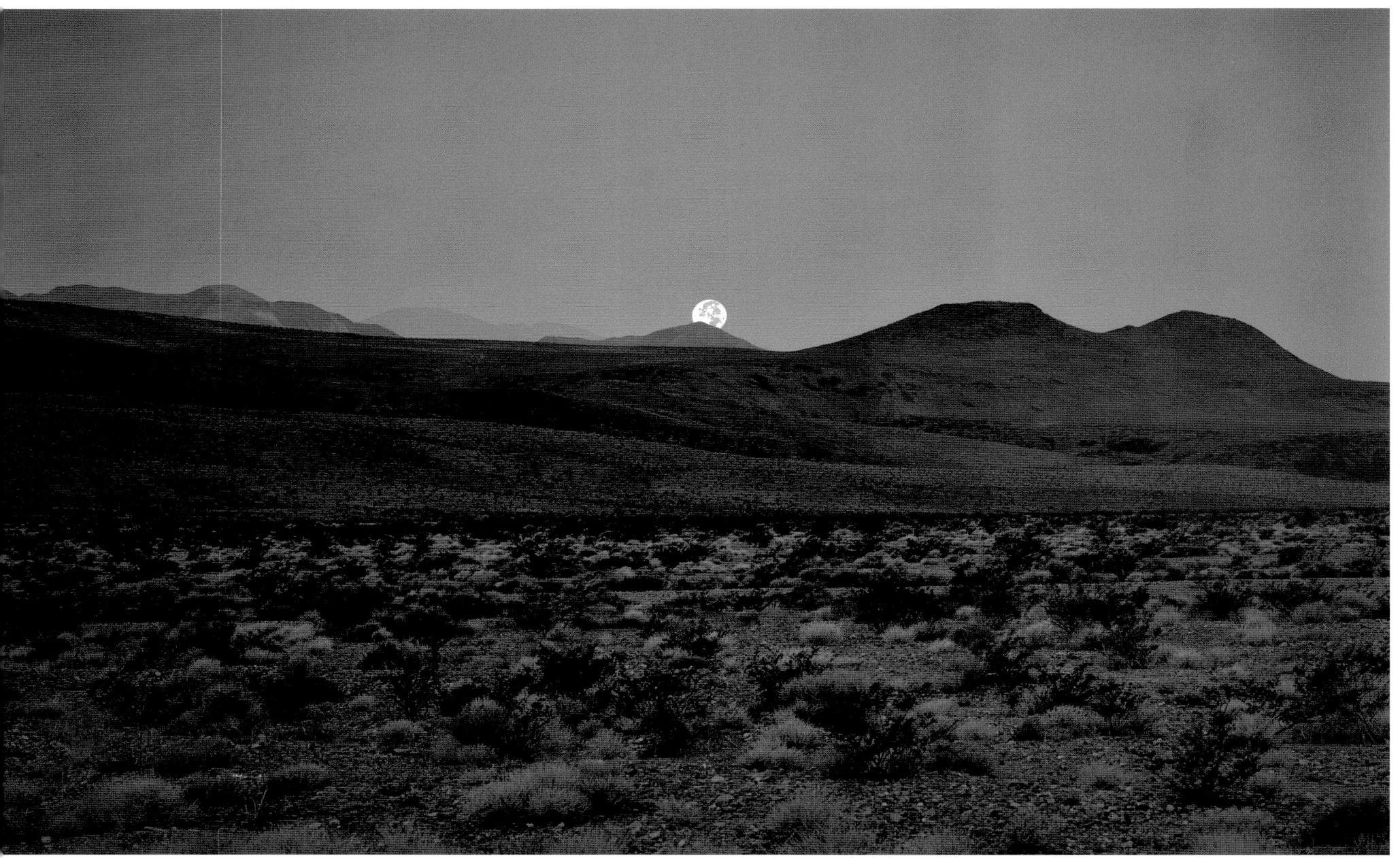

Moonset over Death Valley, California, 9-27-1999; Linhof Technika V 4x5 camera; 300mm Schneider Xenar lens; Ilford HP5+ 4x5 film; PMK Pyro developer.

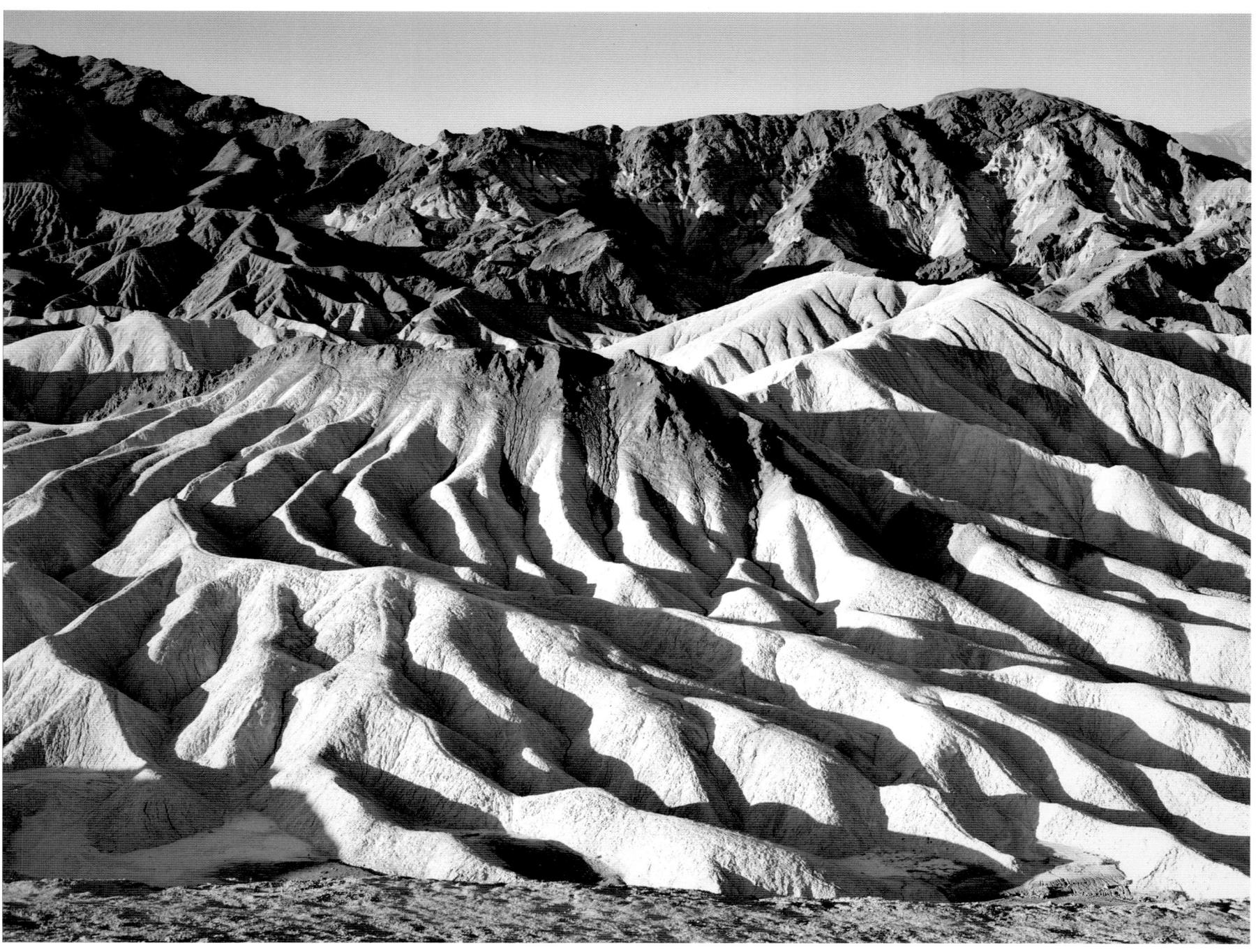

Death Valley, Calfornia, 9-26-1999; Linhof Technika V 4x5 camera; 210mm Schneider Apo Symmar lens; yellow K2 filter; Ilford HP5+ 4x5 film; PMK Pyro developer.

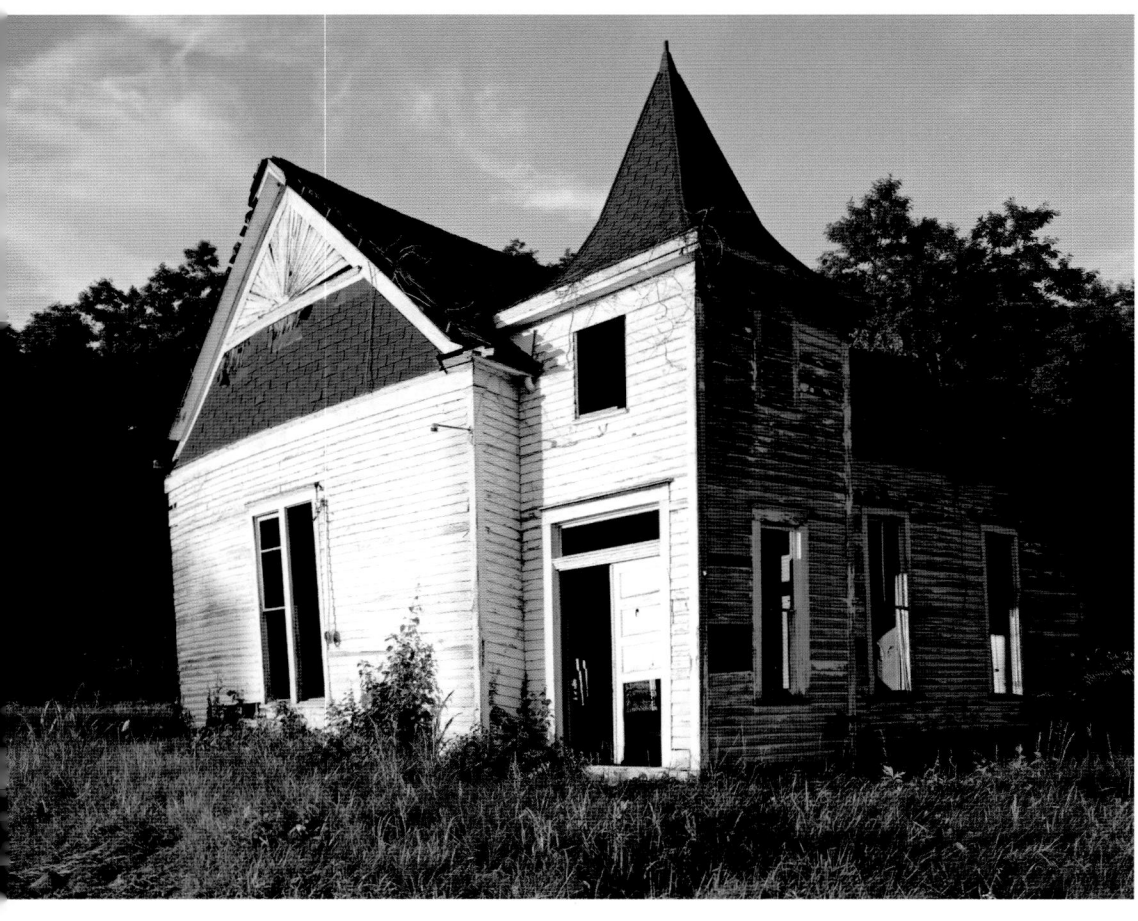

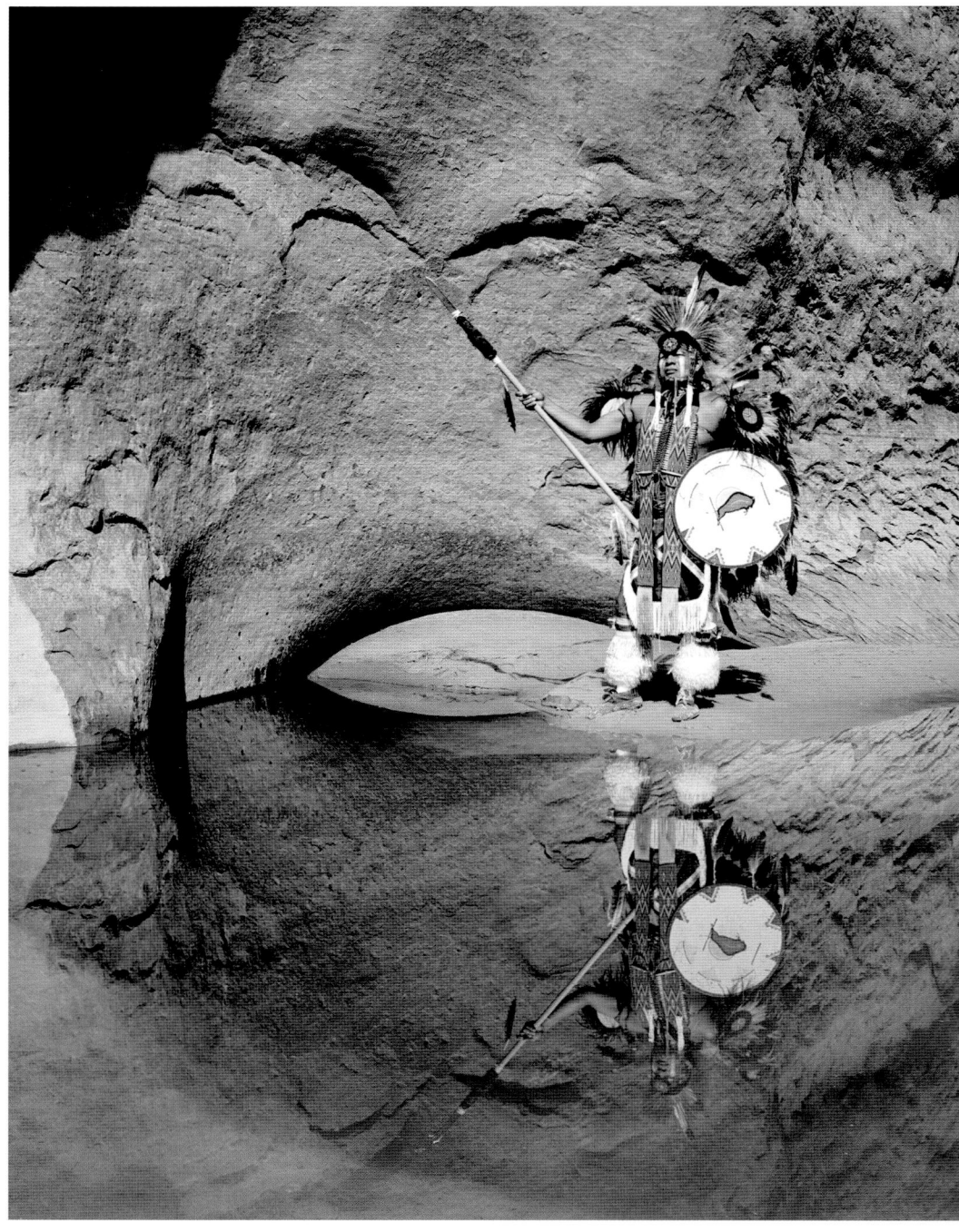

Above: Abandoned church in Rocheport, Missouri, 6-1991; Linhof Technika
V 4x5 camera; 120mm Schneider Super Symmar HM lens; yellow K2 filter;
Kodak Tmax 100 4x5 film; Kodak Tmax RS developer.

Right: Navajo American model, West Canyon, Lake Powell, Arizona, 10-3-
1993: Linhof Technika V 4x5 camera; 150mm Nikkor lens; Ilford HP5+, 4x5
film; PMK Pyro developer

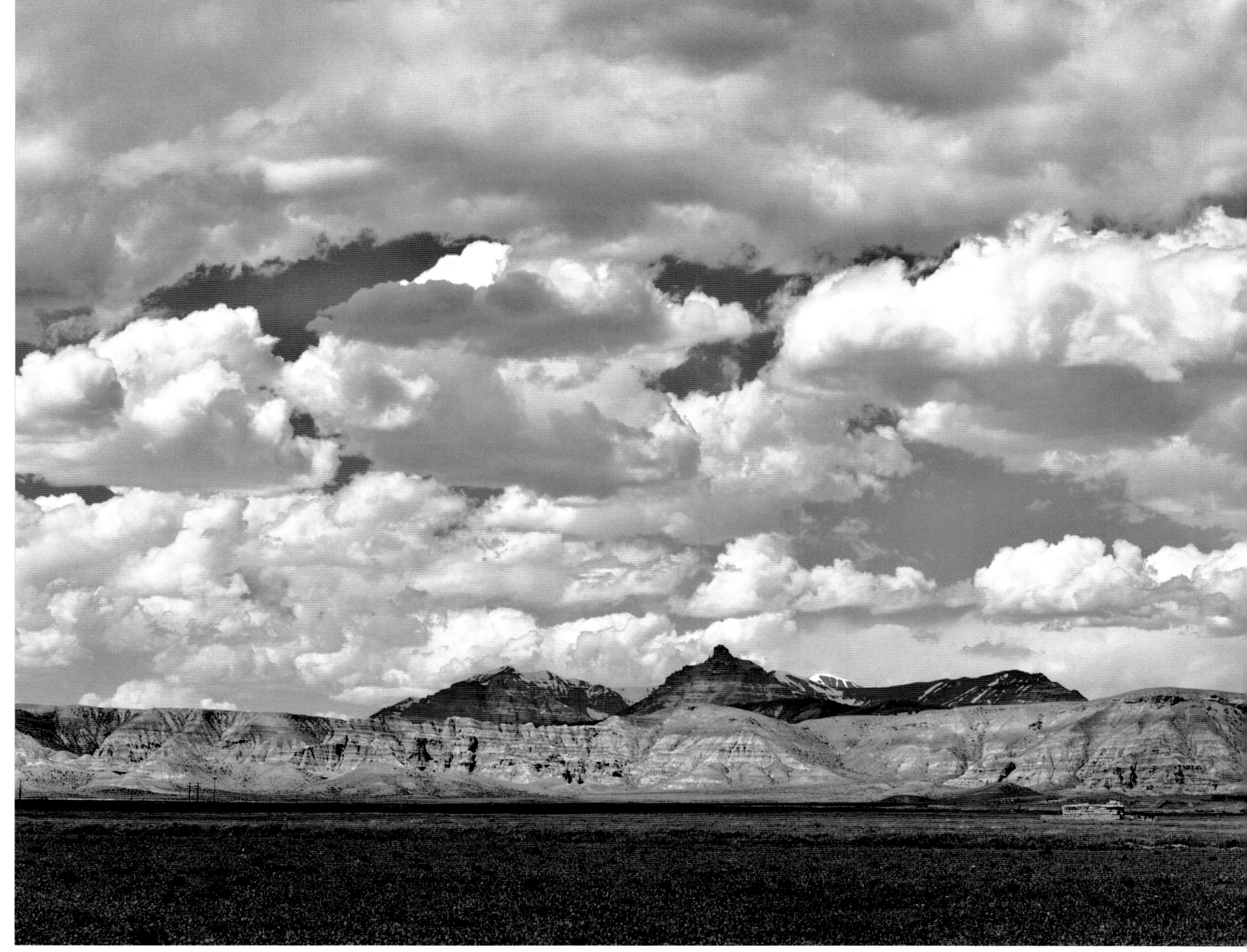

Rural scene near Dubois, Wyoming, 6-1990; Linhof Technika V 4x5 camera; 300mm Schneider Xenar lens; yellow G filter; Kodak Tmax 100 4x5 film; Kodak Tmax RS developer.

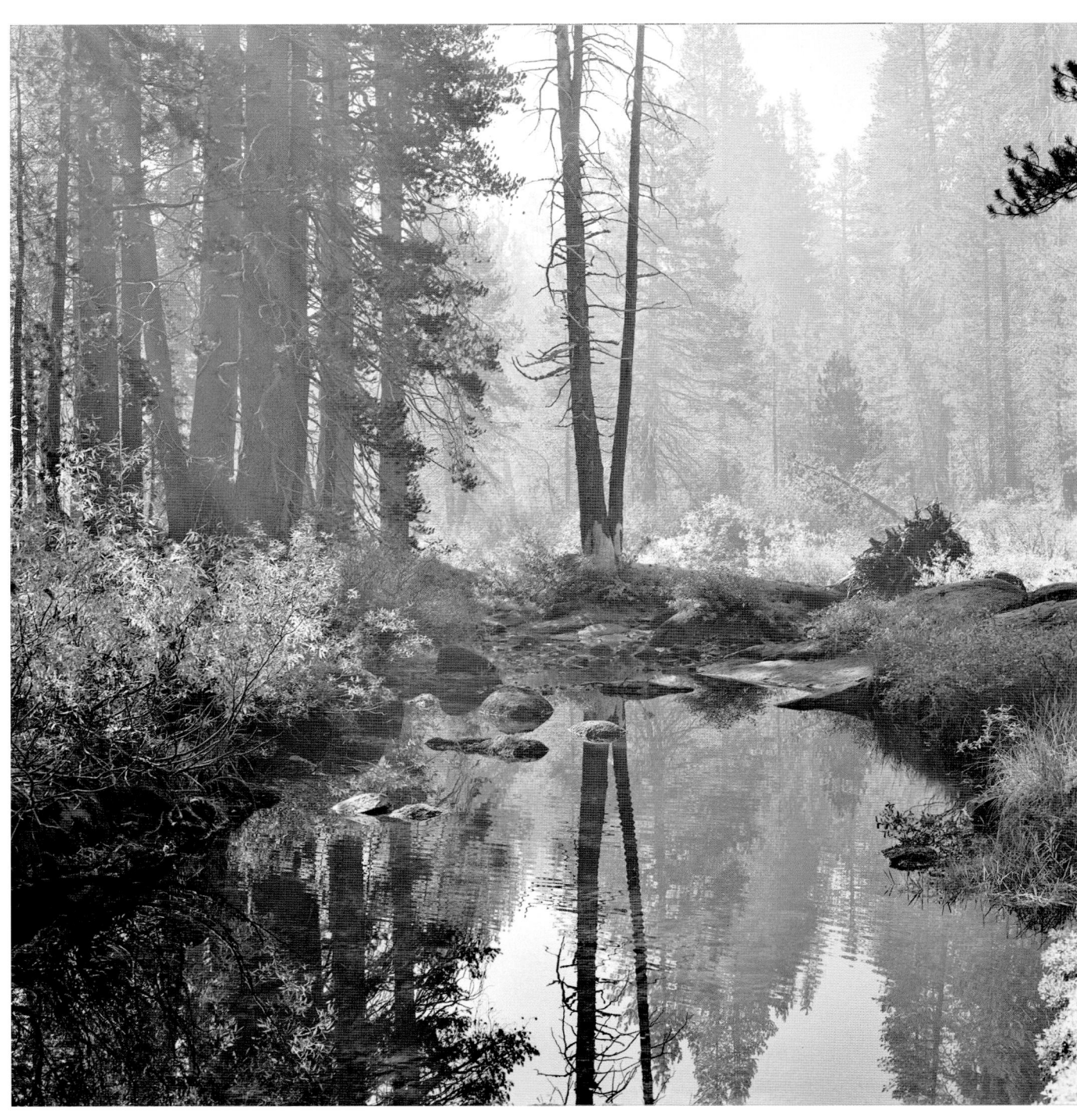

Yosemite National Park, California, 9-1999; Hasselblad camera; 80mm Zeiss Planar lens; Ilford HP5+ 120 film; PMK Pyro developer.

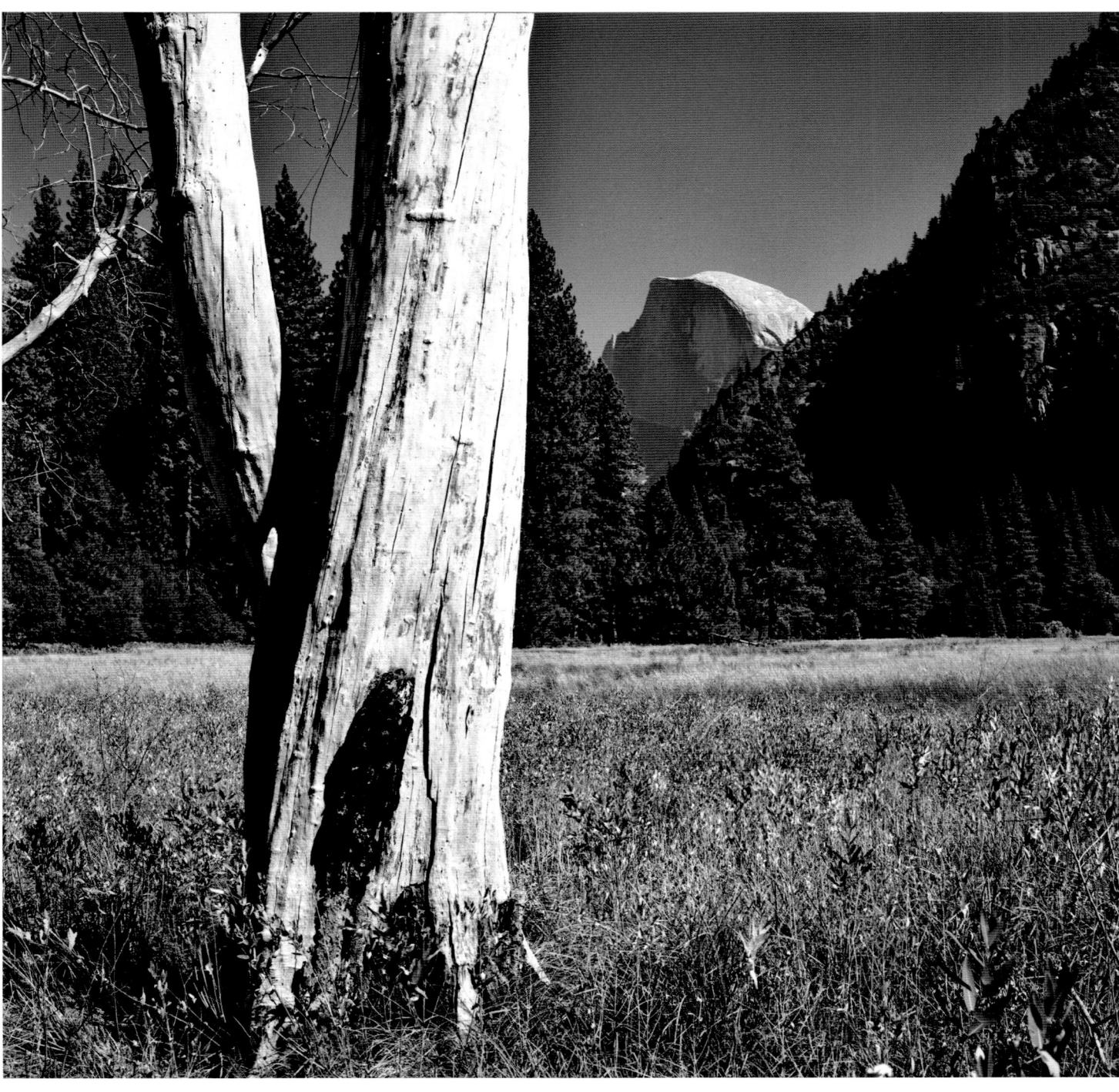

Yosemite Valley, Yosemite
National Park, California,
9-1999; Hasselblad camera;
80mm Zeiss Planar lens;
orange filter; Kodak Tmax 100
120 film; PMK Pyro developer.

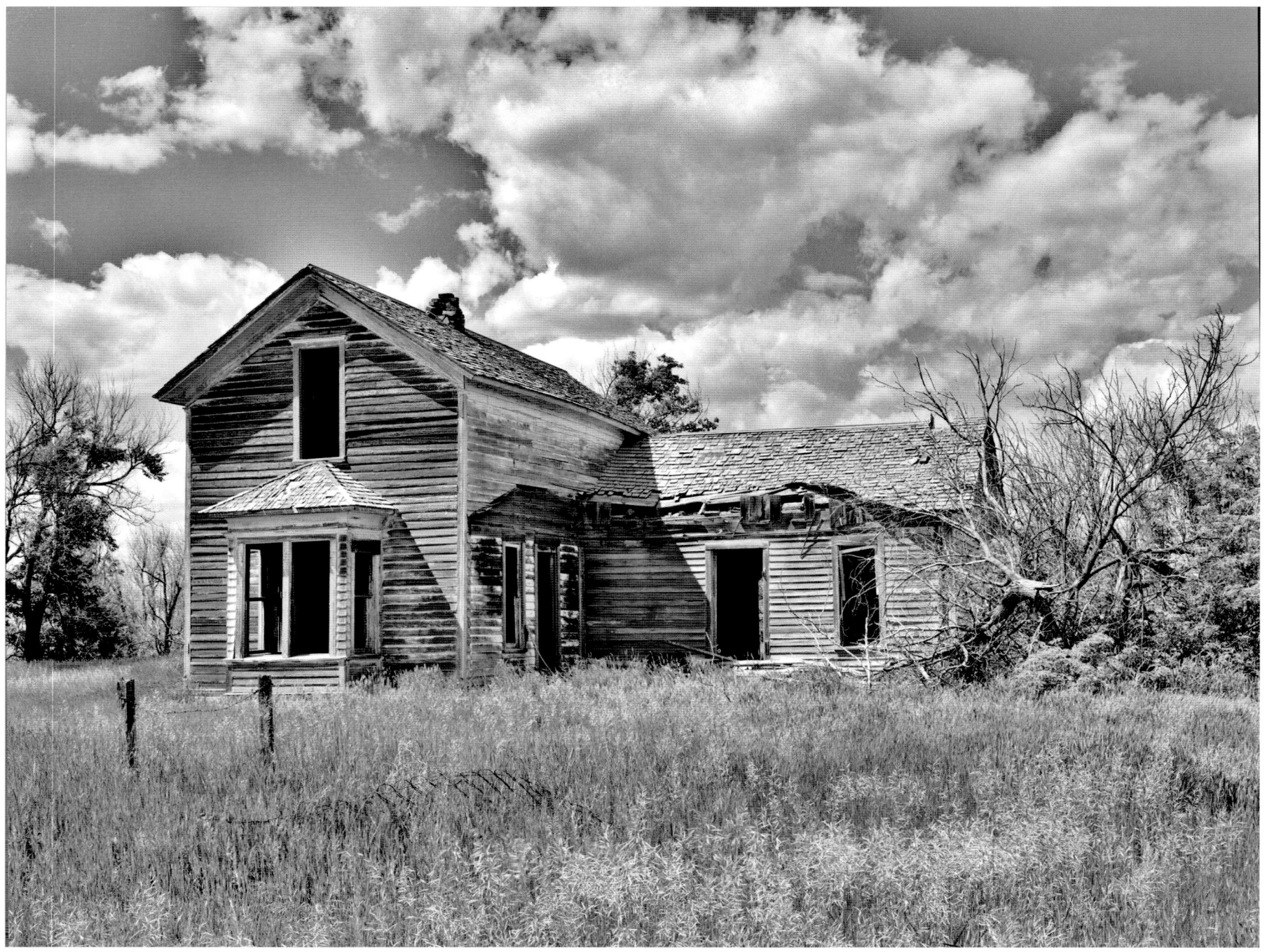

Homestead in rural Nebraska, 6-22-1990; Linhof Technika V 4x5 camera; 150mm Schneider Symmar S lens; yellow K2 filter; Kodak Tmax 100 4x5 film; Kodak Tmax RS developer.

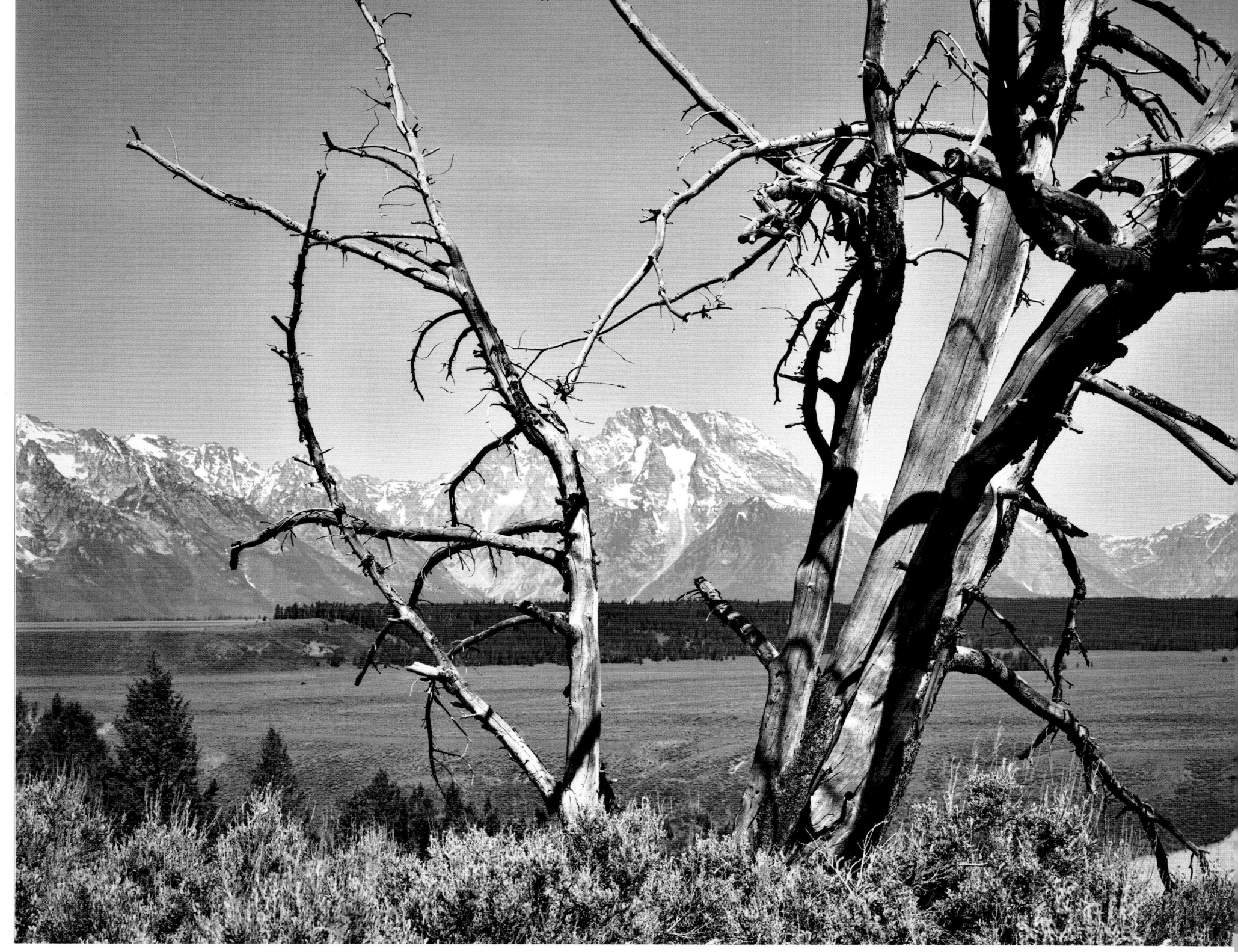

Dead juniper, Grand Tetons National Park, Wyoming, 6-24-1990; Toyo 8x10M camera; 355mm Schneider Gold Dot Dagor; yellow K2 filter; Kodak Tmax 400 8x10 film; Kodak Tmax RS developer.

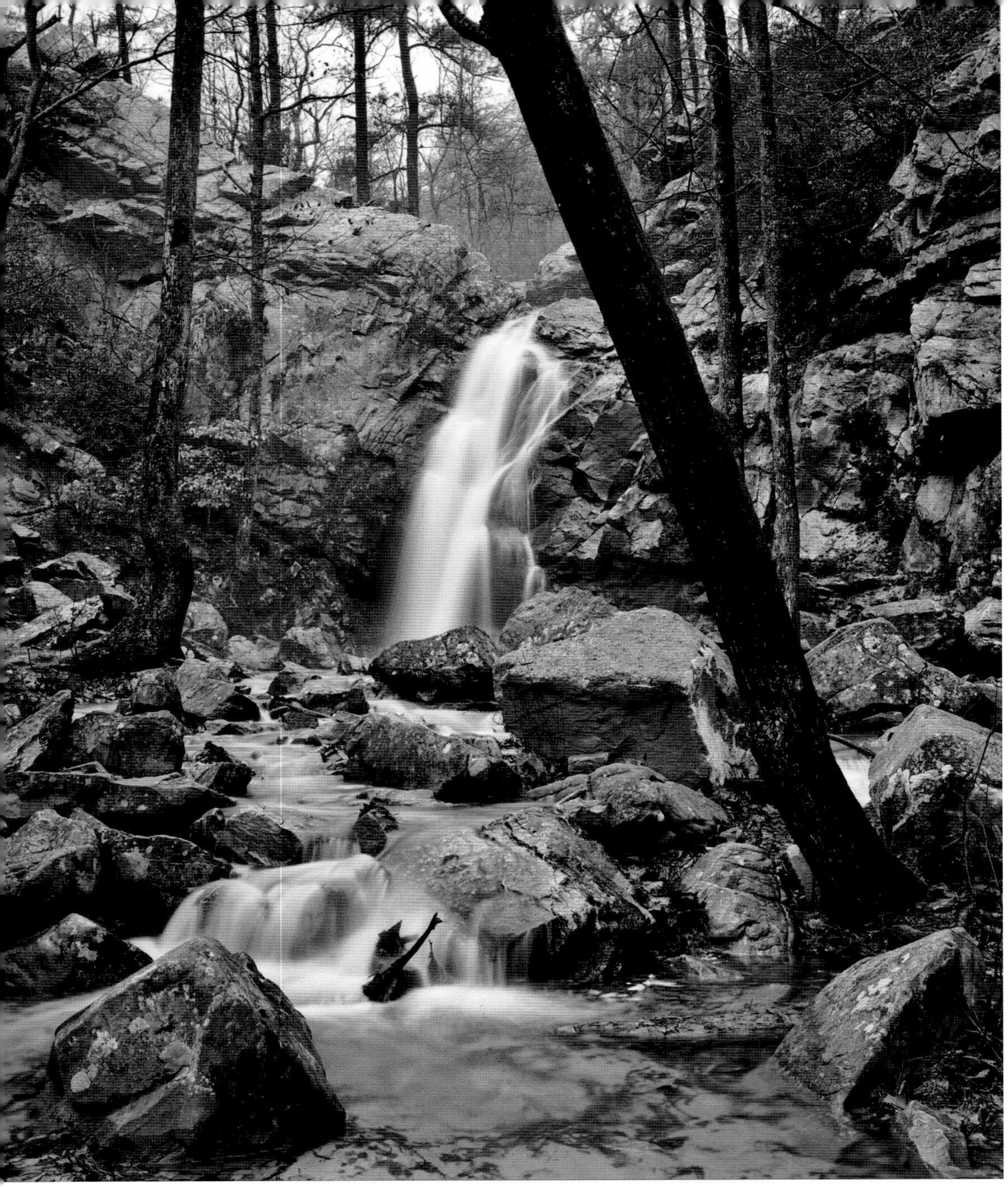

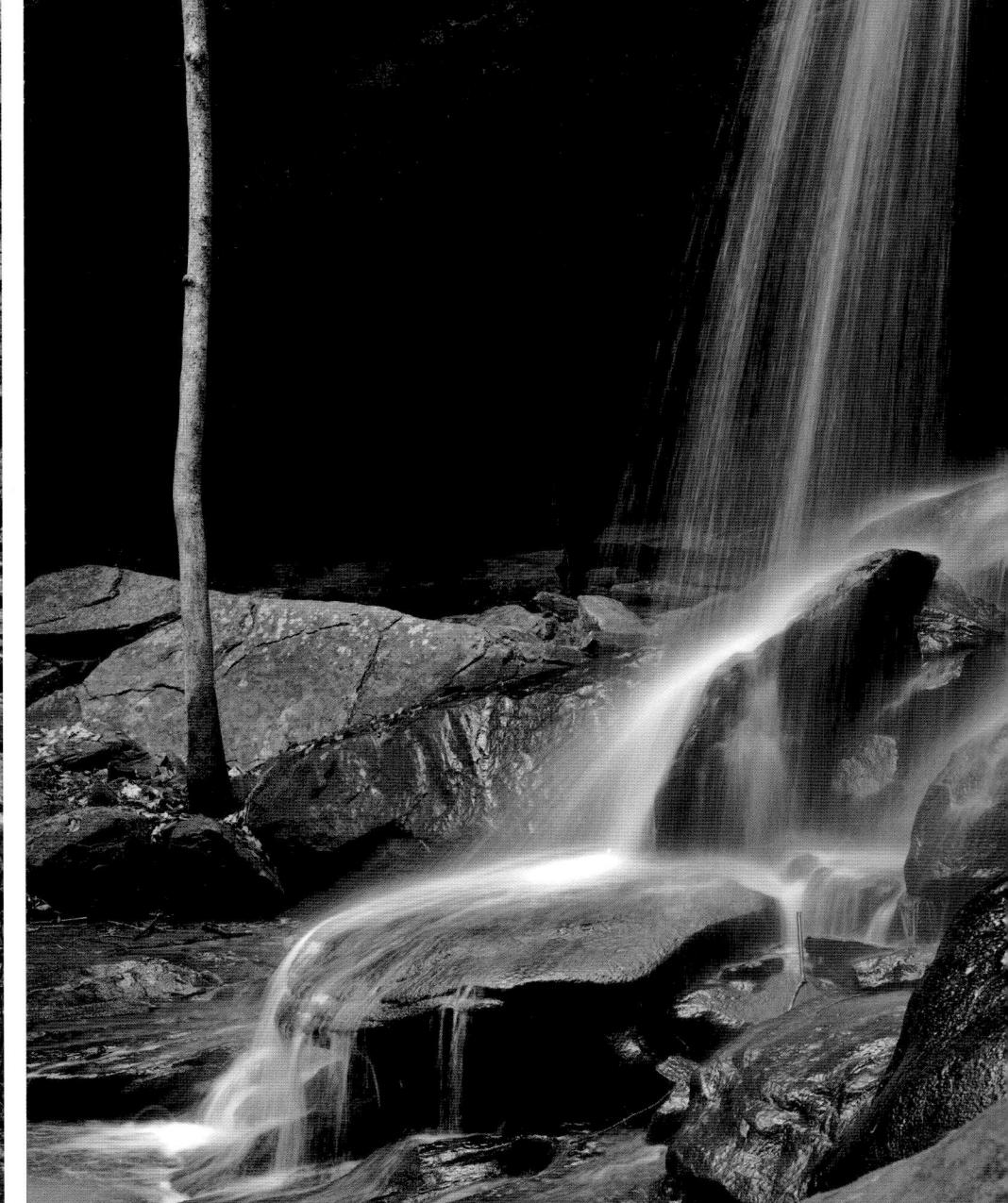

Left: Pevine Falls, Oak Mountain State Park, Alabama, 12-29-1991; Linhof Technika V 4x5 camera; 120mm Schneider Super Symmar HM; Kodak Tmax 100 4x5 film; Kodak Tmax RS developer.

Right: Turkey Foot Falls, Sipsey Wilderness, Bankhead National Forest, Double Springs, Alabama, 2-27-1993; Linhof Technika V 4x5 camera; 150mm Nikkor W lens; Kodak Tmax 100 4x5 film; Kodak Tmax RS developer.

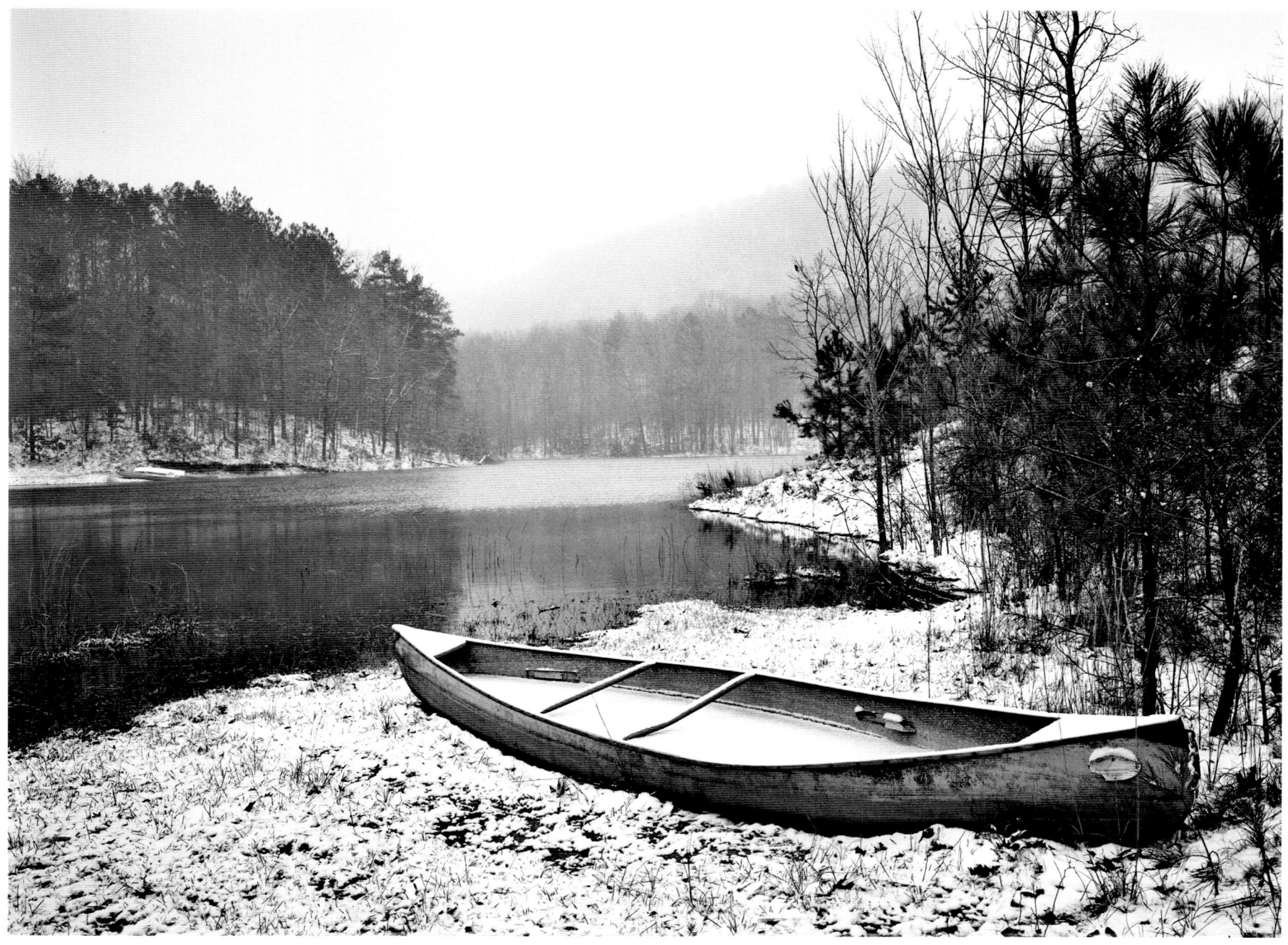

Double Oak Lake at Oak Mountain State Park, Alabama, 1-6-1996; Linhof Technika V 4x5 camera; 90mm Schneider Super Angulon lens; Kodak Tri X Pan Pro 4x5 film; PMK Pyro developer.

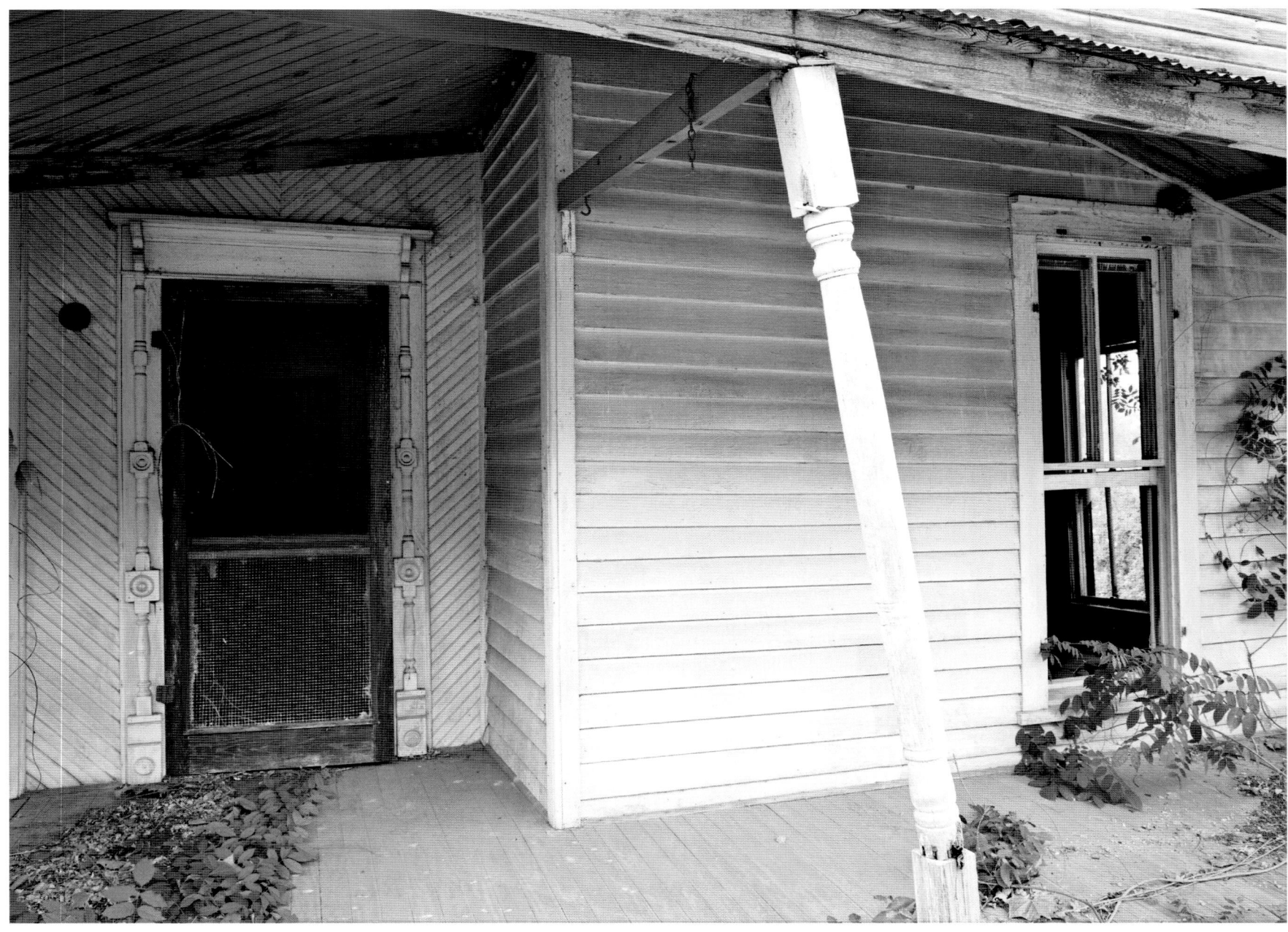

Above: Old house in Maplesville, Alabama, 11-3-1991; Linhof Technika V 4x5 camera; 120mm Schneider Super Symmar HM lens; Kodak Tmax 100 4x5 film; Kodak Tmax RS developer.

Facing page: Cahaba lilies, Cahaba River, Bibb County, Alabama, 5-22-1994; Linhof Technika V 4x5 camera; 120mm Schneider Super Symmar lens; Kodak Super XX 4x5 film; PMK Pyro developer.

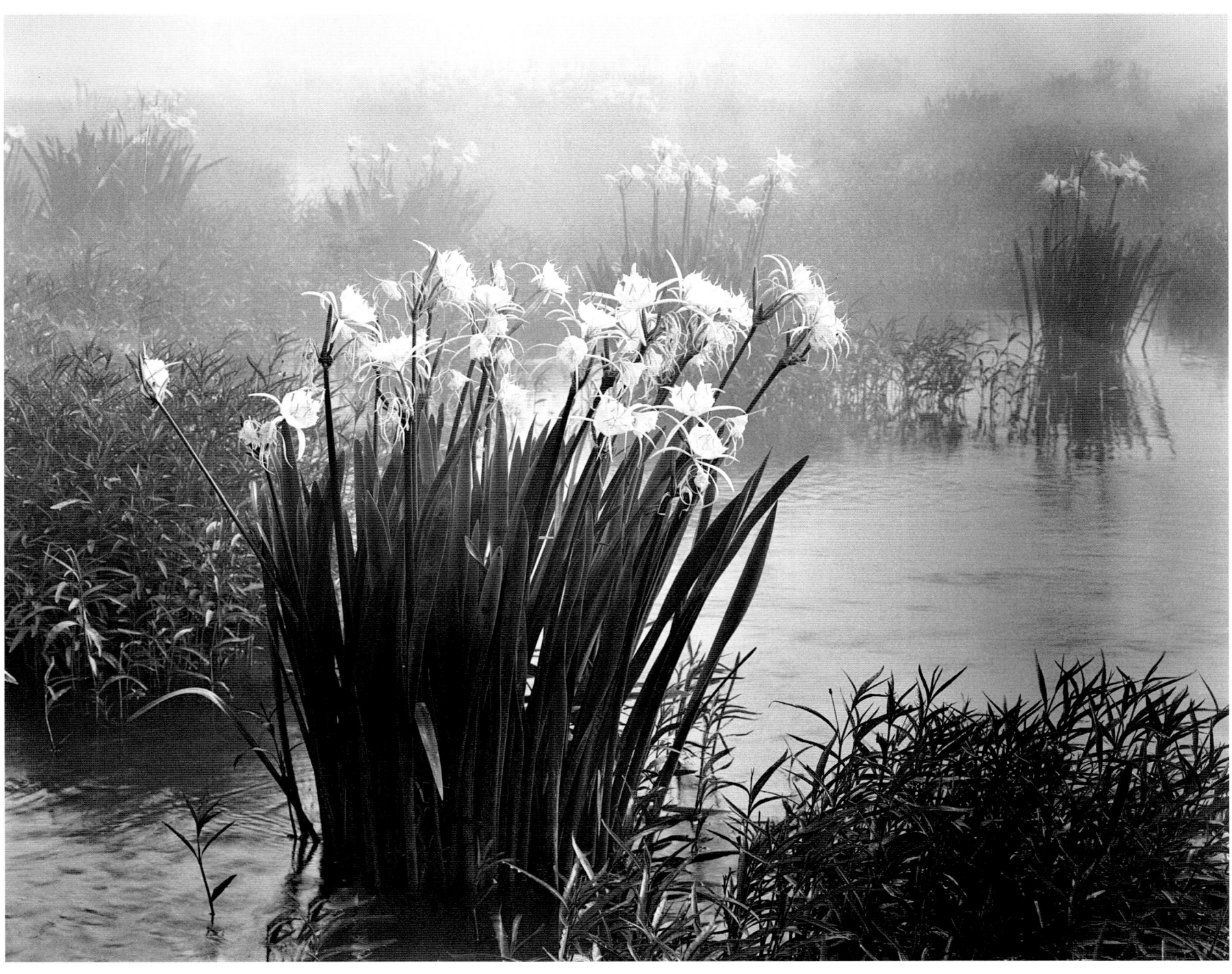

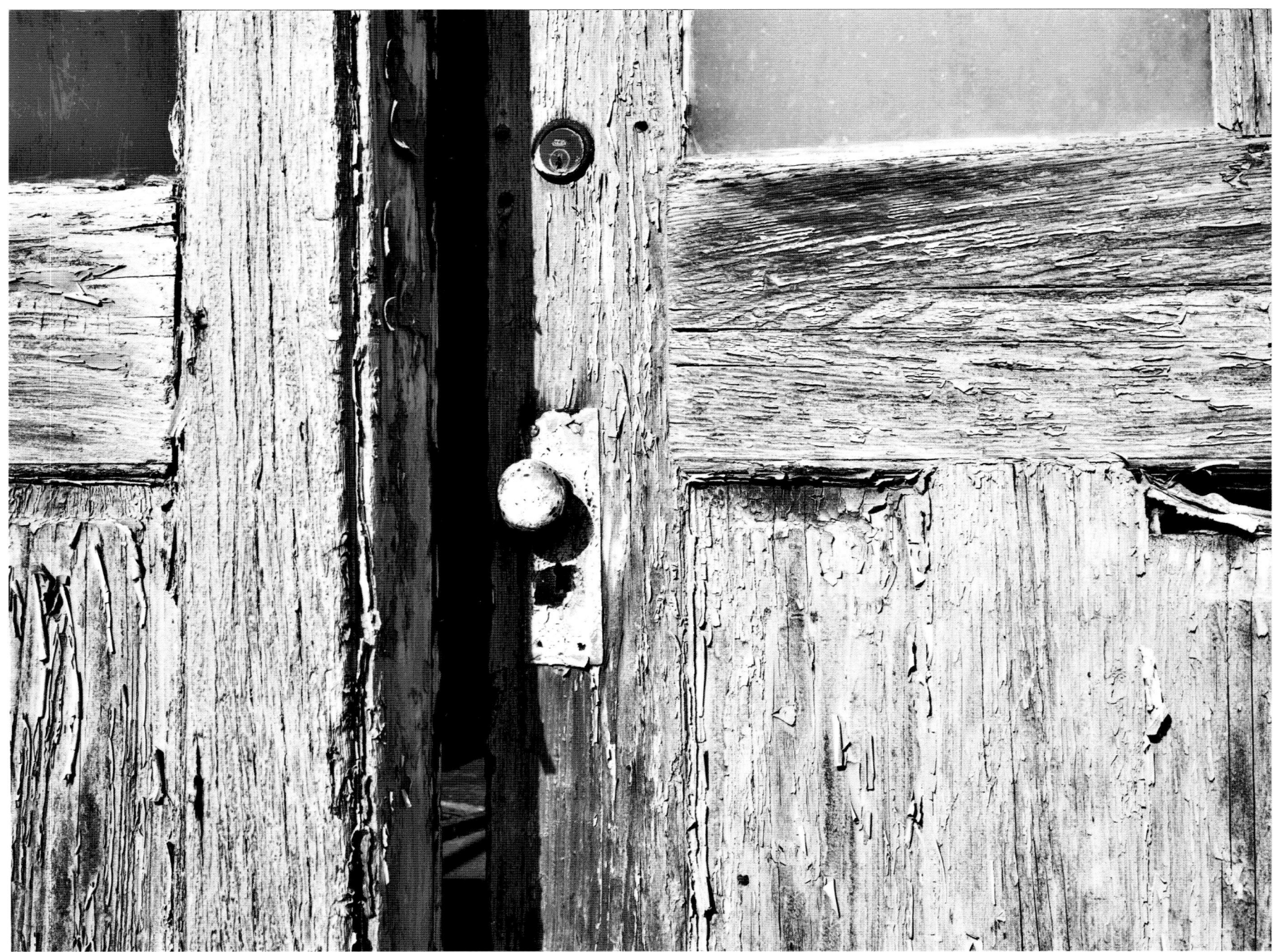

Door in downtown Cairo, Illinois, 3-1-2008; Toyo 8x10M camera; 240mm Schneider G Claron lens; Kodak Tmax 100 8x10 film; PMK Pyro developer.

5

The 2000s: The Journey Diversifies

Y2K never came to fruition, however almost everything I had been doing for a living and in my personal photography seemed to be ending or at least changing course.

The impact of digital photography was wiping out the traditional film, paper, and chemical businesses that traditional film photography required. Digital cameras were getting better and better; megapixels were going up, as were all other quality aspects of digital photography. Now, not only the consumer was satisfied with digital images, so were the professionals.

Kodak began major downsizing in the middle and late 1990s. By 2000, the handwriting was on the wall. There was nothing Kodak could do to stop the decline of film-based photography.

In 2001, Kodak was a hundred and twenty-one years old, and that year it sold more film and processing than each of its prior years. In 2002, that streak ended, and the film business began dropping by the double digits each year. More downsizing, consolidations, plant closings, and restructurings were occurring. After thirty years of Kodak seniority, my department was greatly consolidated, and my job was eliminated. After two more years, the entire nationwide and Canada department was gone.

At the same time my personal large-format film photography seemed dated and doomed. Even my long-term photography friends were going 100 percent digital. I started shooting digital also, but I never stopped shooting film. Film and digital had very different looks. Black-and-white film, for example, delivered deeper, richer images, with more emotional content, tonal values, subtle tones, and greater variations of tone, contrast, and depth, especially with large-format film.

I was shooting more film than ever, but it felt like no one else was. I feared the companies making the products that I used might not survive. I was depressed about this. I was melancholy about the loss of my career, but I equally feared the loss of my life's passion. Digital was easy to use—pictures were sharp and well exposed—but, for me, nothing about digital photography was as fun or as rewarding as film. I loved the whole process of film. I loved not knowing what my pictures would look like until I processed them. I loved the entire crafty darkroom experience and the hard work that went into making the images good. The extra hard work of large-format photography is what I loved best. By comparison, to me, digital seemed sterile, cold, and uninviting. Sitting at the computer on Photoshop was not nearly as rewarding, to me, as darkroom work.

MY FEELING OF JOB and hobby loss remained strong until August 2007, when I got a call from Jennifer Hunt at her gallery in Mountain Brook, a suburb of Birmingham. An old large-format photography friend, Randal Crow, had recommended my work to Jennifer. She called me and was excited at the prospect of an exhibit of black-and-white photos shot on film, especially with large-format cameras. By this time, her photography exhibits were of digitally shot images. All of a sudden, my seemingly antiquated film work seemed new again.

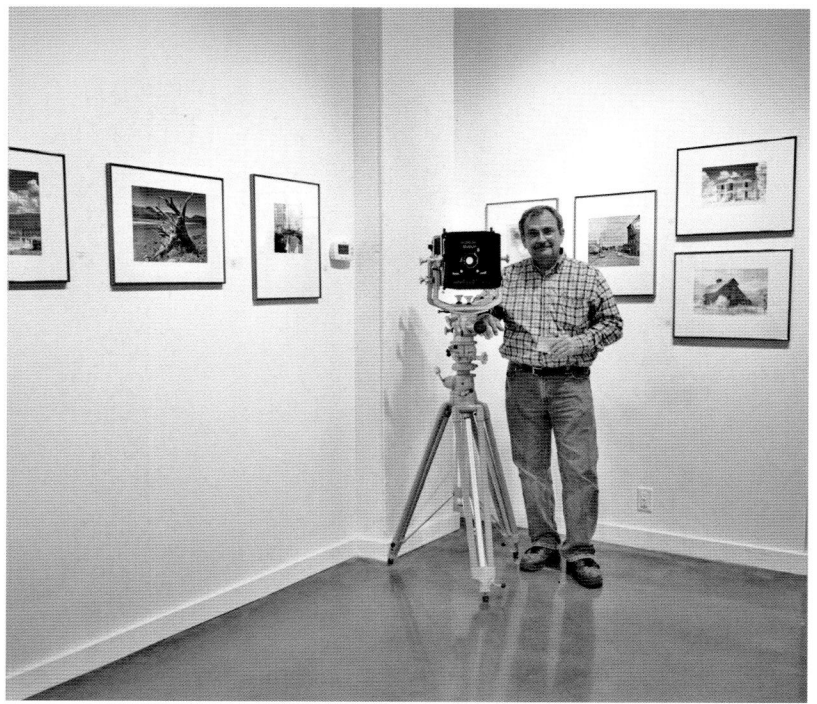

John Dersham exhibit at the Jennifer Hunt Gallery in Mountain Brook, Alabama, 10-25-2007; Hasselblad camera; 50 Zeiss Distagon lens; Ilford HP5+ 120 film; PMK Pyro developer.

The result of our discussion was an exhibit at the Jennifer Hunt Gallery from September 2007 to the spring of 2008. Gallery visitors were able to see something in the prints from film that was more organic, real, and earthy. Film conveyed greater depth and mood than the digital images that were now considered normal. I was reinvigorated by this recognition, and after several years of dejection about the potential loss of film photography, I started to get the feeling that perhaps film was going to stick around.

THE 2000S WAS A big decade for changes for my family and my workplace.

The new decade began with both kids having finished high school. Jennifer moved to Nashville to study cosmetology and Jad soon followed to go to college. Before I left Kodak, I had been able to help Jad get a job. He worked at one of the Kodak-owned minilabs in Target stores. Jad started at the first Target built in Birmingham. He was able to transfer to a store in the Nashville area when he moved. Jad worked his way through college at Middle Tennessee State University while working for Kodak at Target. Soon after he graduated in 2005, Kodak got out of that business and his job ended.

Kodak began closing a lot of facilities in the late 1990s, including mine in Birmingham. Kyle and I had been taking weekend vacations to Mentone on Lookout Mountain in northeast Alabama and the nearby valley town of Fort Payne. Lookout Mountain is not a peak but a ridge—part of the Appalachians—that extends from Chattanooga, Tennessee, to Gadsden, Alabama. The kids were not home anymore so we decided to move to Lookout Mountain. I was still at Kodak and responsible for seven states, but I worked from a home office and was allowed to live in any of my territory's states.

We bought land on Lookout Mountain in 1999 thinking we would go there one day and have horses. Kyle loved horses and we had been boarding one for several years in Birmingham.

In August 2000, we found a repossessed house in Fort Payne

that we decided to buy and fix up ourselves. Our house of eleven years in Hoover had just sold. For the next several months we worked on the Fort Payne house and moved there in early December.

In January 2001, our daughter gave birth to Tristan. Jennifer and her family moved to Fort Payne to be near us.

More and more downsizings were happening at Kodak, and in March 2002, my career came to an end. I learned this just after Kyle and I decided to build a house on our land on Lookout Mountain so we could have horses there. On Thanksgiving weekend 2001, we broke ground for a house, separate garage/studio/

Tristan Rose Dersham (granddaughter) learning photography in the studio with a Rolleiflex 2.8FX TLR camera, 3-16-2003; shot with a Rolleiflex 2.8.F TLR camera; 80mm Zeiss Planar lens; Kodak Tmax 100, 120 film; PMK Pyro developer.

darkroom, and a barn. Despite my job loss, we decided to continue construction. Our original house in Fort Payne sold right away. I had earned two years of severance and twenty-one weeks of paid vacation when I left the company.

Kyle and I designed the house and buildings and how they were configured on the property. We also did a lot of the interior construction together. I spent one year without job hunting in order to do this work. Kyle was doing massage therapy and teaching yoga classes at the same time.

AT THE BEGINNING OF my second year of severance from Kodak, I began a job search. After a few months, I got a job as the director

of sales for ImmageTech out of Chattanooga. They serviced the film-based X-ray business and sold refurbished, minilab equipment to retailers. I guess I was still in denial. ImmageTech had no chance of survival. They were in the same boat as Kodak. The minilabs did not sell, and the film-based X-rays were all going digital too.

After leaving ImmageTech, I struggled a few more years to establish a new career. During that time, I moved my elderly father to Fort Payne to an assisted living facility. Mom had passed away in 2000. Dad was in his late eighties and was having regular bouts of pneumonia. I got to spend a lot of time with him since I was not working part of the time he was here. He loved to come to our house and property to enjoy family and dogs. He passed away in 2007.

I was checking job sites and area newspapers looking for a job in late 2007. I filled out an application and sent in my resume for a position as director of tourism for DeKalb County, Alabama, located in Fort Payne. It required five years of tourism experience. I did not have that experience, but thought my job at Kodak possessed many of the same skill sets. My resume was sent to a blind email address with no name attached. I figured I would be ignored, so I began calling people I knew, like our bank president, Steve Eberhart, and real estate agent, Anita Killian, to see if they knew anyone that I could contact about the job. Anita said that she thought Roy Jones from Sequoyah Caverns was on the tourism board. I called him and explained my interest. He asked me to send my resume directly to him. I did that, along with a follow-up letter, a phone call, and then another letter. Two months went by and I was close to starting a job with another company when Roy called and asked if I was still interested in interviewing for the job. I said yes and he told me to come to the tourism information center the next day for an interview.

Roy did not explain that I would be interviewed by the entire tourism board. They asked a lot of questions about my background with Kodak. They especially liked the fact that my wife and I had moved all around the country and Fort Payne was the only move that we had picked—the others were all career moves. I explained we had been coming here as tourists, and we loved the area so much that we decided to live here. I told them with a lot of passion how I felt about our local scenic beauty and great attractions. Many locals had interviewed for the job, and there existed political pressure to give it to a friend, relative, or a well-known local person. Roy and the board did not seem to like that pressure, so the board unanimously voted to offer me the job.

TOURISM BECAME A NATURAL fit for me as a professional manager but also photographically. Within a few months, I was well-known statewide in tourism and actively involved in all of the state and regional tourism organizations. Over the next several years, I became intimately involved in multiple organizations and was soon chairman of several boards and winner of a half dozen regional and statewide tourism awards.

It only took a few months in tourism for the industry to learn about my background in photography. I was soon taking pictures for travel guides, magazines, newspapers, and advertising shots throughout the Southeast. I did the photography for travel guides such as the Waterfall Trail, the Motorcycle Trail, the Hallelujah Trail (churches with services for more than a century), and multiple other publications. I was getting calls and emails almost daily to provide images for particular purposes.

As the 2000s were coming to an end, my family was doing great (in 2008, Jennifer gave birth to our second granddaughter, Aris), my job was wonderful beyond imagination, and my personal photography was reaching an all-time high, including my medium- and large-format black-and-white photography.

In 2009, when Jacksonville State University opened its LEED-certified field school at Little River Canyon National Preserve, my photography was featured in a NASA film done about Little River Canyon. The director, Pete Conroy, asked me to feature my photography in the main hall of the center. He did not ask me to display my color work done for tourism, but rather my large-format film and darkroom work. It was to be a temporary exhibit, but eleven years later, the exhibit was still there and still getting nice comments.

In the spring of 2009, I held my first Jacksonville State University Field School photography workshop at Little River Canyon. It included a Friday night class called "Composition, Lighting, and Impact." On Saturday we photographed in and around Little River Canyon. I have been doing two of these fun workshops twice a year for the park ever since. I meet incredible people that become long-term friends.

The 2000s had many challenges and major life changes. The decade included the loss of both my parents, a move, job changes, the births of two granddaughters, 9/11, and a recession. Even with all the challenges, it proved to be a fulfilling decade for family, work, and photography.

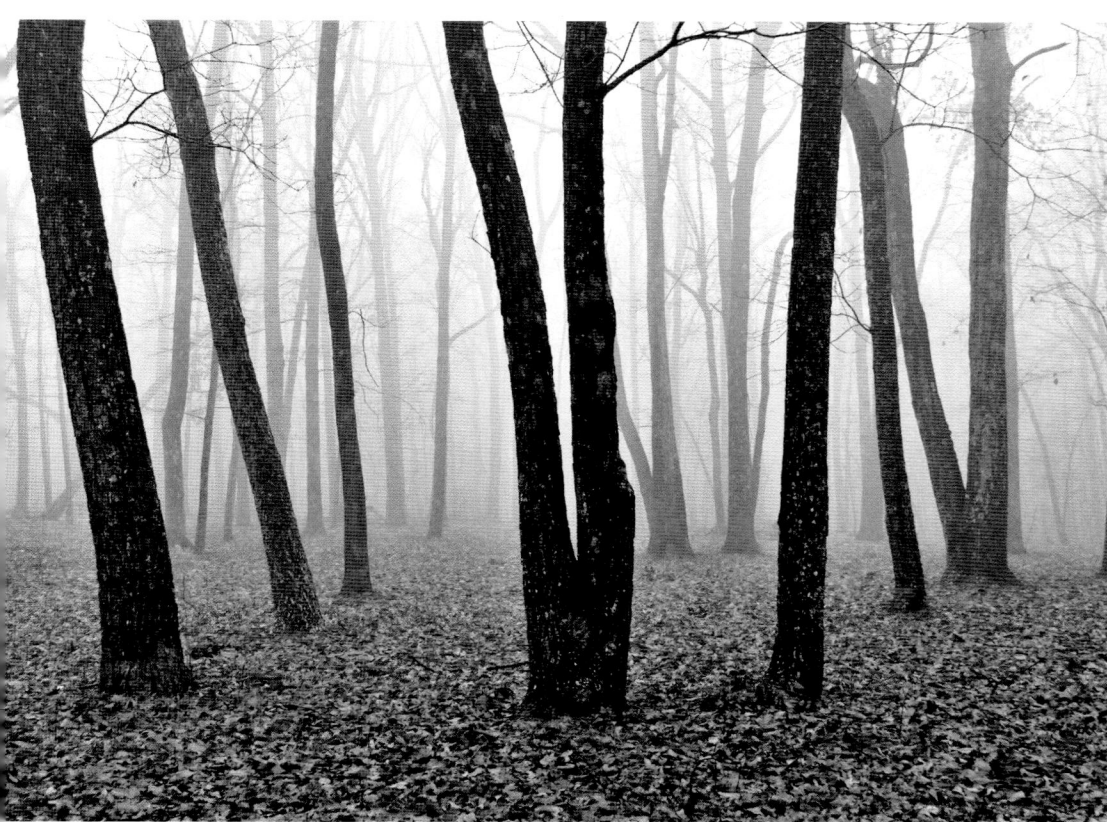 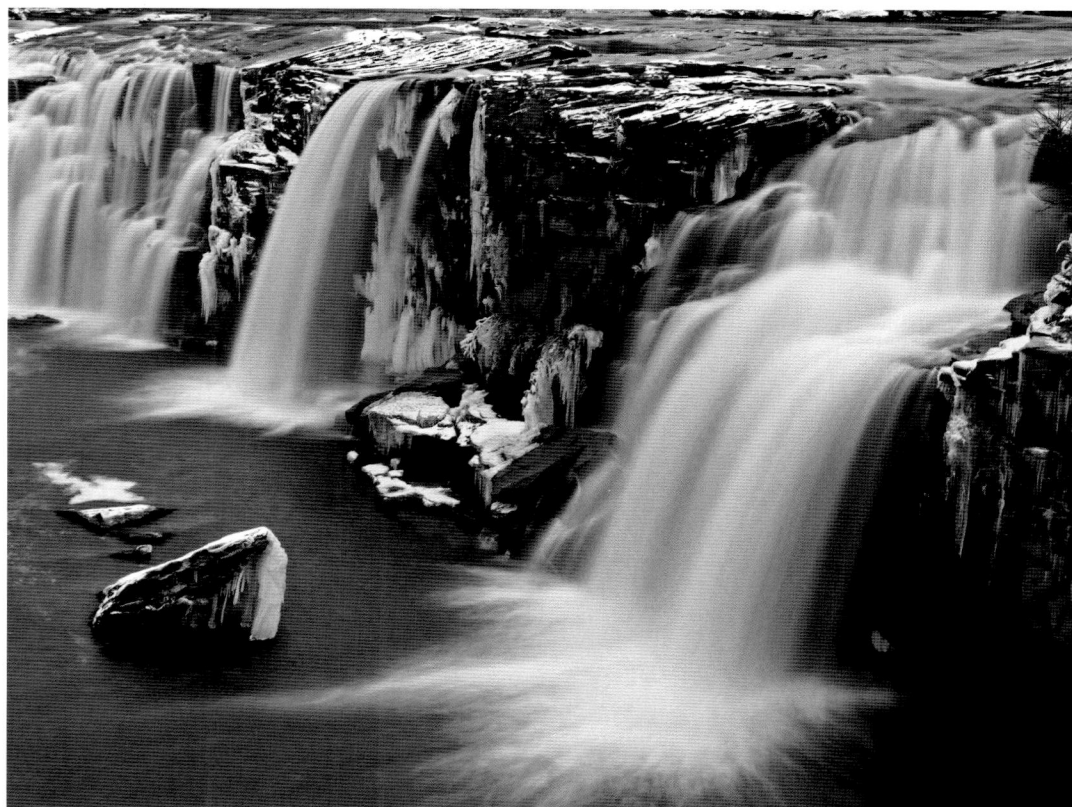

Left: Monte Sano State Park, Huntsville, Alabama, 1-12-2009; Wista DX 4x5 camera; 120mm Schneider Super Symmar HM lens; Ilford HP5+ 4x5 film; PMK Pyro developer.

Right: Little River falls in winter, 1-2009; Pentax 6x7 camera; 105mm lens; Ilford Delta 100 120 film; PMK Pyro developer.

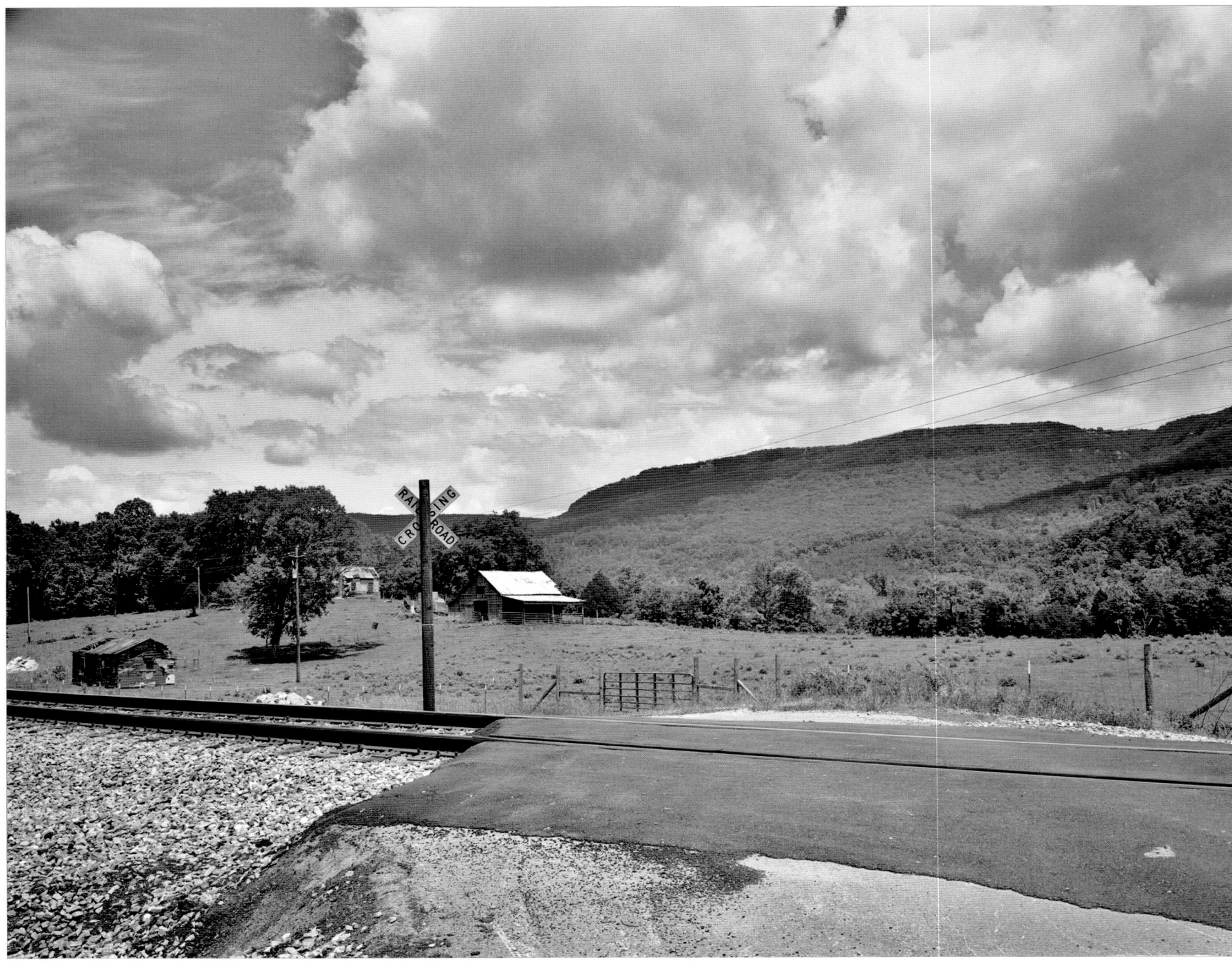

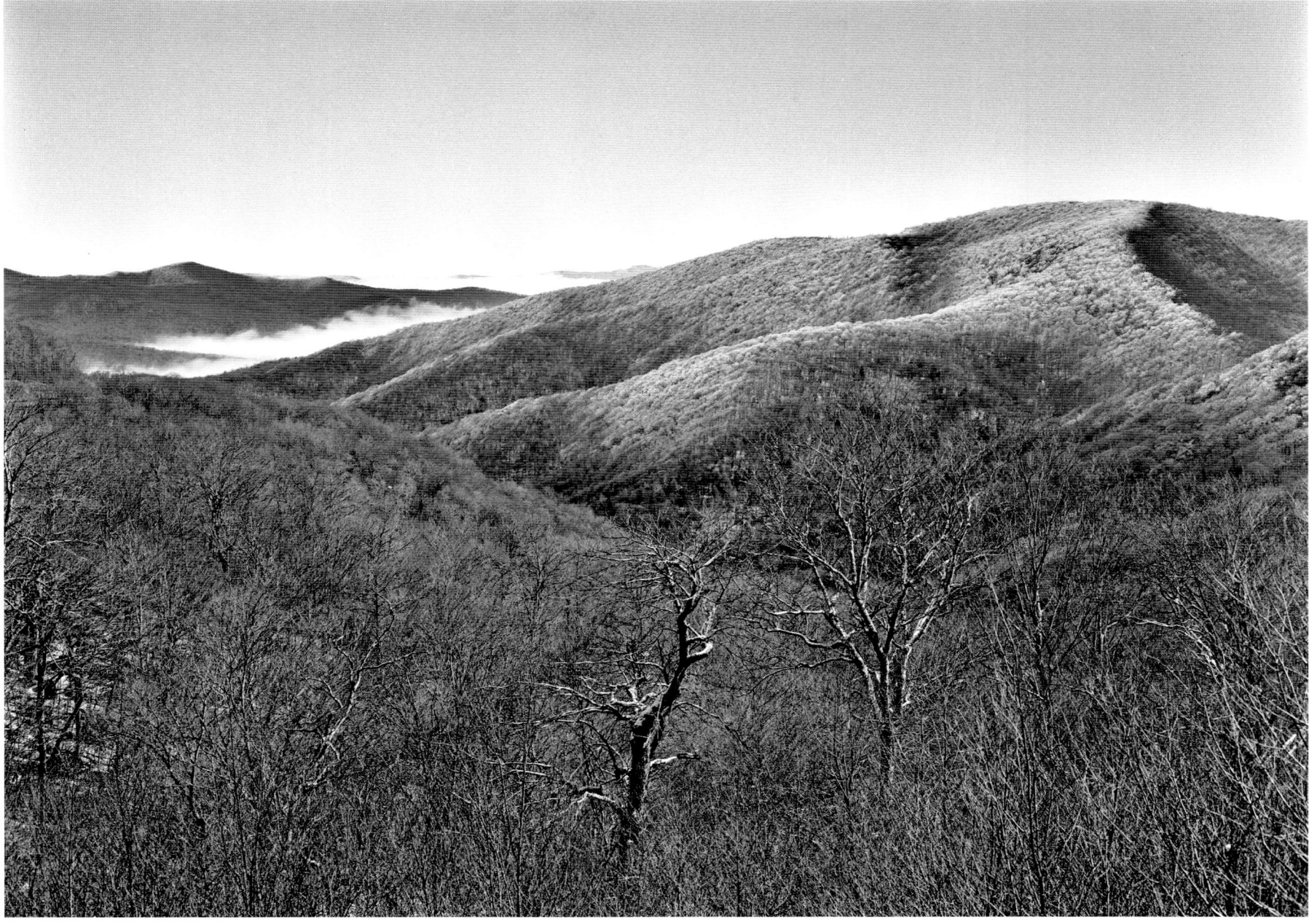

Above: Light snowfall and fog, Cherohala Scenic Parkway, east Tennessee, 3-5-2008; Linhof Master Technika; 150mm Schneider Xenar lens; Ilford HP5+ 4x5 film; PMK Pyro developer.

Facing page: Rising Fawn, Georgia, rural scene facing Lookout Mountain, 5-22-2009; Toyo 8x18M camera; 210mm Schneider Apo Symmar lens; Kodak Super XX 8x10 film; PMK Pyro developer.

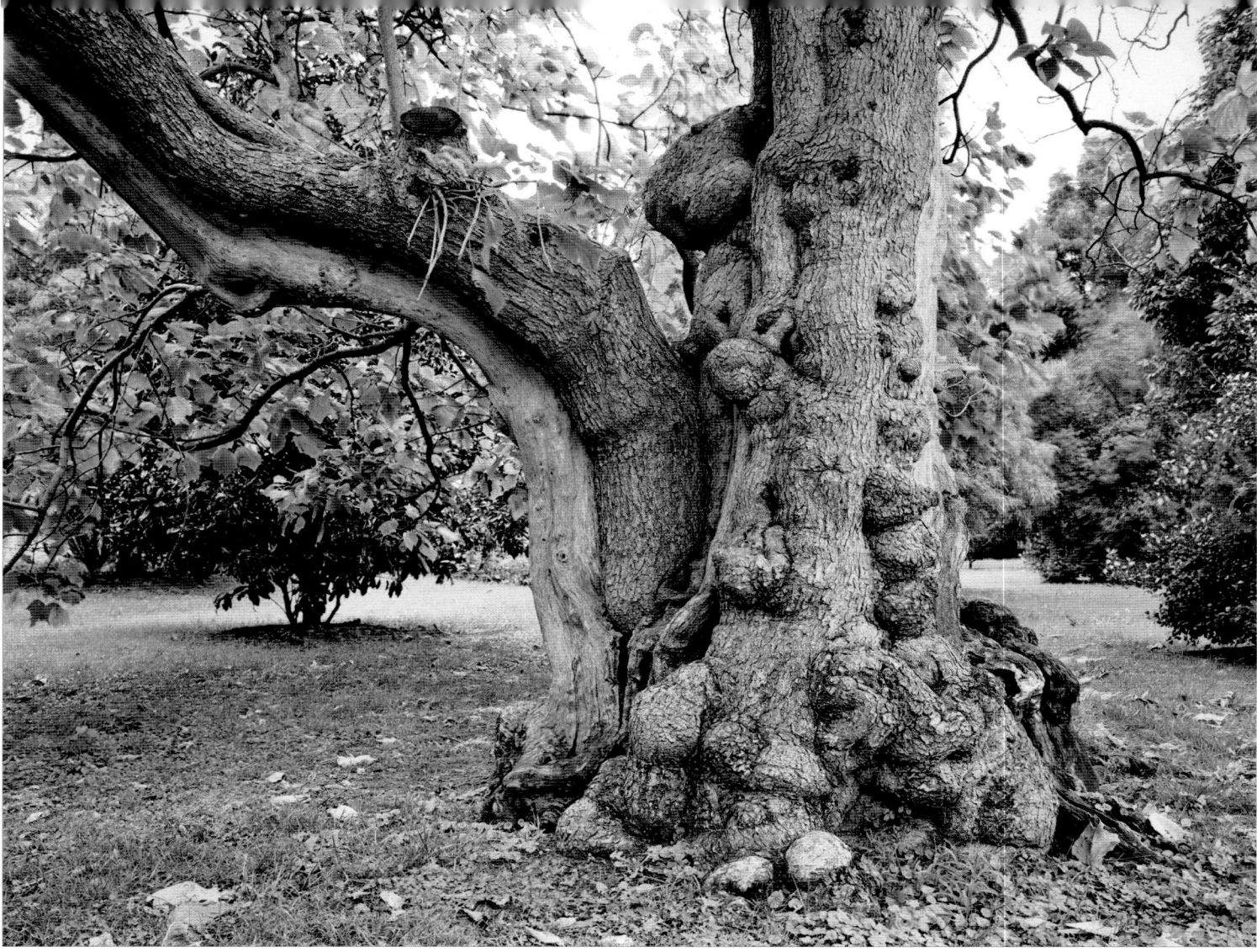

Why Sunrise Instead of Sunset?

I love the morning. I get up early feeling fresh, with positive thoughts and a great feeling about my day ahead. I make a pot of coffee and I hit the road for a day of photography. I load the car with my equipment then grab my coffee for a ride in the dark sipping away till I reach my first destination.

The morning is filled with what I call environmental enhancements which typically do not exist later in the day as the air dries out. Fog, mist, ice, snow, wet grass, dew, frost, low hanging clouds on the horizon, mist and fog rising from the rivers and ponds. In the morning I get overwhelmed with a sense of enthusiasm and energy that are not with me later in the day. The air is cool, the environment is quiet and most people have not begun their day and all around me is quiet, even on the roads. I have always said even if I took no pictures it is worth being out enjoying these beautiful, peaceful scenic moments.

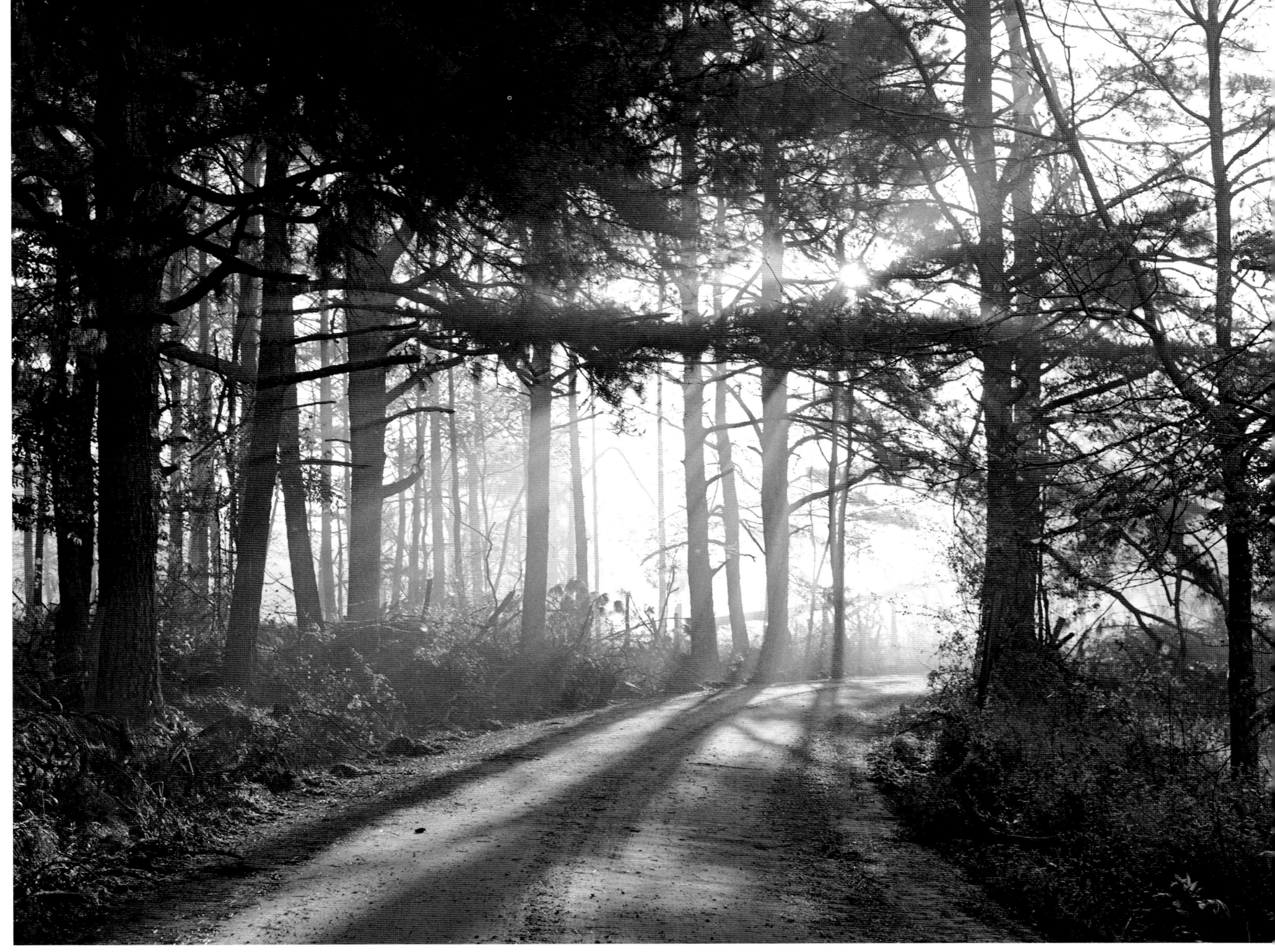

Above: Winter sunrise, near Dogtown, Alabama, 2-2001; Hasselblad camera; 50mm Zeiss Distagon lens; Ilford HP5+ 120 film; Kodak Xtol developer.

Facing page: Catalpa tree in Centennial Park, Nashville, Tennessee, 9-14-2008; Toyo 8x10M camera; 240mm Schneider G Claron lens; Ilford HP5+ 8x10 film; PMK Pyro developer.

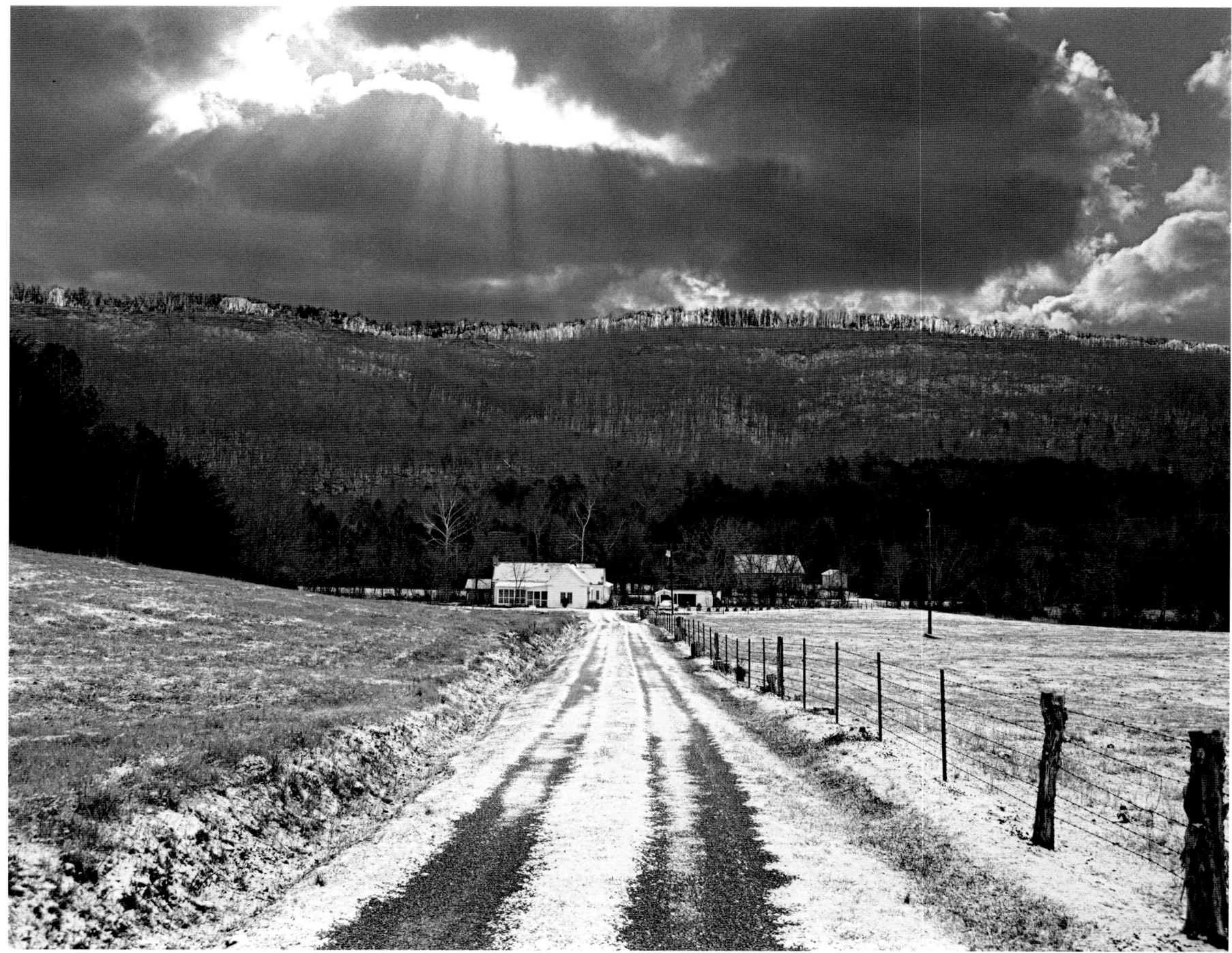

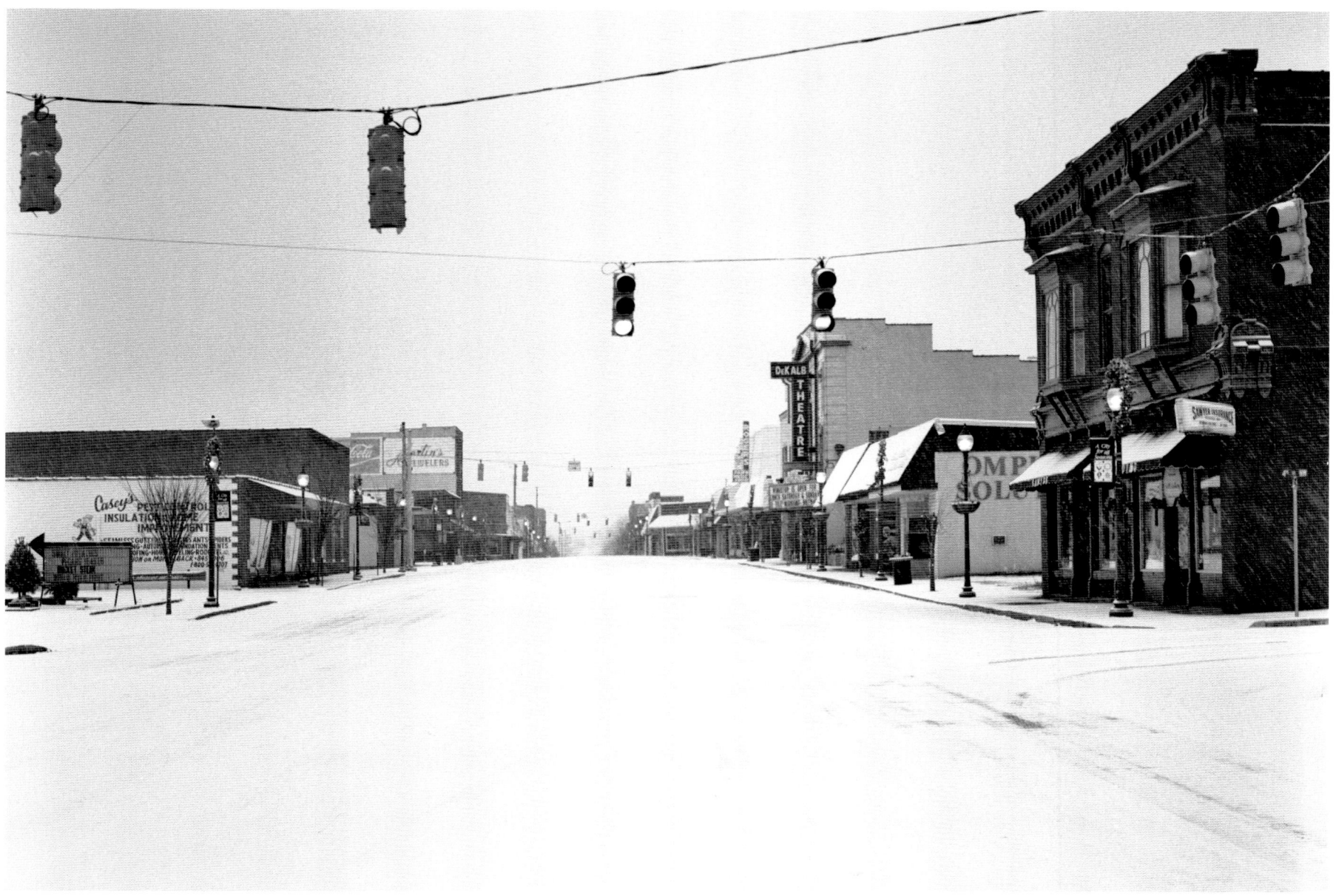

Above: Early morning snow on New Year's Day, Fort Payne, Alabama, 1-1-2001; Rolleiflex 2.8F TLR camera; 80mm Zeiss Planar lens; Kodak Tmax 100 120 film; Kodak Xtol developer.

Facing page: Winter sunrise looking toward Lookout Mountain in DeKalb County, Alabama, 1-2002; Pentax 6x7 camera; 45mm lens; Ilford HP5+ 120 film; Kodak Xtol developer.

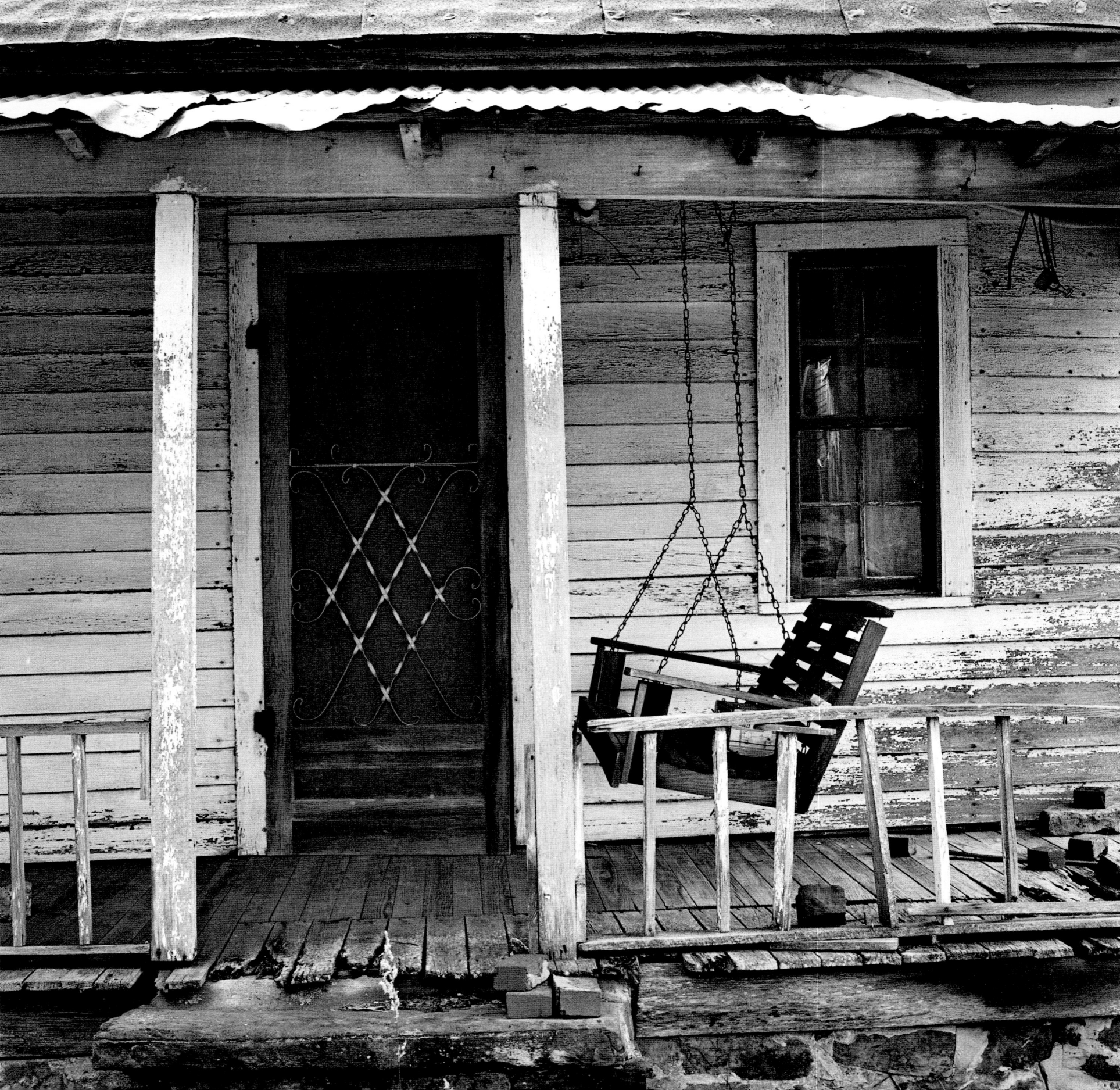

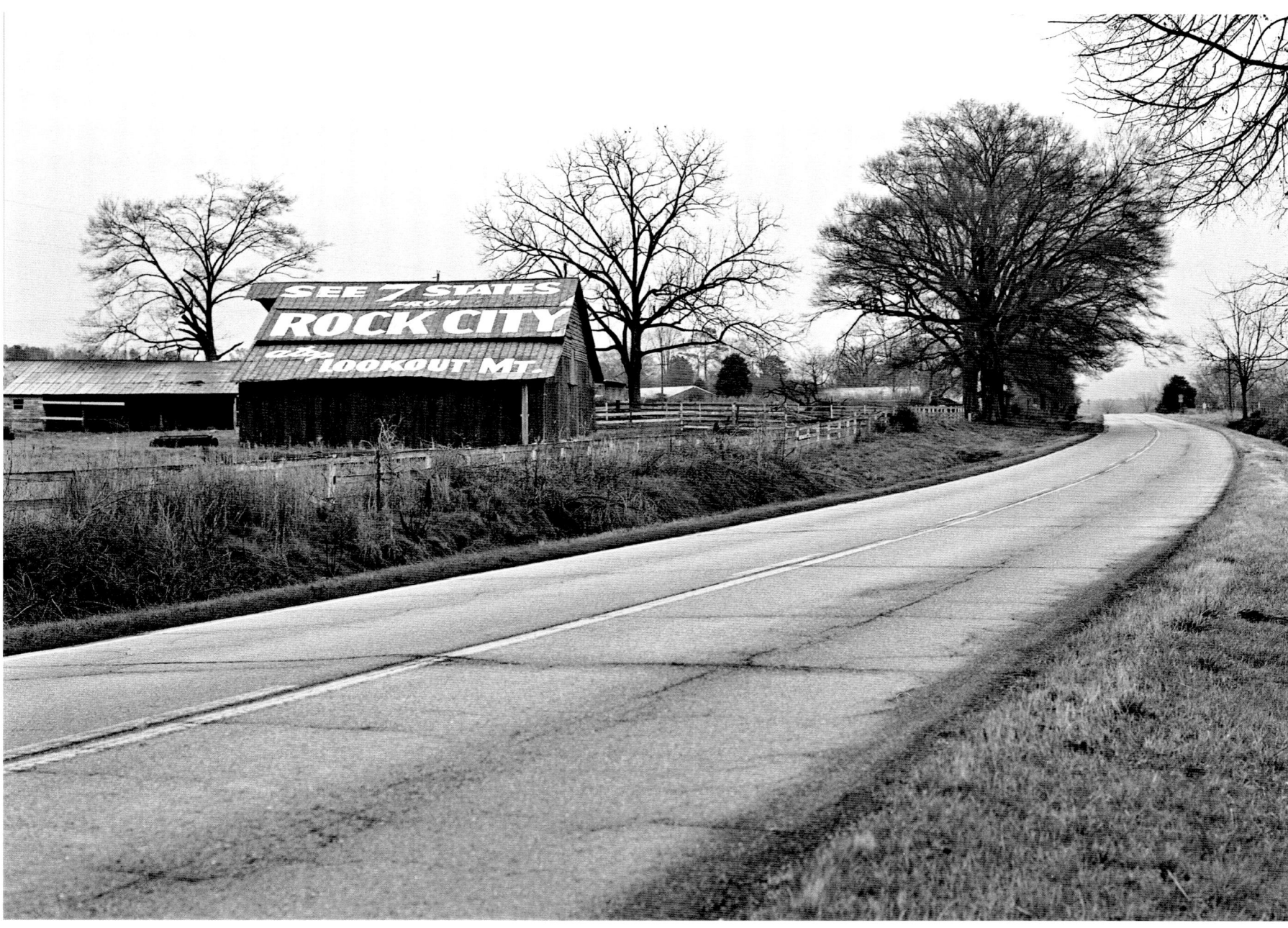

Above: Rock City barn on U.S. 11, DeKalb County, Alabama, 1-15-2001; Hasselblad camera; 80mm Zeiss Planar lens; Ilford HP5+ 120 film; PMK Pyro developer.

Facing page: Abandoned farm house, Jackson County, Alabama, 9-2001; Hasselblad camera; 80mm Zeiss Planar lens; Ilford HP5+ 120 film; PMK Pyro developer.

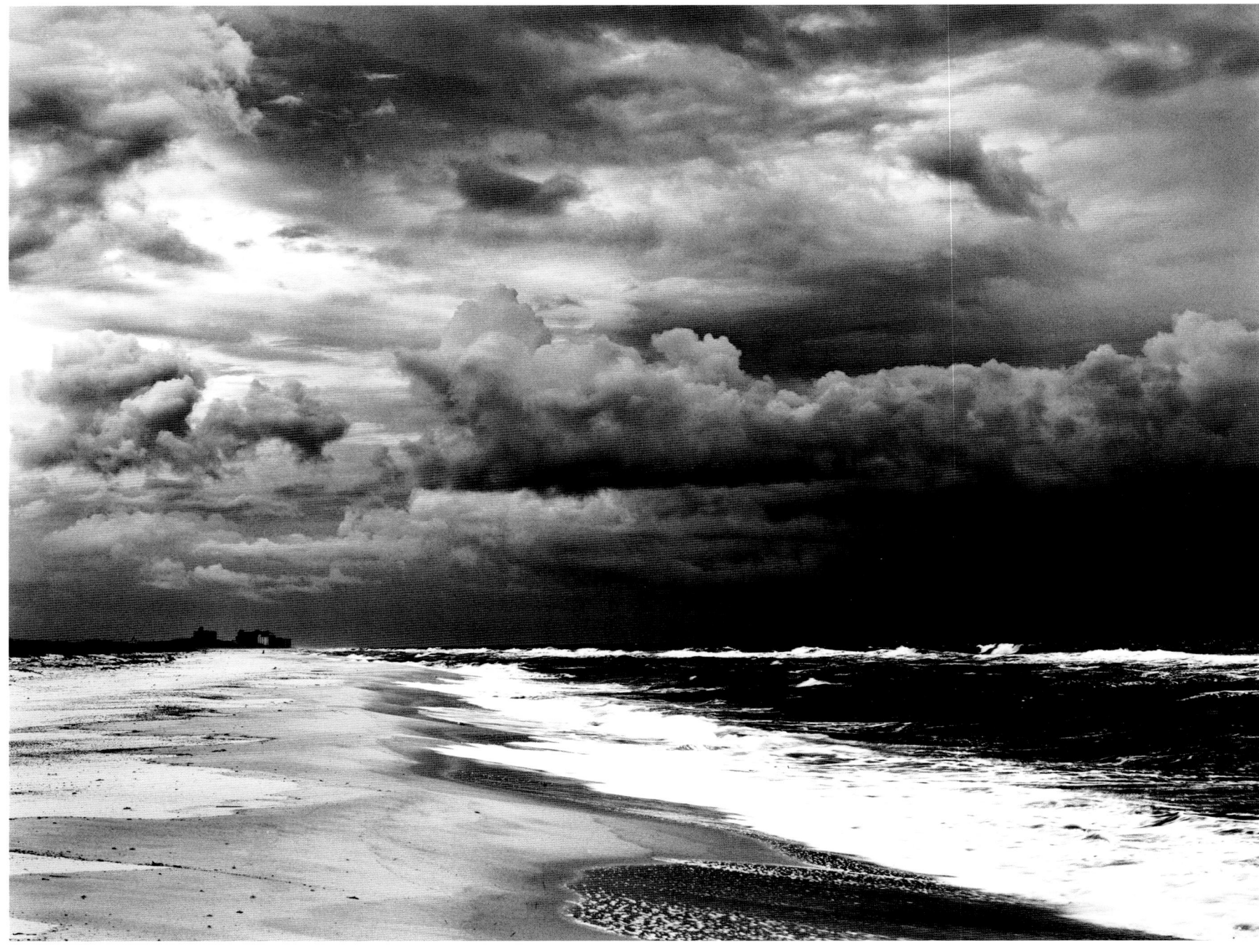

Storm clouds at Perdido Key, Alabama, 9-30-2000; Linhof Technika V camera; 210mm Schneider Symmar S lens; yellow K2 filter; Kodak Tmax 100 4x5 film; Kodak HC10B developer.

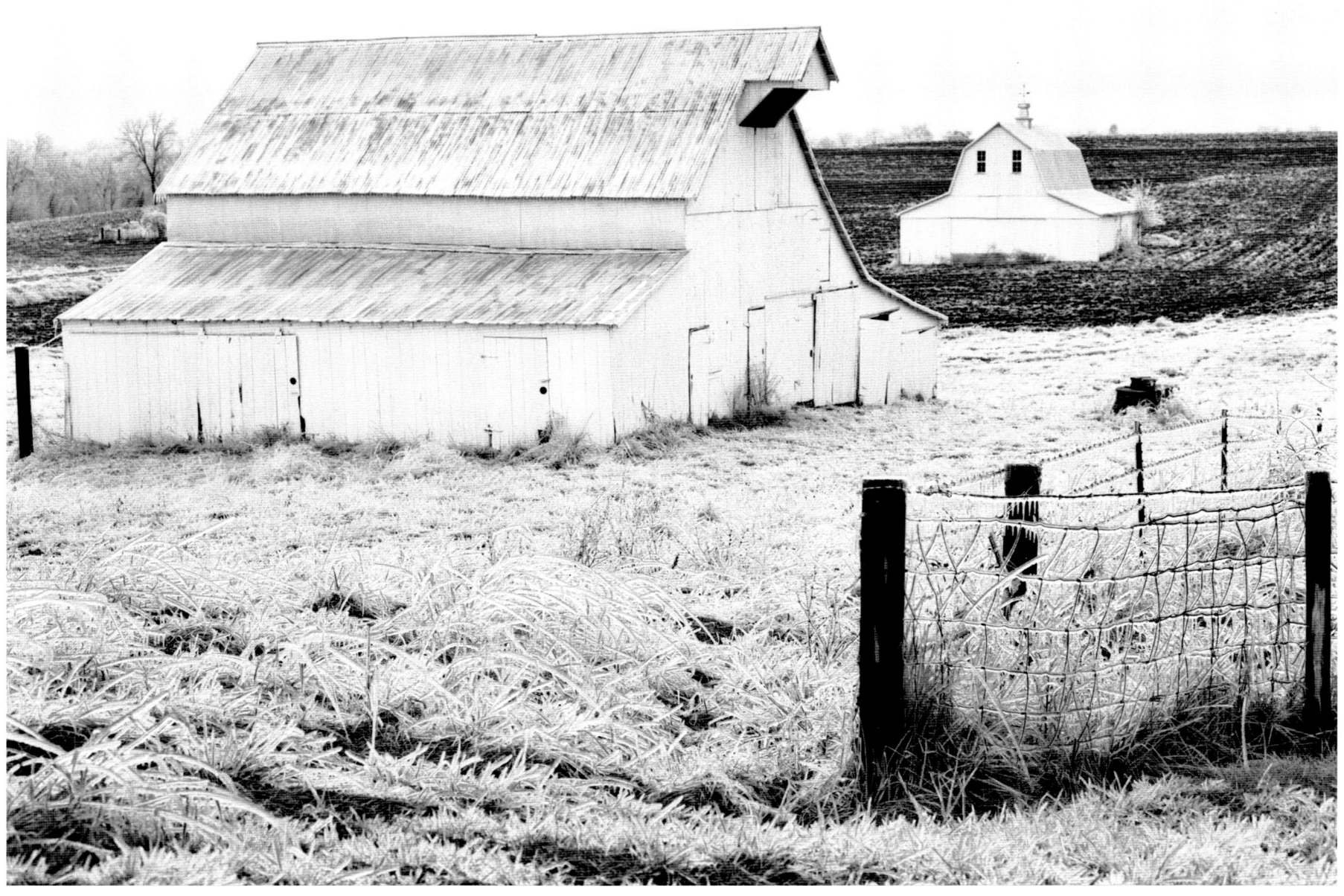

Winter farm scene near Glasgow, Missouri, 2-2002; Pentax 6x7 camera; 75mm lens; Ilford HP5+ 120 film; Kodak Xtol developer.

The Darkroom

The darkroom is a magical place. Unlike digital images where you sit at a computer, the darkroom is a workshop where you create your art. It is hands-on, touching and feeling film and paper, hands in chemicals in the dark, feeling your way to your next masterpiece.

The first thing is to load your camera with film, then go and take some pictures; It may be one sheet at time as with large-format film, or up to 36 pictures on a roll of 35mm. Unlike the seemingly unlimited number of pictures you can take with your digital camera, film will require that you study and plan your compositions prior to taking your pictures since you will run out of frames quickly with film.

Now to the darkroom, where you will load your film into the film-developing tank in total darkness. You will only touch the edges of the film to ensure you do not fingerprint them. Once loaded into the light-tight tank, you can turn on the lights to pour in the processing chemicals. First the developer, then stop bath to halt the development, and then the fixer to make the image stable and permanent. After the fixer you wash the film in a wash tank or in the developing tank in running water for thirty to sixty minutes before you hang it in a dust-free environment to dry. Once dry, you carefully cut it into lengths to fit a sleeve that will keep the negatives clean and dry. Most negative sleeves have a place to write the date, location, and technical details.

Then on to the printing. This is where you see the magic. In the darkroom a certified safelight lets you see your way around just well enough to know what you are doing and where you are walking. You will pick your negative to print, put it in your enlarger's negative carrier, then project it to your easel below, sizing the enlargement to fit your paper size and focusing it to perfection. Then comes a few test prints to make sure your exposure time is correct for the paper you are using. You may dodge or burn in the print to make objects lighter or darker in the scene. You do this with your hands or a dodging tool placed between the enlarger light and the paper below. It will take some time to learn how to control the light so you are only affecting the areas of the scene you want to.

Then you will put the paper in the developer, rock the tray to get the flow even over the paper, and watch as your image slowly begins to appear. You will be so excited and perhaps frustrated at first since you may have to keep making a new print to get the end result just where you want it. Once developed, you put the print in a tray of stop bath, then fixer, and then you wash the print thoroughly.

There are more steps you can take, like giving your prints a sepia or selenium tone. Selenium will add to the life of the print and give a nice warm tone to the image.

Mastering the darkroom takes time, effort and a lot of passion to stick with it and get it right. Once you get the results you like, you will be hooked.

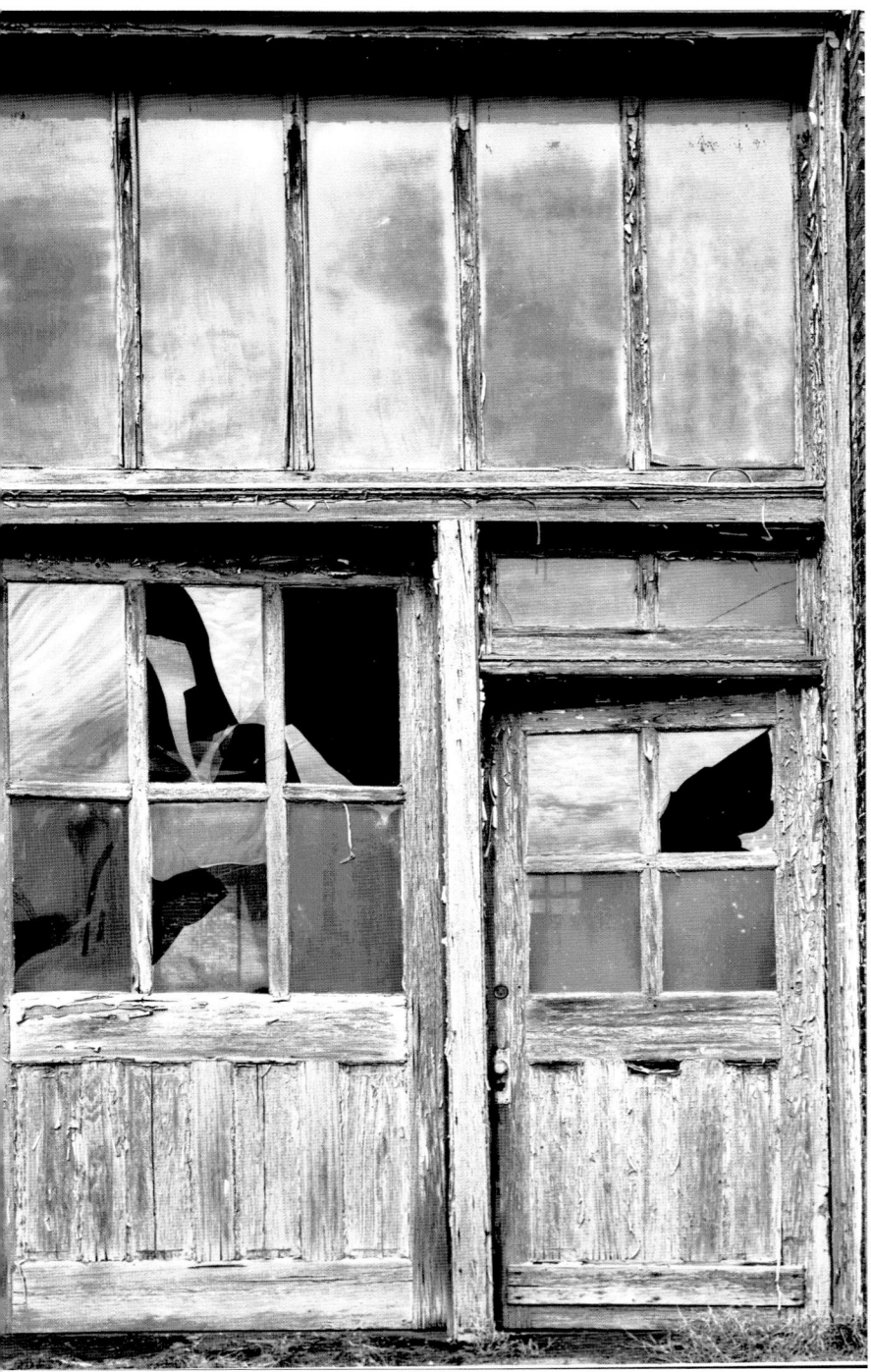

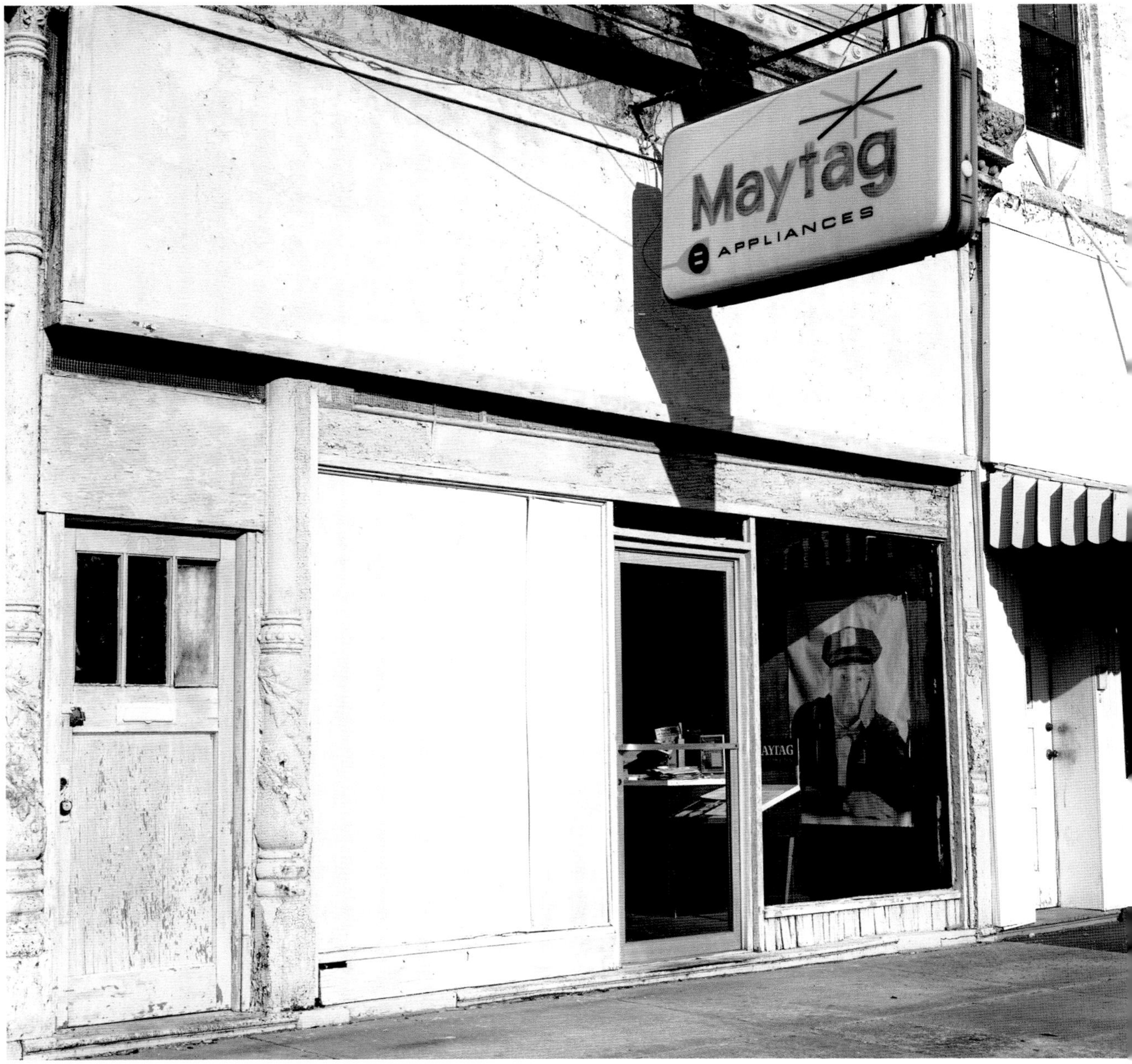

Left: Abandoned building in downtown Cairo, Illinois, 3-1-2008; Toyo 8x10M camera; 240mm Schneider G Claron lens; Kodak Tmax 100 8x10 film; PMK Pyro developer.

Above: Maytag Man in downtown Cairo, Illinois, 3-1-2008; Hasselblad camera; 80mm Zeiss Planar lens; Kodak Tmax 100 120 film; PMK Pyro developer.

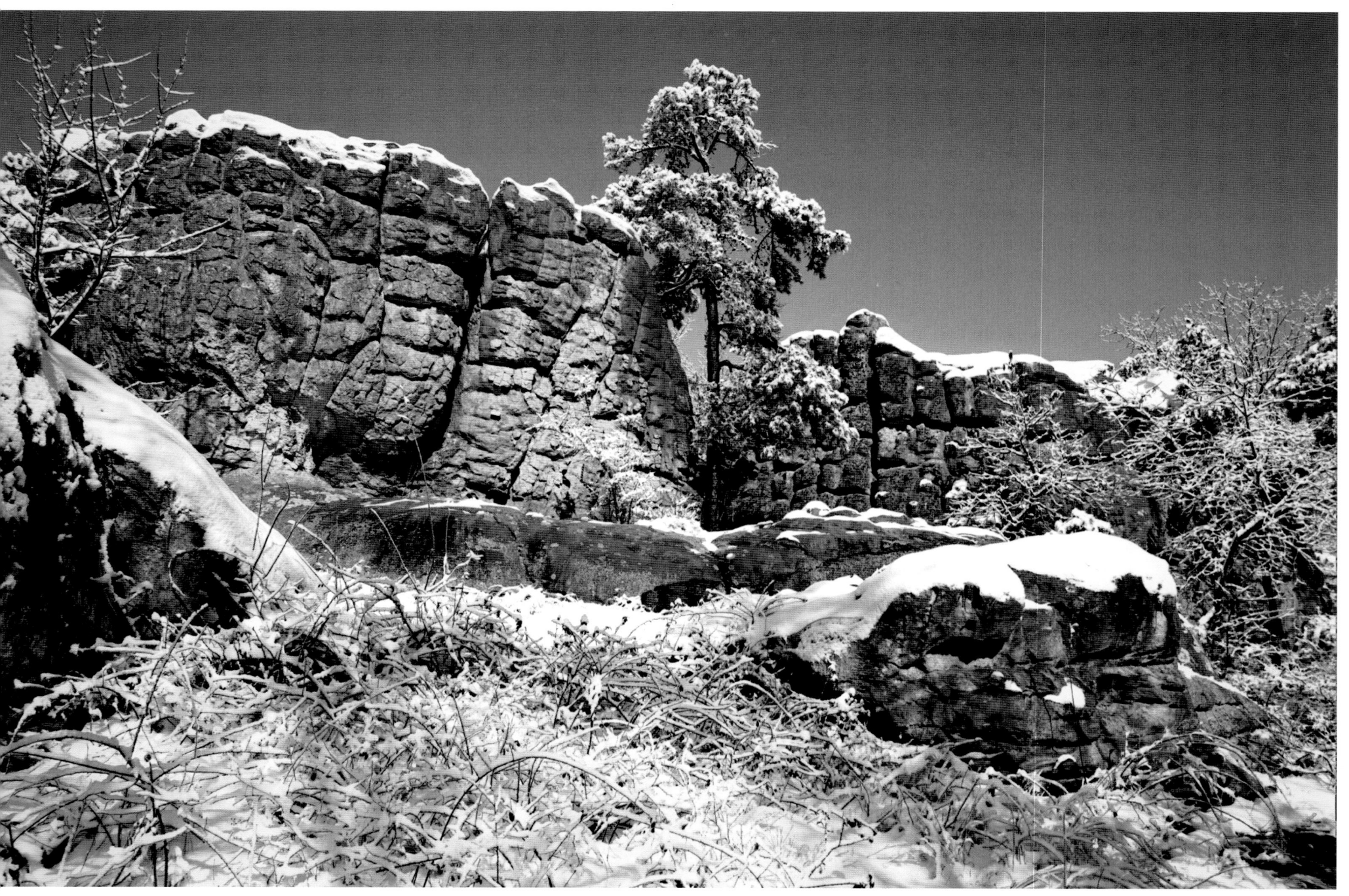

Snow on rock outcrops on Lookout Mountain, DeKalb County, Alabama, 2-2007; Pentax 6x7 camera; 45mm lens; yellow K2 filter; Ilford Delta 100, 120 film; PMK Pyro developer.

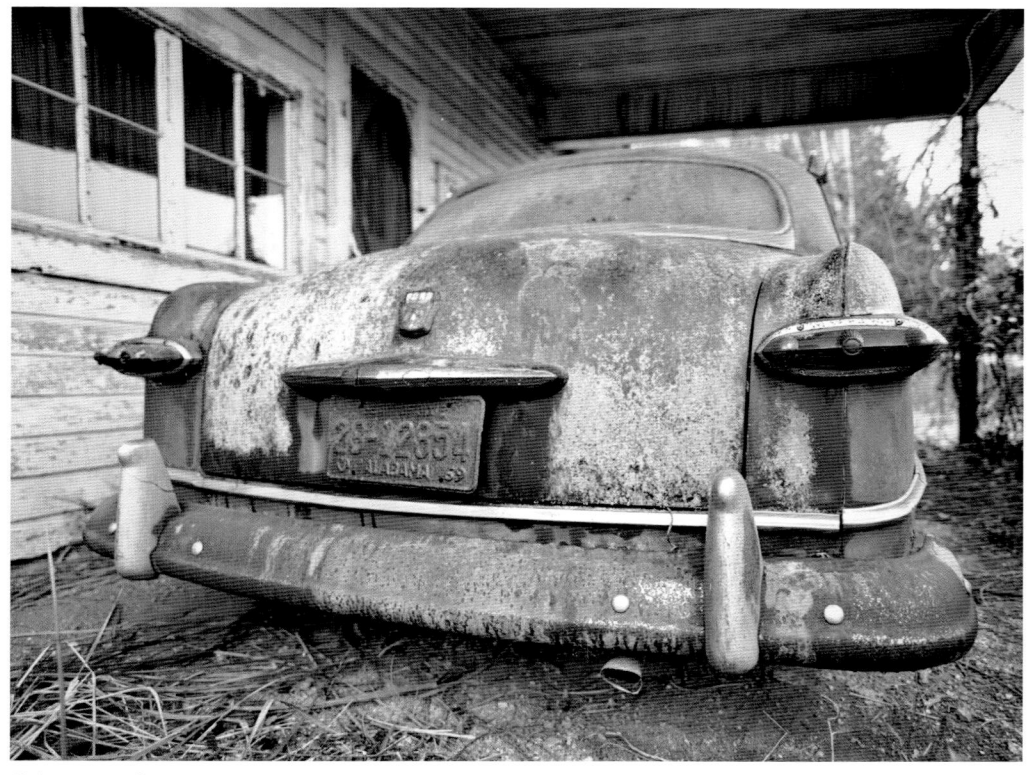

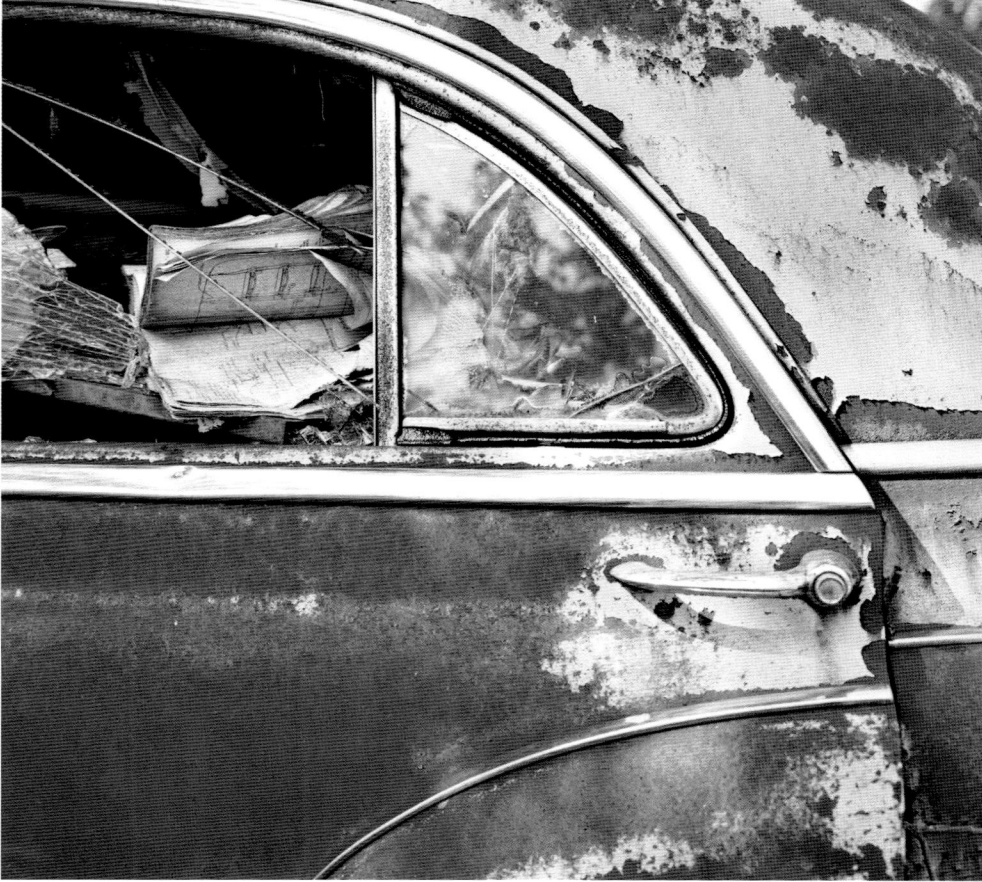

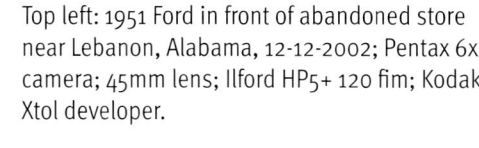

Top left: 1951 Ford in front of abandoned store near Lebanon, Alabama, 12-12-2002; Pentax 6x7 camera; 45mm lens; Ilford HP5+ 120 fim; Kodak Xtol developer.

Top right: Abandoned 1950 Chevrolet with books to read near Dogtown, Alabama, 3-2001; Pentax 6x7 camera; 75mm lens; Kodak Tmax 100, 120 film; Kodak Xtol developer.

Left: Frozen Farmall tractor at a farm near Glasgow, Missouri, 2-2002; Pentax 6x7 camera; 75mm lens; Ilford HP5+ 120 film; Kodak D76 developer.

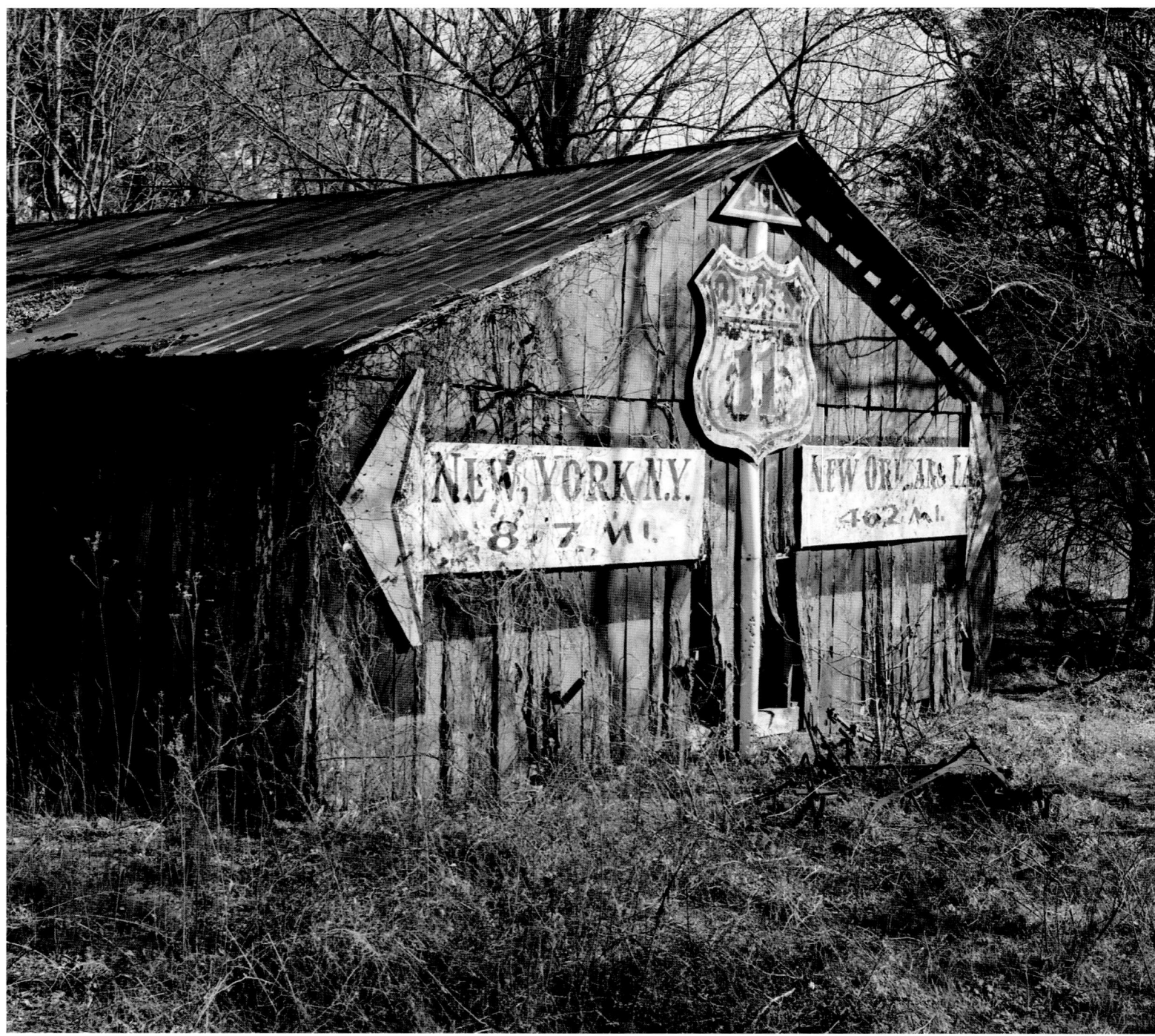

U.S. 11 directional
sign near Sulphur
Springs, DeKalb
County, Alabama,
4-2009; Hasselblad
camera; 50mm
Zeiss Distagon lens;
Kodak Tmax 100
120 film; PMK Pyro
developer.

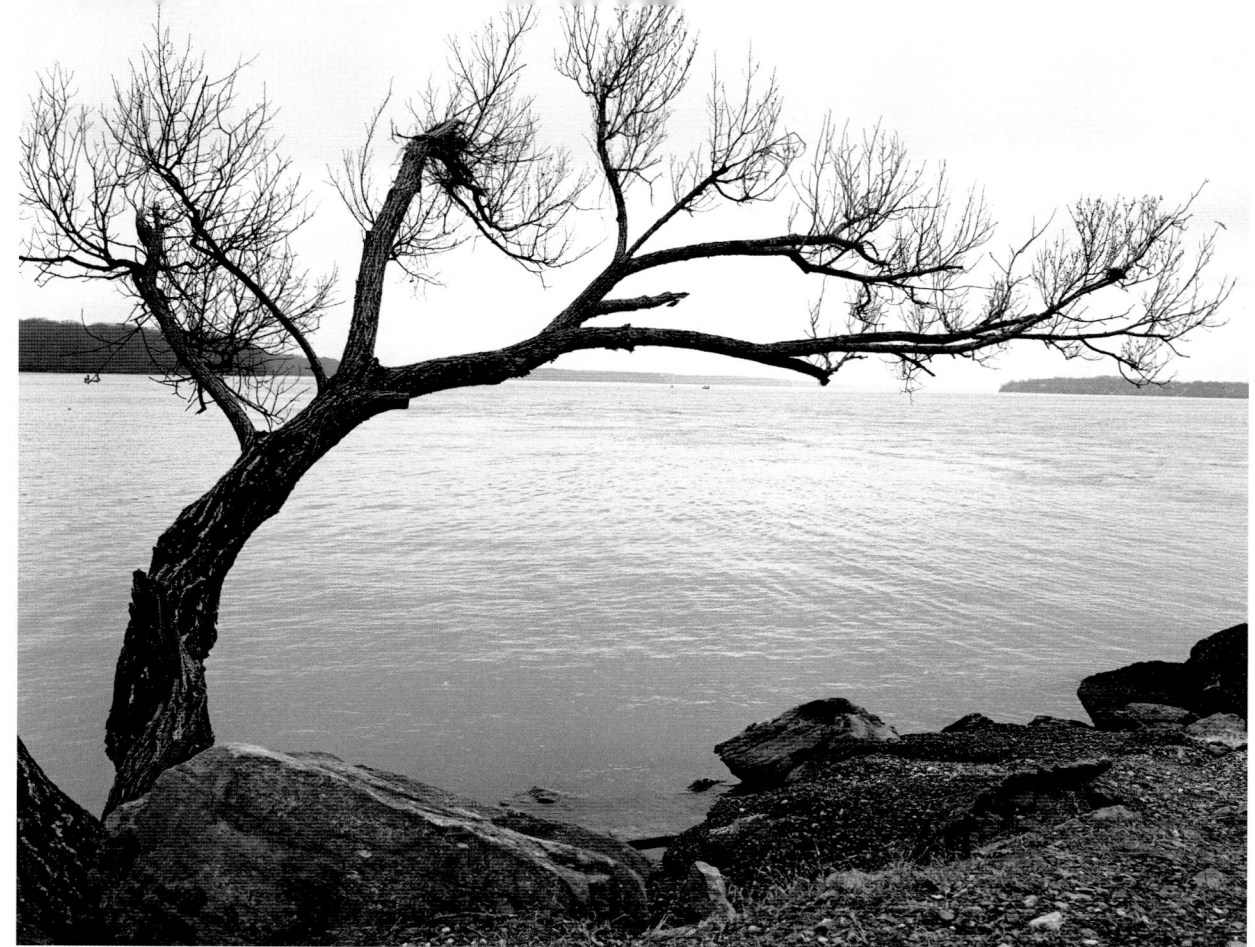

Top: Joe Wheeler State Park, Alabama, 3-1-2006; Hasselblad camera; 50mm Zeiss Distagon lens; Ilford HP5+ 120 film; PMK Pyro developer.

Bottom: Little River at Little River Canyon National Preserve, DeKalb and Cherokee counties, Alabama, 6-13-2009; Linhof Master Technika camera; 120mm Schneider Super Symmar lens; Kodak Super XX 4x5 film; PMK Pyro developer.

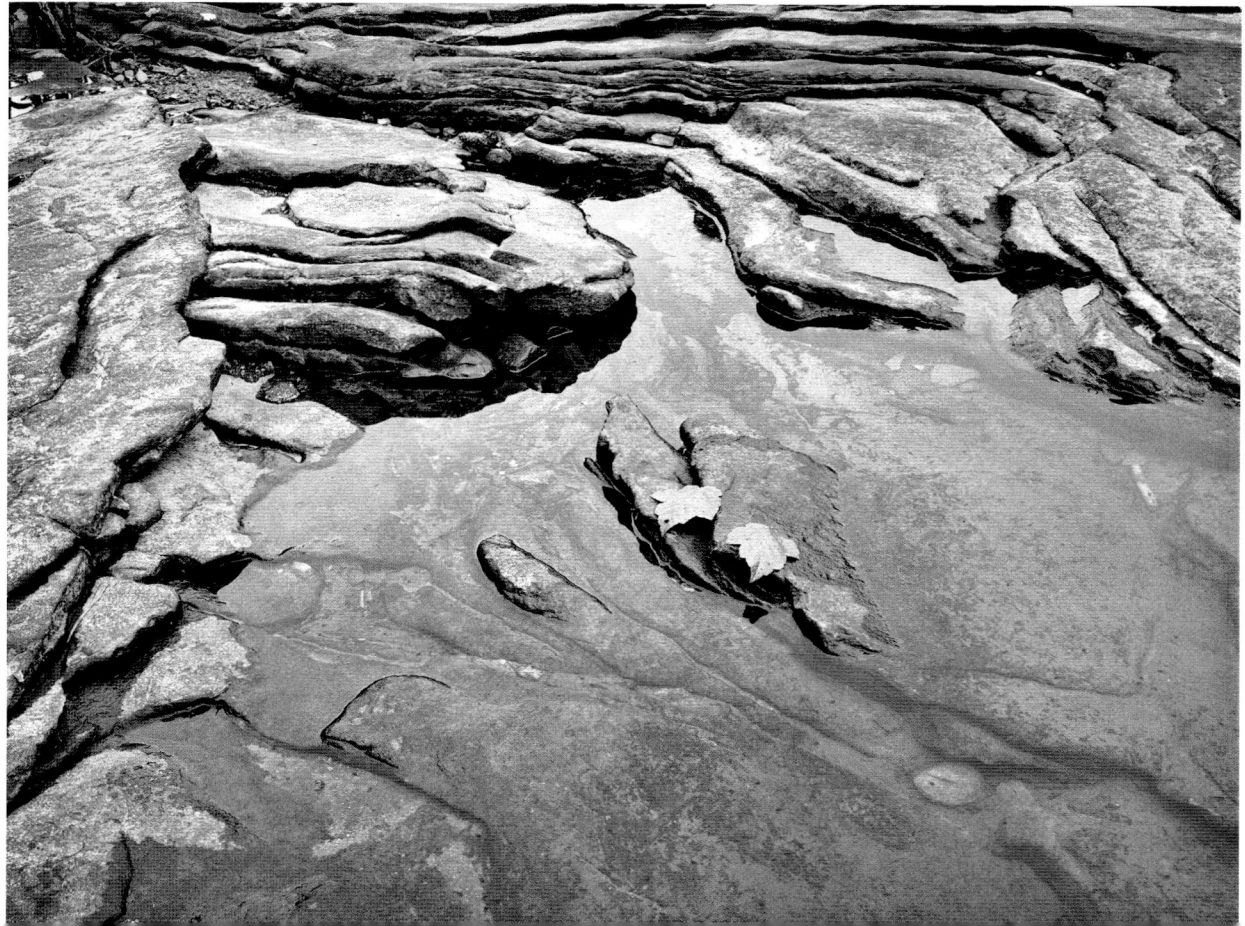

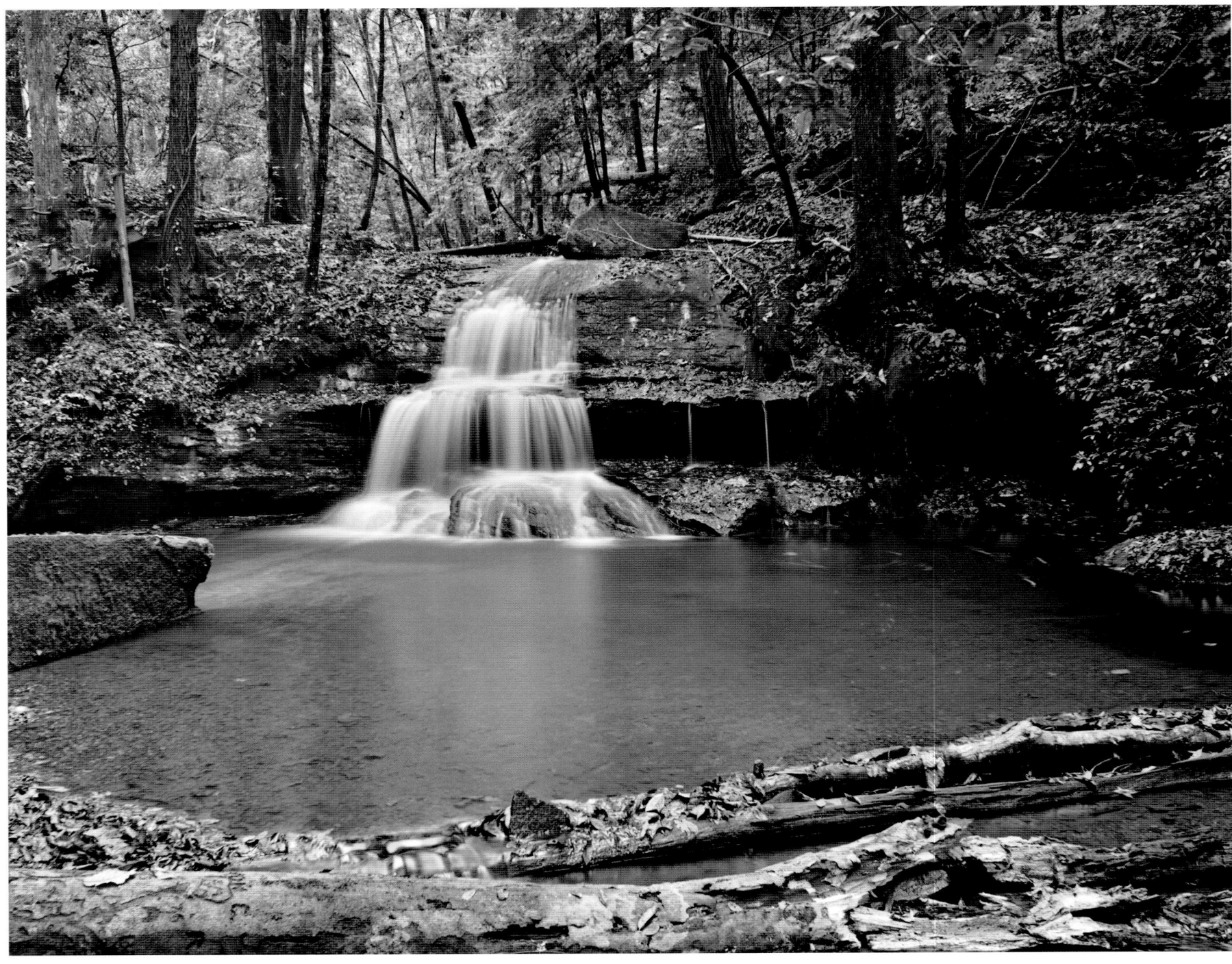

6

The 2010s: Film in a Digital Age

The continuing evolution of digital photography produced better and better single-lens reflex cameras and point-and-shoot cameras, and smartphones were making photography easy for everyone. Good-quality digital images that were easy to take were becoming the norm.

The decimation of the film, paper, and chemical businesses continued. As described earlier, digital killed Kodak's premier color film, Kodachrome. Dwayne's Photo in Parsons, Kansas, the last remaining Kodachrome processing lab in the world, processed the last Kodachrome film. The targeted last day had been December 30, 2010, but thousands of unprocessed rolls came in from around the world, including fifteen thousand rolls of railroad pictures. Dwayne's did not finish till January 18, 2011. I was honored to have four rolls of slides and two rolls of Super 8mm movie film processed in the last batch. One image I shot, a still life of Kodachrome film and various cameras, was used by CNN in a story about the end of this legendary color film. I had made it a practice throughout the decades to shoot my medium- or large-format black-and-white film first on my photo outings. After that, I would shoot color. Most often, my color work was done on 35mm Kodachrome film using a Leica camera.

My career in tourism was doing well, and I continued to grow within the industry, becoming an area president/CEO. My tourism photography was growing too. I provided photographs for books, magazines, and travel guides. In addition, I was getting more and more requests to teach photo workshops for camera clubs, art councils, tourism organizations, and state parks. I have always taught these workshops as two-day events: beginning with a class and then a day of shooting. My primary class for all levels of photography experience is titled "Composition, Lighting, and Impact." This class focuses on taking better pictures, regardless of whether you were using film or digital cameras.

IN EARLY 2013, I was contacted by Randy and Olivia Grider about a new lifestyle magazine for the Lookout Mountain region, which includes northeast Alabama, southeast Tennessee and northwest

Facing page: Mystic Falls at Rock Bridge Canyon, Hodges, Alabama, 11-3-2015; Toyo 8x10M camera; 240mm Schneider G Claron lens; Efke R50 4x5 film; PML PMK developer.

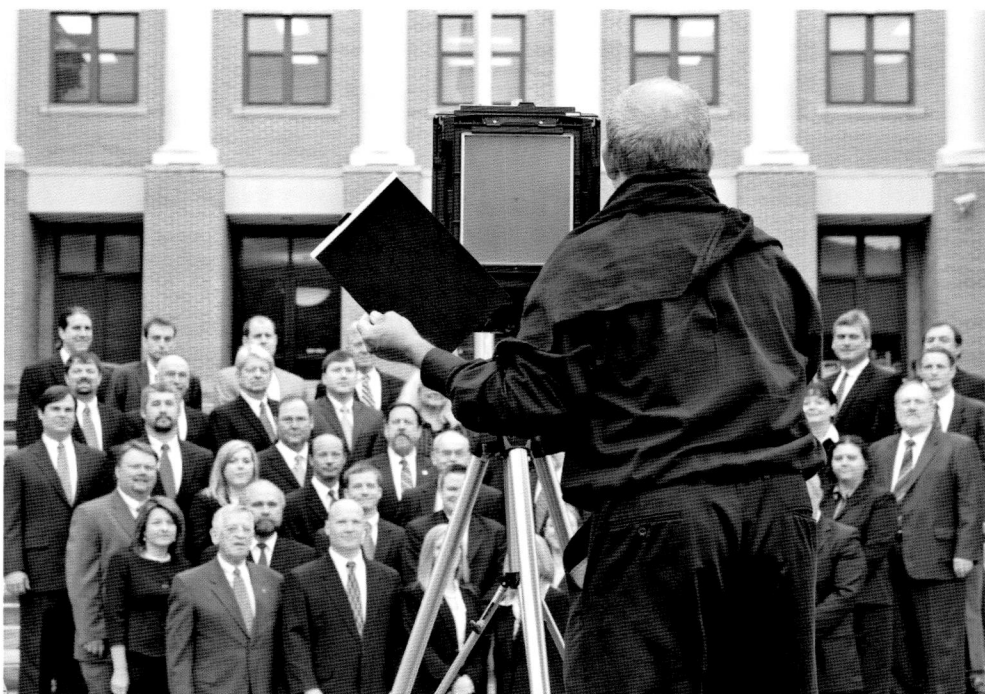

Above: John Dersham shooting the DeKalb County, Alabama, Bar Association on 8x10 film in front of the courthouse, October 12, 2011. Below: John Dersham at the Evelyn Burrow Museum in Hanceville, Alabama, for the opening of his "Changing Moods" gallery exhibit, November 2014.

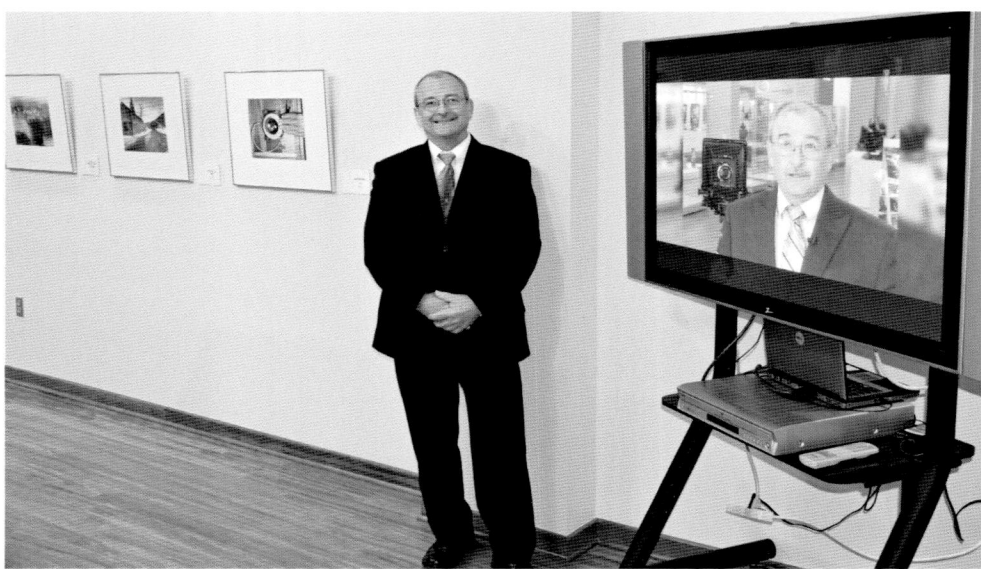

Georgia. *Lookout Alabama* magazine would have an emphasis on attractions, arts and crafts, travel, food, etc. The magazine would published quarterly, corresponding to the season. The first issue appeared in the summer of 2013.

I built an ongoing relationship with the Griders, which led me to writing a column for each issue called "Life on Lookout Mountain." I used my photography in my column, but it was featured throughout the magazine as well. This magazine was a beautiful keeper with a long shelf life and a quickly building collector's market. It was perfect-bound with fantastic print quality on a thick paper stock. The popular magazine was sold by subscription but also in retail stores and big-box outlets like Barnes & Noble and Gander Mountain. At its peak, the magazine was sold across eleven states. Unfortunately, the owners struggled to remain profitable and discontinued publication after three years.

In September of 2014, I had black-and-white exhibit at the Evelyn Burrow Museum in Hanceville, Alabama. This exhibit contained sixty-five large, framed archival darkroom prints of various sizes. The exhibit lasted six months and was heavily promoted, including a short documentary of my work shown in the gallery and on television in Alabama.

Earlier in the decade, I was asked by Arcadia Publishing to write a postcard history book for Fort Payne. Arcadia is the largest publisher of local history books, with a variety themes, including historical postcards. I was not a postcard collector, so I borrowed cards from people who were collectors. For more recent years, when fewer postcards were being produced, I used my photography. Many of those images ultimately wound up as postcards for visitor centers.

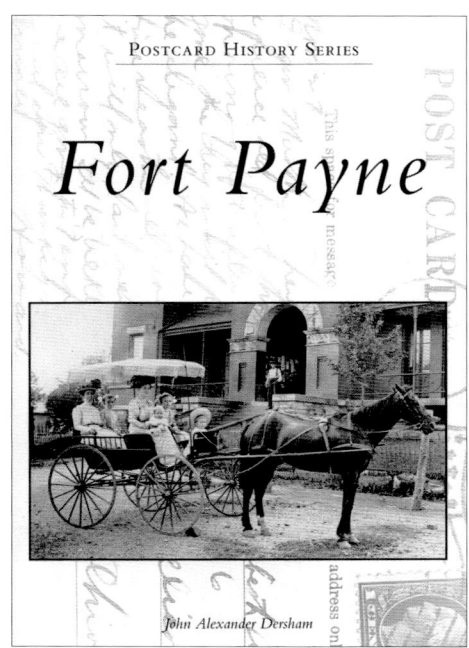

Fort Payne Postcard History book, released March 2016.

IN THE MIDDLE OF the decade, Alabama was beginning to turn its focus to its upcoming bicentennial. The state would reach its two hundredth birthday on December 14, 2019. The Alabama Bicentennial Commission was formed, and the Alabama Department of Travel and Tourism was given the task of developing a three-year bicentennial celebration. This included a certified education program for schools and a traveling exhibit created by the Alabama Humanities Foundation that would visit all sixty-seven Alabama counties for a month. The exhibit would cover our two-century history using touch-screen computers and large attractive fixtures with interesting graphic art that matched the history of the period dealt with each part of the exhibit. There would be lectures, newsletters, and multiple organizations contributing to the Alabama Bicentennial.

In early 2015, I began discussing with tourism and economic development leaders a statewide coffee table photography book that would reflect the beauty and diversity of our state. The book would also contain text discussing the reasons for the state's great amount of scenic beauty: climate, rivers, forests, mountains, lakes, and the Gulf Coast. In conjunction with Jay Lamar, director of the Bicentennial Commission; Nisa Miranda, director of the University of Alabama's Center for Economic Development; and Tami Reist,

president/CEO of the Alabama Mountain Lakes Tourism Association, the project got a nod from Lee Sentell, director of the Alabama Tourism Department. We met with a few publishers to propose the book concept. All were interested, but NewSouth Books in Montgomery was the most excited and immediately offered a firm yes to the book. Sentell and Lamar confirmed the book would be an Alabama Bicentennial-certified book and carry the Alabama Bicentennial logo.

In early 2019, the book was finished. It became an immediate success at Barnes & Noble, Books-A-Million, and most Alabama independent bookstores and gift shops, including the Goat Hill

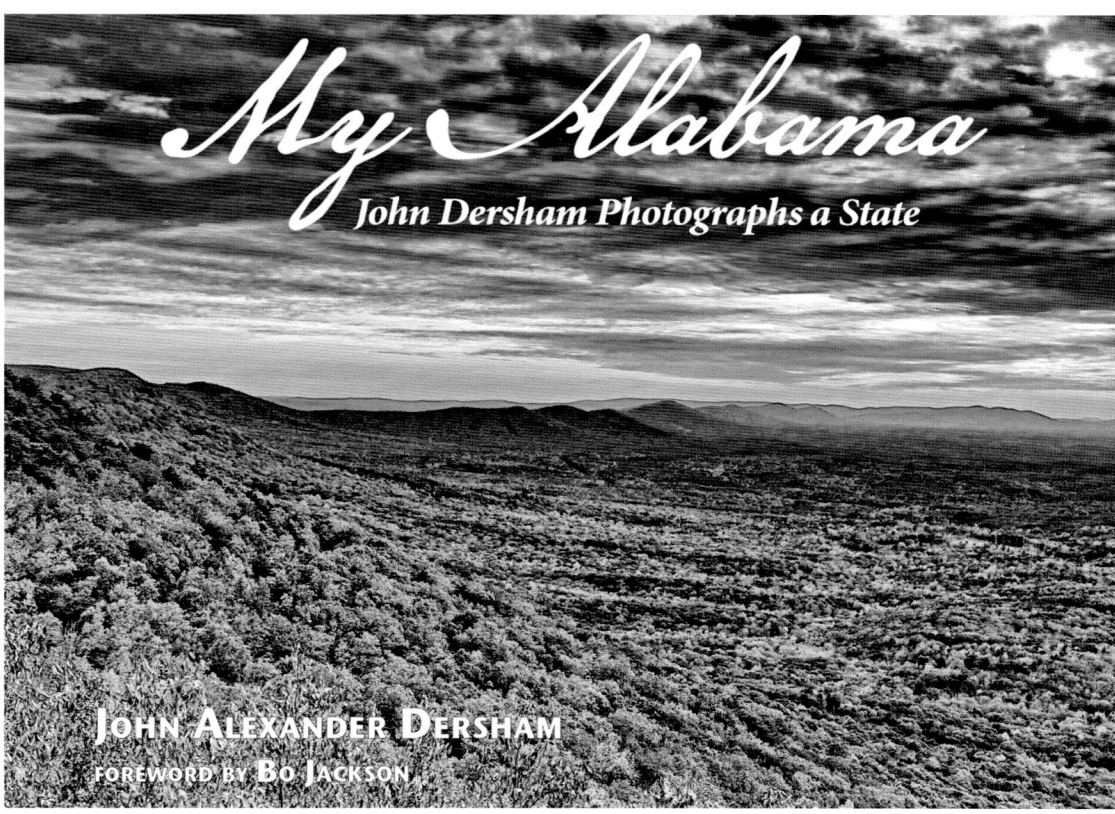

My Alabama was released in May 2019 to coincide with the state's bicentennial.

Below: John Dersham hosted the DeKalb County Alabama Bicentennial celebration in November 2019 and gave Governor Kay Ivey and Country Music Hall of Famer Randy Owens signed copies of My Alabama.

Right: John Dersham on the cover of Alabama Living *magazine, June 2019; the issue featured a story about his new book,* My Alabama.

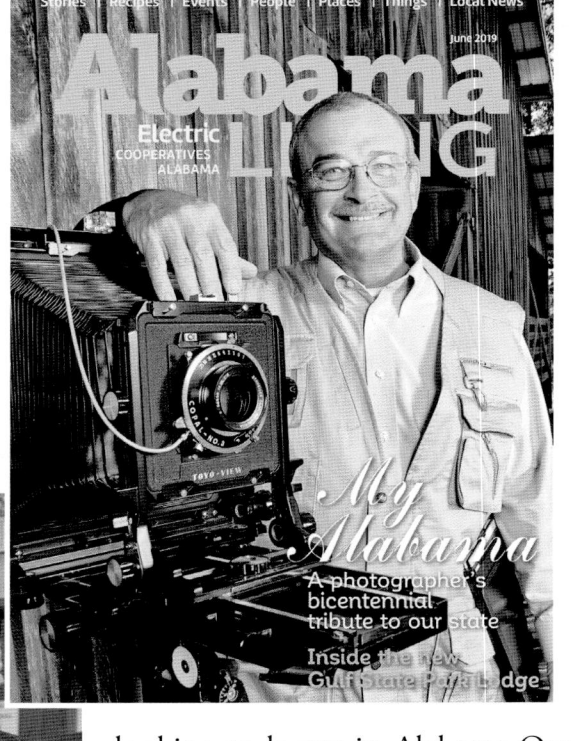

gift store in the State Capitol and gift shops at the various state parks. Sentell bought books for each public library in the state. Tourism organizations who were sponsors of the book gave copies to Alabama congresspersons. The Alabama Senate and House of Representatives bought copies for their elected members. Economic development officials gave the book to industry leaders and executives of companies looking to locate in Alabama. Over the next year, I participated in the Bicentennial author book tour and was speaking statewide at libraries, bookstores, organizations, universities, and camera clubs. I was also doing signings at bookstores and gift shops statewide. (I still am.)

DURING THIS DECADE, I appeared seven times on *Absolutely Alabama,* the popular TV show hosted by Fred Hunter, airing on multiple CBS, NBC, and ABC stations in Alabama. One of the episodes was about my work with large-format film, especially 8x10 film. In 2019, an episode featured my new Alabama Bicentennial book, *My Alabama: John Dersham Photographs a State*, with the foreword written by legendary athlete and Alabama native Bo Jackson. This episode aired as

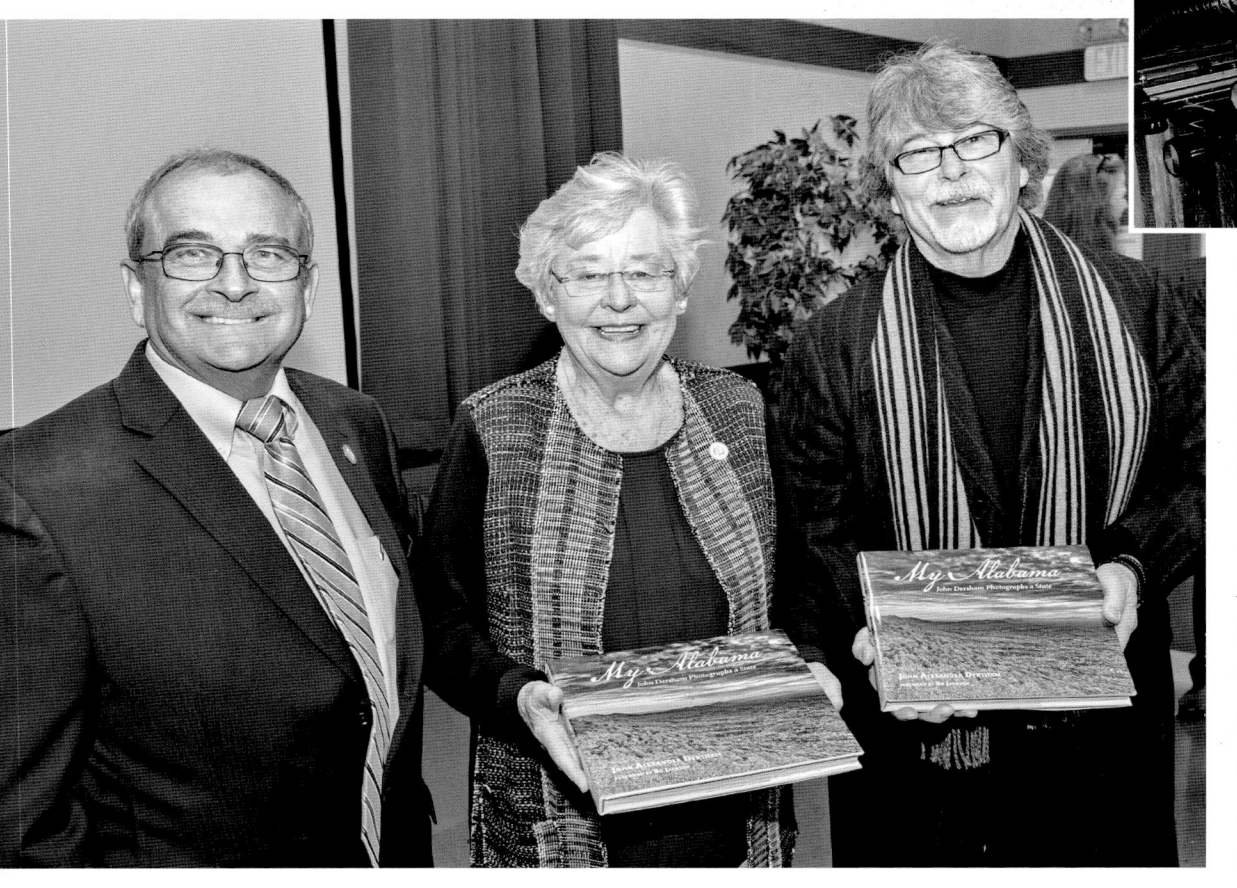

a separate show but was also included in two longer versions used during the Bicentennial celebrations later in 2019.

My Alabama became popular for a few reasons. There had not been any generic Alabama coffee table photography books in a while, especially one that covered the entire state. It could become a valuable keepsake due to its Alabama Bicentennial certification. It was also highly supported and promoted by the tourism and economic development industries in Alabama. NewSouth Books did a fantastic job promoting the book as well. It became a sizable story in four large magazines covering Alabama. One, *Alabama Living*, made it their cover story in June of 2019.

AS THE DECADE MOVED along, the decline of film sales over the last decade and a half began to level out. Towards the end of the decade, the use of film was growing again, and much like the analog vinyl record, film found a new audience among young people who had grown up in the digital age but were finding film interesting, fun, and "real" in comparison with the non-tangible, non-material realm of digital. Film had character, feel, and emotion. It easily showed mistakes, flaws, and imperfections, and it seemed more lifelike and a better suited for us flawed human beings.

My former employer Eastman Kodak and other film companies like Ilford, Foma, Fuji, and Adox were selling more film and finding a new audience for darkroom supplies, paper, and chemicals. There was even enough of a demand for Kodak to reintroduce Ektachome after having dropped it in 2012. Kodak had to find a way to make the film a few thousand rolls at a time instead of a hundred thousand at a time. This took some R&D, but Kodak was successful, and I feel what we now have is the prettiest Ektachrome film ever.

In the last few years of the decade, I began getting requests to teach film and darkroom classes again. My friend Randy Grider, now director of the Mentone Arts & Cultural Center, asked me to teach film and darkroom classes there. It was incredible how many people have wanted to take this class. We cap class enrollment at six participants so that we have space in my darkroom for everyone to make two 8x10 prints. It is a two-day workshop, the first day beginning with loading cameras with Ilford Delta 100 (I provide the film and a loaner 35mm camera for students who need one). After shooting, I show students how to load the film onto a developing reel, in the dark, then process the film. The next day we print it. The students are young people, most of whom have never shot film and some that used to and want to again. I love to teach these workshops.

Even though film will remain a niche business, it appears to be stable and should continue to have enthusiasts for generations to come.

Throughout my many years of holding workshops, I have always encouraged photographers to shoot both digital and film. The two have different looks and levels of quality, but both provide artistic merit to add to one's portfolio of creative efforts.

I always bucked the trend of totally replacing film with digital, since both have their place in photography. I am glad that this is acknowledged among aspiring photographers and photo artists.

As the decade ended, my eldest granddaughter graduated from high school and entered her first year in college, and our youngest was in fifth grade. Kyle, the kids, and I are busy with our own lives. We get together often as a family and rarely miss a holiday together.

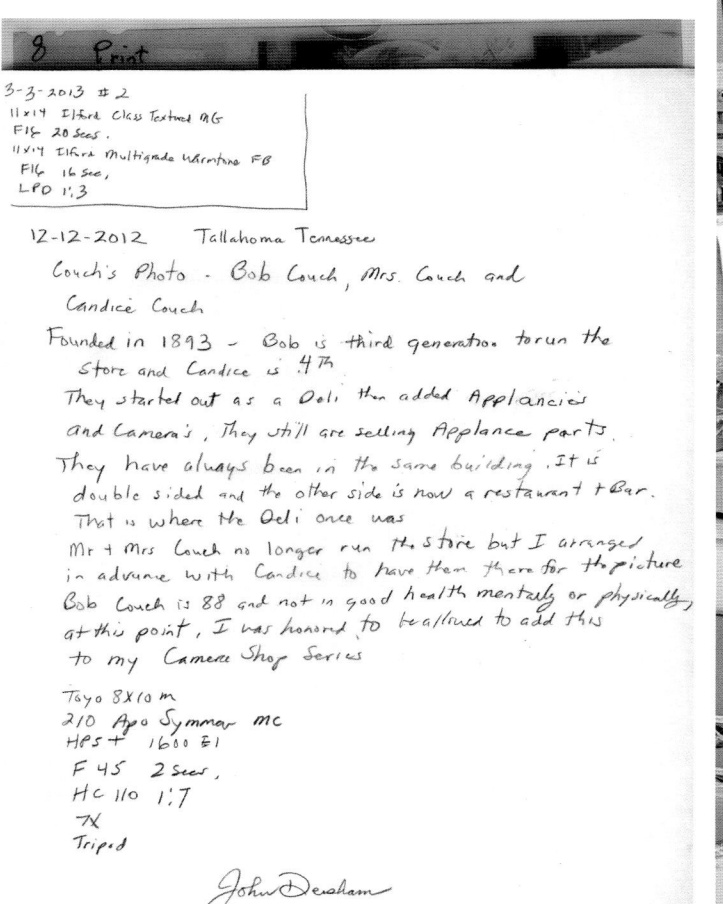

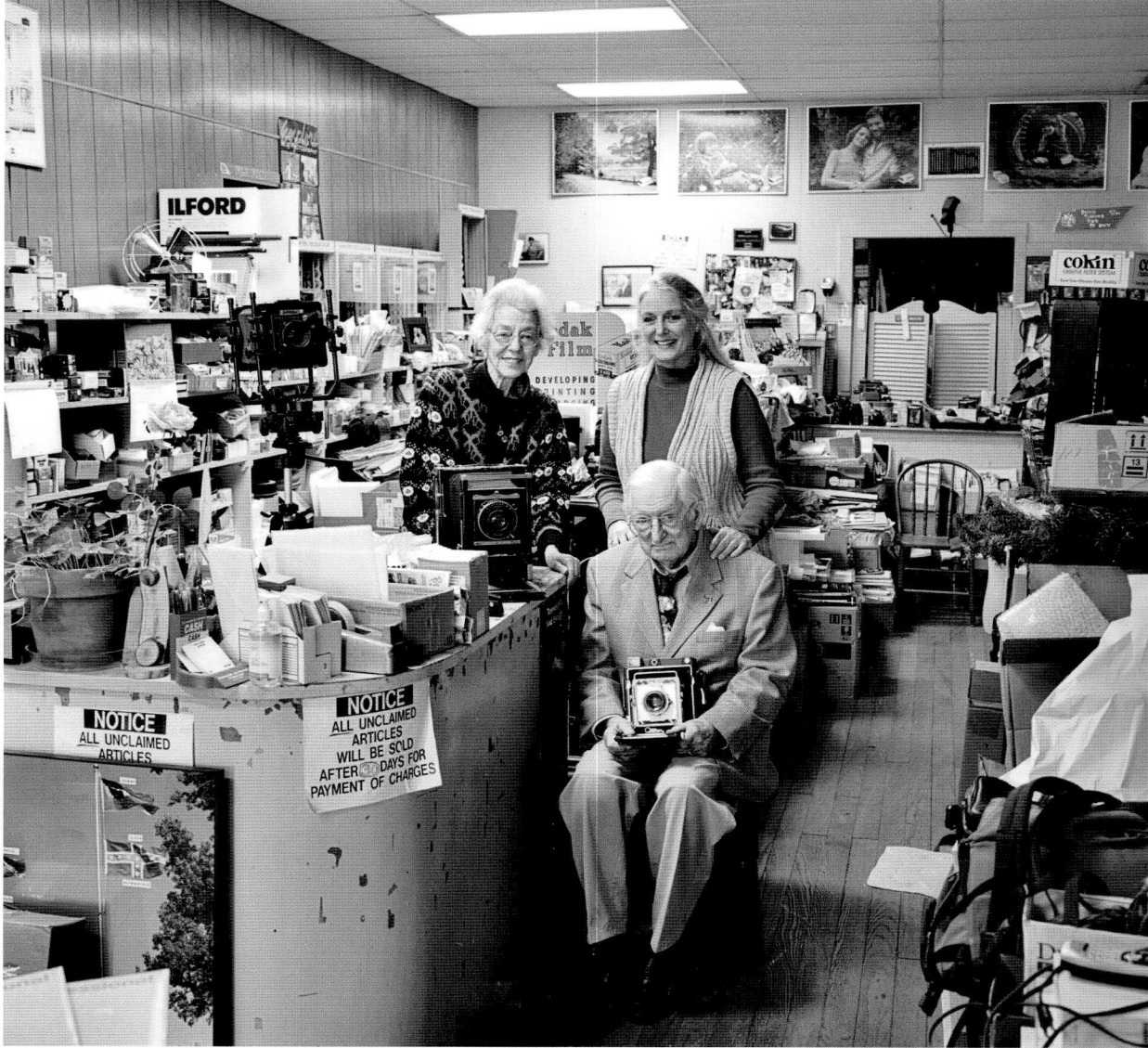

Above: Couch's Camera, Tullahoma, Tennessee, estd. 1893, 12-12-2012; Toyo 8x10M camera; 210mm Schneider Apo Symmar lens; Ilford HP5+ 8x10 film; PMK Pyro developer.

Facing page: Chair at abandoned log house near Joe Wheeler State Park, Rogersville, Alabama, 2-28-2015; Hasselblad camera; 50mm Zeiss Distagon Lens; Ilford Delta 100, 120 film; PMK Pyro developer.

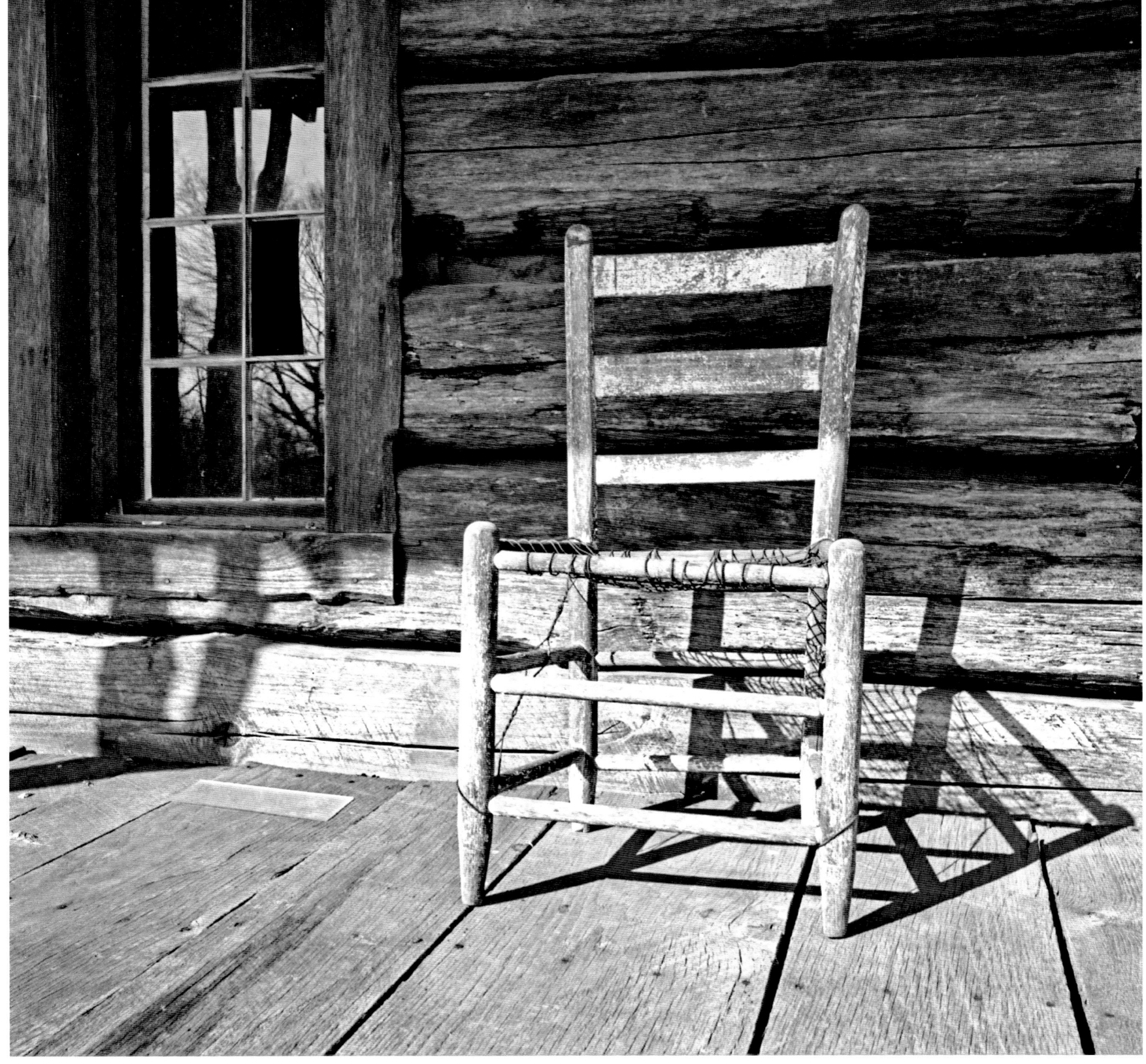

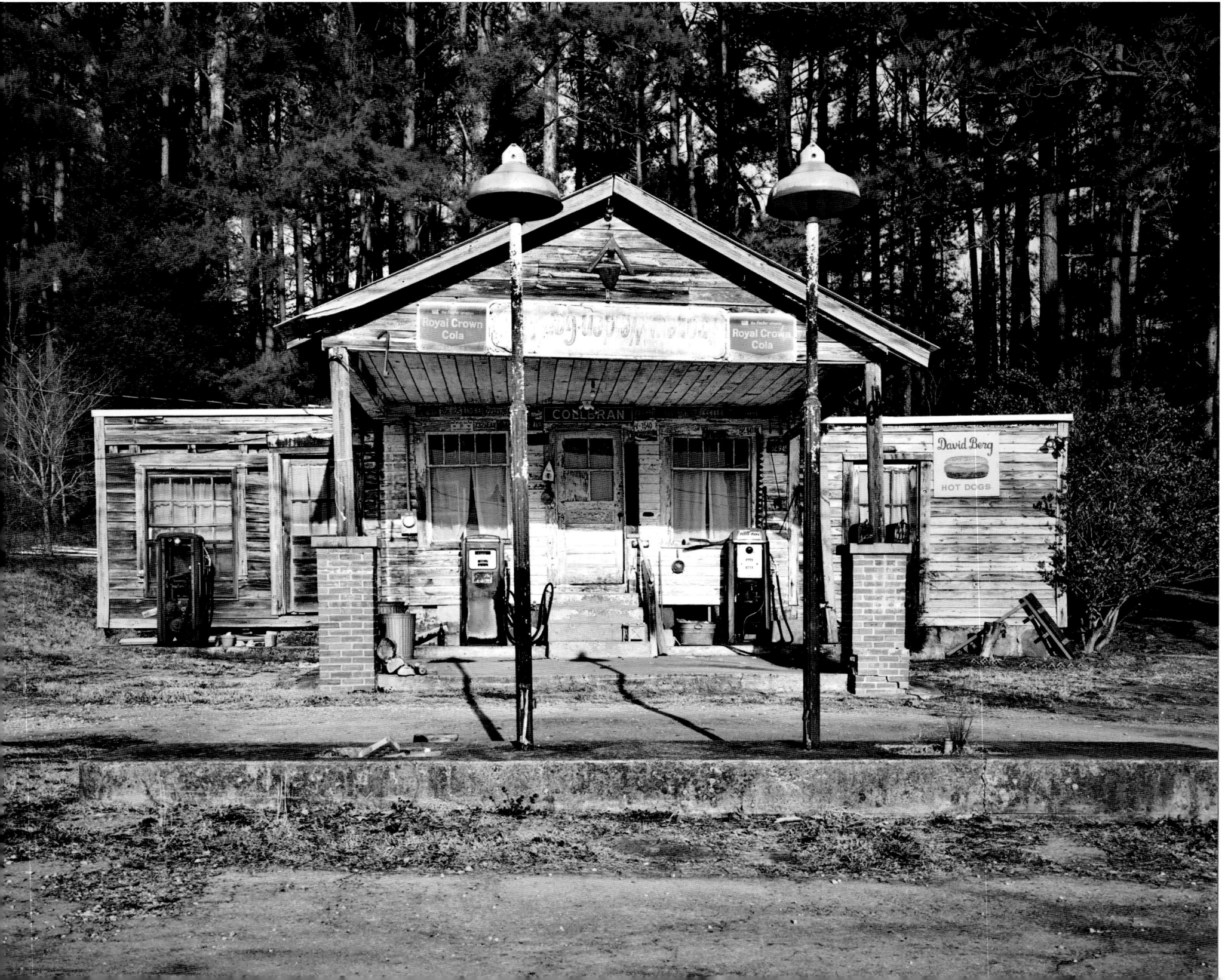

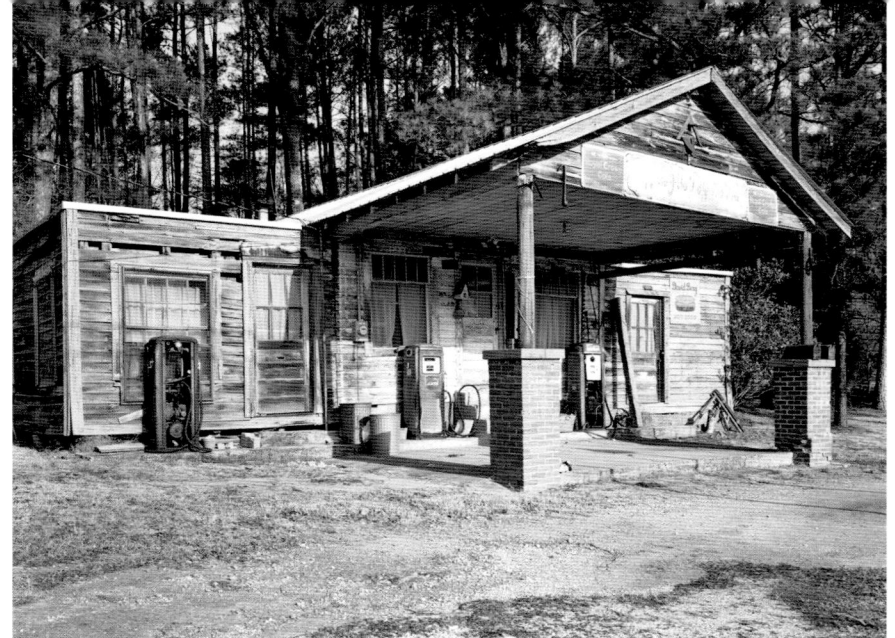

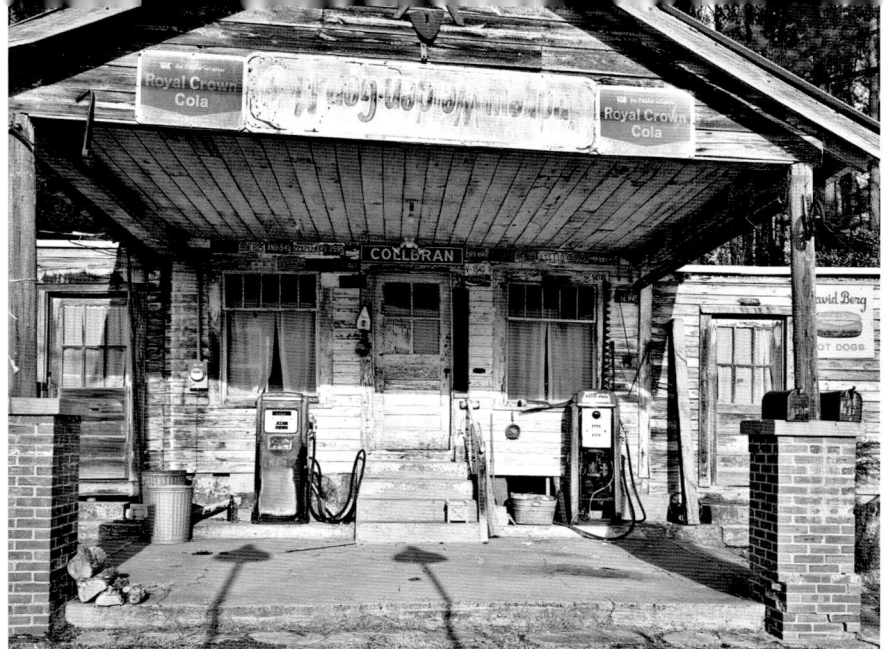

Facing page and above: Killian's U.S. 11, Collbran, Alabama, 3-9-2014; Toyo 8x10M camera; 240mm Schneider G Claron lens; Adox CHS 100 8x10 film; PMK Pyro developer.

1-10-2016 #1
Kentmere Kentona 12x16 #2
F16 9 secs. - LPD 1:7 developer
dodge shadow under entry slightly

3-9-2014 7:00 Am hour - Collbran Alabama

Killian's Korner/Corner - Gad Killian owner recently deceased
He bought it in 1937. It was the Post office and he was
Post Master. His family of whom I have spoken is not sure
if it still handled mail after he bought it and made it a
General store. Later in life Gad made it an Antique store
and though not open to the public late in his life he continued
to sell antiques out of there on yard sale weekends and via
private contacts.
There was a time in the early 1900's that Collbran had 3 general stores,
Post office, railroad station and more houses than today,

Toyo 8x10 M
240 Schneider G-Claron
F 64 v 90 ½ sec.
Adox CHS 100 8x10 (100 EI)
PMK Pyro Developer
7X lupe
Tripod

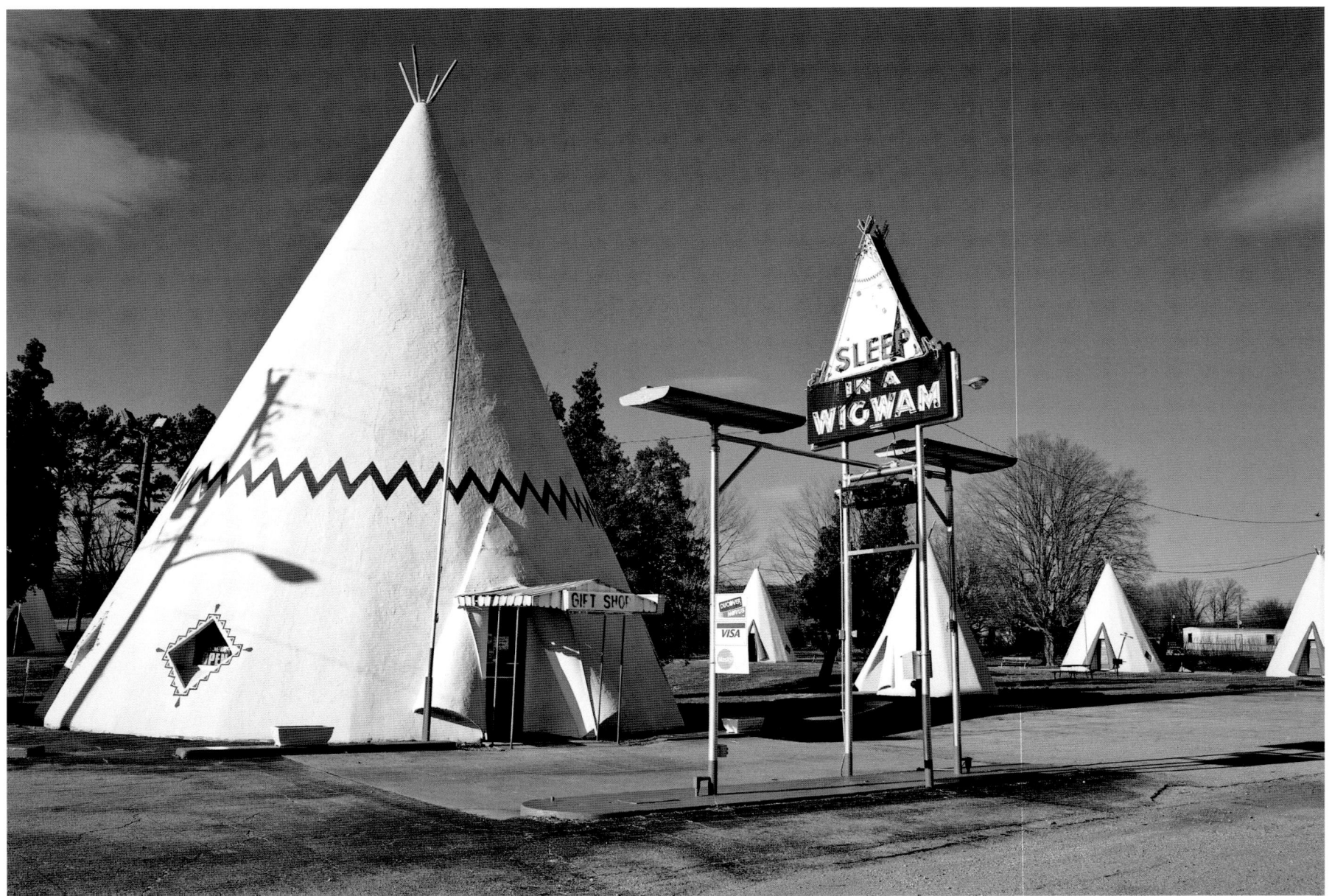

Wigwam Motel Cave Springs, Kentucky, 2-2013; Pentax 6x7 camera; 45mm lens; yellow K2 filter; Ilford Delta 100 120 film; PMK Pyro developer.

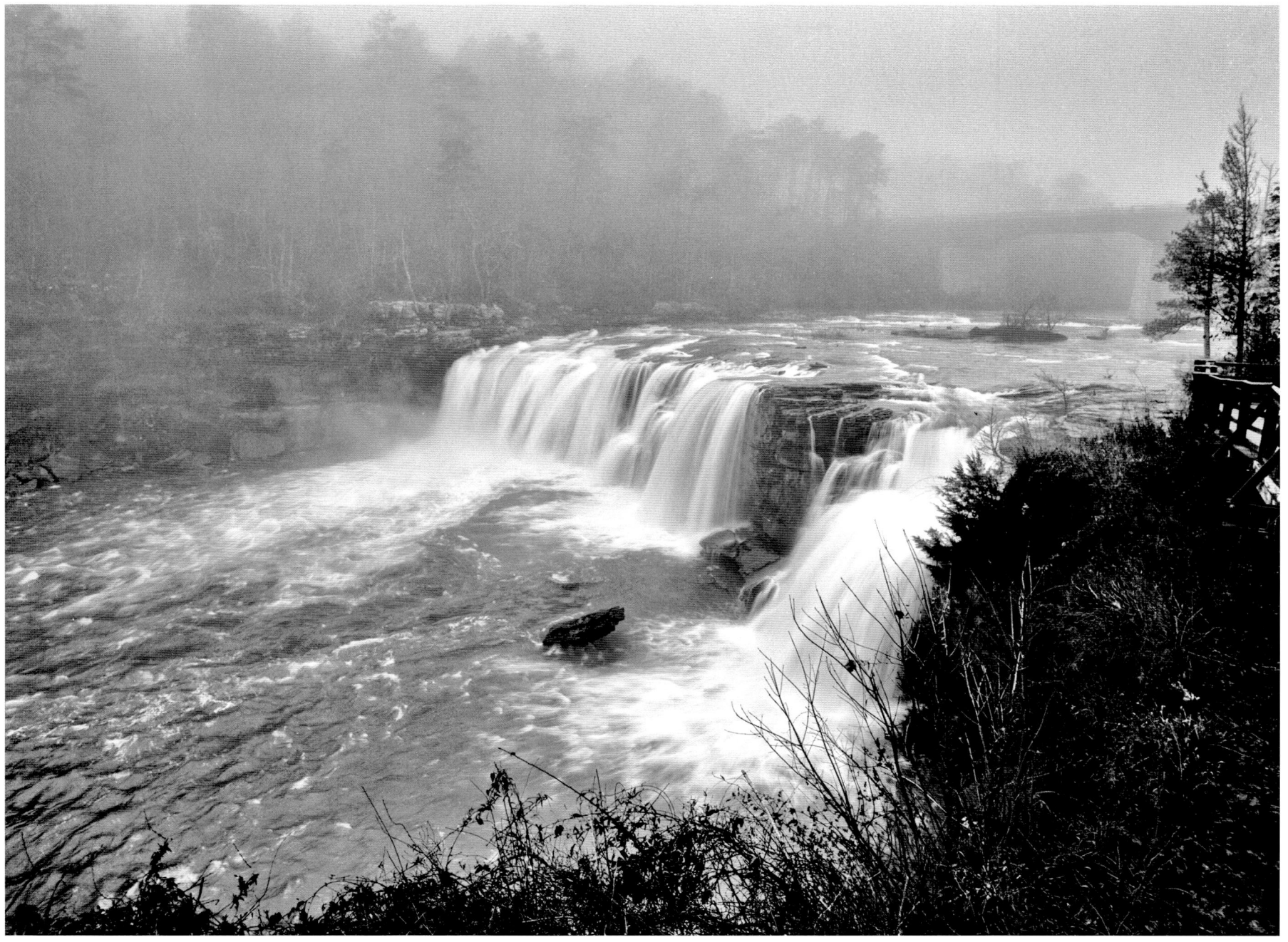

Little River Falls, Little River Canyon National Preserve, DeKalb and Cherokee counties, Alabama, 3-9-2019; Pentax 6x7 camera; 45mm lens; Ilford Delta 100, 120 film; PMK Pyro developer.

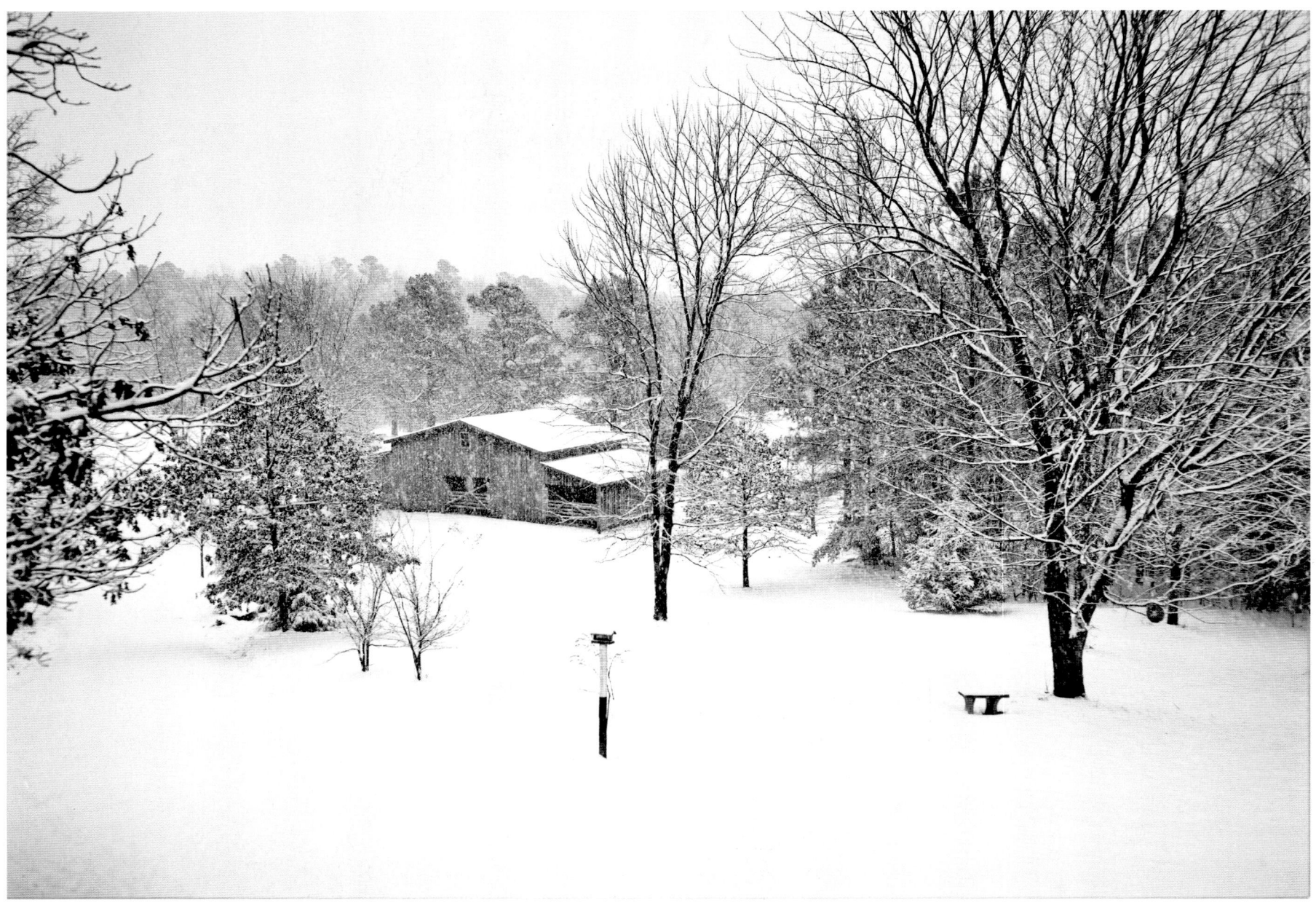

Above: Snow scene from our front window on Lookout Mountain in DeKalb County, Alabama, 2-2104; Crown Graphic 4x5 camera; 135mm Schneider Xenar lens; Ilford HP5+ 4x5 film; PMK Pyro developer.

Facing page: Rural scene near Roanoke, Virginia, 8-28-2012; Wista DX 4x5 camera; 210mm Schneider Apo Symmar lens; yellow K2 filter; Adox CHS 50 4x5 film; PMK Pyro developer.

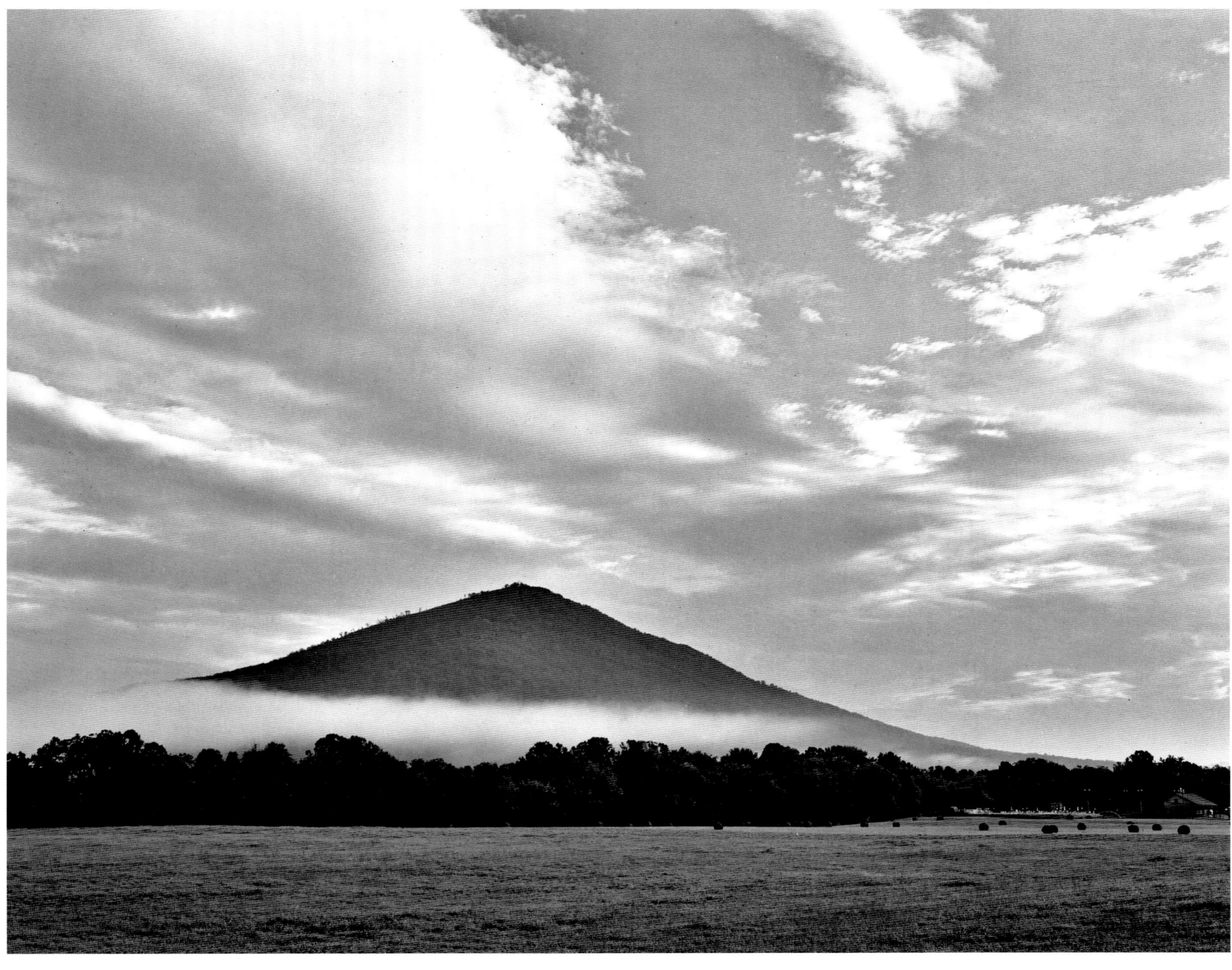

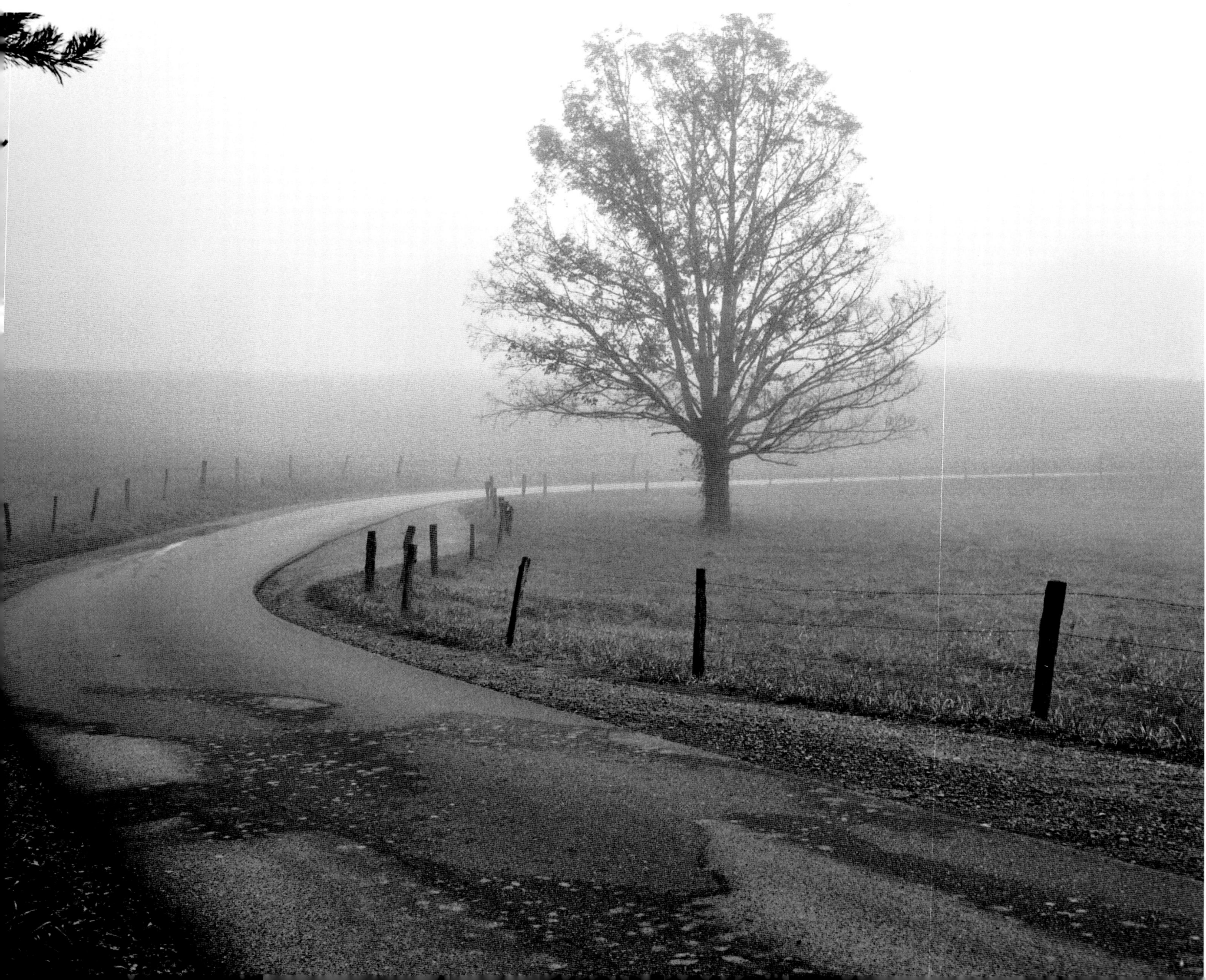

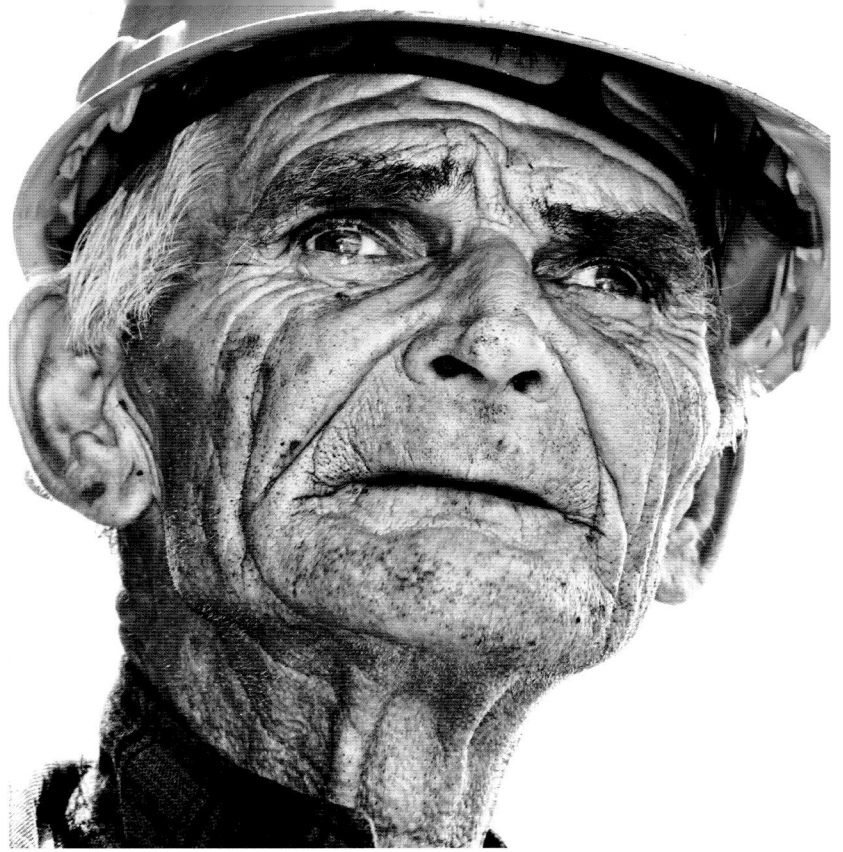

Left: Tom Williams, Hamilton, Alabama, known locally as "Neighbor" due to his calling everyone that when he sees them, 6-19-2010; Hasselblad camera; 150mm Zeiss Sonnar lens; Ilford HP5+ 120 film; PMK Pyro developer.

Below: From that same Hamilton, Alabama, community, the late folk potter Jerry Brown turning his clay the old way with his mule, "Ole Blue," 11-15-2014; Pentax 6x7 camera; 55mm lens; Ilford Delta 100, 120 film; PMK Pyro developer.

Facing page: Cades Cove at daylight, Great Smoky Mountain National Park, Gatlinburg, Tennessee, 10-2014; Pentax 6x7 camera; 50mm lens; Ilford HP5+ 120 film; PMK Pyro developer.

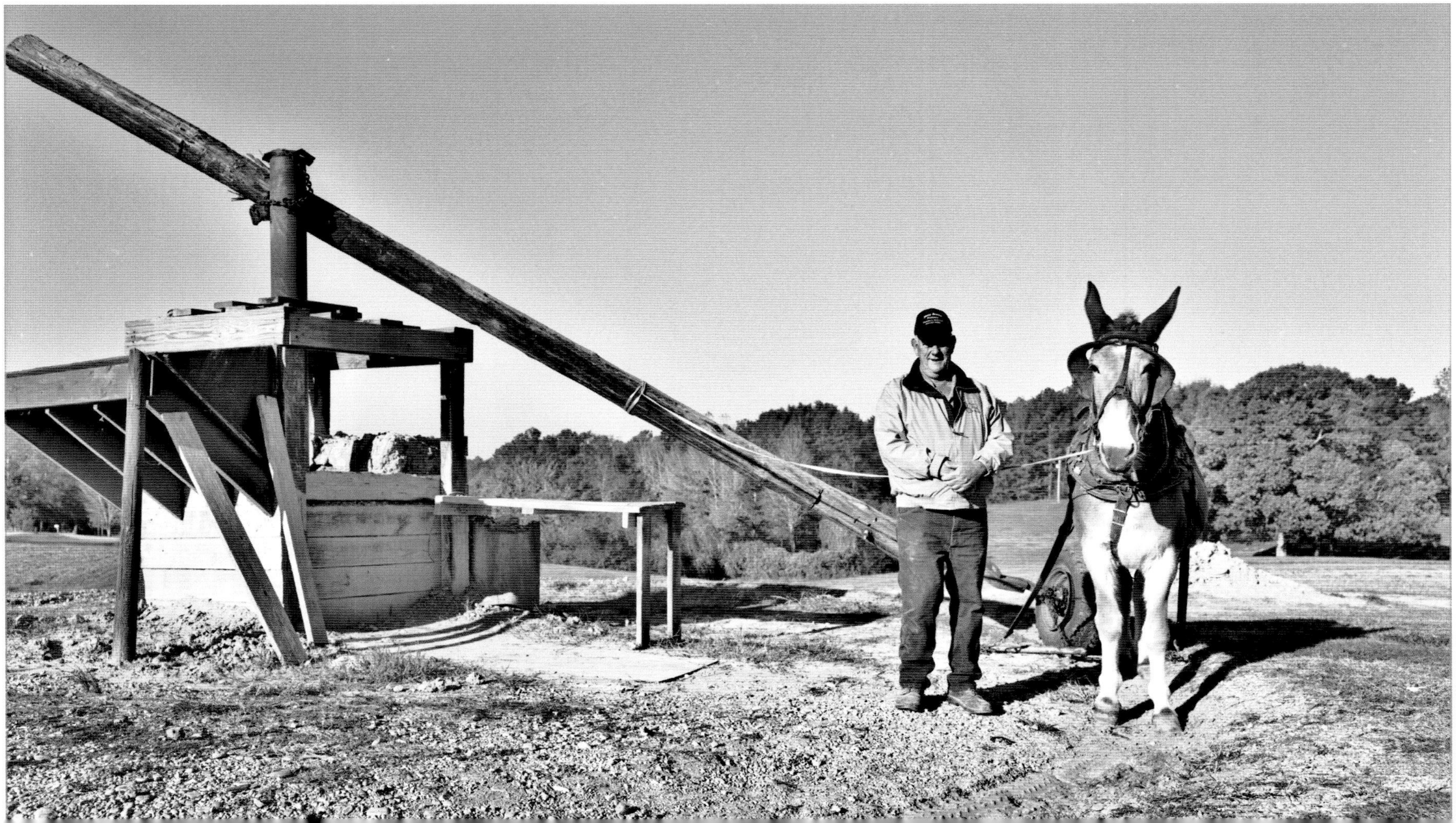

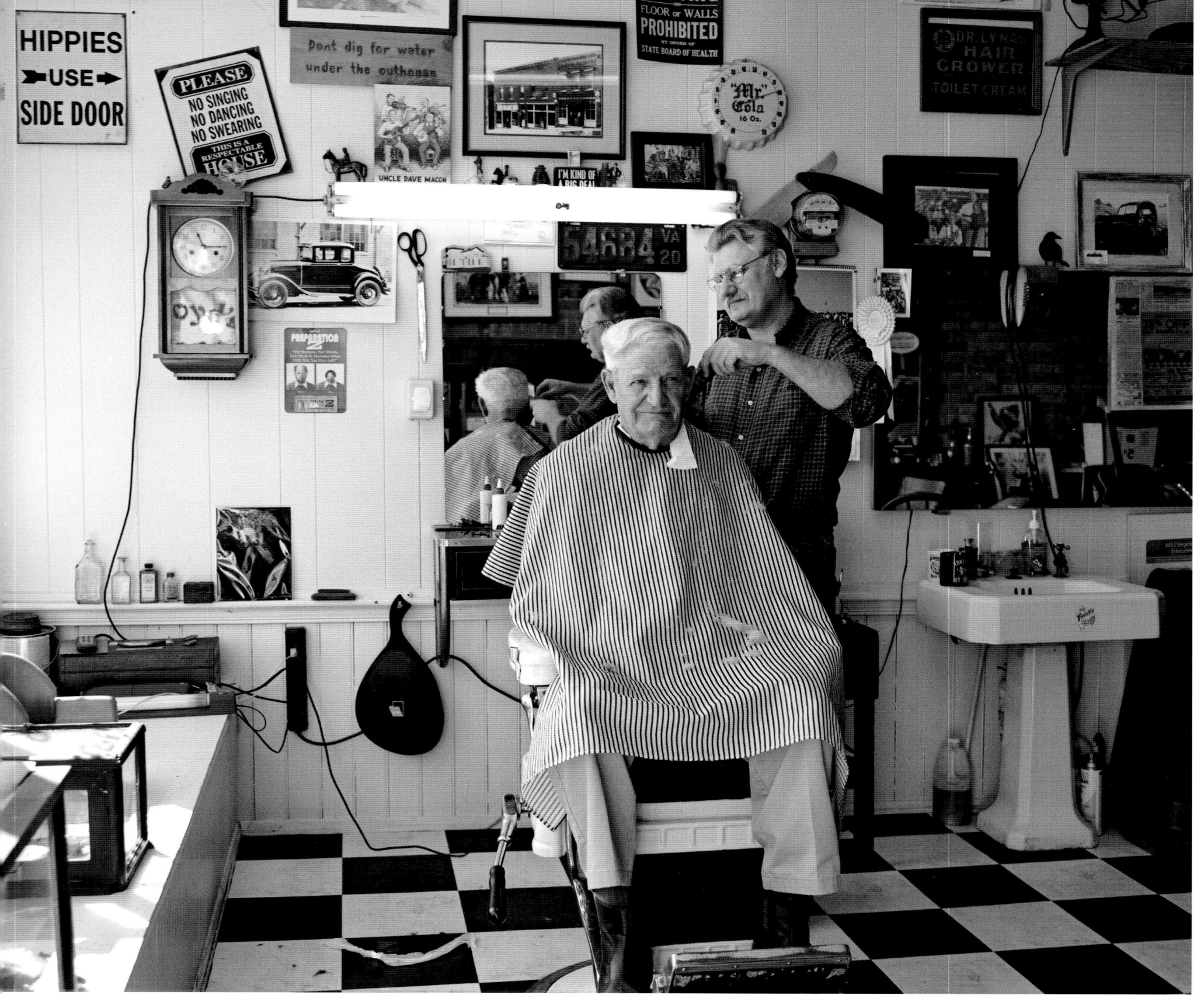

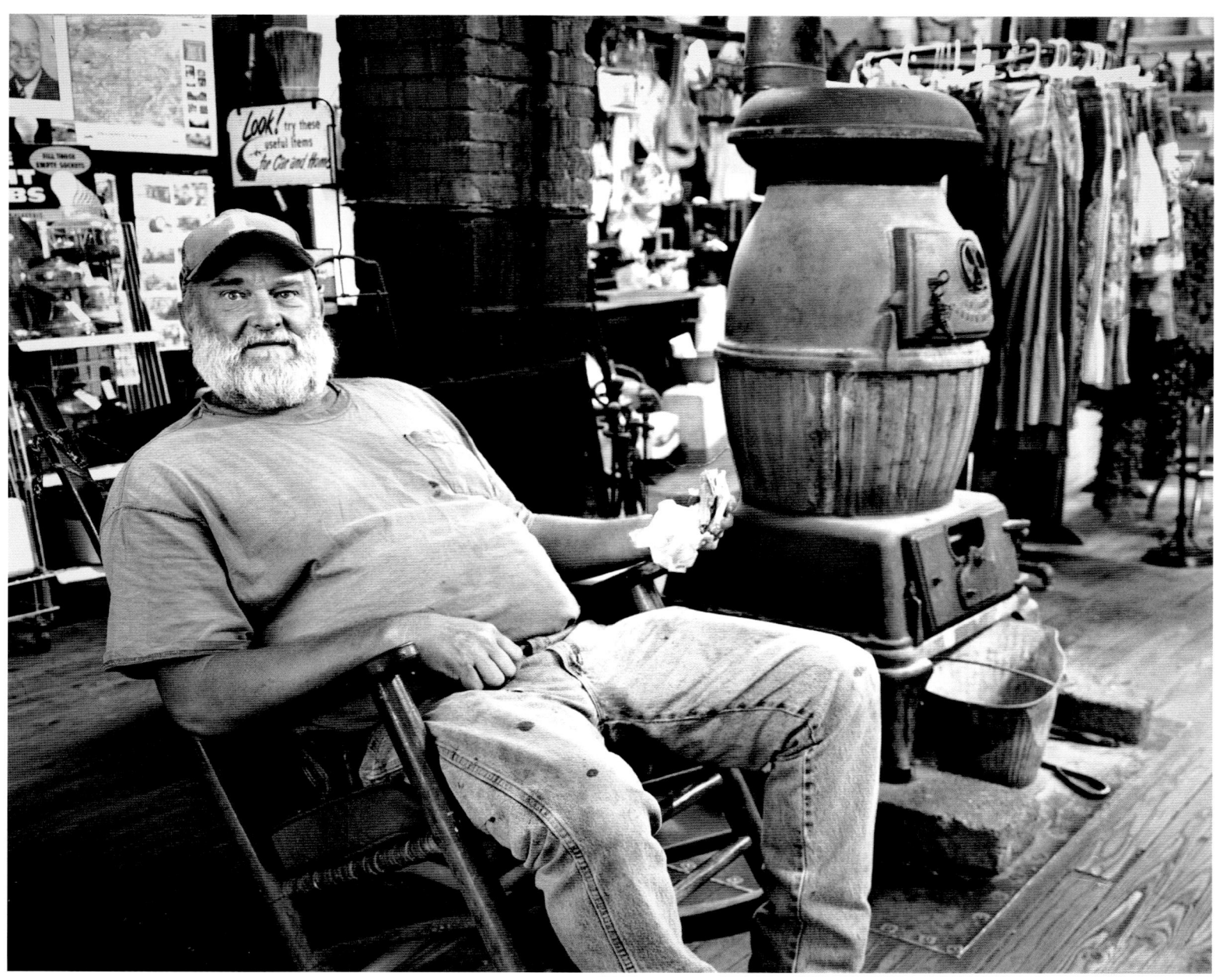

Left: Dwight Smithers at R. M. Brooks General Merchandise, Rugby, Tennessee, 6-10-2016; Wista DX 4x5 camera; 90mm Schneider Super Angulon lens; Ilford HP5+ 4x5 film; PMK Pyro developer.

Facing page: Jim Lloyd cutting hair at his shop in Rural Retreat, Virginia, 10-8-2015; Pentax 6x7 camera; 45mm lens; Ilford Delta 100 120 film; PMK Pyro developer.

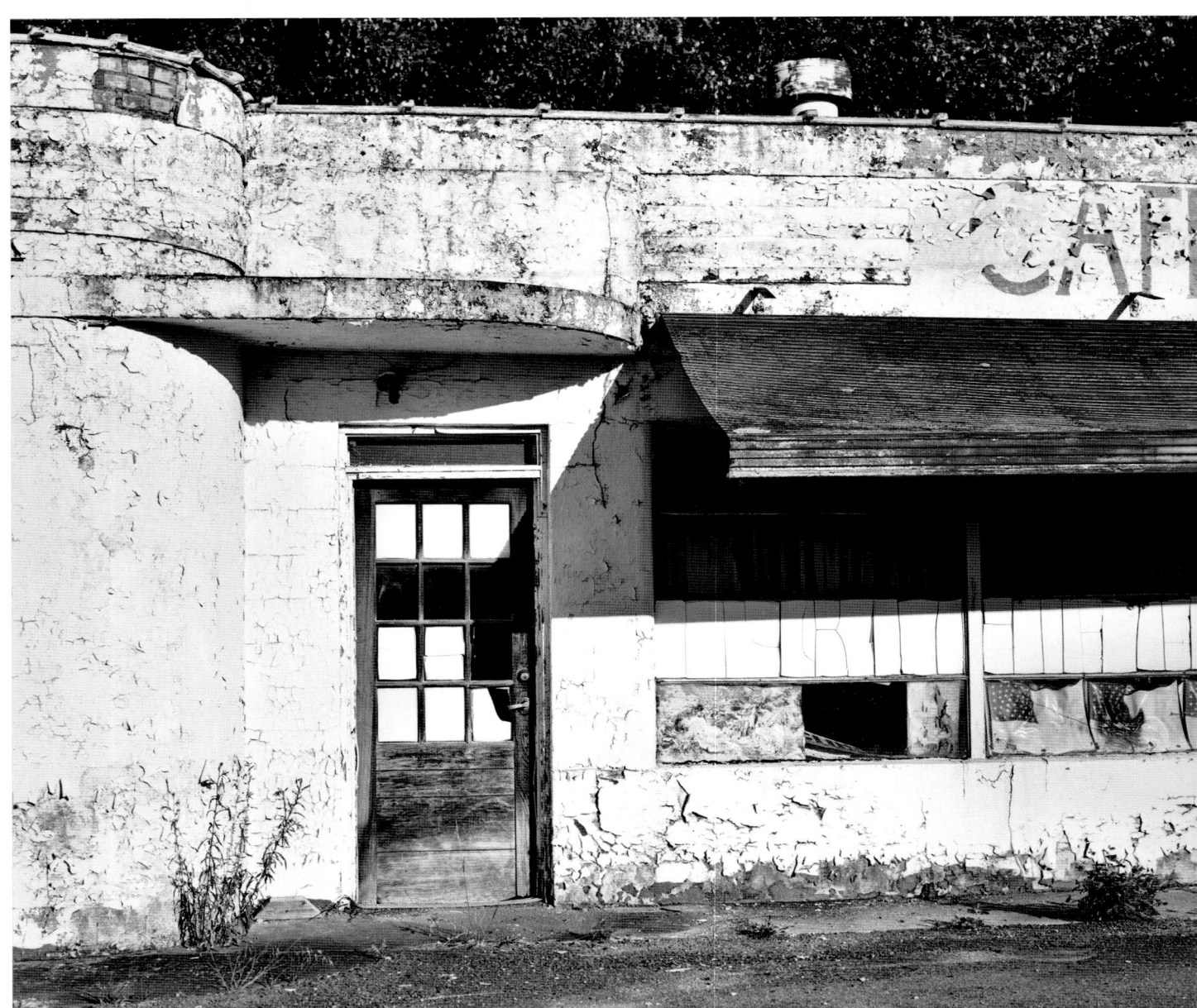

6-10-2016   7:00 P.M. hour
Stillwell Corner   H 30   Southeast Tennessee
John Stillwell and his wife came up while I was shooting this
he is trying to sell the location now.
His dad opened this business in 1951 which is the year
John Stillwell was born. It closed in 1984 after the new highway
was build in front of his location which changed how people got
to his building.
This was the classic service garage building. It had
gas, service, a market and cafe. In its day it was a
great travel stop and truck stop
They were nice people. I always enjoy collecting data about
the sites of my photographs.

Toyo 8x10m
12"1 Kodak Commerical Ektar lens
No filter
F 32~45 ½ sec.
Adox CHS 50 8x10 film (50EI)
7X lupe
Tripod

Stillwell Corner, south of Etowah, Tennessee, on U.S. 411, 6-10-2016; Toyo 8x10M camera; 12-inch Kodak Commercial Ektar lens; Adox CHS 50 8x10 film; PMK Pyro developer.

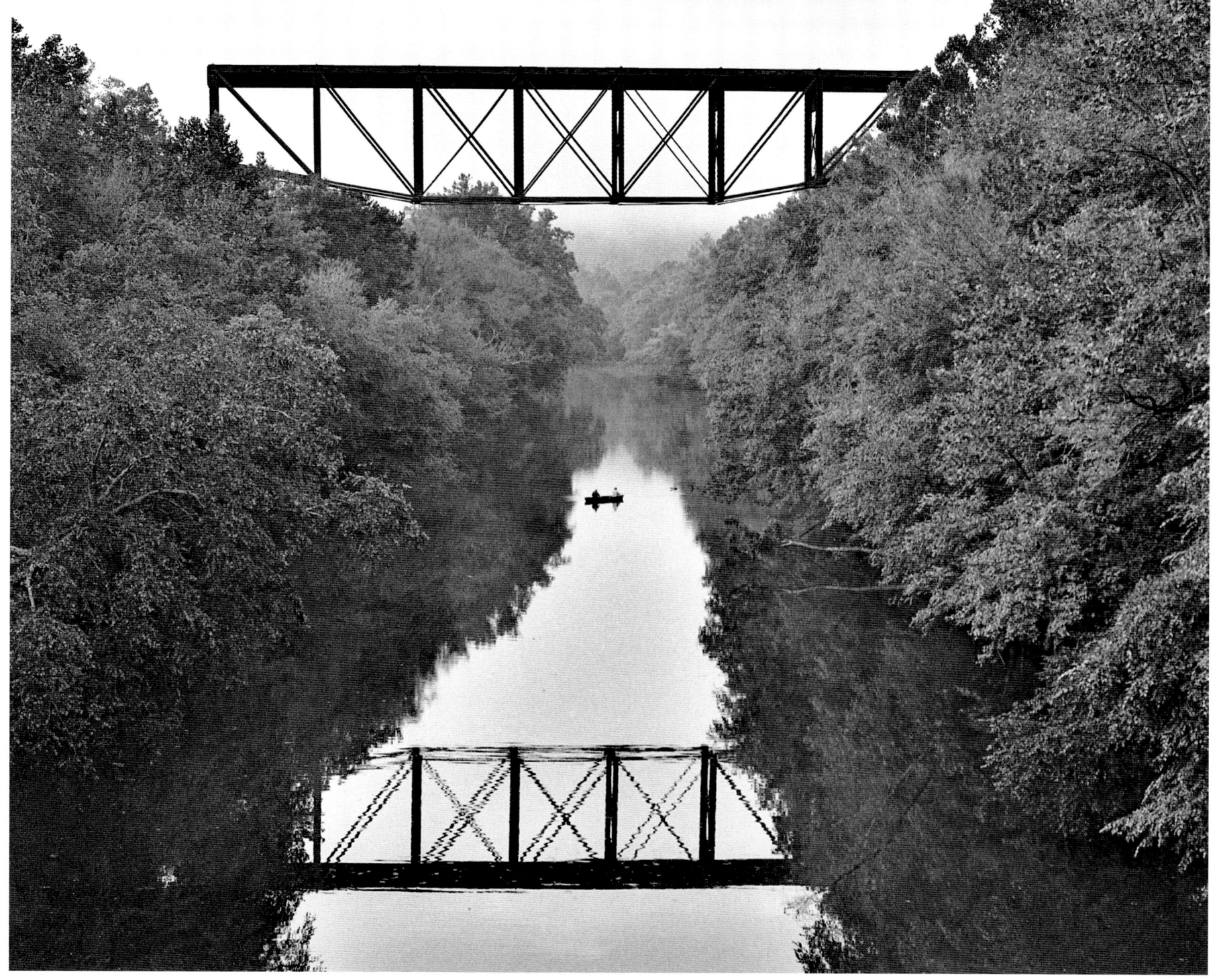

East Tennessee fisherman and bridge reflection, 9-16-2013; Rolleiflex 2.8F TLR camera; 80mm Zeiss Planar lens; Ilford HP5+, 120 film; PMK Pyro developer.

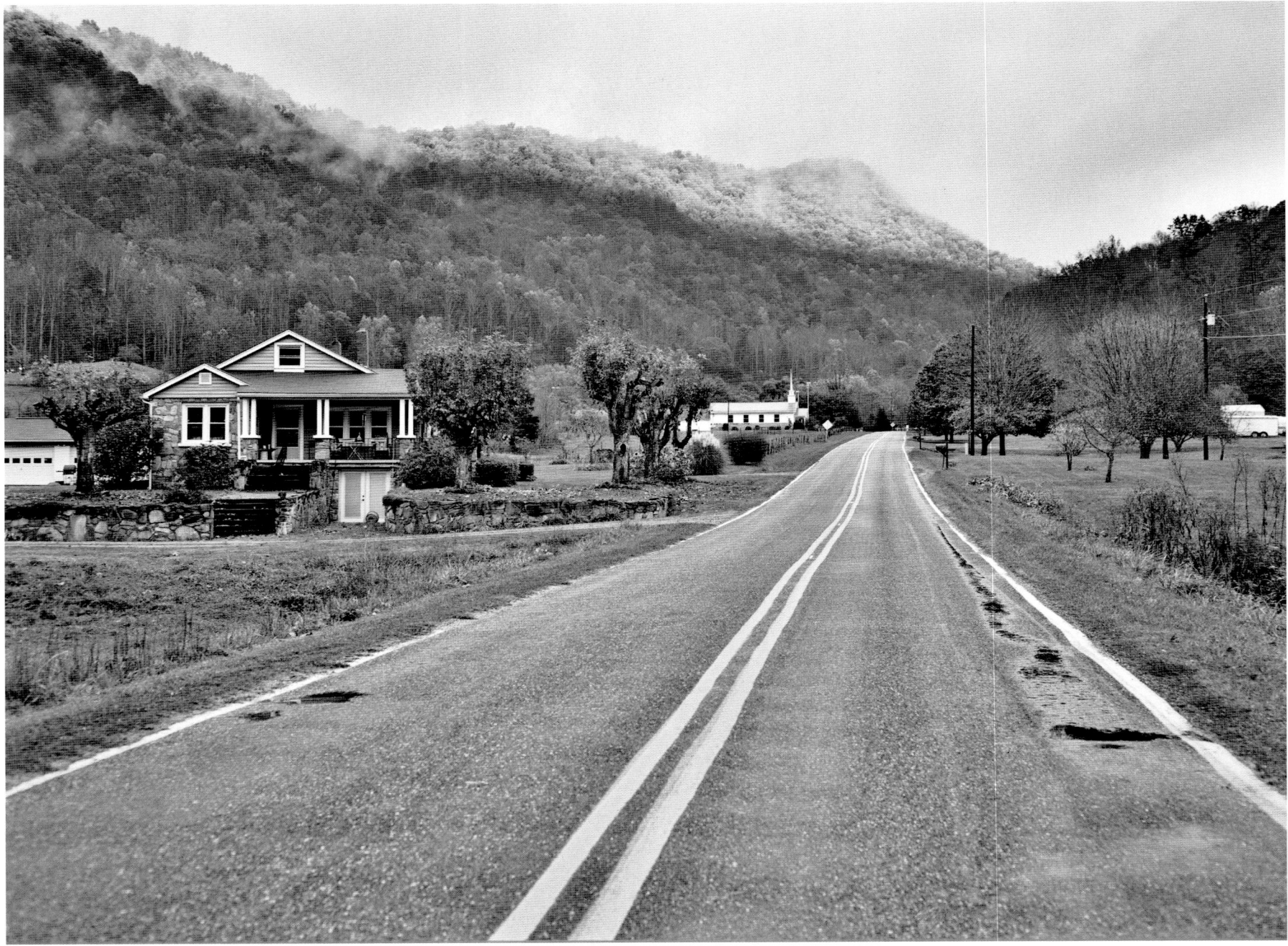

Snow in the mountains near Pensacola, North Carolina, 10-30-2012; Crown Graphic 4x5 camera; 135mm Schneider Xenar lens; Ilford HP5+ 4x5 film; PMK PMK Pyro developer.

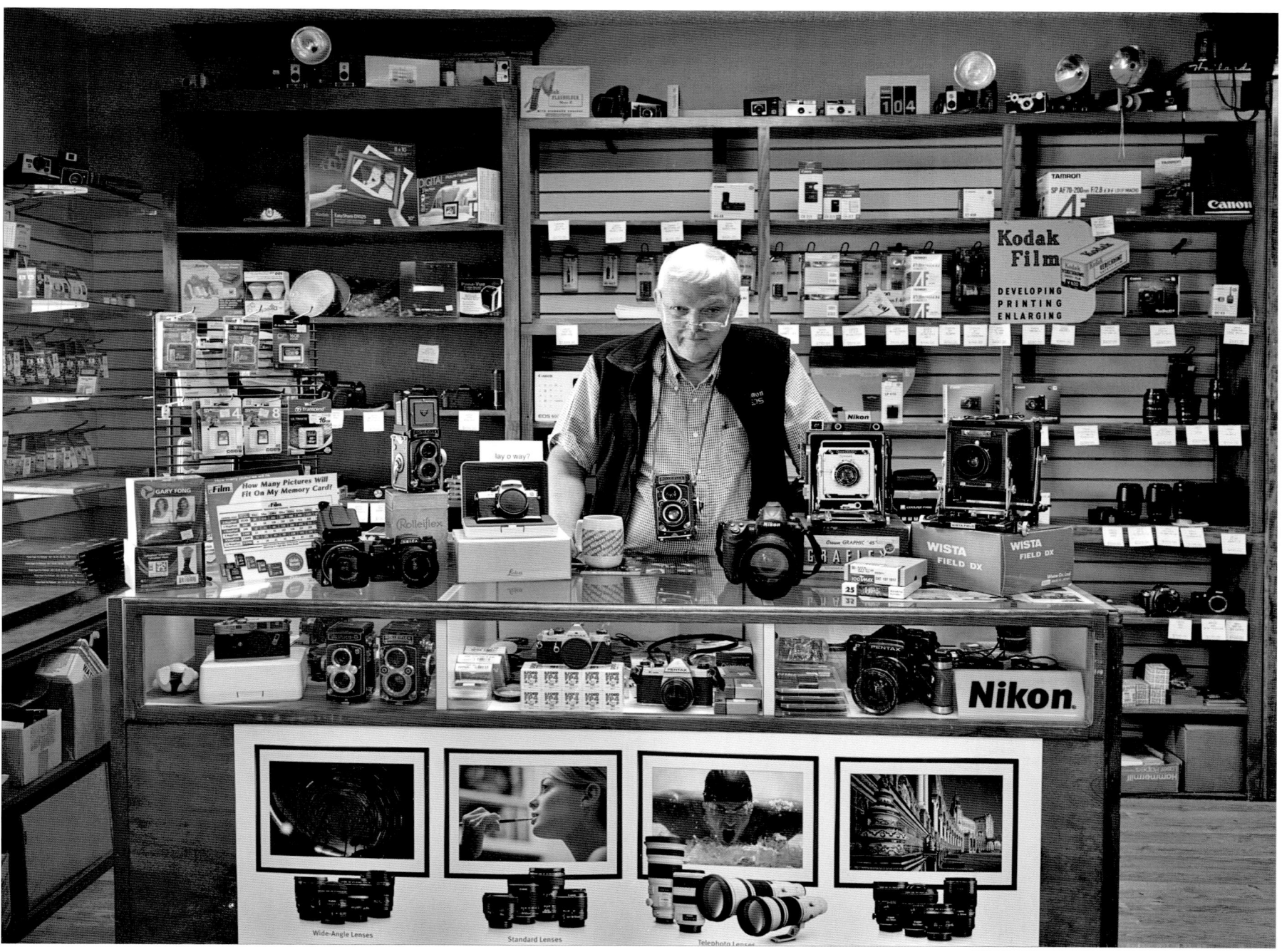

David Brandsma, owner of Camera Inn, estd. 1977, Anniston, Alabama, 4-25-2012; Toyo 8x10M camera; 210mm Schneider Apo Symmar lens; Ilford HP5+ 8x10 film; PMK Pyro developer.

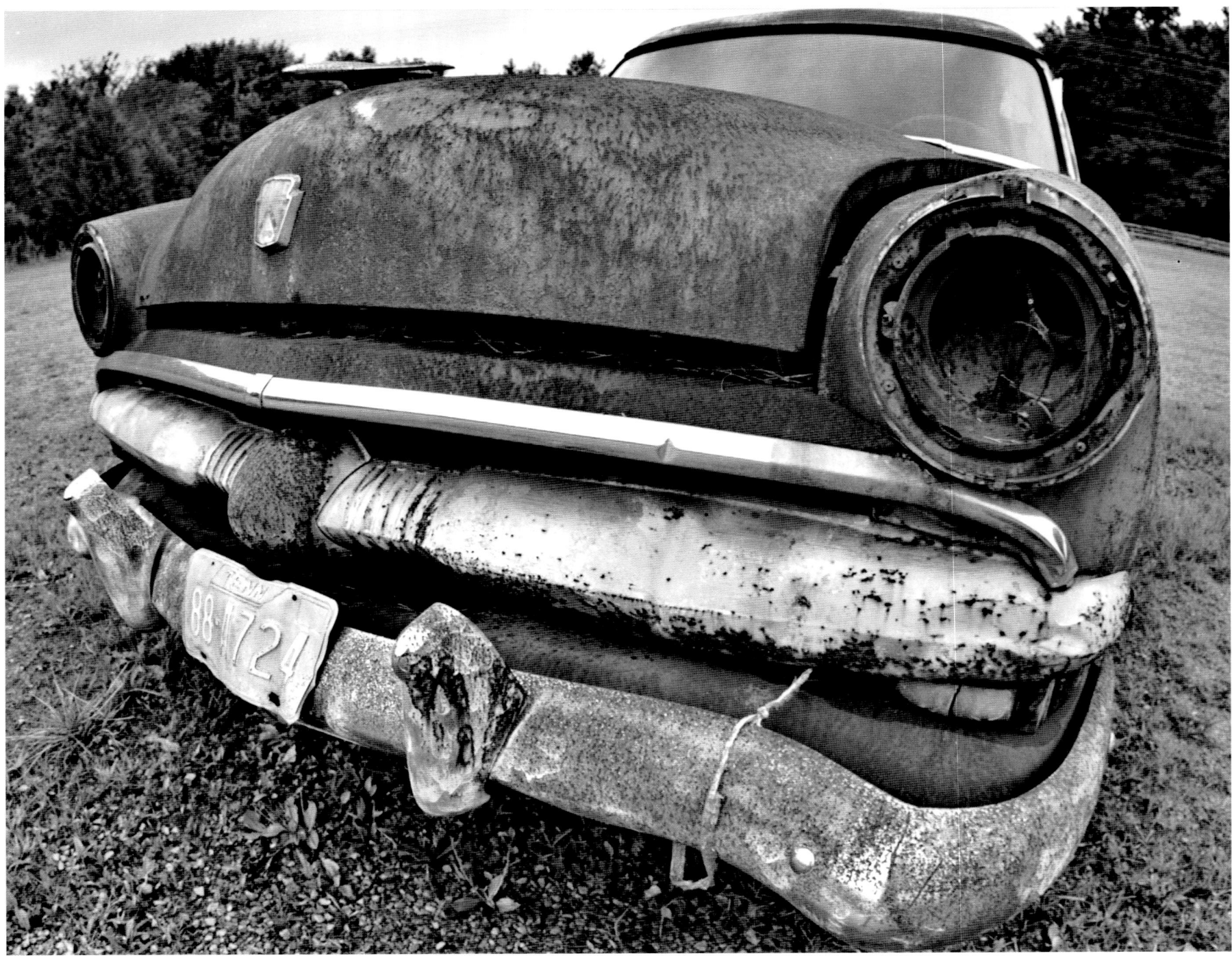

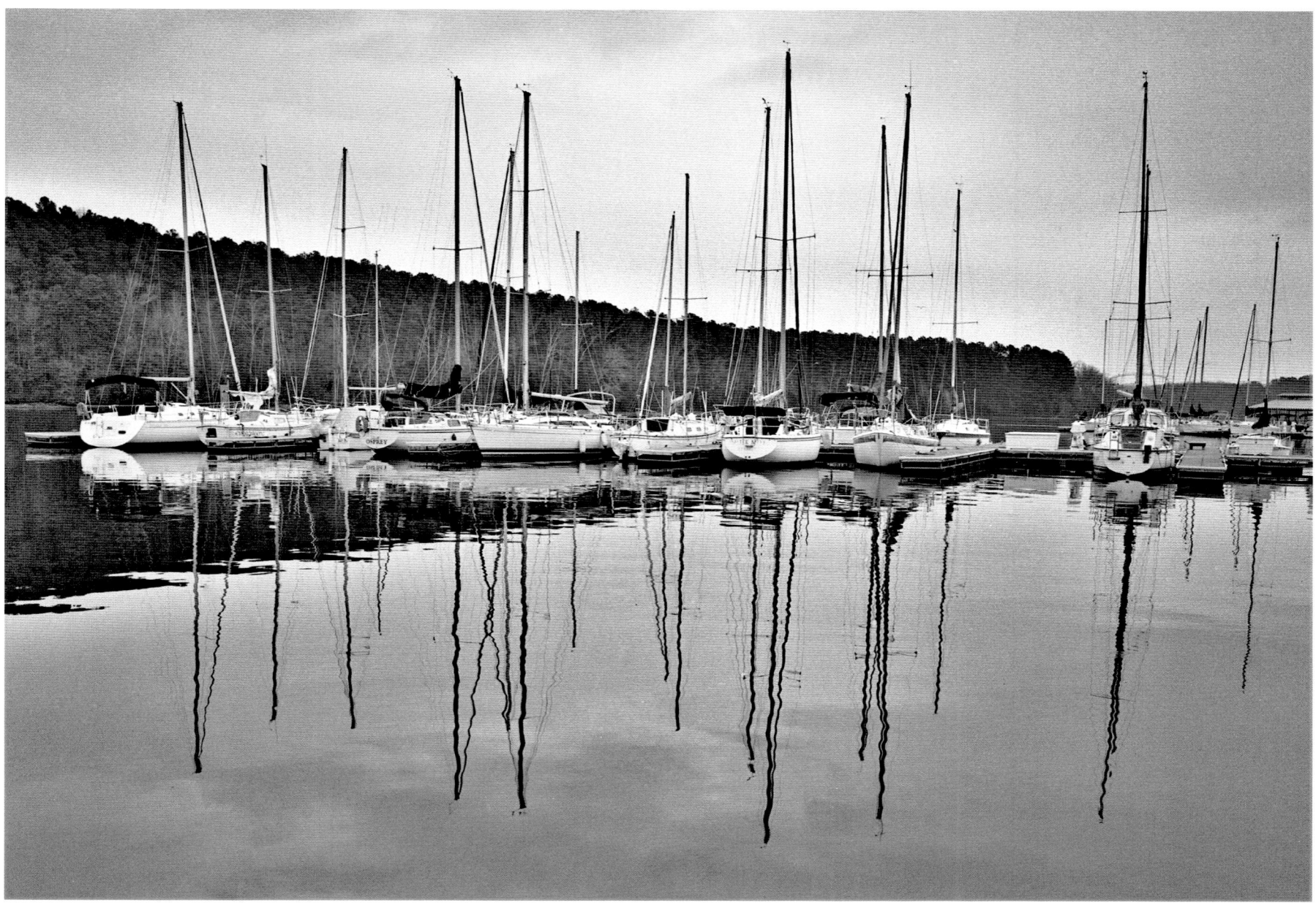

Above: Joe Wheeler State Park, Rogersville, Alabama, 3-1-2014; Hasselblad camera; 50mm Zeiss Distagon lens; Ilford HP5+ 120 film; PMK Pyro developer.

Facing page: 1953 Ford Ranch Wagon, near Dunlap, Tennessee, 7-31-2013; Pentax 6x7 camera; 35mm fisheye lens; Kodak Verichrome Pan 120 film; PMK Pyro developer.

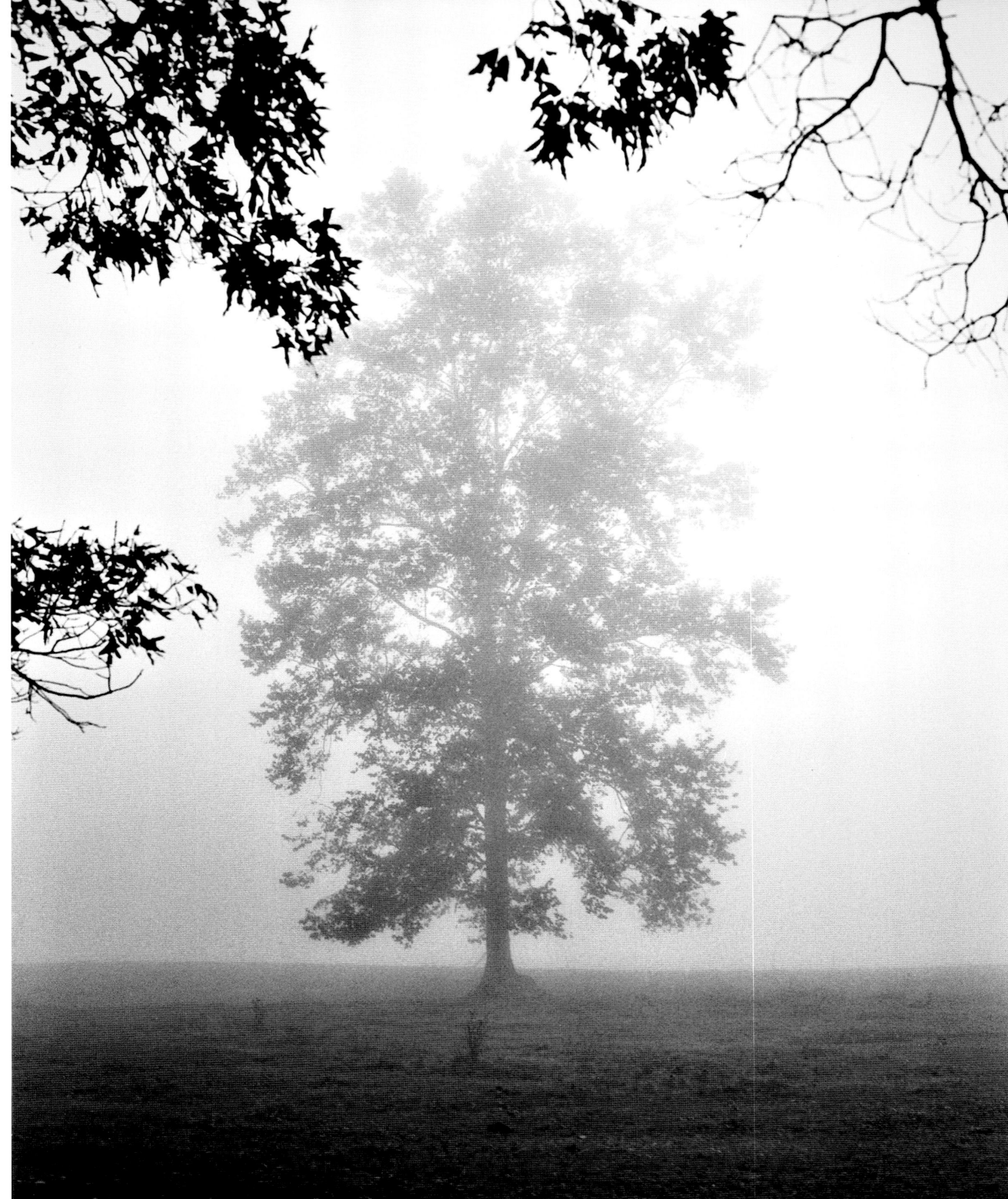

Cades Cove on a foggy early morning, Great Smoky Mountains National Park, Gatlinburg, Tennessee, 10-2014; Pentax 6x7 camera; 50mm lens; Ilford HP5+ 120 film; PMK Pyro developer.

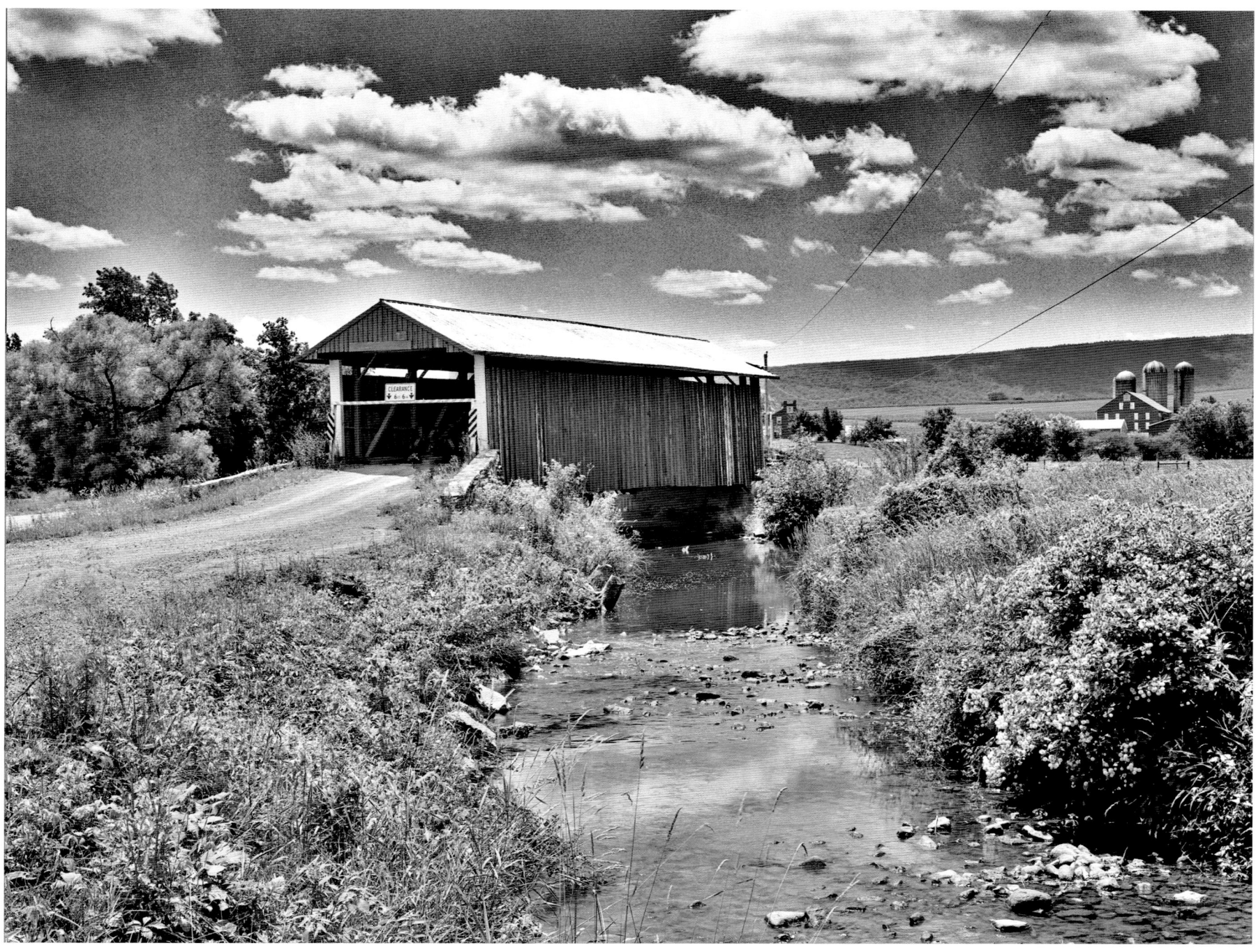

Hayes Covered Bridge, Union County, Pennsylvania, 7-1-2010; Wista DX 4x5 camera; 120mm Schneider Super Symmar HM lens; yellow K2 filter; Efke R100 4x5 film; PMK Pyro developer.

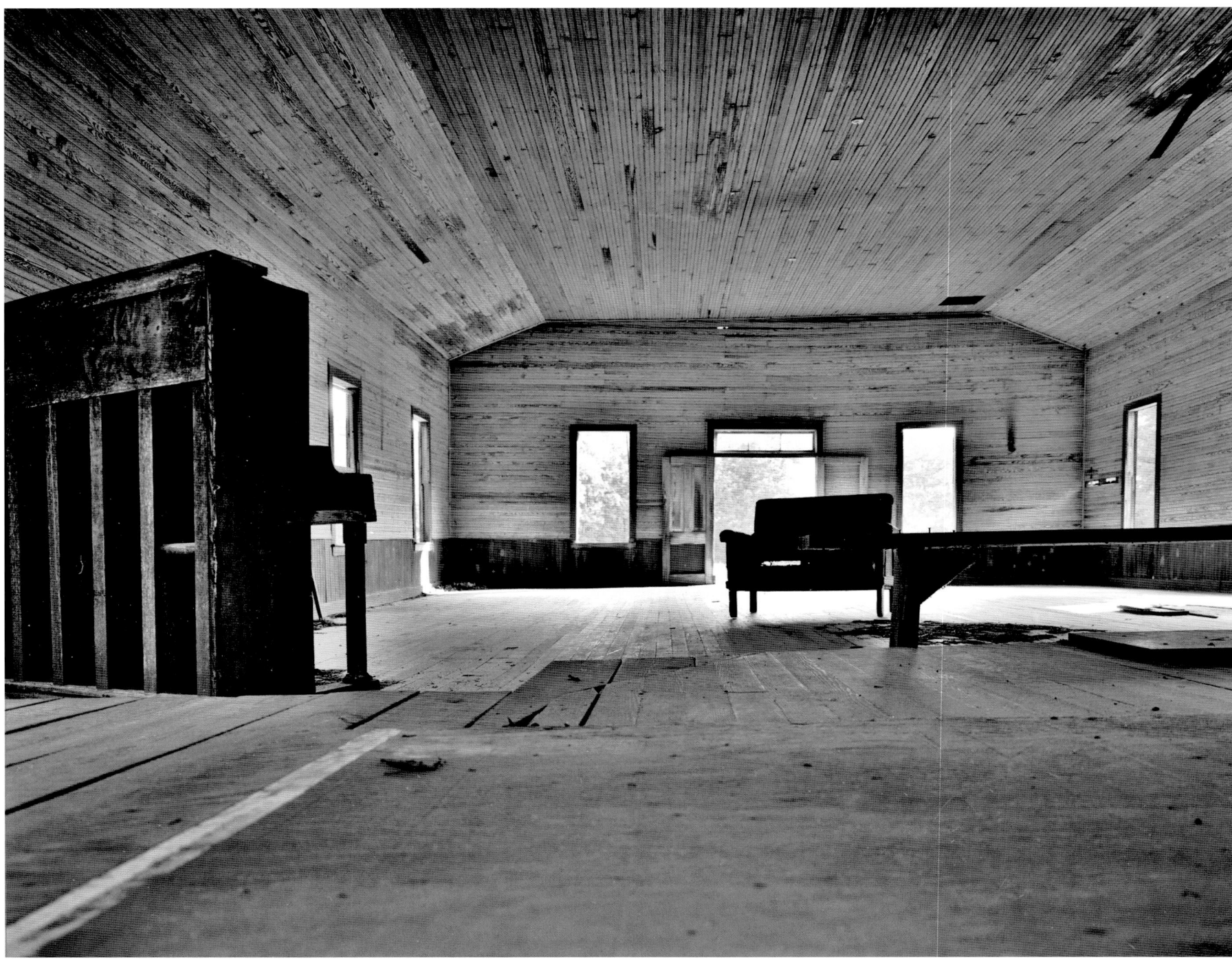

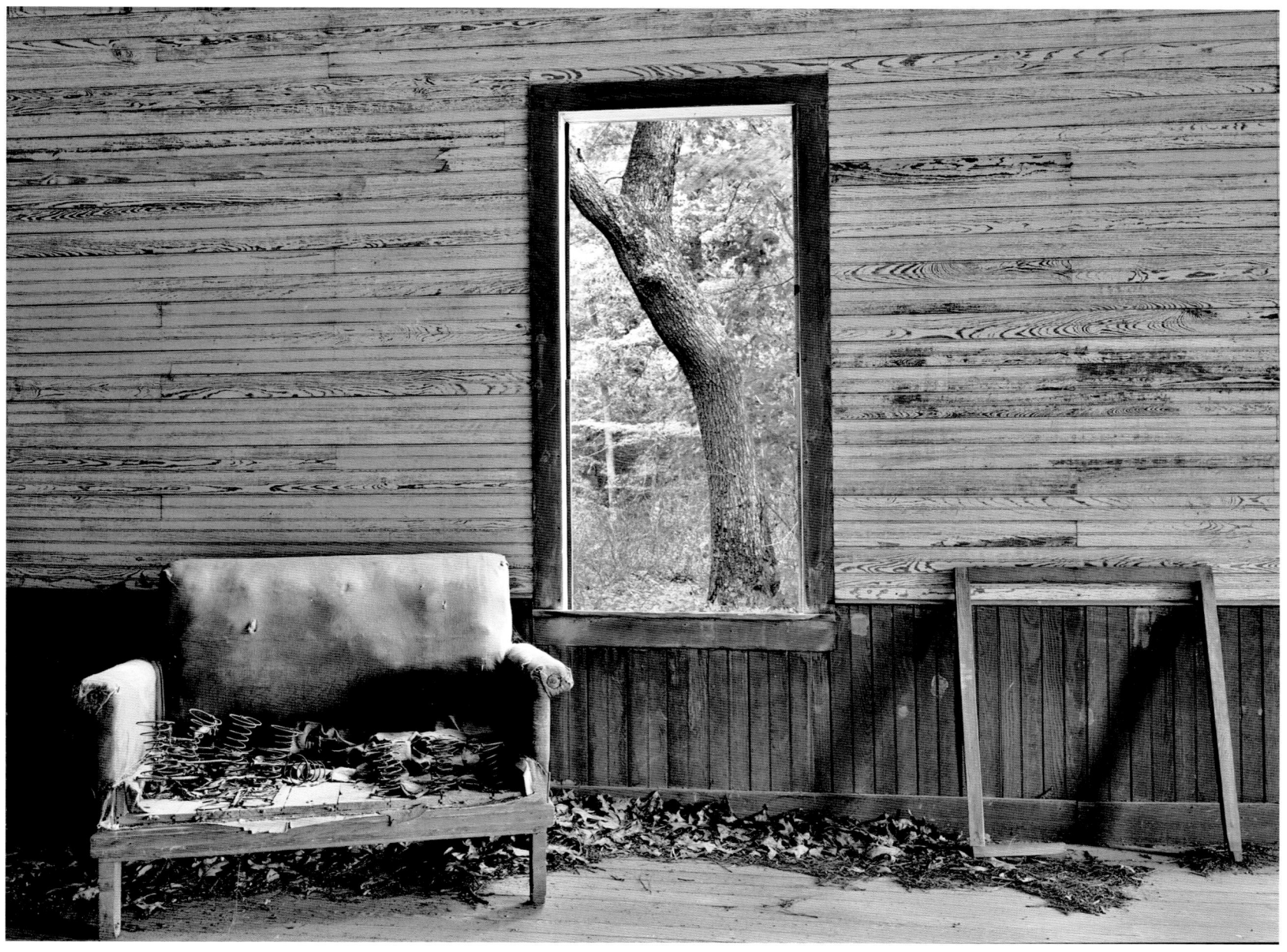

Above: Edna Hill Methodist Church, estd. 1907, DeKalb County, Alabama, 6-24-2016; Toyo 8x10M camera; 210mm Schneider Apo Symmar lens; Kodak Tri X Pan Pro 8x10 film; PMK Pyro developer.

Facing page: Edna Hill Methodist Church, 5-6-2016; Wista DX 4x5 camera; 120mm Schneider Super Symmar HM lens; Adox CHS 100, 4x5 film; PMK Pyro developer.

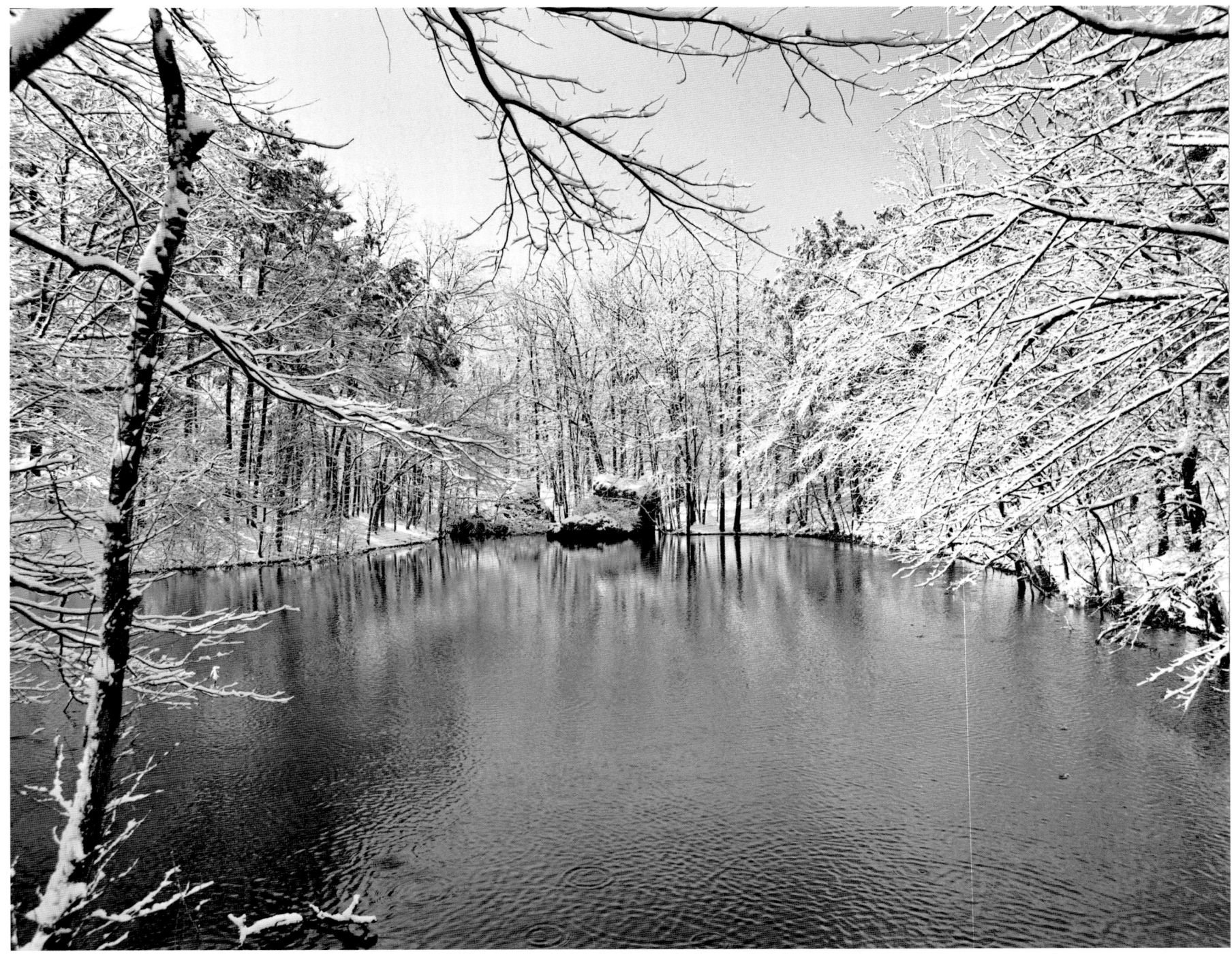

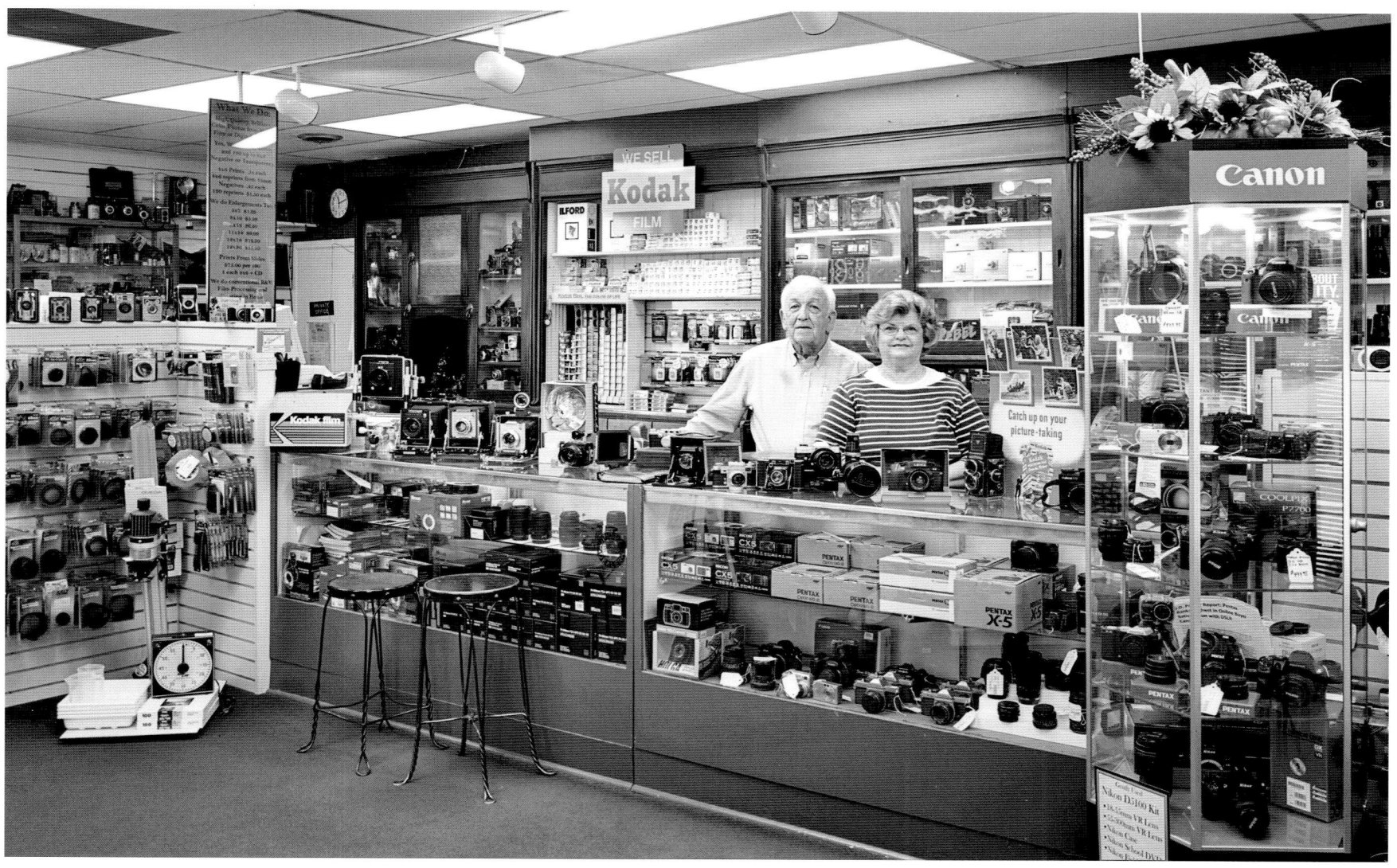

Above: Fiftieth Anniversary picture of Southerland's Photo in Huntsville, Alabama, Malcolm and Betsy Tarkington, owners, 11-29-2012; Toyo 8x10M camera; 210mm Schneider Apo Symmar lens; Ilford HP5+ 8x10 film; Kodak HC110B developer.

Facing page: Snowy pond on Lookout Mountain, DeKalb County, Alabama, 2-13-2014; Pentax 6x7 camera; 45mm lens; Ilford Delta 100 120 film; PMK Pyro developer.

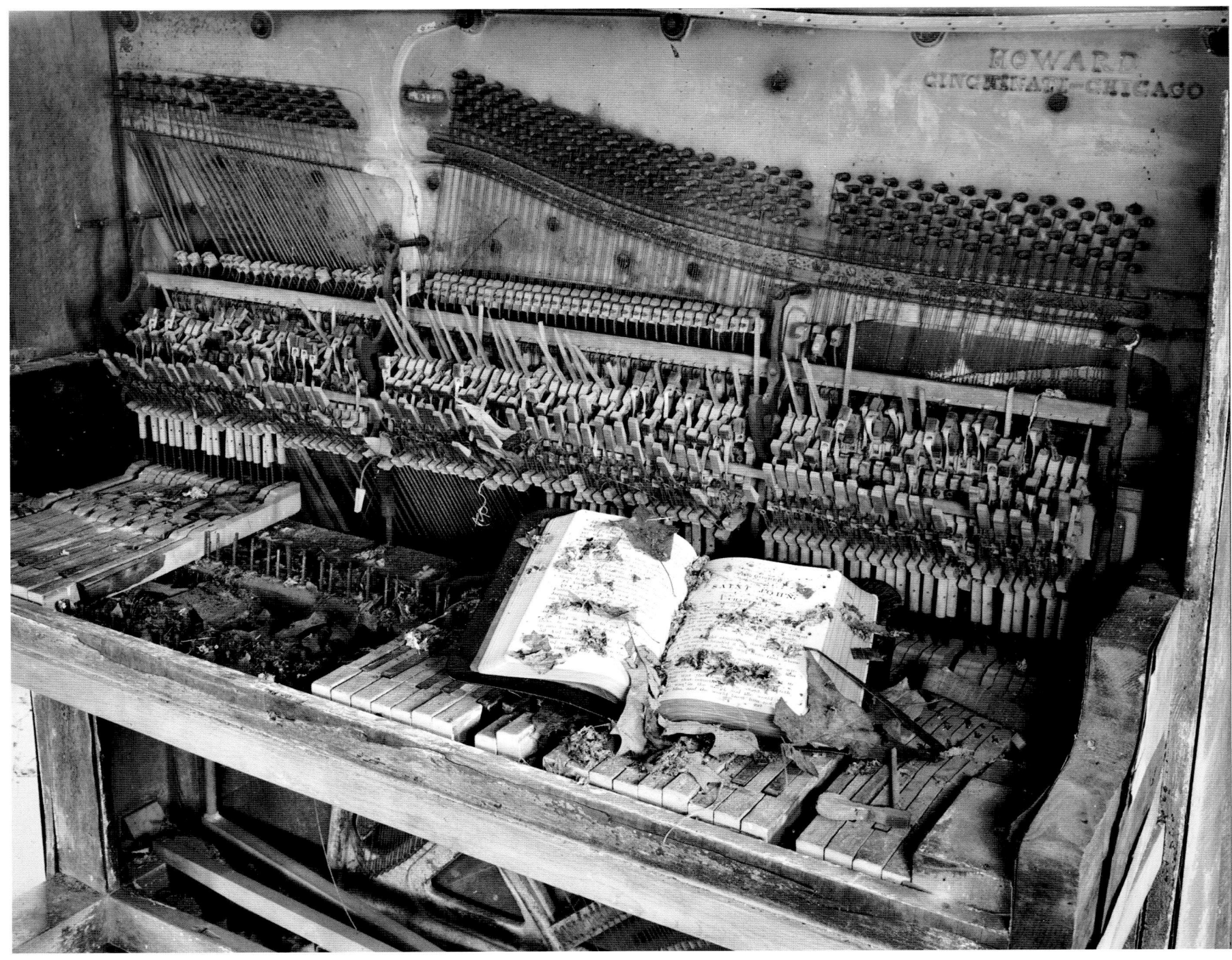

The 2020s: The Seventh Decade Begins

Now in my seventh decade of shooting black and white medium and large format film, I still have the same enthusiasm I had when I caught the bug of handling film, processing it, and printing it in the 1960s. There is something special about the whole process from loading the film in the camera or sheet-film holders to adjusting the totally manually operated cameras on a tripod, then focusing the image and getting the depth of field correct.

The steps go on with unloading the exposed film in the darkroom, processing, drying the film, then carefully putting the negatives in archival protective sleeves and writing the location and technical data about the image on the sleeve, and, finally, selecting the images to make fine-art darkroom prints.

In today's digital age when almost none of the steps I just mentioned are used, you might wonder why I don't shoot all digital. I do shoot a lot of digital. I often shoot the same subjects on both digital and film during the same outing. Typically my color images are from digital, and my black and white are from film. I have been doing it this way for a couple of decades.

The truth is that I like the rendering of black and white images much better from film than from digital, which is usually a color capture and then removing the color. With black and white film, the image starts black and white and stays black and white unless you separately color it manually. The tonal variations and contrast are much more pleasing using black and white from film than from a digital file. In addition, film conveys more depth, mood, and a feeling of being in the picture instead of sitting outside of it looking at the surface.

So as I enter my seventh decade of shooting, it is my intent to keep doing it the way I have been doing it all along and, most importantly, continue enjoying it as much as I have for the previous six decades.

Facing page: Edna Hill Methodist Church, with original piano and a 1890 leather-bound Bible, everything covered in dirt blowing in from the window next to it, 3-1-2020; Toyo 8x10M camera; 240mm Schneider G Claron lens; Kodak Tri X Pan Pro, 8x10 film; PMK Pyro developer.

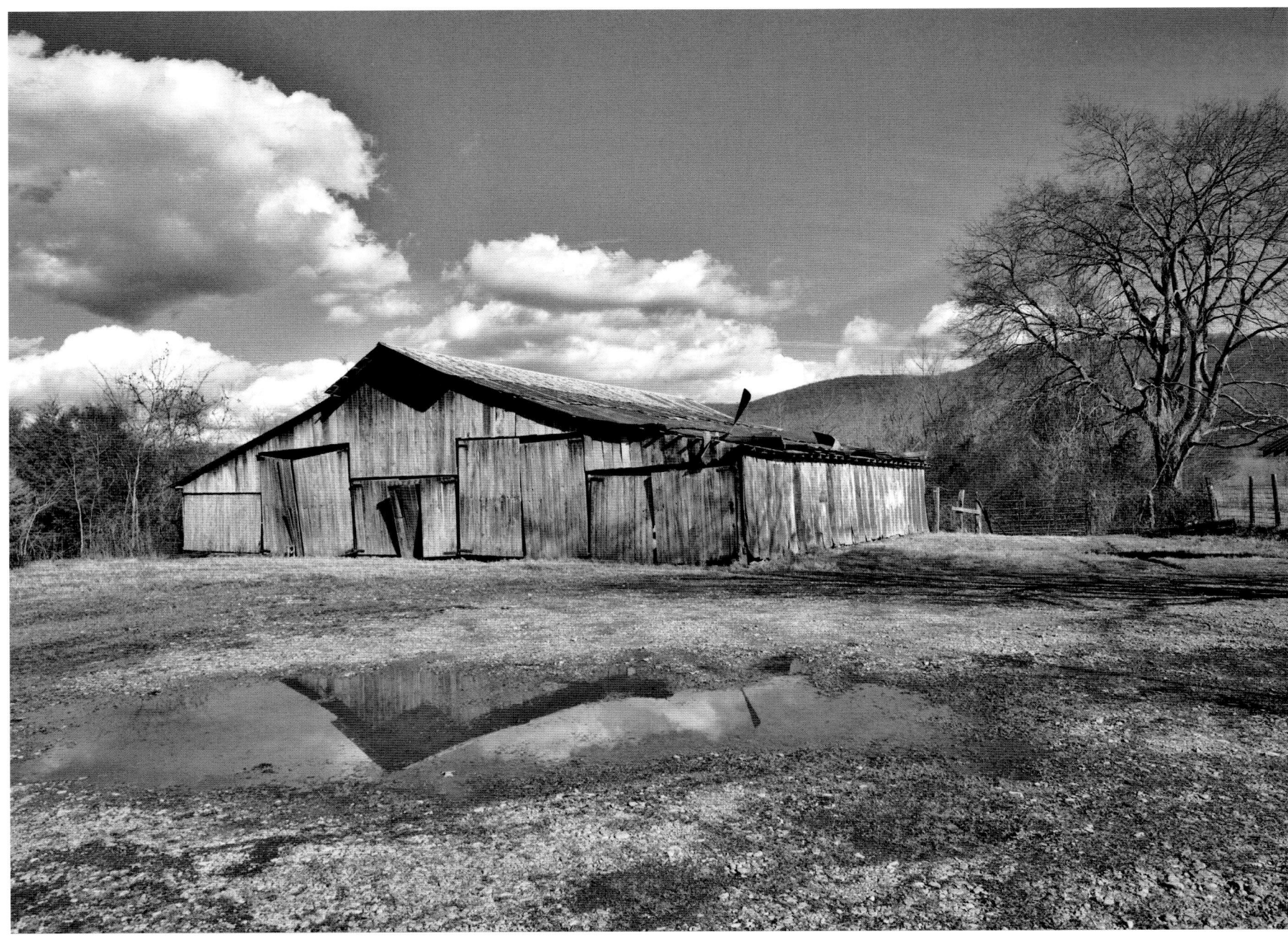

Above: Roy B. Whitaker Paint Rock River Preserve, Paint Rock, Alabama, 2-8-2020; Pentax 6x7 camera; 45mm lens; yellow K2 filter; Ilford Delta 100 120 film; Ilford Ilfotec DD-X developer.

Facing page: Mountains near Murphy North Carolina, 6-2020; Linhof Master Technika; 120mm Schneider Super Symmar HM lens; Efke R50, 4x5 film; PMK Pyro developer.

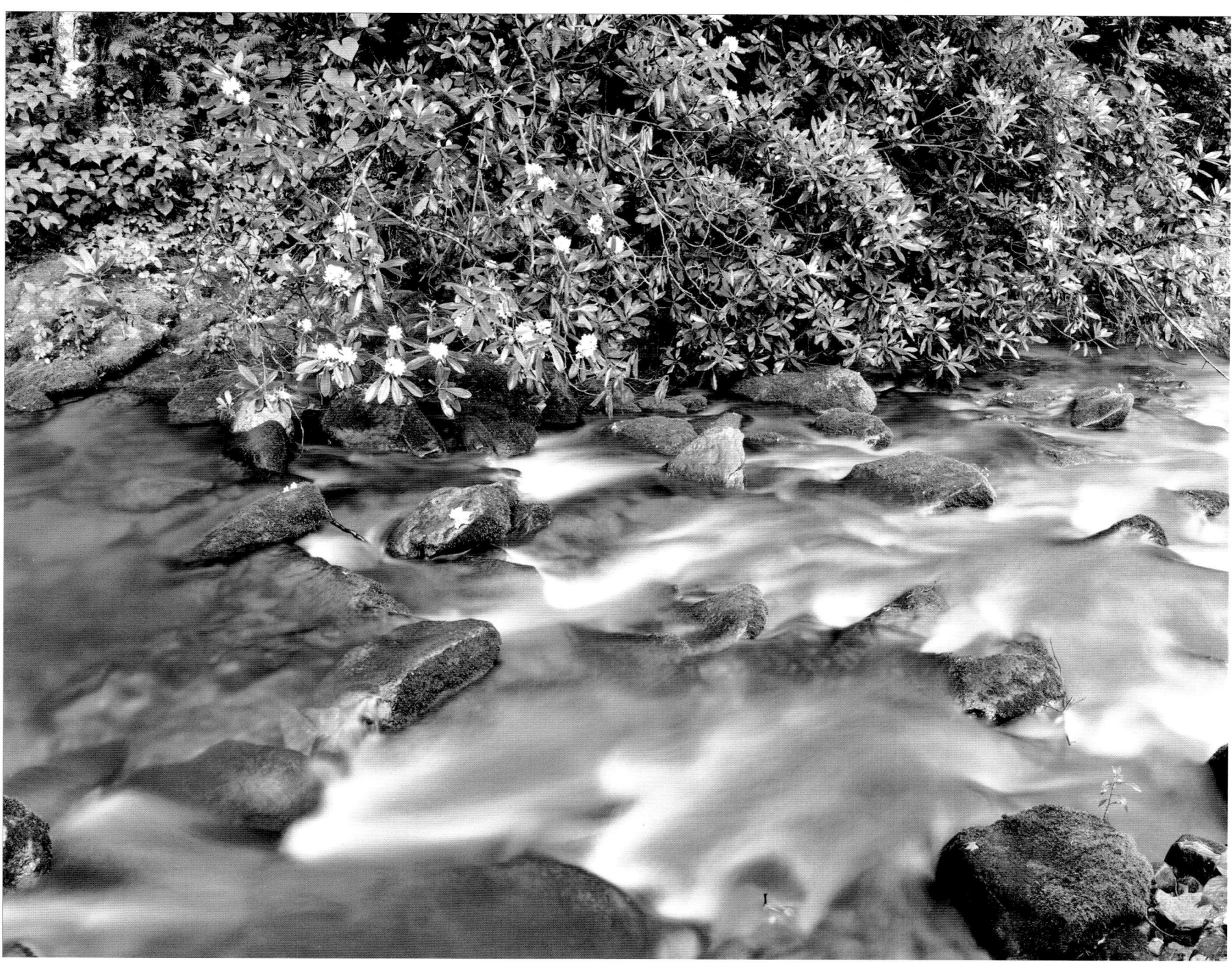

Why Shoot Film?

Film photography requires a great deal more training and practice than does digital photography if your goal is to produce images worthy of an exhibition. Once you produce a digital image, the rest is done on your computer. The image can produce exact copies with no loss of quality. In the case of film, you are shooting it blindly with no LCD screen to immediately check your image quality. If your focus or exposure was wrong when you took the picture, with digital you can shoot another image right away and repeat till you get it right. But if your film image is bad, you would have to go back to the scene to try and recreate it. In many cases, if you were shooting people or events, there would be no second chance.

Shooting film means you need to understand composition, lighting, exposure, aperture, shutter speed, and depth of field prior to taking the picture. You must understand how to set your camera to match the needs of the particular shot of the moment, so you can take one or two exposures that will be correct. Film is costly in comparison to digital, and you only get thirty-six exposures on a roll of 35mm film, less than that on medium format, and only one sheet at a time with large format. Being well trained in composition, lighting, and exposure, film processing, and printing will get consistently positive results when using film.

If you are a serious film photographer, then most likely you process and print the film yourself, because you know the art of photography comes when you start with superior images in the camera and add your expertise in the darkroom. First the film has to be perfectly processed and handled with extreme care not to get dust on it, scratch it, or incorrectly process it. You do not get to see your result until the end since you are doing it in the dark. Once negatives are processed properly, you will print on a wide range of photographic paper based on the look you like, warm or cold tone, resin-coated, or fiber-based paper. There is no end to the choices of developers, toners, paper types, and sizes to create your art.

Once you master the understanding of your equipment and the chemicals and papers you are using, you will start producing beautiful black and white darkroom prints that will last for hundreds of years and are beautiful hanging on your wall, someone else's, or in a gallery.

So why shoot film at all if digital is easier and just as good? Here is why: Digital images, like digital sound, are sterile. They are precise to the point of not having the subtle nuances that make film earthier, more human. Film carries emotional content seen and felt by us emotional humans. It delivers imperfections that look and feel better to the imperfect characters that we are. Digital is unearthly, rigid, without feel. Film has depth of tone, delivering a sense of being in the scene instead of looking at the surface. Film is real and tangible. It is a material item that even as a negative you can hold it up to the window and see the picture. Digital does not exist physically; it only comes to life with an electronic converter of the images' data.

With all this said, film is not for everyone. It is for those who like the artsy differences in film and are willing to work hard to develop their art. Digital has provided everyone the ability to take good-looking images on their smartphones or digital cameras that are lightweight, easy to use, and give the average person a chance to take better pictures than they ever did using film.

For me, black and white film has been a lifelong investment of time and effort with a lifelong ambition to keep improving my art and the craft of photography.

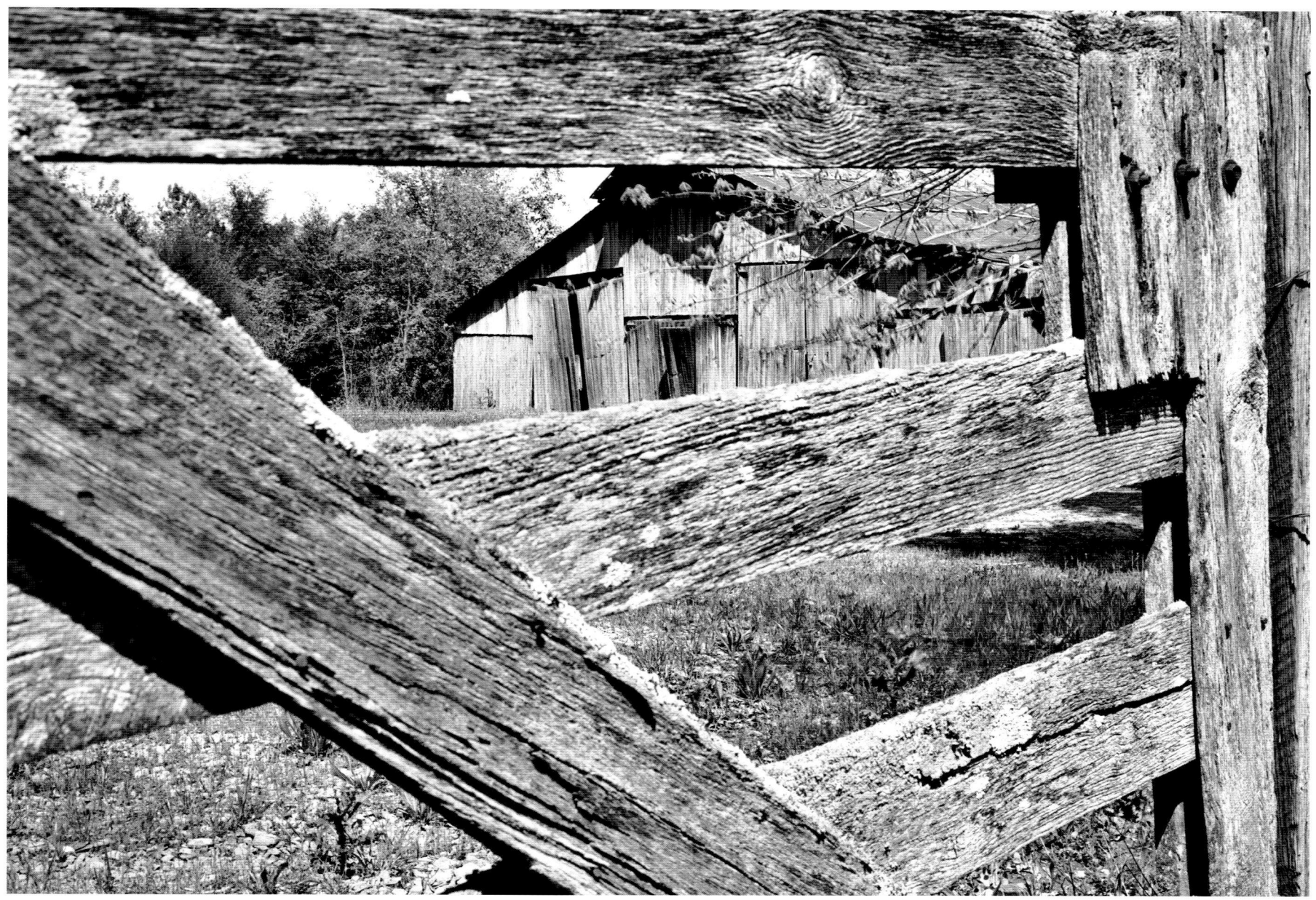

Above: Barn through the gate at Roy B. Whitaker Paint Pock Nature Preserve, Paint Rock, Alabama, 4-11-2020; Toyo 8x10M camera; 240mm Schneider G Claron lens; Tri X Pan Pro 8x10 film; PMK Pyro developer.

Next page: Sunrise at Penn's Landing, Philadelphia, Pennsylvania, 7-17-1983; Linhof Technika V 4x5 camera; 120mm Schneider Symmar S; G filter; Kodak Tri X Pan Pro 4x5 film; Kodak HC110B developer.

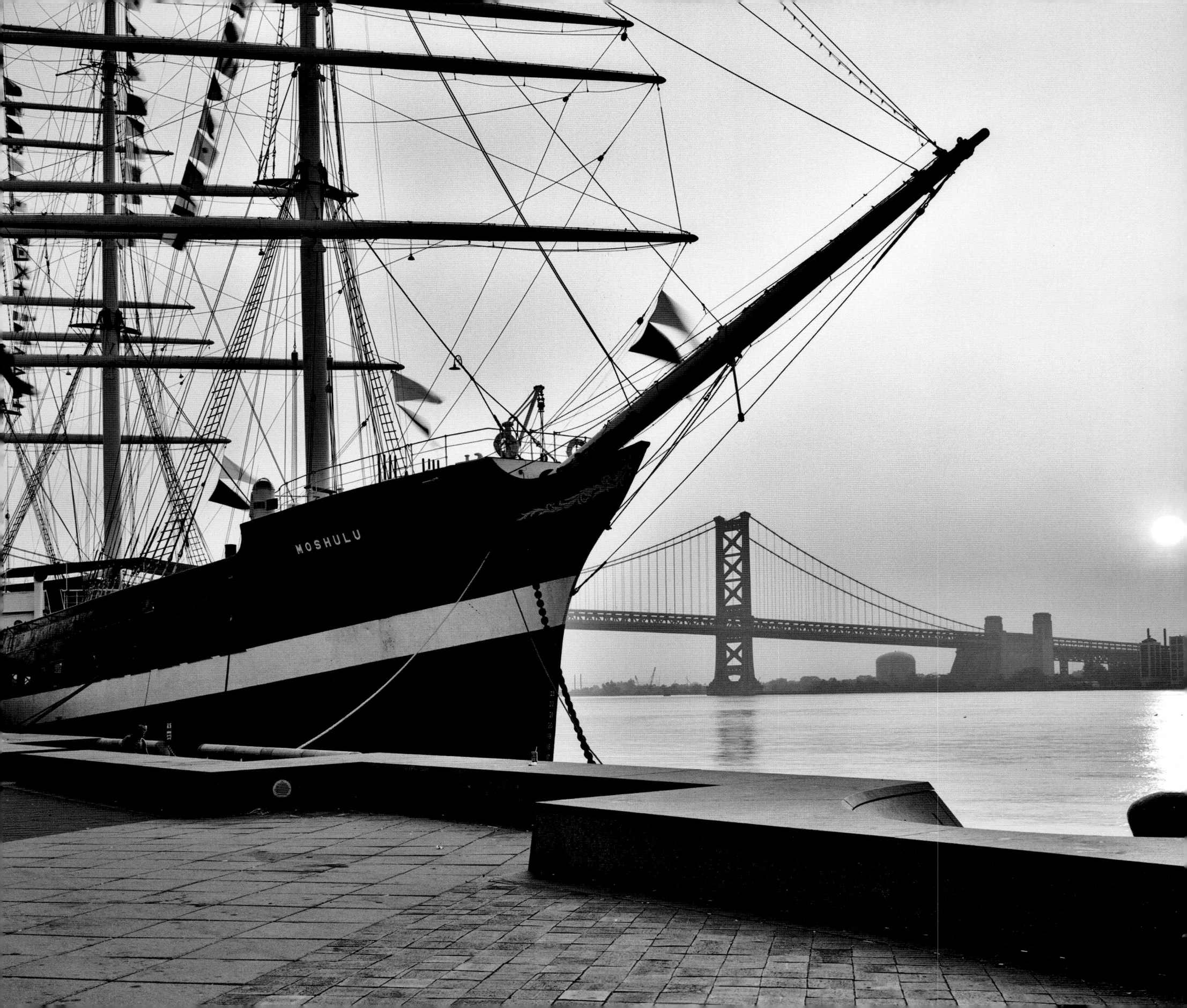